The Threshold

HARVARD-YENCHING INSTITUTE MONOGRAPH SERIES 136

The Threshold

The Rhetoric of Historiography in Early Medieval China

Zeb Raft

Published by the Harvard University Asia Center
Distributed by Harvard University Press
Cambridge (Massachusetts) and London 2023

© 2023 by the President and Fellows of Harvard College

Printed in the United States of America

The Harvard University Asia Center publishes a monograph series and, in coordination with the Fairbank Center for Chinese Studies, the Korea Institute, the Reischauer Institute of Japanese Studies, and other faculties and institutes, administers research projects designed to further scholarly understanding of China, Japan, Vietnam, Korea, and other Asian countries. The Center also sponsors projects addressing multidisciplinary and regional issues in Asia.

The Harvard-Yenching Institute, founded in 1928, is an independent foundation dedicated to the advancement of higher education in the humanities and social sciences in Asia. Headquartered on the campus of Harvard University, the Institute provides fellowships for advanced research, training, and graduate studies at Harvard by competitively selected faculty and graduate students from Asia. The Institute also supports a range of academic activities at its fifty partner universities and research institutes across Asia. At Harvard, the Institute promotes East Asian studies through annual contributions to the Harvard-Yenching Library and publication of the *Harvard Journal of Asiatic Studies* and the Harvard-Yenching Institute Monograph Series.

Library of Congress Cataloging-in-Publication Data
Names: Raft, Zeb, author.
Title: The threshold : the rhetoric of historiography in early medieval China / Zeb Raft.
Other titles: Harvard-Yenching Institute monograph series ; 136.
Description: Cambridge, Massachusetts ; London : Harvard University Asia Center, 2023. | Series: Harvard-Yenching Institute monograph series ; 136 | Includes bibliographical references and index. |
Identifiers: LCCN 2022049727 | ISBN 9780674291379 (hardcover)
Subjects: LCSH: Shen, Yue, 441–513. Song shu. | Rhetoric—Political aspects—China—History—To 1500. | China—History—Liu Song dynasty, 420–479—Historiography. | China—Biography—History and criticism.
Classification: LCC DS748.62 .R34 2023 | DDC 951/.015—dc23/eng/20230110
LC record available at https://lccn.loc.gov/2022049727

Index by the author
∞ Printed on acid-free paper
Last figure below indicates year of this printing
32 31 30 29 28 27 26 25 24 23

Believe the *Documents* completely? It would be better not to have the *Documents* at all.
—Mencius

It is well known that the official dynastic histories of China are more or less influenced by traditional ways of thought. This calls for some criticism regarding their contents. All the information given by their authors must not be taken at its face value; on the other hand the reader must be careful to avoid a hypercritical attitude towards the texts.
—Herbert Franke, "Some Remarks on the Interpretation of Chinese Dynastic Histories"

Contents

Introduction — 1
  The Liu-Song and China in the Southern Dynasties Period   3
  The Historiography of the Liu-Song   7
  Approaches   17
  The Arguments of This Book   25

Chapter 1   Interiority — 30
  The "Absolute" Quality of Historiography   31
  The Historical Actor and the Rhetoric of Interiority   37
  The Threat of Exteriorization and Defense Against It   47

Chapter 2   Exteriority — 56
  Role, Type, and Rhetoric   58
  The Abuse of Liu Muzhi   67
  The Use of Liu Muzhi   72
  Written into History   81

Chapter 3   An Essay in Officialdom — 90
  The Grammar of Officialdom   91
  The Rhetoric of Officialdom   108

Chapter 4   Historiographical Self-Fashioning: The Rhetoric of a Court Debate — 117
  Exigence: Wang Hong Opens the Debate   122
  Exposition: Speakers One and Two Set the Terms   127
  Gentry Reasoning   132
  Speaker Four: A More Perfect Gentry Casuistry   138
  The Righteous Contrarian   145
  The Orchestrator Returns   148
  Into the Historical Frame   162

Chapter 5   The Historical Process   166
    The Documentary Motive   167
    Historiography as Public and Private Interest   175
    The Exigence of Incompletion   190

Conclusion   Epideictic History   200

Appendix   The *Song shu* Biography of Liu Muzhi (360–417)   211

Works Cited   249
    The *Song shu*   249
    Other Premodern Chinese Sources   250
    Secondary Scholarship   252

Index   261

Introduction

Res gestae and *historia rerum gestarum* were beginning to merge, things done with the account of those things...
—Daniel Woolf, *A Global History of History* (chapter 6)

When we want to learn about the past, we turn to artifacts from the past. The problem is that an artifact invariably tells us only part of the truth—and may obscure other parts. More precisely, a given kind of artifact only tells us its own kind of truth, or mistruth. The only way through is to assess the artifact's underlying qualities, understanding the information it conveys in those terms.

It is important to remember that historiography—how historical events were committed to writing—is itself an artifact of history. This is a point of fundamental significance in the study of early medieval China—roughly, the second to seventh centuries of the Common Era—not least because so much of our understanding of this period comes down to us through the lens of histories produced during that time. If we do not grapple directly with the qualities of these sources, we will not use them well. More than that, early medieval China was a great age of historiography, witnessing the compilation of hundreds of historical titles and the establishment of "history" as an independent bibliographical category.[1]

---

1. A modern study demonstrates this development with the following contrast. In the middle of the first century of the Common Era, just eleven historical works, classed under the *Spring and Autumn Annals*, were noted in the bibliography incorporated into the *History of the Han*. Some four hundred years later, more than a thousand historical titles would be listed in the bibliography compiled by Ruan Xiaoxu 阮孝緒 (479–536) and in a special section devoted to history. See Hao Runhua, *Liuchao shiji yu shixue*, 28.

Historiography was a quintessential product of early medieval culture, its qualities very much those of the age itself. Further, and most importantly of all, though we naturally think of historiography as "writing about the past," a great deal of historical writing in early medieval China was highly contemporary. It was the record of the very recent past—and the real-time creation of the "primary sources" that would soon be taken up into that record. This makes historiography an artifact in the strongest sense: not just an account of what happened in the past, or even a reflection of how the past happened, but a key element in the happening itself.

Received characterizations provide some basic footholds for understanding traditional Chinese historiography. The Chinese historian's primary interest, many have observed, was to praise and to blame, in pursuit of moral truths that lie beyond a merely factual record. Alternatively, Etienne Balazs (1905–63) found a more pragmatic didacticism in Chinese historiography: it was "written by officials for officials," to educate its readership in the art of governance.[2] Considering a different dimension of that same readership, Wolfram Eberhard (1909–89) saw a historiography written by the gentry for the gentry, in representation of their own interests, while Hans Bielenstein (1920–2015) and others have emphasized the flip side of that coin: that historiography was an instrument of the imperial state, wielded to acknowledge the men who served its glory and give just deserts to those who had not.[3] Introducing these points of view, Albert E. Dien grants each "some validity," adding to them a higher-level formulation of his own: that Chinese historiography challenges us because its primary concerns were "permanence" and "continuity," as opposed to "process" and "change."[4] Burton Watson (1925–2017), meanwhile, once offered the opposite view: "the essence of human history, as of the whole natural world, was regarded by the Chinese as the phenomenon of change."[5]

There is insight in all these perspectives; when they contradict one another, it is because the Chinese historiographical tradition is too broad

---

2. Etienne Balazs, "History as a Guide to Bureaucratic Practice," 135.
3. See Wolfram Eberhard, *A History of China*, 104, and Hans Bielenstein, "The Restoration of the Han Dynasty: With Prolegomena on the Historiography of the *Hou Han Shu*," 38.
4. Albert E. Dien, "Historiography of the Six Dynasties Period (220–581)," 509–11.
5. Burton Watson, *Ssu-ma Ch'ien: Grand Historian of China*, 133.

and varied to be covered by any single characterization. For any given statement or passage in any given history, we may well run through a litany of questions derived from them: Was this written to praise or to blame? What useful knowledge did it convey to its readers? What gentry interests did it serve? How does it reflect on the interests of the state whose history is being told, or those of the successor state under which the history was finalized? Does the narrative serve to illustrate some transcendent moral rule? Does it reveal some aspect of the eternal mutability of human affairs?

What these assessments share in common, however, is that they all tend to take us *away* from the historical text itself. This is to start off on the wrong foot. Before boiling historiography down to the historical conditions that shaped it, we might first evaluate it as a kind of written representation. That is the idea behind this study, using a close examination of the *History of the Liu-Song* (*Song shu* 宋書), compiled in 487–88 and covering the first three-quarters of the fifth century.

The Liu-Song and China in the Southern Dynasties Period

The dynasty known as the "Liu-Song" 劉宋, to distinguish it from the greater Song dynasty that ruled China half a millennium later, was founded in 420 and expired in 479, enduring for exactly one sixty-year Chinese cycle. Conventionally identified as the start of a "Southern Dynasties" period, in fact the Liu-Song's predecessor, the Eastern Jin (318–420), was entirely a dynasty of the south, and a tradition of dynastic rule in the southeast had been established two centuries earlier by the state of Wu (229–80). Based in the city of Jiankang (modern Nanjing), these southern states ruled primarily over the lower and middle Yangtze regions, with colonial advances into the south and occasional, tenuous conquests of territory in the north and the west. Topography and scale distinguished them from their forebear and model, the Han dynasty (the Western Han, 202 BCE–8 CE, and the Eastern, 25–220 CE): the "fluid" political economy of the river-linked south stood in contrast to the land-oriented empire of the old northern plains and passes, and even at its height—a census from 464 records some five million registered souls—the southern state's control over its subjects compared neither with the Han, which in the first century CE had registered a population of nearly sixty million, nor with the population resources of contemporary regimes in the north.[6]

The southern regimes faced two chief problems. First, their sovereignty swelled and diminished in a functional relationship with the vicissitudes of their adversaries in the north. In 383, the Eastern Jin was nearly overrun by the state known to history as the "Former Qin" (350–94), and the Liu-Song would be confronted with the rise of an even more fearsome foe, the Northern Wei (386–534, established as an imperial dynasty in 399). There is nothing like an external threat, and occasional opportunity, to concentrate, or dissipate, the energies of a state, and in the matter of historiography it is likely that such an external audience contributed to the development of a kind of historical writing that cast the state and its actors in a basically positive, "eulogistic" light.[7] Acute as the external threat may have been, however, the more crucial challenge that was confronted by the dynasties based in the south, and processed in their historiography,

---

6. The best general introduction to the history and culture of early medieval China is Mark Edward Lewis, *China between Empires: The Northern and Southern Dynasties*; see especially 7–14 for the contrast between the political cultures of the old north and the new south. See also Charles Holcombe, *In the Shadow of the Han: Literati Thought and Society at the Beginning of the Southern Dynasties*, 1–24, for a review of influential mid-twentieth-century approaches to understanding this period.

On the population, see Hans Bielenstein, "Census of China during the Period 2–742 A. D.," 145 and plates III, IV, V; and Ge Jianxiong, ed., *Zhongguo renkou shi* 1:498, 557. The actual population of the Liu-Song was probably several times the number of registered persons. Recently an argument has been made, relying on the highest conceivable population estimates, that the Liu-Song was "the largest and most populous state in East Asia at the time" and thus an "empire" in the full connotation of that word; see Andrew Chittick, "The Southern Dynasties," 237, and Chittick, *The Jiankang Empire in Chinese and World History*, appendix 2. The registered population number, however, remains a good index of the scale of the Southern Dynasties state, with the Han, Tang, and the contemporary north the most relevant points of comparison.

7. Studies that use material from the *Song shu* to explore how the northern and southern states presented themselves to their counterparts include Albert E. Dien, "The Disputation at Pengcheng: Accounts from the *Wei shu* and the *Song shu*," which translates a dialog between northern and southern statesmen as it was recorded in northern and southern histories; and Lu Kou, "The Epistolary Self and Psychological Warfare: Tuoba Tao's (408–52, r. 423–52) Letters and His Southern Audience," which analyzes the rhetorical effects of statements made by northern and southern emperors.

was an internal problem: a viable body politic had to be negotiated between the imperial state and what, for lack of a better word, we may refer to as the "gentry."[8]

The state-gentry relationship was a problem with a long history. The foundational empires of the Qin (220–206 BCE) and the Han established this relationship to the state's favor, but the early medieval period was characterized by a tilt toward the gentry. The simple historical reason for this change is that centralized imperial power, having enervated and then imploded over the last century of the Eastern Han, was not easily reconstituted, no matter how much a successor state might desire to do so, the gentry naturally finding greater exercise of self-sovereignty an amenable condition. The power of the gentry only grew with the Western Jin dynasty's (265–316) loss of the northern heartland and the ensuing flight south, where a feeble imperial court was tethered to a succession of dominant clans. Nevertheless, this retrenchment had its limits: the circumscribed imperial state of the Southern Dynasties remained an imperial state, which the gentry might dominate but would never supplant. In fact, in an apparent paradox, it may be said that the state became more important even as the court languished. For one, state emolument was essential to gentry identity, who relied on office-holding for material and especially symbolic sustenance. Further, the state provided a political venue for the development and integration of a complex gentry society—newly arrived families from the north mixing with those that had established themselves in the south centuries earlier, with various social divisions within and across the two groups and, as the southern economy burgeoned, the incorporation of upwardly mobile men who made their way onto the gentry fringe. Gentry actors leveraged the state's authority, to their own advantage or to the advantage of the state over other members of the gentry, but the state as an entity could not tip to the gentry as a class, because the gentry depended on it too much.

In sum, the state-gentry relationship was a vital dynamic in Southern Dynasties China, intensified and not vitiated by gentry dominance. Such

---

8. We need a broad concept to cover the varyingly propertied and privileged class that did business with the state. For this purpose I adopt the term "gentry," on which see the still insightful survey of the early medieval period in Eberhard, *A History of China*, esp. 69–73, 154–57.

was the background against which Liu Yu 劉裕 (363–422, r. 420–22), known in the history of his dynasty and henceforth in this study as "the Founding Ancestor" (Gaozu 高祖, the "high[est] ancestor" worshipped by a given family), rose to power. Liu Yu is often spoken of in terms of his deficient qualifications vis-à-vis the court elite, but he is better regarded as a legitimate power who emerged from the broad late Jin lower and middle gentry.[9] The beginnings of the Liu-Song can be traced to the highly factionalized Jin court of the 390s, with strife between a wayward uncle and an even more wayward cousin of the sitting emperor (the "Peaceful" Emperor, Andi, r. 396–419), on the one hand, and high ministers of greater and lesser ability and loyalty on the other. Meanwhile, widespread dissent—"rebellion," from the perspective of the court and its historiographers—emerged in the thriving but discordant and precarious society that had taken shape in the state's core lower Yangtze region. Through talent and charisma, fortune and fate, the future Founding Ancestor became one of the few men capable of wielding substantive power, playing a key role in suppressing the rebellion and then, in 404, leading the ouster of an erstwhile establisher of a new dynasty, Huan Xuan 桓玄 (369–404). Slowly picking off his civil and military competitors, by 412 the Founding Ancestor had taken full control of the imperial capital. In 416, he led a (briefly) successful prestige raid on the old northern capitals—his rise to power was greatly facilitated by the relative dormancy of the Northern Wei in this decade—and in 420 he duly received the Mandate of Heaven from the Jin emperor known to history as "the Respectful" (Gongdi, r. 419–20).

The Founding Ancestor died just two years into his reign. Following a brief succession crisis, his third son, Emperor Wen (r. 424–53), would rule for a relatively stable thirty years, before pressure from the Northern

9. See Wan Shengnan, ed., *Chen Yinke Wei Jin Nanbeichao shi jiangyan lu*, 119–22, 179–80, and, with a detailed discussion of the office holdings of the family and in-laws from Liu Yu's great-grandfather down, Zhu Zongbin, "Liu Yu mendi kao." Recent scholarship in English has pegged Liu Yu too low: Chittick, "The Southern Dynasties," views him as a "largely illiterate" outsider (238, with a remarkable mid-life transformation at 241); Lewis, *China between Empires*, 70, refers to him as a "commoner"; and the introduction to Scott Pearce, Audrey Spiro, and Patricia Ebrey, eds., *Culture and Power in the Reconstitution of the Chinese Realm: 200–600*, directly incorporates the extremely prejudicial, if informative, biography of Liu Yu in the *History of the Northern Wei* (*Wei shu*), calling him a "shoe peddler" (25).

Wei and factionalism among his thirty sons and daughters led to his assassination. One of those sons, Emperor Xiaowu (r. 453–64), emerged to rejuvenate the dynasty's fortunes, establishing a vigorous, aggressive imperial court for a decade. That revival ended with enormous bloodshed during the brief reign of his young heir, and in the fifteen years that followed, the Liu-Song dynasty did little more than tread water before the Mandate passed on again.

The Historiography of the Liu-Song

The history of the Founding Ancestor's rise and of the dynasty he established was written as it happened. In the final years of the Jin, works were produced that summed up its years of decline and spoke for the men who, resigned to pointless loyalty, continued to identify themselves as its subjects.[10] If they could not, strictly speaking, foresee the exact end point of their dynasty, through the prism of dynastic historiography they could envision its horizon. Correspondingly, the rise of a new dynasty was as much a historiographical phenomenon as a political one. The process by which the Mandate of Heaven was transferred from one house to another was intrinsically historiographical, documents being created and inserted into the record in order to satisfy the narrative arc of orthodox history. The people involved in the dynastic transition were likewise attentive to their own place in this process. The practical realities of their lives—securing family interests, surviving the violent battles of the political arena—were melded together with acts of self-representation as historiographical subjects, fulfilling historiographical roles in the service of an incoming dynasty.

These historiographical representations accumulated like the sediment of a rock bed over the course of the Liu-Song, culminating in the *History of the Liu-Song* by Shen Yue 沈約 (441–513), commissioned eight

---

10. Xu Guang 徐廣 (352–425) is an example; see *Jin shu* 82.2158–60. By the interpretation of the *Song shu*, Tao Yuanming (365?–427), the great "hermit poet" of the late Jin, is another. Not all Jin subjects were so loyal: see the works of Wang Shaozhi 王韶之 (380–435), as discussed in chapter 5.

years after the dynasty's conclusion.[11] Carrying on standard imperial practice, the Liu-Song staffed court offices charged with collecting and processing historical documentation—the Palace Secretary (*mishu jian* 秘書監) and his "gentlemen of composition" (*zhuzuo lang* 著作郎), with their "gentleman assistants" (*zuolang* 佐郎).[12] Occasionally we gain a view into their work, as when, in 433, "the Grand Ancestor (Emperor Wen) had Xiao Sihua (400–455) submit to the court a narrative of his pacification of the Hanzhong region, and passed it down to the officials in charge of historiography" 太祖使思話上平漢中本末，下之史官.[13] The first step toward a formal dynastic history came in 439, when He Chengtian 何承天 (370–447) was tasked with editing a "state history" (*guoshi* 國史) composed of annals, biographies, and treatises.[14] Shen Yue implies that He Chengtian drafted the biographies of the early Liu-Song and relevant late Jin figures, and he says that one of those charged with continuing his work, a man by the name of Su Baosheng 蘇寶生 (d. 458), composed the biographies of men active in the reign of Emperor Wen.[15] Be that as it may, we do not know to what extent they were stitching together received narratives or how their work was re-edited at the next inflection point in the production of the *History of the Liu-Song*. That was the work of Xu Yuan 徐爰

---

11. The most important sources for the history of the compilation of the *Song shu* are Shen Yue's own account, in the last scroll of his work, and the synoptic one in Liu Zhiji (661–721), *Shitong tongshi* ("Waipian," "Gujin zhengshi") 2.319–21. Of various modern reviews, see especially Tang Changru, "Wei Jin Nanbeichao shiji juyao," 279–83, and the integral account in Tang Xiejun, *Shijia xingji yu shishu gouzao: yi Wei Jin Nanbeichao yishi wei zhongxin de kaocha*, chapter 5. For a sympathetic portrait of Shen Yue, see Richard B. Mather, *The Poet Shen Yüeh (441–513): The Reticent Marquis*, supplemented with greater political detail, and less sympathy, by Tang Xiejun, *Shijia xingji yu shishu gouzao*, appendix 2.

12. Li Jutian, "*Song shu* zuanxiu shimo kao," identifies as far as possible all of the men who held these offices in the Liu-Song period. These posts were noted sinecures and stepping stones, but real work still went on in them.

13. *Song shu* 78.2013.

14. See He's biography at *Song shu* 64.1704, which provides the date, and Shen Yue's preface, 100.2467. As Edwin G. Pulleyblank ("The Historiographical Tradition," 154–55) has emphasized, dynastic histories were written during the life of a dynasty and not only after its demise, as sometimes assumed from the example of the received standard histories, which were in fact finalized after the close of the dynasties they cover.

15. *Song shu* 100.2467. There is a brief biographical note for Su Baosheng at 75.1958.

(394–475), a talented lower official at the vigorous but authoritarian court of Emperor Xiaowu. It is said that although Xu Yuan based his version, completed in 462, on earlier compilations, he gave the material his own distinctive stamp, producing an integral history of the half-century from the Founding Ancestor's restoration of the Jin court in 404 up through Xu's own time. According to Shen Yue, the emperor himself contributed biographies for three prominent villains.[16]

One influential characterization of Shen Yue's *History* holds that he was able to complete the bulk of it in a single year because he largely copied from Xu Yuan's work, adding coverage of the dynasty's final two decades.[17] This seems true as far as it goes—but no further. In his memorial to the throne, Shen especially remarks on the biases in the earlier histories, and presumably in Xu Yuan's particularly, and he speaks of his revision in strong terms, saying that "today, your servant has endeavored to establish a different framework, to make a new history" 臣今謹更創立，製成新史.[18] The title line—as preserved in early printings, though no longer in the modern typeset edition—also underscores Shen Yue's authorship, specifying that this is a *History* "newly compiled" (*xin zhuan* 新撰) by his hand. How exactly Shen Yue exercised this authorial agency can only be glimpsed and guessed at—Xu Yuan's work survived into the Tang but is now extant only in fragments. In the annals, at least, he appears to have trimmed the sails of a more heroic narrative. For instance, Xu Yuan's account of the Founding Ancestor's defeat of the "rebel" Sun En 孫恩 (d. 402) reads:

> Though he had suffered a rout, [Sun En] still had many supporters to rely on and thus (*sui*) he proceeded directly to attack the capital. *The court, shaken*

---

16. *Song shu* 100.2467. See also *Song shu* 94.2308–9, which quotes the memorial in which Xu Yuan sets out the principles of his work.

17. See Zhao Yi (1727–1814), *Nianer shi zhaji jiaozheng* 9.179–80; Tang Xiejun, *Shijia xingji yu shishu gouzao*, 105–7, calculates that only 92 out of a total of 238 treatises and biographies in the *Song shu* are limited to events before the year 464. Another of Zhao Yi's criticisms is that Shen Yue's *History* glossed over the true history of how the Song overthrew the Jin and was again too polite in its telling of how the Song fell to the Qi. Yet the whole idea of a dynastic history was to show how the Mandate of Heaven was duly transferred from one legitimate imperial house to another, and then on again at its expiration.

18. *Song shu* 100.2467.

> with fright (*zhen ju*), made Liu Yu Establishing Martial General and Prefect of Xiapi. Commanding a naval unit, Liu Yu pursued Sun to Yuzhou, where he again inflicted a great defeat upon him.

> 雖被摧破，猶恃眾力，遂徑向京師。朝廷震懼，以高祖為建武將軍、下邳太守，帥舟師討恩于郁洲，復大破之。[19]

The parallel passage in Shen Yue's *History* tracks this closely, but with a different tone:

> Though he had suffered a rout, [Sun En] still had many supporters to rely on, and he proceeded directly to attack the capital. But headwinds stalled his tall-masted ships, and it took him ten or so days to reach Baishi, and then he found that Liu Laozhi had returned *and that the court was well prepared* (*you bei*). Thus (*sui*) he was forced to flee toward Yuzhou. In the eighth month [of 401], the Founding Ancestor was made Establishing Martial General and Prefect of Xiapi. Leading a river brigade to Yuzhou in pursuit of Sun En, he again inflicted a great defeat on En, who fled south.

> 雖被摧破，猶恃其眾力，徑向京師。樓船高大，值風不得進，旬日乃至白石。尋知劉牢之已還，朝廷有備，遂走向鬱洲。八月，以高祖為建武將軍、下邳太守，領水軍追討至鬱洲，復大破恩。恩南走。[20]

Where Xu Yuan had glorified the Founding Ancestor, rescuing the court from a state of shock, Shen Yue reserves due dignity for the Jin court, presented as well prepared. The exigence of the situation is toned down through a displacement of "consequence," in the shift of "thus" (*sui*) from Sun En's threat to its abatement.

In prefaces to the treatises, which required much labor and were incorporated into the work some time after the rest was presented to the throne, Shen Yue explains why he chose one topic and not another, and how he made use of his predecessors' scholarship. But for the biographies, though we may at times perceive certain editorial choices—such as the

---

19. *Taiping yulan* 128.1b–2a.
20. *Song shu* 1.3. Liu Laozhi (d. 402; biography at *Jin shu* 84.2188–91) was the most powerful military commander of the late fourth century. In the turmoil of Huan Xuan's coup he committed suicide, and the Founding Ancestor, who had served under Liu's command, emerged to take his place.

pairing of the higher- and lower-born statesmen in the first biography proper (the subject of chapters 1 and 2 in the present study) or the special inclusion of certain documents (as in chapter 4 here)—more frequently we cannot confidently distinguish Shen Yue's authorial voice from the older biases he left intact in his work. Yet the historian's hold over a historical work was subtle anyhow. The work Shen Yue crafted was more decorous and courtly than pointed and analytical: the short historical disquisitions appended to each biographical chapter, for instance, read as neat designations of praise and blame in due proportion, together sketching out a simple picture of a dynasty that rose by great deeds and fell through grievous foibles.[21] The *History* was not primarily an expression of Shen Yue's own historical interpretation, but a robust and respectful transmission of historical source material—"the splendid canons of an entire era" 一代之盛典 in his own description—stocked with informative detail.[22]

Shen Yue surely had his views, but the greater meaning of the *History of the Liu-Song* lies rather in the form of historiography he was working with. There were two major historiographical forms in Shen Yue's time. Chronological history, a type associated with the *Spring and Autumn Annals*, the terse record of antiquity ostensibly edited by Confucius, sought to present the history of a dynasty or period in a relatively concise series of events. This was not the dominant form, however, and a number of well-known chronological histories are in fact abridged reorganizations of the chronicle's more important counterpart—the history of "annals and biographies" (*ji zhuan* 紀傳).[23] This model was established by the great Sima

---

21. For an interpretation of the view of Liu-Song history implied in Shen Yue's *History*, see Kawai Yasushi, *Nanchō kizokusei kenkyū*, chapter 6.

22. *Song shu* 100.2468.

23. The annals and biographies framework includes several other elements, some uncommonly used, the most significant of which were the "tables" (*biao* 表) and the "treatises" (*zhi* 志). Tables condense historical data into an easily surveyed format organized by topic and chronology. This element was abandoned in the early medieval period, but it was used to great effect by Sima Qian and Ban Gu, and its utility was rediscovered after the Tang. For discussions, see Watson, *Ssu-ma Chʻien*, 112–15, and Grant Hardy, *Worlds of Bronze and Bamboo: Sima Qian's Conquest of History*, esp. 29–34. Treatises were something like "monographs" on various subjects relevant to imperial governance in the *Shiji*, but by this period they had become copious repositories of historical records or documentation, edited and introduced by the historian. Jiang Yan 江淹 (444–505), a poet-historian

Qian (145/135–86 BCE) at the teetering height of the Western Han, while Ban Gu (32–92) made it a strictly dynastic model with his *History of the [Western] Han (Han shu)*, a book that furnished a stately patrimony for the "Eastern" or "Later" Han. Thus established, dynastic historiography became a key feature of the Chinese state all the way up to the twentieth century, even if its relative valence within the wider field of historical sources diminished, first with the move to compilation by committee under the Tang, then with the advent of print culture in the eleventh century. For early medieval China, however, the prevalence of this model again presents an apparent paradox: that a historiographical form that had taken shape as a part of a grand empire thrived under the auspices of southern heirs not a tenth its size. One might have thought that the weakness of the state would have opened the way for other kinds of history. Instead, the court-oriented annals-biography form remained the pole star of early medieval political culture, and even the other types of history that arose in the period, such as local history, maintained its characteristic state-gentry political orientation.

The essence of the annals and biographies history lies in a conceptual relationship between the two elements that constitute its name. Annals were the hoariest kind of formal historiography, associated with the court scribes of the Zhou. Closely shorn court records, they only by exception—for instance, in the long narrative of the Founding Ancestor's rise in the *History of the Liu-Song*—offered anything resembling an integral historical account. This concision became a key feature in their historical application: in the more manifest form of the term used by Sima Qian, annals are the "basic threads" (*benji* 本紀) upon which all else depends, the word for a strand of silk or cord of gathered strands, *ji* 紀, being cognate with the

---

contemporary of Shen Yue, is said to have remarked that the compilation of treatises was the art of historiography's greatest challenge, and they make up a full thirty of the *History of the Liu-Song*'s hundred scrolls, covering the calendrical sciences, imperial ritual, lyrics for court performance, administrative geography, government bureaucracy, and natural omens of varying sorts. See Balazs, "History as a Guide to Bureaucratic Practice," 134, and B. J. Mansvelt Beck, *The Treatises of Later Han: Their Author, Sources, Contents, and Place in Chinese Historiography*, 55.

word used for "classic," *jing* 經, literally the "warp" on which cloth, or a text, is woven.[24]

The idea of a "biography" (*zhuan* 傳, literally, "what has been passed down") in imperial China took shape against this conception of the annals. These biographies are not "lives" but "commentaries" (also *zhuan*) to an annals/classic. Set out (to again use Sima Qian's terminology) in an "array" (*lie* 列, cognate with 烈, "shining" or "outstanding"), individuals were put on display in the textual halls of the imperial houses for their accomplishments in the sphere of the imperial state and the culture it sustained. Like the three *zhuan*-commentaries to the *Spring and Autumn Annals*, biographies in early medieval China eclipsed their annalistic classics in bulk and in impact but never departed from their weave.[25]

Instantiating the relationship of state and gentry, the annals-biography form establishes the most important characteristics of early medieval historiography. With the annals supplying the basic chronological framework and the various biographies filling in the historical detail, the form nullifies any expectation that history should be told in a straightforward fashion. This fundamentally open structure does not gather facts relevant to a given event in one place but spreads them across any number of different biographies, important events narrated not once but over and over. This means that readers, up until they have absorbed the entire *History*, must always wonder whether a certain event will be cast in a different light elsewhere, or, complementarily, whether a particular telling within a particular biography might hold some particular interpretative significance. This leads

---

24. The classic-to-commentary relationship of the annals to the biographies was observed by the Tang historical critic Liu Zhiji (*Shitong tongshi* 2.43, "Liezhuan"); see Twitchett, "Chinese Biographical Writing," 97–98, and Twitchett, "Problems of Chinese Biography," 26, 32–33. The point is endorsed and expanded in Mark Edward Lewis, *Writing and Authority in Early China*, chapter 7 and 334; also Zhu Dongrun, *Badai zhuanxu wenxue shulun*, 22–23; and Chen Shih-Hsiang, "An Innovation in Chinese Biographical Writing," 50. It is unclear, however, how certain we should be that Sima Qian explicitly had such a model in mind, and Burton Watson (*Ssu-ma Ch'ien*, 120–27) rejected the association.

25. The two studies by Denis Twitchett cited in the preceding note remain insightful introductions in English to Chinese biography, this historiography's richest vein. For another useful overview, see Brian Moloughney, "From Biographical History to Historical Biography: A Transformation in Chinese Historical Writing," 2–13, which cites Pierre Ryckmans for the association of *liezhuan* with "exemplary" lives.

into two somewhat dubious yet culturally significant templates of historical interpretation. One is that the historian, following the laconic lead of Confucius in the *Spring and Autumn Annals*, might make use of "subtle words" (*wei yan* 微言)—the selection or absence of specific diction or detail—to convey a historical judgment. It can be hard to positively identify such judgments, and to distinguish the extent to which historians use oblique expression as a technique to convey historical interpretation from their use of it as a crutch, excusing themselves from the precariousness of forthright judgment, or from the embarrassment of having presented an insufficiently complete historical account; but the effect on the readers of a history is functionally the same, imploring them, and us, to discern judgment in what the text says or does not say.

Related to "subtle words" is the idea of a "theory of mutual illumination" (*hujian fa* 互見法). Identified much later but clearly present in early medieval historiography, this technique relies on the juxtaposition of parallel narratives in a work to produce what one modern scholar has described as "a higher level vision developed through an interplay of perspectives."[26] This manifold historical perspective is best explained by two separate but intertwined factors. Historians, having accepted a "normalized role" for a biographical subject, were wont to place disjunctive, often negative, portrayals elsewhere in a history, "to maintain consistency" and to ensure decorum.[27] The main origin of those disjunctive materials, meanwhile, lay not with the historian but in the variously biased sources from which histories were assembled, and though he would prune and select from these sources, the dutiful historian was committed to relaying them in some degree of completion.[28]

Both "subtle words" and "mutual illumination" suggest to the reader that meaning is somewhere to be found hidden in the historical text, but

---

26. See Wai-yee Li, "The Idea of Authority in the *Shih chi* (*Records of the Historian*)," 397.
27. Twitchett, "Problems of Chinese Biography," 32.
28. Grant Hardy argues that Sima Qian's different and not infrequently contradictory accounts are due to an unwillingness to overturn one source on the basis of another, a motive that applies to the early medieval historian as well; see Hardy, *Worlds of Bronze and Bamboo*, esp. 82–85. To similar effect, Wai-yee Li, "Pre-Qin Annals," 431–34, connects the rich variation of perspective in the *Zuozhuan*, the most extensive early historical narrative, to that work's "complex textual history."

we should not overlook the significance of what historical texts present to us most directly. Above all, the annals-biography form establishes the idea that the words and deeds of men (and sometimes women) as relayed in a biography had historical import. On the surface, this point may seem banal—for whence does history derive if not, mainly, from human deliberation and action? The distinction lies in the most salient quality of early medieval Chinese historiography: the integration of historical action with historiographical representation. What the gentryman did or said was envisioned and executed with the annals-biography form somewhere in mind.

The biographies, and historical action itself, were constructed of three major elements or modes of representation—the anecdote, the document, and the narration of "officialdom." Of these, the anecdote has received the most attention.[29] Droll or piquant little stories, anecdotes are beyond the realm of truth and falsehood, a status that perpetually confounds studies that seek to make use of dynastic biographies to tell real history. They are miniature allegories, spun up, in some certain proximity to historical fact, to illustrate the character of a biographical subject or to shed light on a historical event or situation. The key issue raised by the anecdote is bias, as various stories about individuals and events compete to portray them in a positive or negative way. This happened in the happening of history itself, as tales were told, and perhaps even staged, to influence the outcome or interpretation of events major and minor. Thus the anecdote is lodged halfway between historical mimesis and historiographical representation, and must be examined for its motivations on both ends of that continuum. It must also be stressed that the historian did not generally

---

29. The anecdote has been identified as "the basic unit of narrative" (David Schaberg, *A Patterned Past: Form and Thought in Early Chinese Historiography*, 164 and chapter 5 generally) in pre-imperial Chinese historiography, and its use has been the subject of much discussion, including essays in Paul van Els and Sarah A. Queen, eds., *Between History and Philosophy: Anecdotes in Early China*, and, on the medieval period, Jack W. Chen and David Schaberg, eds., *Idle Talk: Gossip and Anecdote in Traditional China*. Note, however, the dissent of Yuri Pines: "The pervasive presence of anecdotes in the historical and quasi-historical lore of the Warring States period has created the wrong impression that they define all early Chinese historical writing." See Pines, "Zhou History and Historiography: Introducing the Bamboo Manuscript *Xinian*," 323, and the fuller discussion of the relationship between anecdote and "informative history" in Pines, *Zhou History Unearthed: The Bamboo Manuscript "Xinian" and Early Chinese Historiography*, 73–80.

concoct anecdotes, but inherited them from his sources, guiding if not transforming history's vectors of bias through the arts of selection, omission, and editing—or finding himself guided by them.[30]

The anecdote may supply much of historiography's "enargia," strongly influencing the reader's impressions of historical actors and events, but it was the historical document that formed the true core of the historiographical tradition. *Shi* 史, the category term for "history," originally meant "scribe," and Confucian lore held that early historical records were in the charge of scribes who sat to their lords' left and right, respectively responsible for documenting his deeds and his words. The most common generic term in the titles of dynastic histories, *shu* 書, means "written document," and those titles can be construed not just as "the History of . . ." but as "the full documentary record of . . . ." This documentary lifeblood coursed through the *Shiji* and the *Han shu* and only gained in vigor in the early medieval period, when documentation came to constitute an outsize proportion of the historical narrative; the trend reached an apex with the *Song shu*, where nearly a third of the biographical section is composed of quotations from documents. Later historical critics would savage Shen Yue for the unwieldy bulk of his *History*, but his unparsimonious approach is a great boon to the historian, both for its preservation of period detail and perspective and because that very abundance points us toward a better understanding of what "historical writing" really was in early medieval China.

This documentation was no longer the domain of court scribes but a republic in which the lettered men and women of early medieval China performed historical action. Its greatest glory lies in poetry and belletristic prose, produced, to paraphrase the traditional formula, in order to give public voice to the author's state of mind in a given socio-political situation. An analogous framework underpinned the production of a wider range of writing and (recorded) speech, more or less artistic, inherently rhetorical, often practical, but never divorced from the author, representing his ideas in writing and allowing his writing to represent himself, speaking to his

---

30. The extent to which the speeches and anecdotes recorded in historiography are fictional is examined at length at Bielenstein, "The Restoration of the Han Dynasty," 49–61. Unsurprisingly, Bielenstein finds that a great deal of it is invented, but his inquiry cannot pin down where in the historiographical process this invention occurred.

contemporaries and, as if in soliloquy, to the audience of history. The key implication of this documentary "motive" is that if "history" is essentially retrospective, the historiography we are dealing with here was eminently contemporary, historical actors writing history as they lived or created it. In this respect again, the *History of the Liu-Song* provides a model example: compiled, apparently with a light hand, within a century of the events it relays, it provides a clearer view of the bond between history and historiography than we may obtain from sources with muddier timelines, most notably the *History of the Later Han* and the *History of the Jin*, both re-edited from earlier sources several centuries after the periods they cover.

"Officialdom"—the government of early medieval China and its representation in language—may pale beside the vivacity of the anecdote and the rhetorical richness of the document, but in its ubiquity it was peer to both. Annals and biographies alike brim with zero-degree records of promotion, demotion, and transfer across the official ranks. As a matter of historical realia, this historical element has much to tell us, if in coded form: we see who held power when and where, and better understand historical individuals through the types of offices they held during their careers. But is there not a deeper historiographical significance to officialdom, insofar as it was a central feature of the landscape across which historical actors traveled? Its glistening, lapidary surface seems to be more than just an index to the careers of mortal men.

Approaches

"Through its form," Burton Watson remarks of Sima Qian's *Shiji*, "the history passes judgment upon its material."[31] This imprint pressed deeper and deeper as the annals-biography form took root in the culture of early medieval China, shaping not just historical narrative but the production of the historical material itself. But here we face a problem of interpretation. An appreciation of the impact of the form is essential to reading early medieval historiography, lest we fall into the "hypercritical" approach to our sources warned of by Herbert Franke (1914–2011), for we cannot expect

---

31. Watson, *Ssu-ma Ch'ien*, 112.

early medieval biography to be anything more or less than what it was.[32] At the same time, what is necessary is not necessarily sufficient: the judgments carried in a historiographical tradition do not fully overlap with the judgments we the readers, knowing better than to take this historiography at "face value," will wish to make. To put the problem generally: no text is ever read solely on its own terms, but only against some structure of interpretation, mapped out according to some set of ideas. The question, then, is what tools might be employed to pry open the form of early medieval historiography. In this study, I propose and make use of two: a political model and a rhetorical one.

From the production of primary sources to that material's assembly into completed and imperially ratified works of history, Chinese historiography was embedded in and deeply concerned with political culture. Thus, our interpretation of historiography must be informed by this politics, the logic of which has been aptly articulated in spatial terms by the modern scholar Mark Edward Lewis as an "authority of the inner over the outer," in which progress toward the interior represents the accrual of political power.[33] This formation began with, or culminated in, the way power in the Han dynasty imperial system gathered around the emperor in the "inner court" of the palace, to the disadvantage of the bureaucratic organs of the "outer court." At once physical and conceptual, this interior-exterior division marked the organization of power structures as varied as the city, the household, and the tomb.

Thus, a model so conceived starts with two poles: the interior, strong and good, and the exterior, weak and low. These are not fixed points, however, but a relation that existed at any moment for a historical actor, an interior-exterior dynamic that shaped political action, a motive that informed the production of historiographical narrative in real time and in retrospect. To elucidate the operation of this dynamic, we may fill in two further features: the central position of the "threshold" and the key mechanism of the "prompt." The threshold represents the boundary line

---

32. Herbert Franke, "Some Remarks on the Interpretation of Chinese Dynastic Histories," 113.

33. Mark Edward Lewis, *The Construction of Space in Early China*, 114, with discussion of different spaces so organized at 114–18, and in chapter 2 on the power paradox of gendered space, noted below.

between interiority and exteriority; crossing it meant power or deprivation of power, and control over it—a point of security, safe from the danger and instability of directly held political power, or a staging ground for timely interior advancement—proved one's mastery of the political art of the interior-exterior. And how did one cross the threshold? The deep mover of interior progress might have been the human drive for power—or its complement, the drive to expel others—but that general cause took effect through the human drive to narrative, the "plotting out" of a political career. These plotted points were "prompts," serving to advance one toward interiority or push others to the outside.

The most interesting thing about the interior-exterior dynamic is that while it is simple in constitution, in operation it was complex and unstable. One reason for this is that interior and exterior space is configured differently in arenas that are different, but overlap. In a discussion of the status of women in early imperial China, for instance, Lewis observes that their physical location in the interior of the household or the palace often gave women authority over family or state affairs from which they were nominally prohibited. In the social sphere of the early medieval period we encounter an analogous power potential paradox, of men from the middle and lower gentry who by their social status were excluded from the rarefied realm of the true gentry elite but for that very reason were able to draw closer to powerful patrons, including the emperor and the imperial kinsmen. Interaction between different configurations of interior and exterior produced a subtle political interplay.

A second factor in the complexity of interior-exterior dynamics is an inherent confusion in the way interior and exterior relate. Truth and power lie in the interior, but when we speak of the interiority of an individual we refer to something—their personality and values—that is inaccessible and inscrutable except through the exterior dimensions of representation and action. By analogy, when facing a building we may affirm that what matters is what happens inside, that that is where the power resides; but how crucial its exterior, as the facade that manifests its eminence or the fortification that ensures its dominance. In this sense, as a representation of the interior, the exterior boasts an interiority of its own. Exteriors, however, can be false facades. That again makes the exterior inferior to the interior essence—but external falsehood also furnishes a new articulation of power. That is the strange power of irony, where exterior holds interior in check, lest its true nature be revealed, while the exterior persists only as long as it performs that concealing function. This enigmatic insistence of the exterior is crucial to our understanding of early medieval historiography because historiography was an exterior wrapping around the interior historical action it represented, while at the same time this external representation was part of the action. Inevitably, readers will seek a historical reality held within the written form, but it is equally important to recognize the reality of the historiographical surface: it was the public face of that interior world, the dignified visage of its internal organization, sometimes revealing, sometimes concealing, but always constitutive, never displaced by what lies beneath it.

To navigate this exterior surface and the strong currents that run beneath it we turn to the tools of rhetoric, by which is meant not the narrow analysis of diction and style, though consideration of literary tropes is involved, but the global art of persuasion. Speaking on the documentary record, historical actors sought to persuade their audiences to adopt their positions or sympathize with their interests. Anecdotes were shaped and reshaped as stories for or against their protagonist's good repute. Presenting an account of events, the historian implicitly or explicitly formulated a judgment for his audience's consideration. At the deepest level, undergirding all of these local instances of persuasion, lies a rhetoric of historiography—the ways of persuasion that molded the historical events and their representation alike. This is to say that, from action in the world to inscription on the page, history and historiography conspired in a process of argumentation.

The analysis of argument is the province of the rhetorical "topic." The topic, particularly in the study of literature, has come to be associated with what are also known as "specific topics" or "commonplaces"; the image of "a world turned upside down" is a stock example, while for our subject we might point to the commonly invoked "good historian" (liang shi 良史), conveyor of a truthful record, no matter the dangers that might entail.[34] But the specific topic is a narrower connotation of a broader concept. A mainstay of the rhetorical tradition since Aristotle, topics involve not

---

34. For an influential introduction to these specific topics, see chapter 5, "Topics," in Ernst Robert Curtius, *European Literature and the Latin Middle Ages*, including 94–98 on "The World Upsidedown."

specific statements but the general logical forms from which arguments may be derived—a typology of arguments to which a given speaker, in a certain culture or context, may profitably refer. Aristotle lists hundreds in his *Topics*. In the *Rhetoric*, he gives a (rather various) list of twenty-eight, these apparently singled out for their utility in the contexts he was concerned with. The later tradition further winnowed and rationalized the scope—Cicero (106–43 BCE) listed sixteen topics, while one modern scholar has found twenty groups in the influential scheme of Boethius (477–524).[35] But if the rhetorical topics are to be a practical interpretative tool, they must be reduced further still, and that is what one group of mid-twentieth-century American teachers of rhetoric did, identifying a basic, intuitive set of four topics.[36] Slightly modifying their formulation, I will here articulate historiographical argumentation against four topoi: definition, consequence, analogy and contrast, and circumstance.

Definition is an account of what a thing or a situation *is*, comprising both definition in the strict sense of the term—a fair account of the thing's

---

35. Otto Bird, "The Tradition of the Logical Topics: Aristotle to Ockham," 311–12, which also cites numbers for Aristotle. Useful overviews of the topic and its complexities include Richard Graff, "Topics/Topoi"; Christof Rapp, "Aristotle's Rhetoric," which also discusses the enthymeme; and Quentin Skinner, *Reason and Rhetoric in the Philosophy of Hobbes*, 111–19, which concisely summarizes the shifts in the meaning of the term. A direct inspiration for the approach adopted in the present study is the work of Mary Garrett, a pioneer in the study of Chinese rhetoric who has investigated the use of "topics" in early Chinese persuasive speech; see Sharon Bracci Blinn and Mary Garrett, "Aristotelian *Topoi* as a Cross-Cultural Analytical Tool." For some recent approaches to argument in pre-modern China, but not from this perspective, see Garret P. S. Olberding, ed., *Facing the Monarch: Modes of Advice in the Early Chinese Court*, and Joachim Gentz and Dirk Meyer, eds., *Literary Forms of Argument in Early China*.

36. See Manuel Bilsky et al., "Looking for an Argument." Their topics are: genus (i.e., definition), consequence, likeness and difference, and testimony and authority. The scheme is primarily identified with, and was possibly initiated by, Richard M. Weaver (1910–63), a reactionary figure who advocated a "rectification of names" style program. For an early, succinct summary of his philosophy, see Weaver, "To Write the Truth"; for an early, succinct critique, see W. E. B. Du Bois, "Is Man Free?" His work on rhetoric may be read with Sharon Crowley, "When Ideology Motivates Theory: The Case of the Man from Weaverville," and with the copious gathering of political (e.g., 555–58) and rhetorical (e.g., 290–99) essays in Weaver, *In Defense of Tradition: Collected Shorter Writings of Richard M. Weaver, 1929–1963*.

essence—and in the widened sense of the "properties" or qualities that something inherently possesses or instantiates. Definition is the seat of rhetoric, the basis of all persuasion—for who would act on a falsehood?—and its end, insofar as (almost) all human action is undertaken to bring reality into coherence with some perceived truth. The only problems are that definitions are not always correct, their application is not always ethical, and the truths they point to are multivocal. These are critical weaknesses, if not ones generally recognized by those who would hold to a particular definition, or to definition itself as their master trope.

Two important aspects of the topic of definition are the enthymeme and what may be called the "quality of the absolute." An enthymeme is an argument that assumes a premise that is generally accepted by, or "endoxic" to, all reasonable members of its audience.[37] The enthymeme is an essential part of argumentation because much of human communication (fortunately) involves elements that are assumed and passed over in silence. Filling out these enthymemes with their implicit definitions, however, can help us arrive at a deeper understanding of the qualities, motivations, and implications of a given culture of argumentation. The quality of the absolute, meanwhile, reflects the persuader's confidence in the defining scheme he or she works within. Once put in accord with a definition, an event or action or judgment takes on the air of certainty and finality. The narratives of dynastic historiography exude this quality.

The topic of consequence is a matter of cause and effect, comprising both the prior causes of a given thing and the effects that will later issue from it. Rhetoric itself is a kind of consequence, persuasion causing a change in the audience's psychological state. In historiography, consequence is a topic of significance because narrative is tasked with organizing events into cause-and-effect relationships. On one hand, the development of consequence works hand in glove with definition, as historical action is narrated with a sense of inevitability, which is to say, with an "absolute" quality. In this respect, dynastic historiography frequently employs what can be called a "pluperfect" mode, in which the earlier and later parts of a historical "event" lock together in a grammatical certainty, and it typically renders historical action with an "immediate" sensibility, binding events

---

37. See George Kennedy, trans., *Aristotle: On Rhetoric; A Theory of Civic Discourse*, 41–42, 297–98.

together rapidly and indubitably. The certainties of consequence, however, cannot evade some fundamental issues of historical narrative. First, while historical events happened one way and not another, it is always true that they *could* have happened otherwise, and no "good historian" can be entirely unattuned to such contingencies. Second, historical causation, to the extent we can identify it at all, is more complex than simple notions of consequence would allow. The upshot of this is that historiography balances its absolute deployment of consequence with more artful forms. In the historical mimesis, this happens when actors make subjunctive arguments of "contrary consequence" about what would certainly happen *if* a (wrong) course of action were to be pursued, or what would have happened had a correct one been adopted. At the level of historical narration, it is the open annals-biography form itself that leavens the certainty of its exposition, by preserving the possibility that some other causal constellation may be found elsewhere.

Analogy and contrast—the juxtaposition of things similar and dissimilar—informed premodern Chinese historiography in a wide variety of ways, from "correlative thinking" in the early period to a "historical-analogistic attitude" that would later undergird some of the tradition's most trenchant historical thinking.[38] Perhaps most importantly, analogy and contrast accounts for an important aspect of the use of "roles" and "types" in historiographical action and representation—reaching into the past for points of comparison or projecting a present moment into the future. More generally, this topic again communes with something essential to the nature of rhetoric: it summons a meeting of minds. Analogy is the move that calls upon someone to join into a common imagination. Look, it is to say, at this thing we speak of and that thing you know—are they not similar? Contrast asks the complementary question: look—do you not see that they are different? These are the techniques of "association" and "disassociation" that lie at the center of the "new rhetoric" of Chaïm Perelman (1912–84) and Lucie Olbrechts-Tyteca (1899–1987), conjuring up an audience that perceives a manifold situation and aggregates

---

38. Robert M. Hartwell, "Historical Analogism, Public Policy, and Social Science in Eleventh- and Twelfth-Century China," 708.

or disaggregates its parts for comparative judgment.[39] In this sense, analogy and contrast is complementary to definition and consequence: not statements or actions alone, but as they are perceived and evaluated in relation to other statements and actions. This process of perception is suggestive and open, always—for better or for worse—leaving way for a new analogy or contrast to be raised.

Starting with definition as the strongest topic, we can perceive a progressive weakening in the unnecessary associations of consequence and the arbitrariness of analogy. To link our political and rhetorical models together, it is a progress from interiority to exteriority, and this progress culminates in our fourth topic, circumstance.[40] Circumstance refers to the willy-nilly world around us that constitutes the beginning and end of the whole rhetorical process, the cognitive environment for our formulation of the other topics and the ground upon which we act. It is the weakest topical state insofar as, in order to take on meaning, *mere* circumstance must be alchemized into something more than itself. But the import of circumstance is more subtle than that. Stylistically, circumstance populates the "story world" of the historical mimesis with contextual detail, delivering vitality to the arguments proper. Moreover, in argumentation, circumstance supplies a negative capability that is key to the rhetoric of dynastic historiography. For the historical actor and the historian alike, "thresholding"—positioning oneself on the cusp of "interior" power, within reach of it but beyond its inherent dangers—is a self-circumstantialization, demurring when a strong claim to definition might have been made. On the other hand, they were also easily circumstantialized, carried off in the floods of the historiographical rivers in which they swam. This ambivalence plays out on the conceptual level as well. In one sense, historiography's relationship to underlying reality is circumstantial: it is merely an external surface, a veneer under which very different things certainly occurred on

---

39. Chaïm Perelman and Lucie Olbrechts-Tyteca, *The New Rhetoric: A Treatise on Argumentation*, 190–92, and 371–410 on analogies in a more limited sense, including discussion of how analogies tend to be extended and amended.

40. This is a substitution for "authority" in the received framework. As its originators conceded, the topic of authority differs in nature from the preceding three: it is better viewed as a "warrant" within a definition, or part of the "ethos" of the rhetor.

the interior. At the same time, that surface had its own potency—as vehicle for eulogy and veil for irony, the processes on which interior action relied so greatly. More broadly still, while historical writing may be about defining what happened, about determining, often absolutely, who was responsible for what, as a form of representation it untethers itself from the task of definition, circumstantializing the signification of some separate historical reality in favor of its own self-sustenance.

The Arguments of This Book

The first two chapters of this study use the first individual biography in the *History* to explore how the interior-exterior dynamic worked—the push and pull of positive and negative rhetorical acts that made historiographical action and formed the historiography we read today. Chapter 1 reads the biography for its depiction of interiority, as a narrative of the rise, from humble origins to lofty heights, of Liu Muzhi 劉穆之 (360–417), founding minister of the Liu-Song. To the extent that threats of exteriorization lurk in the shadows of this narrative, he faced those challenges down with rhetorical aplomb, retaining his interiority by positioning himself on its threshold. In chapter 2, however, we re-read Liu's "life" with a focus on his experience of the forces of exteriorization. This alternative narrative is buried deep in the biography, but more manifest elsewhere in the history—most notably in the biography of the man with whom he shares the space of scroll 42 in the history. The exteriorizing perspective sees Liu Muzhi die estranged from the Founding Ancestor, his influence having gradually been supplanted by that of the elite gentry who would guide the actual establishment of the dynasty some four years later. But is the alienation of Liu Muzhi a fall, or is it a sublimation into something with its own circumstantial potency? Just as historical actors temporize in defense of their interiority, thresholding themselves to safer exterior positions, so Liu Muzhi's loss of agency over his own narrative also brings gain. Sacrificed to the elite gentry, he does the work of a good client, "prompting" his patron's interior progress. This is the transition from the naively conceived historical actor, or what Kenneth Burke (1897–1993) referred to as the "the symbol-using, symbol-making, and symbol-misusing animal," to the actor as a well-used symbol in the enactment of a discourse—the historiographical subject as fully realized through the annals-biography form.[41]

The third chapter is an "essay"—an attempt to address something in a new way. "Officialdom" appears to be nothing more than basic historical data, the condensed and bone-dry record of the structure of the government and the identity of its occupants. Its interpretative impenetrability is emblematic of, and partly responsible for, the resistance the dynastic biographies present to the reader who would wish to recover real human personalities from them. With the interior-exterior dynamic in hand, however, we come to see officialdom as a semiotic system brimming with rhetorical energy. This energy begins with its "grammar"—the rhetorical qualities harbored in the standard set of terminology used to narrate progress across the official ranks. That terminology, it is argued here, cleaves along an interior-exterior axis and features "thresholding" points of balance. Out of this grammatical potential develops a "rhetoric," in the more realized sense of how the official system was put to persuasive use by historical actors—and how they were suspended in its persuasive dispositions. Analysis of this system reveals a portrait of Southern Dynasties political culture: a state-oriented system leveraged by the gentry in their own interests and against the interests of their peers. Threshold positions in the realm of officialdom were key both for individual actors, for whom political interiority was possible but inherently precarious, and for the state itself, which had to exercise due tact in its hold on the gentry. For these purposes, the glossy surface of officialdom, not as system of government but as mode of representation, was a potent resource, if also an unpredictable one, leaving its participants to its whims.

Chapter 4 shows how early medieval historiography's most important element, the document, operated on multiple levels. A court debate from the 420s, something like a transcript of which is recorded in our *History of the Liu-Song*, offers a window onto the foundational socio-political issue of the time—the mutual dependence of the state and the gentry, and the latter's distinction, or lack thereof, from the commoners of the realm. It is also a showcase for the art of rhetoric in this period. Narrowly construed,

---

41. Kenneth Burke, *Language as Symbolic Action: Essays on Life, Literature and Method*, 4.

this is the rhetoric of court oratory, with each speaker—some better than others—making topically grounded and artfully embellished arguments. Widening our view, we find that the individual speeches of the extended document do not exist independently, but as parts of a whole, as the speakers respond to and draw on those who spoke before them, while setting "prompts" for those yet to speak. When the debate's convener returns with a long peroration, we perceive the whole as an orchestrated historiographical act, in which the eminent statesman parades his commitment to the formation of a gentry that operates under and for the state. He produced this document for the ears of his contemporaries but also for the historian of the future, who duly takes it up—but in a frame of his own making, one that pointedly leaves Wang Hong's 王弘 (379–432) self-fashioning efforts unconfirmed, and even ironized.

Having covered the interior-exterior dynamic and the key elements of officialdom and the document, in chapter 5 I turn to a more synthetic approach, presenting three general arguments about the nature of early medieval historiography. First, I identify historiography as a process, with the document—not the finished book of history—as the basic unit of production. This provides a useful reorientation of an old controversy about the status of Chinese historiography: the extent to which the dynastic histories were just "scissors and paste" compilations of received materials. The culture of historiography in this period was, from the start, a culture of the document. Second, I place historiography in a balance between public and private interests, emphasizing that although historiography was often a private endeavor in this period, its cultural profits accruing to individuals and their families, as a value it constituted a public standard. This offers a different perspective on another common discussion point: the ostensible flourishing of privately compiled histories. Finally, I stress the significance of incompletion in the process of historiography. While it is easy to regard incompletion as a condition of our own perspective—from bibliographical records we can see that only a small fraction of the vast number of texts produced and/or circulating in this period has survived—incompletion is not merely the condition of the modern scholar of the period, for books and documents were appearing and disappearing even then. Incompletion is an inherent feature of the open process of historiography, and the idea of incompletion played an important functional role in the historiographical culture, providing "rhetorical exigence" for historical actors.

The conclusion identifies the major "mode of emplotment" of this historiography. As a kind of rhetoric, history was an "epideictic" art: it was less about judging the past or determining future action than displaying and manipulating common values. This is "praise and blame" historiography in a new light. The role of blame, in the form of the good historian's critical judgment but even more so in historiography's ironies, acknowledged and unacknowledged, was to temper the praise, couching simple eulogy in the complexity of the interior-exterior dynamic. The epideictic perspective emphasizes historiography's representational qualities—the interior power of its exterior surface—over its referential content—the historical reality that was, in reality, interwoven with its exterior.

Hegel had the idea that historical writing could be divided into three stages. At the bottom is "original history," written by people who had lived through the events or were so close to them in experience that the "cultural formation" of historian and event were "one and the same." From that basis comes the common "reflective history," which evaluates the past from a later, exterior vantage point. On top of that there ought to emerge the true "philosophical world history": an account neither relayed in its own terms nor analyzed otherwise, but manifesting the universal "spiritual principle" that is "the guide of individual souls, of actions and of events."[42]

Standing Hegel on his head, or shaking him up a little, this triad provides the ingredients for a good definition of the qualities of early medieval Chinese historiography. The dynastic history is not, for the most part, "reflective history": completed as it was after the fall of a dynasty, in some ways it does present a retrospective assessment, but that point of view is only lightly superimposed upon historical materials that were first compiled during the life of the dynasty—the "annals and biographies [that] took shape very shortly after the event, when passions might still run high."[43] Further back lay the true "primary sources"—the fundamentally

---

42. G. W. F. Hegel, *Lectures on the Philosophy of World History, Volume 1: Manuscripts of the Introduction and the Lecture of 1822–23*, 134, 140. For a discussion, see Hayden White, *Metahistory: The Historical Imagination in Nineteenth-Century Europe*, 97–105.

43. Twitchett, "Problems of Chinese Biography," 30.

biased and historically involved documentary, anecdotal, and archival materials that would supply the marrow of later compilations.

This historiography, then, was at once "original," in the sense that its historians were one with the age they recorded, and "philosophical," the unfolding of historical events being driven by a consciousness that the historiography instantiates. Writing documents, confecting anecdotes, tracing out profiles on the canvas of public life—historical actors participated in the realization of what would become the past, working within a philosophical unity—or concert, or confusion—of historical action and historiographical representation.

ONE

Interiority

> Thus, official biography became in practice the imitation of eulogistic memorial writings.
> —Denis Twitchett, "Chinese Biographical Writing"

Life begins in its background, so a biography—a "life"—might be expected to start with an account of its subject's family, giving us some understanding of the social setting into which he or she was born, and to follow with a treatment of childhood experience, in which we should see the formation of the aims and the deeds that the adult will pursue. Biography in the historiographical tradition of early medieval China gestures toward these needs: it sets out an ancestry, sometimes with outlines of the lives and careers of the father, grandfather, and possibly siblings, and it not infrequently supplies a character-revealing, and possibly fictitious, childhood anecdote or two. The focus, however, is invariably on the political career of the adult, and more specifically, on the part the adult played in the life of the dynasty.

The biography of Liu Muzhi presents a paradigmatic example of this special focus. He is dignified with a genealogy that links him to a Western Han king half a millennium in the past, but even his father is left unmentioned. It is said only that "for generations" his family had lived in Jingkou 京口—modern Zhenjiang, a bastion of northern immigrants just downriver from the capital. His early life is passed over with the remark that he was well read, and the beginning of his career, under a man with whom he apparently had family connections, is merely noted. Liu Muzhi's historiographical life does not begin in earnest until he is forty-five years old, when his stream merged into the river of the *History*'s historical narrative. Joining the Founding Ancestor's cause in 404, Liu Muzhi helped oust the "usurper" Huan Xuan and restore the weak Jin emperor to the throne. Toiling by the Founding Ancestor's side for over a decade, he played pivotal roles in his patron's arrival in the capital in 408 and in the extermination of competing powers there in 412, serving as the future emperor's right-hand man up until his death in his fifty-eighth year. That was three years before the official founding of the Liu-Song dynasty, but for his great contributions to that great enterprise, Liu Muzhi would be posthumously recognized as one of the dynasty's founding ministers and accorded a preeminent, emblematic position in its history—the subject of its first proper biography.[1]

The "Absolute" Quality of Historiography

The running theme of Liu Muzhi's biography is the accrual of the "interiority" of political authority. At the pinnacle of his career, he governed the capital region, with an armed guard to protect him, and headed the imperial Secretariat, holding control over official appointments throughout the land. The incline of Liu's rise was steeper than what we see in many other biographies in the dynastic histories, but the issues it addresses are common to all: how was power acquired, how was it maintained in the face of "exterior" pressure, and how was this interplay of interior and exterior fashioned out of and into the forms of historiographical representation.

Liu Muzhi's interiority has a preordained aura from the start of his political journey. This is evident in the account of his initial meeting with the Founding Ancestor, which exudes an absolute quality, represented through two important modes: the "pluperfect" (in bold below), locking together prior and consequent events, and the "immediate" (underlined), giving the sense that whatever happens, happens decisively and irrevocably.

> **In the beginning**, Liu had once dreamed that he was boating on the sea with the Founding Ancestor. A great wind <u>suddenly</u> arose, frightening him, but

---

[1]. The preceding scroll, nominally the first of the biographical section, belongs to empresses, an exceptional category.

when he looked down from the boat, he found two white dragons escorting them on either side. Then they came to a mountain, its peaks towering beautifully, its shrubbery growing dense. He found it most delightful.

Then, upon the conquest of Jingkou, the Founding Ancestor spoke to He Wuji (?–410): "I <u>urgently</u> require a chief of staff. Where shall I look for one?" Wuji replied: "There is none better than Liu Daomin." "**Ah, I too know him**," said the Founding Ancestor, and immediately he <u>rushed</u> a messenger off to summon him.

<u>At that time</u>, Liu Muzhi heard a ruckus coming from within Jingkou. <u>At dawn</u>, he arose and went out to the field-path [to see what was happening], and <u>at that moment he happened to meet up with</u> the messenger. Liu Muzhi stared at him for a long while, saying nothing. Then he returned to his house, where he <u>tore his cloth skirt</u> apart to make a pair of [warrior's] pants and set out to see the Founding Ancestor.

The Founding Ancestor spoke to him: "My uprising to defend the grand righteousness of the empire <u>has just begun</u> and <u>right now</u> I face many difficulties. I <u>urgently</u> require an officer for my army—would you, sir, know anyone up to the task?"

"As your esteemed generalship has <u>just been established</u>," Liu Muzhi replied, "a talented officer is indeed needed. <u>In this moment of haste</u>, perhaps my abilities will not be surpassed by those of another?"

Smiling at this, the Founding Ancestor replied: "If you can condescend yourself to do it, **then the success of my enterprise is certain.**"

And <u>immediately at that sitting</u> Liu Muzhi accepted the appointment.

初，穆之嘗夢與高祖俱泛海，忽值大風，驚懼。俯視船下，見有二白龍夾舫。既而至一山，峯崿聳秀，林樹繁密，意甚悅之。及高祖克京城，問何無忌曰：「急須一府主簿，何由得之？」無忌曰：「無過劉道民。」高祖曰：「吾亦識之。」即馳信召焉。時穆之聞京城有叫譟之聲，晨起出陌頭，屬與信會。穆之直視不言者久之。既而反室，壞布裳為袴，往見高祖。高祖謂之曰：「我始舉大義，方造艱難，須一軍吏甚急，卿謂誰堪其選？」穆之曰：「貴府始建，軍吏實須其才，倉卒之際，當略無見踰者。」高祖笑曰：「卿能自屈，吾事濟矣。」即於坐受署。(II-B)[2]

---

2. Parenthetical references here and in the following discussion are to the section and paragraph divisions in the translation of Liu Muzhi's biography (*Song shu* 42.1303–8) presented in the appendix.

The pluperfect supplies the macrostructure of this anecdote. The phrase "in the beginning" (*chu* 初) is a standard figure of thought in Chinese historiography, used to reinforce the truth value of a given event by linking it, in a quasi-cause-and-effect relation, to some prior event, a "beginning" that makes the end a natural consequence, here expressed as "then, upon…" (*ji* 及).[3] Thus, the establishment of a patronage relationship with the Founding Ancestor is defined as fact, their absolute bond confirmed by the dream said to have occurred "in the beginning."[4]

Inside this structure, local instances of the pluperfect motivate the two main sections of dialogue, before and after Liu Muzhi enters the scene. The first section has the Founding Ancestor consulting He Wuji, one of his earliest confederates and a powerful general in his own right. The Founding Ancestor asks a question—what men of talent are available?—and receives an answer—Liu Muzhi—but this is less an answer than a "prompt" for the patron to demonstrate his prior knowledge—"I too know him." A similar mechanism underpins the second section, describing the first encounter of the Founding Ancestor and Liu Muzhi, where the link between past and present is projected into the future: when Liu agrees to join his cause, the Founding Ancestor rejoices, "certain" of success, using the completive particle *yi* 矣. Indeed, as the "Founding Ancestor," he *will* be successful, chaining past knowledge, present situation, and future result together in a historiographical absolute. Put in terms of our fourfold set of rhetorical topics, the pluperfect transforms the potential of "circumstance" into the certainty of "consequence."

---

3. See the discussion of the word *chu* ("in the beginning") in early historiography in Schaberg, *A Patterned Past*, 205–6, where it is identified it as analepsis, "a pluperfect mode of narration." On uses of the pluperfect in the western tradition of historiography, see Jonas Grethlein and Christopher B. Krebs, eds., *Time and Narrative in Ancient Historiography: The "Plupast" from Herodotus to Appian*. Related is the use of a "sense of an ending" in Mark Laurent Asselin, *A Significant Season: Cai Yong (ca. 133–192) and His Contemporaries*, to explain the motivations of literary composition in the late second century.

4. This absolute bond is bolstered with a more intimate metaphor in an alternative version of the dream, in which the greatness of a mountain is replaced by the union of "two boats coming together to form one double-boat." See the note to this passage in the appendix.

The second vehicle of the absolute quality of historiography in this passage, the sense of "immediacy," ensures that events do not simply follow one from another in a raw, meaningless kind of consequence. Rather, they do so with the force of defining change, like the transformation in state caused by the flip of a switch in an electric circuit. This feeling of immediacy is palpable throughout the passage. In the dream, the wind arrives "suddenly" (*hu* 忽). The Founding Ancestor's need for a chief of staff is "urgent" (*ji* 急), and when the two men meet they share gestures toward this immediacy, referring to an enterprise "just begun" (*shi* 始, also a pluperfect gesture toward future success), to the difficulties of the here and "now" (*fang* 方), and to the current "moment of haste" (*cangcu* 倉卒). A messenger has been "rushed off" (*chi* 馳), and Liu Muzhi, at dawn—that is, at day's immediate incipiency—"happened to" (*shu* 屬) meet up with him—the serendipity that arises from the immediate intersection of two narrative moments. The historian's narration of Liu Muzhi's encounter with the messenger accents the sense of immediacy with some artful contrastive coloring. Narrative time is suspended with a dramatic pause, "the long while" (*jiu zhi* 久之) in which Liu Muzhi stares silently at the messenger, cast into reverie by the fulfillment of his dream, and it resumes with a mimetic act of immediacy, as he decisively transforms his civilian clothing into garb suitable for a martial endeavor. This act is confirmed when Liu Muzhi "immediately" (*ji* 即, "then, with a sense of immediacy") joins the Founding Ancestor's uprising after their conversation.

The absolute goes on to provide the main motif in much of the remainder of Liu Muzhi's biography, beginning with the very next passage, which sees the Founding Ancestor, with Liu Muzhi's able assistance, ousting Huan Xuan:

> He joined in the capture of the capital. When the Founding Ancestor first took the city, the major decisions were all made, in the immediate moment, on the initiative of Liu Muzhi. Thereupon, the Founding Ancestor entrusted to him responsibility for the most vital tasks, and was certain to consult him on every single move. And Liu Muzhi, for his part, also exhausted himself in his sincere dedication to his patron, leaving absolutely nothing unattended or concealed.

從平京邑，高祖始至，諸大處分，皆倉卒立定，並穆之所建也。遂委以腹心之任，動止咨焉。穆之亦竭節盡誠，無所遺隱。(III-A)

The point of this summary is to establish the absolute efficacy of Liu Muzhi and the absolute nature of his bond with his patron.[5] Liu Muzhi does not just make *some* decisions, he makes *all* of them (the construction *zhu* 諸 ... *jie* 皆 ...), and in the immediate moment at that (*cangcu* again). His patron does not merely trust him, he entrusts him with utmost interiority, the "vital tasks" (*fuxin zhi ren*) literally being the affairs of the "stomach and heart," the body's most central organs. He consults him "on every single move"—conveyed by the all-encompassing compound *dongzhi* 動止, "whether in motion or at rest"—and does so as an absolute consequence (the emphatic conjunction *sui* 遂, "thereupon") of his client's abilities. Liu Muzhi, for his part, requites his patron's trust in equally absolute terms. By "exhausting" (*jie* 竭 ... *jin* 盡 ...) himself, he funnels all his natural talent—his interiority—into the interior space of his patron, reserving nothing (*wu suo yi yin* 無所遺隱) for himself or others.

The historian continues with a compact "argument" illustrating Liu Muzhi's interior efficacy at that moment:

> At that time, the rule of the Jin court had grown lax, its awe and authority no longer heeded. Powerful clans and men of ill-gotten riches wielded their power with no compunctions, while the common folk suffered in extreme poverty, with no place even to stand their feet. More than that, the edicts issued under [the debauched prime minister] Sima Yuanxian (382–402) had been full of error, while the regulations promulgated by [the usurper] Huan Xuan had been too overbearing.
>
> [Responding to this,] Muzhi gave careful consideration to the needs of the times and set things straight using proper methods. And in not ten days, the customs of the realm were completely reformed.

---

5. Patronage has been identified as one of the most important political factors in early medieval China, and one that is often veiled in our sources. The classic work on the patron-client nature of the bonds between officials and their subordinates (*li*, the word used in our passage) is Kawakatsu Yoshio, *Rikuchō kizokusei shakai no kenkyū*, part 2, chapter 5. More recently, the signal importance of patronage relations to our understanding of early medieval political culture has been explored in Andrew Chittick, *Patronage and Community in Medieval China: The Xiangyang Garrison, 400–600 CE*.

時晉綱寬弛,威禁不行,盛族豪右,負勢陵縱,小民窮蹙,自立無所。重以司馬元顯政令違舛,桓玄科條繁密。穆之斟酌時宜,隨方矯正,不盈旬日,風俗頓改。(III-B)

The passage neatly presents a full set of argumentative topics. The phrase "at that time" (*shi* 時) introduces the dying Jin dynasty as a circumstantial ground for Liu Muzhi to distinguish himself upon. The description of Jin failings traffics heavily in hyperbolic consequence: the court absolutely powerless, the elite absolutely wanton, the innocent common folk absolutely miserable ("no place even to stand their feet"). Drawing closer to the scene, a contrast is constructed: the court stewards of the 390s were too lax, while Huan Xuan corrected the excesses too harshly, and these twin aberrations prompt the arrival of our Goldilocks figure, getting the balance just right. In all, the late Jin turmoil supplies the perfect "rhetorical exigence"—"an imperfection marked by urgency ... a defect, an obstacle, something waiting to be done, a thing which is other than it should be"—in the face of which Liu Muzhi emerges as a *defining* power, setting the age to rights.[6] And by his consequential force, all the "customs of the realm" are reformed immediately ("not ten days") and absolutely (*dun* 頓, "completely" or "suddenly").

The biography's middle portion wends along a path of the absolute. As his patron's key advisor, Liu Muzhi tells the Founding Ancestor everything, "great or small" (III-G), and as chief of staff he is said to "stop at nothing" in promoting men of his choosing (III-J). As the Founding Ancestor moves, in 411–12, to vanquish his last remaining military competitors, Liu Muzhi is shifted to a position of absolute importance—Prefect-Martial of the capital region (III-L), where his authority is unquestioned (III-N), and backed by extraordinary armaments (III-O, Q). Atop the imperial bureaucracy, his rule is likened to "a river-like flow, obstructed in no matter" (III-R), and there his interiority reaches its climax, epitomized in the following anecdote:

---

6. The idea of "exigence" as a key component of rhetoric is from Lloyd Bitzer, "The Rhetorical Situation," quotation at p. 6. Bitzer formulates a rhetorical triad, the other two components of which are the audience and the "constraints"—including the topics of argumentation—that a speaker finds in or brings to a situation.

> Guests gathered like spokes around the hub of a wheel, petitioning him for all kinds of favors, and the requests he faced, in the court and outside, stacked up on his stairways and filled his rooms. But Muzhi's eyes no sooner glanced over submissions of testimony than his hand wrote out the administrative rejoinders, and as his ears took in the requests so responses issued from his mouth. No confusion resulted, and each and every matter was properly handled.
>
> 賓客輻輳，求訴百端，內外諸稟，盈堦滿室，目覽辭訟，手答牋書，耳行聽受，口並酬應，不相參涉，皆悉贍舉。(III-S)

An interior power in his own right, the "hub" around whom all others, "in the court and outside," gather, Liu Muzhi exudes an absolute efficacy, acts of mental processing—what he reads and what he hears—leading to immediate consequence in political action—what he writes and what he says. All is exterior to his interior command. (But is there a shade of shadow in this eerie automation of eye and ear?)

The history continues with a variation on the same anecdote:

> Also: he often gave banquets for his favored guests, carrying on his conversation and appreciative laughter for hours on end, never growing weary.
>
> 又數客暱賓，言談賞笑，引日亙時，未嘗倦苦。(III-T)

Though his banqueting is, assuredly, done for the benefit of his patron, it is figured as a kind of excess, the abundant conviviality of a newly ascendant patron regaling his blossoming entourage. The "hub of a wheel" rolling toward his own aggrandizement, as a center of power he assumes the prerogatives of a patron, shedding his sanctioned definition as a trusted client of the Founding Ancestor. This absolute interiority is precarious. But Liu Muzhi was well aware of that, and quite adept at deflecting such dangers.

The Historical Actor and the Rhetoric of Interiority

A prime example of the historical actor engaging in the production and maintenance of interiority is found in this biography's biggest set piece, a long speech delivered at the end of the year 407 (III-D and E).

The circumstance of the speech, its "exigence," is a turning point in the Founding Ancestor's rise to legitimate authority. After the restoration of the Jin emperor in 404, the Founding Ancestor retreated to his home base in Jingkou, where he strategically deferred the higher court appointments that were offered him. The imperial court was left under an elite figurehead, Wang Mi 王謐 (360–407), while the Founding Ancestor's erstwhile comrades in the restoration—men of greater stature and nearly comparable military might—held key offices in the capital. The death of that figurehead in the last month of 407 forced a reassessment of this situation, described in the historical narration as follows:

> In the regular order of things, the Founding Ancestor should have entered the capital region to assist (i.e., take control over) the court, but Liu Yi (d. 412) and the other powers did not want the Founding Ancestor to do so, so they proposed appointing Xie Hun (d. 412), General of the Central Army, as Governor of Yangzhou. Others wanted to grant the governorship to the Founding Ancestor but have him hold it in Dantu (i.e., Jingkou), turning over control of the court to the Director of the Secretariat, Meng Chang (d. 410). They sent the Second Assistant to the Secretariat, Pi Chen, to confer with the Founding Ancestor on these two plans.
>
> 高祖次應入輔，劉毅等不欲高祖入，議以中領軍謝混為揚州。或欲令高祖於丹徒領州，以內事付尚書僕射孟昶。遣尚書右丞皮沈以二議咨高祖。(III-D)

Foreshadowing the central line of argument Liu Muzhi will deploy in his speech, two courses of consequence are put in opposition here. The first is the "regular order of things" (*ci* 次, "sequence"), by which the Founding Ancestor would assume the position that, through strategy or caution, he has thus far resisted taking. The opposing course is sub-divided into a pair of alternate strategies. By one, the deceased figurehead would be replaced by another elite figurehead. This is to keep the *definition* of the situation as it has been. With the other, the "regular order" will be followed in name but not in actuality, the seat of the governorship being removed from the capital, the office literally "going to" the Founding Ancestor. In this way, the defining power of the governorship of the "divine province"—Yangzhou, the capital region, stretching east to the sea and south through the rich lands of modern Zhejiang—would be rendered merely *circumstantial*.

Such are the potential paths of consequence that follow from the death of Wang Mi. How will Liu Muzhi maneuver them to his patron's advantage? His persuasive act begins not with the speech itself but in its prelude, in which our orator mimetically models the deployment of a "prompt"—the means by which one advances toward greater interiority.

> Pi Chen was first received by Muzhi, to whom he explained the views of the men at court. Pretending to excuse himself for a trip to the toilet, Muzhi sent off a secret communique to the Founding Ancestor. It said: "Pi Chen has just arrived. Do not agree to anything he says."
> When the Founding Ancestor received Pi Chen, he sent him to wait outside and called for Muzhi. "What did you mean when you said not to agree to anything proposed by Pi Chen?"
>
> 沈先見穆之，具說朝議。穆之偽起如廁，即密疏白高祖曰：「皮沈始至，其言不可從。」高祖既見沈，且令出外，呼穆之，問曰：「卿云沈言不可從，其意何也？」(III-D)

The prompt functions as it did in the scene in which Liu Muzhi first established a relationship with the Founding Ancestor, but here it is acted out literally. There, the Founding Ancestor asked He Wuji a question, eliciting a reply that then prompted his own display of knowledge. The Founding Ancestor exteriorized himself, giving He an opportunity to show interior knowledge; but his exteriorization was strategic, the provisional interiority of his conversation partner—He Wuji's knowledge— serving only to prompt the Founding Ancestor's leap further interior. In this passage, Liu Muzhi first exteriorizes himself, going to the "outhouse" being a stock historiographical ploy, openly acknowledged with the word *wei* 偽, "pretending to."[7] With this, Pi Chen moves interior, to an audience with the Founding Ancestor. From his exteriorized position, however, Liu Muzhi sends a secret message—a superior form of interiority— arranging Pi Chen's ejection and Liu Muzhi's entry into the interiority of private dialogue with his patron. And not just dialogue, but soliloquy. Make a show of your interior knowledge, his patron prompts him.

---

7. Notable examples of "going to the restroom" as a plot point include *Shiji* 7.313 and 86.2519, and *Han shu* 32.1837.

40 Chapter One

Pretend that I am a politically inept fool and give a speech to display your interiority to the world and to history! And that is what Liu Muzhi does.

Liu Muzhi's argument comprises seven well-articulated parts. An introduction is followed by the statement of a general rule, or an "enthymeme," and this is followed by a second enthymeme. The fourth section examines the first of Pi Chen's proposals in light of the first enthymeme, while the fifth uses the second enthymeme to address the second proposal. The rhetor then proposes a novel course of action as a solution to the crisis, concluding with a brief but topically significant envoi.

The "exordium" to his speech is a paean to his patron, based in the topic of contrast:

(1) In the [not so distant] past, the rule of the Jin court went awry, and it has been so for not just a single day. On top of this, Huan Xuan usurped the throne—the Mandate of Heaven had already begun to shift. [But now] Your Excellency has revived the imperial fortunes, and for this your merit shall tower over ten thousand antiquities.

昔晉朝失政，非復一日，加以桓玄篡奪，天命已移。公興復皇祚，勳高萬古。(III-E)

In a move that echoes—or perhaps is echoed in, insofar as historians drew cues from the documents they quoted—the preceding historical narration, the wanton Jin court and the iniquitous Huan Xuan work as foils, against which the great deeds of the Founding Ancestor shine brightly. Eulogy, however, is not equivalent to flattery. "You are great," he is saying, but in the background of such praise lies a warning: "You are great—for the moment." Action must be undertaken to preserve the praised qualities, and the source for that action will be provided by the speaker: "You are great, for the moment—and if you heed my good counsel, you shall remain so." And his counsel so heeded, Liu Muzhi, the able rhetor, will himself become the object of eulogy.

He then introduces the first of two enthymemes:

(2) Having accomplished great deeds, you have attained a position of great prominence. [But] a great position and towering merit cannot be maintained for a long time. Given Your Excellency's current situation, how could you

possibly make yourself humble and weak, remaining a mere general in charge of a border region?

既有大功，便有大位。位大勳高，非可持久。公今日形勢，豈得居謙自弱，遂為守藩之將邪？(III-E)

That is: power is inherently precipitous. The second enthymeme, that equal powers will destroy one another, is the finale of a longer statement:

(3) Liu [Yi], Meng [Chang], and the other Excellencies rose up from ordinary life together with Your Excellency, standing up with you on the side of great Righteousness [i.e., the revival of the Jin house]. At the root, their desire has simply been to use the merit they acquired in the restoration of the monarch to acquire riches and nobility. [But] every enterprise has its necessary sequence, and so they have momentarily deferred their claims to great deeds [awaiting the better time to assert them]. It is not that they have sincerely submitted to anyone's authority, or truly resigned themselves to being subjects to any master. Balanced in power and circumstances, they will eventually devour one another.

劉、孟諸公，與公俱起布衣，共立大義，本欲匡主成勳，以取富貴耳。事有前後，故一時推功，非為委體心服，宿定臣主之分也。力敵勢均，終相吞咀。(III-E)

Not only is power precipitous, but the bearers of power are destined to come into conflict, bringing one another to destruction. Building up to this point, Liu Muzhi again provides a model for action in the interior-exterior dynamic, in the form of the Founding Ancestor's chief competitors, notably Liu Yi and Meng Chang. These men have interiority—"riches and nobility"—on their minds. Power is their "root" (*ben*, "original") motive, that which is internal to whatever branches and leaves their conduct may sprout on the exterior. And yet they have recognized that the "sequence" (*qian hou*) necessary to realizing this process involves a temporary self-exteriorization, and so they have shown deference to the court and to the Founding Ancestor, who was publicly acknowledged as the leader of the restoration. This strategic shift to the exterior, like Liu Muzhi's trip to the outhouse, is set down as the prompt that will lead them to the interiority they seek. That is the consequence Liu Muzhi must here thwart.

The fourth section amplifies the first enthymeme, the notion that "power is precarious":

> (4) The root of imperial power is bound to [the capital region] Yangzhou. [As such,] it cannot be granted to anyone else, and that in recent years it was assigned to Wang Mi was a matter of expedience. Should a great strategy, one destined for success, necessarily follow this course of action? If today you again grant this region to another man, then by all reckoning you shall find yourself under the command of others. And once you have lost your grip on the handle of power, it cannot be regained.
>
> 揚州根本所係，不可假人。前者以授王謐，事出權道，豈是始終大計必宜若此而已哉。今若復以他授，便應受制於人。一失權柄，無由可得。(III-E)

The passage builds back up to the enthymeme, intensifying it: "once you have lost your grip," then all hope is lost. Responding to the first proposal brought by Pi Chen—to replace the old figurehead with a new one—Liu Muzhi dismisses the recent practice of proxy appointments from the court elite as mere circumstance (*quan*, "expedience"). Circumstance is not to be submitted to haphazardly. Rather, it falls to the Founding Ancestor to act to define the circumstances such that they will serve him: he must seize this opportunity to gain control of Yangzhou, the "root" of the empire, pivot of imperial interiority. Consideration of the second proposal comes to the same conclusion in the light of the second enthymeme—that equal powers will destroy each other, or, more to the point, that they will destroy *you*:

> (5) Furthermore, with your towering deeds and weighty merit, Your Excellency is not easily disposed of. Their fears of you and their suspicions will intermingle, and malevolent intentions will arise from all sides. How could you fail to consider the dangers that lie in the future?
>
> 而公功高勳重，不可直置，疑畏交加，異端互起，將來之危難，可不熟念。(III-E)

Ignoring the predicament is not an option—and it is the Founding Ancestor's good fortune to have this able client here to consider the dangers and help him plot a good path to interiority.

The climax of the speech is the revelation of Liu Muzhi's strategy, using a speech-within-a-speech staging that once again enfigures the theme of interiority:

> (6) Today, the opinion of the court is such as it is and you must respond to it, but were you to insist that the appointment go to you, that would be a difficult argument to make. Rather, you should say:
> The divine province [of Yangzhou] is the root of governance, and the Prime Minister [who rules it] is a position of lofty importance. This is the "stairway" for revival or for disaster, and as such it should be a matter for careful selection. Given the great importance of this matter, it is not to be discussed in the abstract, so I will provisionally enter the court to discuss the alternatives exhaustively together with you.
>
> 今朝議如此，宜相酬答，必云在我，厝辭又難。唯應云「神州治本，宰輔崇要，興喪所階，宜加詳擇。此事既大，非可懸論，便暫入朝，共盡同異」。(III-E)

Liu Muzhi's clever plan involves a shift in the argumentative ground, a change, in rhetorical terminology, of the "stasis," or the framing of the issue under discussion. Formerly, the issue was direct: who shall become governor of Yangzhou? Now, he sets that issue in a deeper focus: what are the conditions under which a decision on that issue can be made? A new enthymeme is brought in: that crucial decisions must be discussed thoroughly, not determined "in the abstract" (*xuan lun*, a discussion hanging in thin air). From such a rule, it follows that the Founding Ancestor must enter the capital for face-to-face parley. The actual question at debate is exteriorized, circumstantialized in favor of a prior order question, and with this trick the Founding Ancestor is given a way to literally interiorize himself, bringing him to the capital to grasp the defining power he seeks. This is confirmed in the speech's concluding line:

> (7) When Your Excellency reaches the capital, it is a clear certainty that they will not dare to pass over Your Excellency in favor of some other person.
>
> 公至京，彼必不敢越公更授餘人明矣。(III-E)

Speaking in the same absolute terms his patron had used when they first established their bond, Liu Muzhi casts his argument into a pluperfect relation with the future, declaring his strategy a "clear certainty"—the words *bi* ("certain") and *ming* ("clear"), with the completive particle *yi*. The historical narration framing the speech then grants it the absolute status of historical causation:

> The Founding Ancestor followed his advice, and thus he came to enter the capital to assist the court.
>
> 高祖從其言，由是入輔。(III-E)

"And thus"—*you shi*, literally "from this," an expressly causal statement—the proper order of things was achieved.[8] Meng Chang and Liu Yi would be absolutely exteriorized, the former committing suicide—admitting defeat but preserving his family's fortunes—in 410, the latter meeting his ruin in 412. The Founding Ancestor was on his path to glory—with his prime client in tow.

When he shifts the grounds of discussion from a direct question to a question about that question, or when he tactfully excuses himself to go to the outhouse, or when he issues a faint self-demurral in his initial interview with his patron—Liu Muzhi is proving himself adept at "thresholding," rhetorically playing weaker spaces off stronger ones. An anecdote displays this technique in ekphrasis:

> Muzhi established the protocol for all of the Founding Ancestor's activities. [For instance,] the Founding Ancestor's calligraphy was naturally clumsy, so Muzhi said to him: "This may be a minor matter, but you are sending your handwriting far into the four directions. I beseech Your Excellency to pay a bit of attention to it." But the Founding Ancestor was not able to put his mind to it, and at any rate his natural abilities limited him, so Muzhi took a different approach: "Just write your characters large, letting your brush go as it will. Even if your characters are a foot across, it is no cause for concern. For, being large, they will show an accommodating nature, and

---

8. More specifically, this might be identified as an instance of "causal interaction," wherein two causative "processes" (the militarized enterprise of the Founding Ancestor and the rhetorical action of Liu Muzhi) have come into contact, altering the outcome of both. See Anton Froeyman, "Concepts of Causation in Historiography," 118.

the display of natural propensity will be quite beautiful."[9] Following his counsel, the Founding Ancestor would fill up a sheet of paper with just six or seven characters.

高祖舉止施為，穆之皆下節度。高祖書素拙，穆之曰：「此雖小事，然宣彼四遠，願公小復留意。」高祖既不能厝意，又稟分有在。穆之乃曰：「但縱筆為大字，一字徑尺，無嫌。大既足有所包，且其勢亦美。」高祖從之，一紙不過六七字便滿。(III-I)

This little episode stands as a miniature allegory of the Founding Ancestor's rise: like his handwriting, he is rather uncouth, but that very quality will be packaged in such a way that the gentry elite can be persuaded to accept him. This "low," sometimes even boorish side of the Founding Ancestor's reported character may be a true representation, but it also, as a role, resonated with the Founding Ancestor of the great Han dynasty, who was known, among other things, for urinating in the caps of Confucian scholars.[10]

The rhetoric of this anecdote turns on the dual identity of calligraphy, as both the manifestly exterior marks of ink on paper and, as the emanation of the person who produces those marks, an embodiment of the interior. Putting this distinction into action, Liu Muzhi first lets his patron's maladroit hand serve as a prompt: he purports to intervene on the obvious level of the external sign, only to "discover" that the clumsiness is natural to his patron, an essence that cannot be improved by "paying a bit of attention." This failed intervention is the feint that releases a true demonstration of his mastery of the art of interiority, by addressing the issue at a higher level. In this more clever semiotic intervention, Liu Muzhi no longer seeks to control his patron's natural signs but channels them in a more natural route, "letting them go" (*zong* 縱) to produce exterior signs on a new scale and with a new quality. This shifts the stasis from the crude perceptual judgment of clumsiness to the transcendent aesthetic qualities of "magnanimity" (*bao* 包, literally "encompassing") and "propensity" (*shi* 勢, or "momentum," "natural disposition"), qualities that stand over and above their

---

9. The received *Song shu* reads "fame" (*ming* 名) for *shi*, "propensity." This is possible, but Wang Zhongluo (1913–86) emends based on the *Nan shi* and one instance in the *Cefu yuangui* (722.4b). The latter contains a further variant not accepted by Wang: "the display of natural propensity will be *awe-inspiring* (*wei* 偉)."

10. See *Shiji* 97.2691–93, which also involves a reformation.

physical representations, and with this reorientation of perspective he transforms the Founding Ancestor's calligraphy into a sign of distinction rather than deficiency.[11] The Founding Ancestor is not redeemed but redoubled—and with him goes Liu Muzhi, exercising absolute control over all his patron's activities.

This interplay of higher and lower states of perception is brought into a description of Liu Muzhi himself:

Muzhi and Zhu Lingshi (379–418) were both skilled in official correspondence. Once,[12] he and Lingshi were responding to letters in the presence of the Founding Ancestor. From dawn to noon, Muzhi sent out a hundred replies to Lingshi's eighty—and was able to keep up the conversation all the while.

穆之與朱齡石並便尺牘，嘗於高祖坐與齡石答書。自旦至日中，穆之得百函，齡石得八十函，而穆之應對無廢也。(III-K)

The first stage of this argument by anecdote evokes our protagonist's character with the topic of analogy / contrast: the two men resemble one another in their administrative capabilities, but Liu Muzhi is superior, his counterpart playing the foil, prompting him to prove his interiority. But that is not enough of a contrast. In the second stage, an objective, quantitative comparison—the numeric ratio of a hundred letters to eighty, measured over a fixed period of time—gives way to a more elevated distinction, through a unit of measure—conversation, sometimes competitive yet never quite a competition—that transcends measurement by

---

11. For a wide-ranging study of the Chinese concept of *shi*, see François Jullien, *The Propensity of Things: Toward a History of Efficacy in China*, esp. 76–79 and 133–36 on its use in the discourse of calligraphy, and chapter 9 on *shi* in historical understanding. Chapter 30 of the *Wenxin diaolong* is devoted to the concept; see Stephen Owen, *Readings in Chinese Literary Thought*, 230–39. *Shi* was also a word for the male sex organ.

12. The early printings read "regularly" (*chang* 常, or "always"), a graphically similar homophone for "once" (*chang* 嘗). Encyclopedia citations suggest this is an error, but "regularly," deployed repeatedly in the biography, does serve to reveal the *absolute* superiority of the protagonist's character: always quicker and more nimble in the task, Muzhi's talents were absolutely superior to those of his competitors. "Regularly" is likewise the modifier for Liu Muzhi's (more realistically occasional) allusion to Xun Yu 荀彧 (163–212), discussed in chapter 2.

unit. The distinction is also rendered as an absolute one, marked by the closing particle *ye* 也, denoting a statement of fact—here, the observation that outstrips a superficial data point. No longer defined by quantifiable practical talents, Liu Muzhi's true definition, like the one he staked out for his patron, is qualitative and sublime.

The Threat of Exteriorization and Defense Against It

As Liu Muzhi observes, power is precipitous, and as he shows, it cannot be maintained directly, but only through the rhetorical concert of interior and exterior forces. The artful historical actor must endeavor to keep himself in the interior and to wield the forces of exteriorization against others—and to position himself deftly between the two.

Ideally, the shadows of exteriority can be directly leveraged for interior progress:

> Liu Muzhi was always in the commander's tent helping devise strategy, making resolute decisions on all sundry affairs. Liu Yi and the others resented the favor shown to Muzhi, and at every opportunity they casually insinuated that his power had grown too great. But the Founding Ancestor only trusted him more and more.
>
> 常居幕中畫策，決斷眾事。劉毅等疾穆之見親，每從容言其權重，高祖愈信仗之。(III-F)

This is Liu Muzhi as the Founding Ancestor's key advisor in his war campaigns of 409 and 410. His hold on his patron's decision-making nearly absolute, fierce competitors circle around him, full of suspicion and ready with calumny. By the rule Liu Muzhi himself expressed in his grand speech, these powerful men should, as a matter of consequence, devour him. Instead, this turns into a case of "contrary consequence": not only does their plot fail, but it has the opposite effect, as their suspicion and calumny lead to his further interiorization, being "trusted more and more."

The manipulation of exterior suspicions is played out in a complex fashion in a passage that marks a decisive moment in Liu Muzhi's ascent—his patron's extermination of this very Liu Yi, and his assumption of unquestioned control over the state apparatus, in 412. While the Founding Ancestor led the imperial armies up the Yangtze to vanquish his foe, Liu Muzhi was left back in the capital, where oversight of the home base had been granted to another powerful general, Zhuge Zhangmin (d. 413). The historical narration sets the stage, establishing a pluperfect macrostructure for the anecdote.

> Suspicious of Zhuge Zhangmin's loyalties, the Founding Ancestor left Muzhi to assist him, adding the Establishing Awe generalship to his titles, granting him a staff and assigning troops under his command. And indeed, Zhangmin did have disloyal intentions—but he hesitated, unable to bring himself to action.
>
> 高祖疑長民難獨任，留穆之以輔之。加建威將軍，置佐吏，配給實力。長民果有異謀，而猶豫不能發。(III-M)

The Founding Ancestor is suspicious, but unlike the suspicion Liu Yi had directed toward Liu Muzhi, which not only failed to come to fruition but led to the contrary result, the suspicions of the hero of our dynastic narrative are definitely, pluperfectively true—this adversary does "indeed" (*guo*, the "fruits" of consequence) harbor treachery. Most cleverly, in this narrative the traitor himself dramatizes this chain of certainty, slowing down the action with his show of hesitation, unable, even in treachery, to achieve simple consequence in a set of actions.

Set in this pluperfect mold, the anecdote's mimetic section initiates a choreography of irony and truth. Zhuge Zhangmin begins by sending everyone else out of the room in order to speak with Liu Muzhi in a private, interior space. He addresses him:

> "All the rumors have it that the Grand Commandant (i.e., the Founding Ancestor) and I are not on good terms. How has it come to this?"
> "His Excellency has gone upriver on a distant campaign, and he has entrusted his elderly mother and young children under your banner," Muzhi replied. "If his trust in you were anything less than fully complete, how could he have done such a thing?"
> And so Zhangmin's mind was somewhat put at ease.
> When the Founding Ancestor returned, Zhangmin was put to death.

乃屏人謂穆之曰:「悠悠之言,皆云太尉與我不平,何以至此?」穆之曰:「公泝流遠伐,而以老母稚子委節下,若一毫不盡,豈容如此邪?」意乃小安。高祖還,長民伏誅。(III-M)

The introductory passage established two competing definitions of Zhuge's political status at this time: on the surface, he was the powerful man left in charge of the capital, beneath it, the *bad* powerful man *nominally* left in charge of the capital. Here, Zhuge seizes on the latter definition, knowing that it is true but hoping it is not. He emphasizes his exteriorization—"everyone says" (*jie yun*)—but he also hints at a resolution of the matter by circumstantializing that ubiquitous definition, casting it as part of the unorthodox world of "rumor" (*youyou zhi yan*, "talk in the distance"). In response, Liu Muzhi gives Zhuge Zhangmin what he wants, assuring him that he remains a trusted affiliate. He winds the irony tight with a figure we may call the "synecdoche of the absolute," spotlighting a certain detail—the Founding Ancestor has left his mother and his sons behind in the capital, vulnerable to a political coup—and from this drawing a whole inference—that the Founding Ancestor's trust in Zhuge could not be anything other than "complete" (*jin*, "exhausted," the same word used earlier to describe Liu Muzhi's absolute devotion to his patron). Here the historical narration chimes in: "And so (*nai*) Zhangmin's mind was somewhat (*xiao*) put at ease." The simple consequence of "and so" bolsters the irony, while "somewhat" leaves a clue that his belief was far from absolute. The narration then goes on to coldly lift the veil off this dramatic irony, revealing the truth in a degree zero rhetoric: "When the Founding Ancestor returned, Zhangmin was put to death."[13] Liu Muzhi, with the historiography working in concert with him, has

---

13. The pieces of this story appear in a different configuration in Zhuge Zhangmin's brief biography in the *Jin shu* (85.2212–13), where he is portrayed as a craven military man who grew too powerful. In that account, when the Founding Ancestor returns to the capital he summons Zhuge, luring him deep into his confidence by sharing with him—in an echo of an anecdote from the present biography, discussed below—"all his intimate details." Then, as they enjoy themselves, a bondservant seizes Zhuge from behind and strangles him, and the people, we are told, rejoice at his death. Our version has Liu Muzhi strangle him figuratively.

gently pushed a real definition to the exterior, but only to set the stage for its dramatic and decisive return, as the Founding Ancestor's suspicions reach their pluperfect conclusion.

But what happens when the mechanism of suspicion—the threat of exteriorization—is turned onto Liu Muzhi himself? Suspicions were aroused when Liu Yi criticized Liu Muzhi for his undue influence on the Founding Ancestor, but there the suspicion was only apparent, for Liu Yi is a villain, and a villain has no historiographical right to suspicion. The exterior pressure he applied was merely a prompt for further interiority. Elsewhere, Liu Muzhi must defend himself more actively. This is illustrated by a pair of anecdotes—adjacent passages woven from the same narrative yarn, even using a common figure of thought to convey the quality of the absolute. The first reads:

> Whatever Muzhi heard from outsiders, whether great or small, he never failed to certainly relay on to his patron, without omitting anything, even (*sui fu*) the gossip and invective of the wards and villages, or minor happenings on the roadsides. The Founding Ancestor always made a show of knowing every little thing there was to know about the comings and goings of the common people—and all this knowledge came from Muzhi.

穆之外所聞見，莫不大小必白，雖復閭里言謔、塗陌細事，皆一二以聞。高祖每得民間委密消息以示聰明，皆由穆之也。(III-G)

The focus here is on Liu Muzhi's interiority and he exudes the absolute. We see definition by full extension (*da xiao*, "whether great or small"), by consequential certainty (*bi*, "certainly"), by an adverb of the absolute (*jie*, "whatever," or "everything"), by full enumeration (*yi er*, literally "one, two [and so on to the end]," here rendered as "without omitting anything"), and by the double negative's elimination of any potential middle ground (*mo bu*, "he never failed to"). At the center of the whole lies an *a fortiori* synecdoche of the absolute: if "even" (*sui fu*) the apparently inconsequential gossip was conveyed to his patron, then how much more so would he have fully relayed information of real importance.

The problem lies in the inherent polyvocality of interiority. The absolute quality of Liu Muzhi's actions translates into an absolute control over his patron: "all his knowledge came from Liu Muzhi." Thus, the devoted client risks usurping the defining authority that properly belongs to the patron. This problem is reformulated and resolved in the adjoining counterpart anecdote:

> Also, Muzhi was fond of social gatherings, his receptions always full of guests. [In this way] he spread about people to serve as eyes and ears, so he was certain to know everything about people's opinions at court and beyond, and he would submit all of these to the Founding Ancestor's attention without concealing anything, even (*sui fu*) the peccadilloes of his intimate associates. For this someone once criticized him. "With His Excellency's perspicacity," he responded, "he would surely come to know of it anyway. And having received His favor, Honor forbids me from concealing anything: that is why Zhang Liao (169–222) reported on Guan Yu (d. 220) when the latter was about to rebel."
> 又愛好賓遊，坐客恆滿，布耳目以為視聽，故朝野同異，穆之莫不必知。雖復親暱短長，皆陳奏無隱。人或譏之，穆之曰：「以公之明，將來會自聞達。我蒙公恩，義無隱諱，此張遼所以告關羽欲叛也。」(III-H)

This anecdote intensifies the synecdoche of the absolute: the "everything" that he reports includes not just ordinary gossip but the intimate details of people who would have had his confidence. Nor is the avenue by which he collects his intelligence beyond reproach: sponsoring "social gatherings" is the activity of a patron, not a client. Thus he becomes the object of criticism, which is to say, people seek to exteriorize him. The trick is to receive the threat of exteriorization as a prompt, a rhetorical exigence used to bolster his position. As he did in his reformation of the Founding Ancestor's calligraphy, here Liu Muzhi "thresholds" with a shift in the source of definition, which again involves a double parry. First, he deferentially returns the power of definition to his patron: his supply of information is inessential, he claims, because his able patron "would surely come to know of it anyway." Affirming the Founding Ancestor's rightful pluperfect sequence, he *circumstantializes* his own knowledge and agency. He then proceeds to outdo his own argument by shifting the grounds of the definition to a higher level, locating the explanation for his actions not in a person, be it himself or his patron, but instead deriving it from the abstract ideal of Honor (*yi* 義, a technical term for the duty owed to a patron by a client).[14] Putting himself outside the threshold, he makes himself a (mere) *consequence of* the defining force of Honor. Now, anyone who would dare denounce him will be forced into dispute with an endoxic ideal.

The narrative of Liu Muzhi's service as his patron's preeminent agent in the capital, a position of unquestionable interiority, continually gestures to the potential for transgression, yet to the end Liu Muzhi proves himself a master of the rhetoric of the interior-exterior. The biography's final anecdote trumpets his triumph over this threat, again with intimations of excessive banqueting providing the exigent ground:

> By nature he was wantonly extravagant, certain to demand a full banquet for every meal. Even his breakfasts were invariably made for ten men. Fond of entertaining, Muzhi never dined alone, and whenever mealtime drew near he would regularly gather ten or so guests to dine in his quarters. Such was his regular habit.
>
> 性奢豪，食必方丈，旦輒為十人饌。穆之既好賓客，未嘗獨餐，每至食時，客止十人以還者，帳下依常下食，以此為常。(III-V)

"By nature," "certain to," "never," "not once": the terms are both absolute and negative ("wantonly extravagant"). This constitutes an attack on his character—the suspicion that had centered on Zhuge Zhangmin is now turned on him. But it is also the prompt for his final quoted words:

> He once sought to explain himself to the Founding Ancestor:
> I, Muzhi, come from a poor and lowly family that often struggled even to get by. Since gaining your favor, I have always tried hard to be frugal, but my daily needs have indeed been rather excessive. Yet apart from this, I have never let you down in the slightest way.

---

14. His argument relies on an analogy to a validating historical precedent, using a third-century story in which Zhang Liao weighed his obligations to his peer, Guan Yu, and his patron, Cao Cao (155–220), and chose to give greater weight to the latter. See *Sanguo zhi* 36.939–40, and the note to this passage in the appendix. The tone of the allusion here resembles its formulation in the commentary to the *Sanguo zhi* that was submitted to the throne in 429, just as the early *Song shu* biographical materials were beginning to take shape.

嘗白高祖曰:「穆之家本貧賤,贍生多闕。自叨忝以來,雖每存約損,而朝夕所須,微為過豐。自此以外,一毫不以負公。」(III-V)

The suspicion of Liu Muzhi implied here recalls the example of Xiao He 蕭何 (257–193 BCE), the key advisor to the founder of the Han dynasty, who in his biography repeatedly has to face his patron's doubts about his loyalty. Not only does Xiao He overcome those suspicions, the Han emperor, in the end, openly claims that his aspersions allowed Xiao He to prove himself the great prime minister that he was.[15] The Founding Ancestor is likewise giving Liu Muzhi such an opportunity here.

As was the case with his patron's calligraphy, banqueting is not a thing significant in itself but a sign that leads us back to a certain defining essence. The threatening definition here is that it is a sign of poor character, his "extravagant excess," from which it follows that the Founding Ancestor would be wise not to trust him fully. As before, Liu Muzhi begins by shifting the source of the sign. No longer something *definitive* for him, reflective of his "nature" (*xing*), it is ascribed instead to the formative yet *circumstantial* fact of his family's relative poverty.[16] From this perspective, his extravagance is merely a compensatory consequence of his early misfortune—blame it all on childhood—and that consequence becomes the prompt that lets our protagonist manifest his humble self-awareness. Taking the argument a step further, he declares that "always" (*mei*) he has "tried hard" (*cun*, "kept alive in his mind") to minimize this deficiency. This is to transform excessive banqueting into the positive ethos signal of the earnest man grappling sincerely with a shortcoming.

Not that Liu Muzhi, master of the rhetoric of interiority, or is it his historiographical avatar, will rest there. His concluding line—"apart from this, I have never let you down in the slightest way"—reforms the defect one more time, deploying the synecdoche of the absolute in inside-out form. Where the figure of synecdoche takes a small part and has it stand

---

15. See *Shiji* 53.2013–20.

16. This point reveals a productive tension between social and cultural history in this period: a "poor and lowly" family background was as rhetorically powerful in early medieval China as it was socially disadvantageous. It was a circumstantial misfortune that could "prompt" recognition of a good gentleman's definite worth.

for the whole, here a small part is *just* a small part, decidedly *not* representative of the whole, and the whole is something *absolutely different* from the part. Liu Muzhi's whole person is defined by a high ideal—the client's bond of Honor—that no minor blemish could affect, and indeed that blemish, like a sort of beauty mark, serves to accent that perfection through the addition of a reassuring touch of the ordinary. The flaw places him on the threshold.

Based on a study of Tang dynasty historiography but describing a practice that he would trace all the way back to Sima Qian, Denis Twitchett pointed to the use of commemorative accounts compiled by the family and friends of the decedent as the main source material for "official" biographies in the orthodox histories. Thus he came to stress the fundamentally eulogistic orientation of the Chinese biographical tradition.[17] A contemporary study reached similar conclusions, speaking of the "deeply magical significance" those original sources, offered as they were to the dead, brought to biographical writing.[18] Carrying these observations one step further, we may emphasize that the eulogistic quality of the dynastic biography was due not just to the material on which they drew, but to the form into which that material was drawn—"commentaries" to a dynastic history, the dignified, even "magical" visage of an imperial house.

But the biography in early medieval China was something more than just praise and glory. In the life of Liu Muzhi—the first biography proper in the *History of the Liu-Song*, a place of great distinction—we see that biography was a species of politics, the negotiation between differential positions of power that molded an individual's life and afterlife. Biographical politics was naively eulogistic to the extent that for good (or successful) men, the dynamic interplay of interior and exterior resolved on the side of interiority. For this, Liu Muzhi provides a good example: a consummate politician, skilled in the use of words to achieve his ends, from his position

---

17. See Twitchett, "Problems of Chinese Biography," 27–30; and Twitchett, "Chinese Biographical Writing," 109–13.
18. Peter Olbricht, "Die Biographie in China," 234.

of power he—and the historiography on his behalf—dealt deftly with exterior challenges, using them to prompt himself further inward and upward. And yet those challenges persisted, up to the very end of the account of his life. Was he, the man and his historiographical twin, always so uncommonly able to preserve his interiority, or to place himself in effective threshold positions? In his final words of self-justification, does Liu Muzhi not perhaps protest too much? The forces of exteriorization are not so easily fended off. Eulogy invites irony.

TWO

Exteriority

The influence of the "Spring and Autumn Annals" upon later history has been enormous. To it may be traced the first authoritative expression of the idea that political morality should be upheld by the historian, that it is a function and responsibility of his calling to apportion praise and blame in due measure, not by extended personal comment, but by the manner and emphasis of his record.

—Charles S. Gardner, *Chinese Traditional Historiography*

L iu Muzhi's biography relates his death in most understated terms:

In the thirteenth year (417), his illness became severe. By imperial edict, a standing Doctor of the Yellow Gate was sent to treat him. In the eleventh month he died, in his fifty-eighth year.

十三年，疾篤，詔遣正直黃門郎問疾。十一月卒，時年五十八。(IV)[1]

This is an unremarkable punctuation to a remarkable political career—but an alternate account lies just in the shadows. Two "lives" are arrayed in scroll (or "chapter") forty-two of the *History of the Liu-Song*. With Liu Muzhi stands Wang Hong, an elite statesman some fifteen years his junior who joined the Founding Ancestor's cause and would play an important role in the accession of Emperor Wen (r. 424–53), under whom the

---

1. Parenthetical references in the following discussion are again to the section and paragraph divisions in the translation of Liu Muzhi's biography presented in the appendix.

dynasty's fortunes were consolidated. Wang Hong's biography tells the death of Liu Muzhi rather differently:

> In the eleventh year of Righteousness Resplendent (415), Wang Hong was called to the capital to serve as Senior Aide on the [Founding Ancestor's] Grant Commandant staff. He was promoted to First Senior Aide.
> [In 416] he accompanied the northern campaign. The vanguard took Luoyang (the old Jin capital), but no one in the capital sent forth the Nine Bestowals, so Wang Hong led a return mission, to make the court aware of what orders ought to be issued. At that time, Liu Muzhi was in charge of affairs in the capital—but here were orders coming from the north. Shamed and frightened by this, Muzhi took ill and died soon thereafter.
> 義熙十一年,徵為太尉長史,轉左長史。從北征,前鋒已平洛陽,而未遣九錫,弘銜使還京師,諷旨朝廷。時劉穆之掌留任,而旨反從北來,穆之愧懼,發病遂卒。[2]

The "Nine Bestowals" was a set of ritual implements that was presented, along with a complement of documentation recording the gift for history, by a weakened throne to a rising power as a symbol of the incipient transfer of the dynastic mandate to a new house.[3] As recorded in the imperial annals, the Nine Bestowals documents—the annals quote them in full—were drawn up in the tenth month of 416, after the Founding Ancestor captured Luoyang, the old northern capital. It would be the sixth month of 418, however, nearly two years later, and seven months after the death of Liu Muzhi, before the Founding Ancestor received and accepted them.[4] The annals say nothing about Liu Muzhi failing to facilitate this, and if he held it back it was likely yet another well-considered political maneuver on behalf of his patron. But that is not what happens here. By underscoring Liu Muzhi's apparent hesitancy to initiate the Nine Bestowals process, the narrative in Wang Hong's biography points to a fault line that is mostly hidden in Liu Muzhi's biography. There, in both life and afterlife, Liu Muzhi wields a full rhetorical agency, dazzling the audiences he addresses. Here he becomes the audience, "shamed and frightened" (*kui ju*), exteriorized from the grand

---

2. *Song shu* 42.1312.
3. See the discussion of the documentary nature of dynastic transition in chapter 5.
4. *Song shu* 2.36–44.

narrative in which he had seemed so omnipotent. Allegedly, it is the shock of his replacement by a more naturally interior power—the gentry elite, finally sidling up to the Founding Ancestor—that provokes the illness that "soon thereafter" (*sui*, a strong marker of consequence) kills him.

The issue these dueling narratives of the death of Liu Muzhi raise is the function of irony in early medieval historiography. The dynastic biography of a good man was basically eulogistic in orientation, and the historian was responsible for maintaining that orientation. The classical injunction was to "conceal the failings of worthy men" (*wei xianzhe hui* 為賢者諱), a principle noted and explained seven times in the Gongyang commentary on the *Spring and Autumn* classic, the ancestral source of the historiographical tradition. But while this discretion could entail the elision or neutralization of negative aspects of a positively regarded historical figure, the "good historian" was still tasked with the production of a truthful account. This meant delivering such negative information in more indirect ways, through euphemism or, in the manner of "the theory of mutual illumination," by distributing the negative material to other parts of the history.

That is to speak of the historian's side of the historiographical ledger—but the power of irony did not reside solely, or even mainly, with the historian. The interior-exterior dynamic that informed early medieval political culture generated historical accounts positive and negative. There was no neat division between the two kinds of material: if negatively charged information about Liu Muzhi was placed outside his biography, traces of it are hardly absent from the account of his life proper. There was, further, no clean distinction between historical judgment and historiographical activity—the systole and diastole of interiority and exteriority and the silent resting points between the beats, the mutually constitutive actions and dispositions of different players at different points in time. And just as interiority was not an unalloyed good—power is precarious—so we shall see that exteriorization in this culture was not absolutely vitiating.

Role, Type, and Rhetoric

Liu Muzhi's "first" death is a direct representation of a simple sequence of events. He got sick and he died. The same cannot be said for the antagonistic version: Liu Muzhi's death from shame is not a freestanding historical account, but a story calqued on the legend of the death of Xun Yu, a statesman who lived and died almost exactly two centuries earlier and who played a vital part in the establishment of the Cao-Wei dynasty (220–65), much as Liu Muzhi did for the Liu-Song. Here is how Xun Yu's death is told in his biography in the *Records of the Three Kingdoms* (*Sanguo zhi*), a history compiled in the late third century:

> In the seventeenth year of Establishing Peace (212), Dong Zhao and the others thought that the Great Ancestor [Cao Cao] should have his fief advanced to Duke of State, and that the Nine Bestowals should be prepared, to manifest his outstanding merit. They quietly discussed this with Xun Yu. Xun Yu, however, thought that the Great Ancestor had raised up righteous troops in order to restore the Han court and bring peace to the land, and that having acted out of a loyalty most sincere he would insist on declining any honors; that, as the gentleman regards care of the people as a virtue in itself (and not a means to self-aggrandizement), the promotion and gifts were not appropriate. Because of this, the Great Ancestor came to hold a grudge against Xun Yu.
>
> 十七年，董昭等謂太祖宜進爵國公，九錫備物，以彰殊勳，密以諮彧。或以為太祖本興義兵以匡朝寧國，秉忠貞之誠，守退讓之實；君子愛人以德，不宜如此。太祖由是心不能平。[5]

Xun Yu's refusal to endorse the award of the Nine Bestowals—that is, his refusal to acquiesce to a plan to set Cao Cao on the path to becoming emperor—is the first stage in a pluperfect demise. His biography continues:

> Then, when the Great Ancestor went on his campaign against Sun Quan (182–252), he submitted a memorial to the throne requesting that Xun Yu come to deliver rewards to the army in Qiao. Thereupon he kept Xun with him as Advisor to the Military Affairs of the Prime Minister (i.e., Cao Cao himself), with the titles of Attendant in the Palace and Grand Master for Splendid Happiness, Carrying the Imperial Tally. When the Great Ancestor's forces proceeded to Ruxu [on the northern bank of the Yangtze], Xun Yu stayed behind sick in Shouchun [on the Huai River], where he died of

---

5. *Sanguo zhi* 10.317.

worry (*you*), in his fiftieth year. He was granted the posthumous title of "the Respectful Marquis." And the following year, the Great Ancestor indeed became the Duke of Wei.

會征孫權，表請彧勞軍于譙，因輒留彧，以侍中光祿大夫持節，參丞相軍事。太祖軍至濡須，彧疾留壽春，以憂薨，時年五十。諡曰敬侯。明年，太祖遂為魏公矣。⁶

Cao Cao takes Xun Yu along on campaign, but Xun Yu is no longer the trusted advisor of old. He is only—as Cao Cao states in a memorial to the throne quoted in the *History of the Latter Han* version of this event—a token of imperial authority. Marching to the Yangtze to battle the forces of Sun Quan, the rising potentate pointedly leaves his former client behind at his Huai River base, where he lay ill, and that may have been the whole of the actual story—but illness seeks a better story than that. Xun Yu's historiographical "life" ends by relating how he "died of worry" (*you*)—and how his death clears the way (*sui* again, here translated as "indeed") for Cao Cao's ascent as the "Great Ancestor" of a new dynasty. In another version of the story, Xun Yu's alienation from his patron's political glory is conjured up with a more vivid mimesis: "Cao Cao sent Xun Yu a feast, but when he opened the vessels he found them—empty. Thereupon, he drank a poison potion and died" 太祖饋彧食，發之乃空器也，於是飲藥而卒。⁷

Liu Muzhi's second death, then, occurs as analogy: like Xun Yu, he was a trusted advisor to a rising dynastic founder but failed to rise with

6. *Sanguo zhi* 10.317. Compare Xun Yu's biography at *Hou Han shu* 70.2290, and the parallel account of the *Xiandi chunqiu* 獻帝春秋 (Annalistic history of Emperor Xian), quoted in Pei Songzhi's 裴松之 (372–451) commentary, where the pluperfect structure is placed further back, Cao Cao's resentment of Xun Yu beginning with an earlier episode and manifesting itself in their disagreement over the Nine Bestowals.

7. *Sanguo zhi* 10.317, commentary, citing the *Weishi chunqiu* 魏氏春秋 (Annalistic history of the ruling family of the Wei), a fourth-century chronicle and thus, perhaps, an embroidering of the basic narrative. This piquant story is incorporated into the *Hou Han shu* account. In a still more baroque variation, the *Xiandi chunqiu* features a claim, said to have been brought to Wu by a refugee from Wei and then spread by the leader of Wu into the kingdom of Shu, that Xun committed suicide because Cao Cao had commanded him to assassinate the Han empress.

him to the end. But there are some strange things in this analogy. First of all, it appears not just with the negative version of Liu Muzhi's death, but positively in Liu Muzhi's own biography, where we in fact find allusions to Xun Yu in at least four places.[8] The most prominent of these is a typical illustration of Liu Muzhi's rhetorical art:

> When Muzhi sought to promote someone, he would stop at nothing. "Though I may not promote good men as well as the Gentleman Director Xun [Yu] did," he would regularly remark, "I do not promote the *not good*."
>
> 凡所薦達,不進不止,常云:「我雖不及荀令君之舉善,然不舉不善。」(III-J)

The narration emphasizes the absolute quality of his interiority, "stopping at nothing" to advance the careers of men of his choosing, and we have seen how this kind of representation serves to hint at an unbridled interiority. He will be criticized for favoring certain men to the disadvantage of others. He will be perceived as having assumed too much interiority, taking on patron powers that ought not belong to a client. These implicit criticisms provide the "prompt" for the remark at the center of the anecdote, which shows Liu Muzhi handling criticism with his customary aplomb.

Framed by the historiography as an argument Liu Muzhi made "regularly" (*chang*)—an odd proposition to take literally—the remark is brief but full of argumentative complexity, tacking from interior to exterior along the threshold line. The analogy is set up as a contrast: he is *not*, Liu Muzhi avers, the match of Xun Yu. This is a thresholding move, deferentially distancing himself from this historical paragon, but in that way establishing a sense of equivalence. Moreover, having said this—or rather, before even making the statement—he brackets it ("although . . .") as a statement secondary to his real point, which is the self-definition in the second clause, where he uses, again, the logic of the threshold. He does promote worthy "good" men, but he states this using the rhetorical figure of litotes, the understatement by contrast—"I do not promote the *not*

---

8. Connections to Xun Yu's biography less obvious than the one discussed here include, as noted in the appendix, Liu Muzhi's speech in section III-E (note 34), his diction in another anecdote (III-H, note 40), and a description of his actions that may contain an irony (III-U, note 65).

good."⁹ By defining what he is not, he leaves it to others to find the correct contrary conclusion, and so it is that in the mind of his audience the analogy he has just humbly denied is fulfilled, and that audience, playing its part in his rhetoric, accedes to his interiority.

The analogy drawn up between these two historical figures brings us to a perennial problem in the interpretation of Chinese historical sources: the use of "roles" and "types," an alchemical compound that scholarly solutions only rarely succeed in separating. "Role" refers to the historical models that the premodern elite more or less consciously emulated in the conduct of their lives and careers. "The molding power of example," according to a foundational formulation of this concept, "favored the establishment of certain fixed roles in life, which the young were exhorted and trained to play." These roles were distinguished by "the fullness of their delineation in classical injunctions, in history, and in literature. As one man after another down the centuries played out a role, it accumulated more and more nuances of gesture and attitude."¹⁰ In this sense, Xun Yu was a model strategist and administrator in a time of crisis, well worthy of emulation in a parallel age. Indeed, in the early fourth century we find Wang Dao 王導 (276–339), the prime minister responsible for the reestablishment of the Jin dynasty south of the Yangtze, comparing himself to Xun Yu.¹¹ It is entirely conceivable that Liu Muzhi would have seen himself

---

9. Syntactically, this phrase (*buju bushan*, not promote the not good) is parallel to *bujin buzhi* ("would stop at nothing," or, "if they did not advance, he would not stop [until they had]"), used in the narrative introduction to this anecdote. Grammatically, they are entirely distinct, but the syntactic identity reflects a common interplay between the diegetic and mimetic portions of the historiography, with historiographical narration troping off its "primary sources," with verbal structures generating echoes across the historical record. Bielenstein, "The Restoration of the Han Dynasty," 45–47, observes this correlation between documents and narrative and regards it as a guarantee of factuality, but there is a deeper and more idiosyncratic "documentary motive" at work.

10. Arthur F. Wright, "Values, Roles, and Personalities," 10, 12. Though the terms "role" and "type" have sometimes been used interchangeably, I suggest it is useful to keep them distinguished.

11. *Jin shu* 65.1746. While this could well be a retrospective representation (that is, the application of a "type"), the self-comparison comes in a quoted document (a "missive" *jian* 牋), somewhat bolstering our confidence, and it appears in early versions of the *Jin shu*; see *Jiujia jiu Jin shu jiben*, 111. For a discussion of Wang Dao as a model minister "type" in

in and played this "role," modeling himself on Xun Yu directly, or through an intermediary like Wang Dao.

The counterpart to the "role," acted out by the historical actor, is the "type," deployed by the historian to represent a historical individual. Such "set categories," "stereotypes," and "topoi" range across the dynastic histories, ever leaving the reader to wonder: "how far were the roles we find so clearly depicted actually chosen by the subjects and played out in their lives, and how much was ascribed to the life by the Chinese biographer?"[12] From the view of the "type," Xun Yu, key advisor to a rising leader, may merely have been an easy and sensible form into which historical narrative cast Liu Muzhi, and not a model he really emulated. Yet it is clear that role-versus-type was a continuum: practically because a semi-conscious role might be etched a little too deeply when it was represented in story or in writing, and more fundamentally because in a culture in which historical action and historiographical representation were so tightly linked, role and type were simply projections onto a common horizon from different vantage points. The truth to the problem of role and type is that the pair cannot be dissolved at all—a discomforting truth that, however we may wish otherwise, overlays another kind of historical truth—the undeniable difference between something that really happened and something that is said to have happened, but did not.

Acknowledging the inextricability of role and type does not mean we cannot think about the rhetoric in which role and type operated. Grant it that Liu Muzhi indeed played the role of Xun Yu, saying and doing things that fostered an analogy—or that he played no such role at all, but could scarcely have been surprised, or disappointed, to see himself represented through the prism of his much-admired predecessor. Either way, the

---

the eyes of Tang (but also earlier) historiographers, see Matthew V. Wells, "From Spirited Youth to Loyal Official: Life Writing and Didacticism in the *Jin shu* Biography of Wang Dao."

12. Twitchett, "Problems of Chinese Biography," 35, recognizing this as "one of the least tractable problems in the interpretation" of Chinese historical materials. For examples and discussion, see also Bielenstein, "The Restoration of the Han Dynasty," 61–67. The interplay of role and type in early medieval religious traditions is a focal point of Robert Ford Campany, *Making Transcendents: Ascetics and Social Memory in Early Medieval China*, where early medieval culture as a whole is characterized as "a macro-repertoire of resources and roles" (41).

crucial question is how the positive, interiorizing deployment of the Xun Yu model in Liu Muzhi's biography relates to the exteriorizing appropriation of a Xun Yu story to narrate his death in the biography of an erstwhile peer.

The rhetoric of role and type can be described from two aspects, each of which starts with the positive and turns, potentially, toward the negative. On one side is a "passive rhetoric," by which an individual identifies or is identified with a certain exemplar in a restricted sense—as Liu Muzhi likely looked upon Xun Yu as a model statesman—only to have the boundaries of that comparison expand to include elements that are no longer positive. This is a natural development when a culture's historical ideals are not concepts but human beings, mortal creatures whose auras will always—even Confucius had ugly stories told about him!—include negative elements. It is also dialectical, in the sense that a positively inflected story always implies a negative one waiting in the wings. In this view, Liu Muzhi's death just as his patron was consolidating his authority presented the circumstance that allowed the analogy to spread beyond its normal import.

On the other side is an active rhetoric, which is not an alternative to passive rhetoric but the leveraging of it by human agents. From this perspective, it does not really matter if Liu Muzhi actively played Xun Yu, or if he was "typed" that way in retrospect, or if he was already being typed through such representations in his own lifetime. What matters most is that his competitors found rhetorical potential in the fateful circumstance of his death and they brought out the ominous overtones of the analogy. With that, all of the normal, positive representations became tinged with dramatic irony, Liu Muzhi analogizing himself to Xun Yu without knowing how much he would really resemble him in the end.[13] With this irony in hand, Liu Muzhi's adversaries would have eagerly endorsed the projection of the positive type, letting the eulogies of a life serve as the pluperfect backing for the death of a man out of his political depth.

That, however, is the second odd thing about the analogy: that representing Liu Muzhi's death as a reflection of the representation of Xun Yu's

---

13. In the Wang Dao biographical corpus we also find an ironized application of the Nine Bestowals, different to but perhaps cognate with the stories of Xun Yu and Liu Muzhi; see *Jin shu* 65.1752 and *Jiujia jiu Jin shu jiben*, 111.

death does not work very well. This is not to say that there were not remarkable similarities between the two men, in life and, uncannily, in death, and they were probably also similar in ways obscured by these stories. There is no reason to believe Liu Muzhi expired estranged from his patron, and passages in his biography and elsewhere attest that he was already known to be unwell.[14] Likewise for the historical Xun Yu: perhaps he was cautiously seeking the most opportune moment for the ascendance of his longtime patron—elsewhere Cao Cao is full of praise for Xun Yu, and he had married a daughter to Xun Yu's son—and perhaps his death from illness at that time was just that. "We cannot judge his full intentions," a study of Xun Yu's death aptly concludes, "nor, as with any human being, can we be sure he always acted with consistent motives."[15]

Nevertheless, whatever Xun's associations with Cao Cao, both he and his family had close connections with the Han imperial court, and the story of his death was meant to illustrate those connections. The "worry" that is supposed to have killed him is not concern that his patron has abandoned him but the distraught realization that, with his own naive aid and abetting, Cao Cao had maneuvered to usurp the Han throne. With the superficial exception of his inclusion in the Records of the Three Kingdoms, Xun Yu's historical reception was entirely as a minister of the Han, not of the Wei: a man who had joined with Cao Cao when the latter seemed the best hope for a restoration of the Han but distanced himself when Cao's ambitions became clear. When latter-day historians debated how history should judge him, what they were questioning was not his loyalty to the Han but the quality—noble, or vain, or fatuous—of his loyal death.[16] This was the understanding reflected in the posthumous name granted to him after his death, "the Respectful Marquis" (Jing hou 敬侯),

---

14. *Song shu* 46.1394.

15. Rafe de Crespigny, "A Question of Loyalty: Xun Yu, Cao Cao and Sima Guang," 59. De Crespigny surveys the historical evaluations of Xun Yu; on Xun's reception in the early medieval period, see also Guo Shuo, "'Han chen' yi huo 'Wei chen': shijia bixia Xun Yu shenfen de liubian."

16. Guo Shuo, "'Han chen' yi huo 'Wei chen,'" 62, shows that Xun Yu was never recognized as a Wei subject. Although he did come to be included in the Wei section of the *Sanguo zhi*, Chen Shou's evaluation (10.332) there still presents him as a subject of the Han, unable to foresee the consequences of his support for Cao Cao.

that is, respectful of *imperial* authority—and resistant to Cao Cao's usurpation.[17] This was the view emphasized throughout the Jin, as in an encomium written by the historian Yuan Hong 袁宏 (328–76), which stresses the meaning of his final act: "In the beginning, he sought to rescue the masses, *and in the end he became a shining example of good conduct*" 始救生人，終明風槩.[18] The same assessment carried on into the Liu-Song, his association with the Han observed by Pei Songzhi in his commentary to the *Records of the Three Kingdoms* and by Fan Ye in the biography of Xun Yu in his *History of the Latter Han*.

In light of this, while Liu Muzhi may have died at an analogous moment, in no other respect did he match up well with Xun Yu in death. He had no connection at all to the Eastern Jin court, and no cause whatsoever for loyalty to it, a dynastic house that anyway was far removed from the greatness of the Han. He was his patron's confederate through and through, a fact that would be recognized by his enshrinement first in the Liu-Song ancestral temple—a sharp contrast with Xun Yu in the Wei—and then on the opening scrolls of the dynasty's biographical record. This difference is reflected in the way his death scene does not so much mirror Xun Yu's as trope off one particular depiction of it: the false feast presented to Xun by Cao Cao. Supposedly, this was to show Xun Yu realizing that his patron, having used him to tame the Han court, no longer needed his services. Grafted onto Liu Muzhi, the consternation of a loyal imperial subject is discarded altogether, the focus solely on the disgraced horror of a client who suddenly finds himself estranged from his patron. Xun Yu dies a significant death, defining him as someone who refused to participate in a usurpation of Heaven's Mandate, or at least was excluded from such an unrighteous endeavor. But Liu Muzhi's death is just a frightened

---

17. This must also be the import of the retrospective award of the high title of Grand Commandant (*taiwei*) to Xun Yu in 265, half a century after his death but right on the eve of the Jin displacement of the Wei; as noted in the *Weishi chunqiu*, cited above for the story of his suicide.

18. *Wen xuan* 47.2128. "The masses" (*sheng ren*) alludes (behind a Tang taboo in the received *Wen xuan* text?) to Mao 245 ("Sheng min").

one, the consequence of the shock he suffered upon realizing that the enterprise he had helmed from the start had been taken over by the court elite.[19]

The Abuse of Liu Muzhi

The forces that turned out this analogy were probably partly passive: who could resist a figure as manifest in its circumstance as this one, and with the submission to the court of the Pei Songzhi edition of the *Records of the Three Kingdoms* in 429, shortly before the first efforts were made to write up a Liu-Song history, the model of Xun Yu may have been pushed to the forefront of the historical imagination. But the exteriorization of Liu Muzhi from his own life and legacy, and the undermining of the rhetorical interiority he appeared to possess so fully, must also have been actively pursued, for there are many traces of it left in the historical record.

The adversarial version of Liu Muzhi's death appears in a different form in a cognate anecdote found in the *History of the [Northern] Wei*—the dynastic history of the Liu-Song's giant foe in the north, compiled in 554, but on the basis of fifth-century materials. That anecdote has Liu Muzhi admonishing Wang Zhen'e 王鎮惡 (373–418), a great general, to exert his best efforts in the northern campaign of 416. To this, Wang replies that he is certain to succeed: "I swear to you, if I fail to take Xianyang (the old Western Han capital region), I shall not cross back over the Yangtze again" 吾今不克咸陽，誓不濟江. The *History of the Liu-Song* records this bravado

---

19. At the end of this discussion of the analogy of Liu Muzhi to Xun Yu, we cautiously edge up to a precipice; should we tumble over it, we might find ourselves irretrievably lost in the echoing canyons of traditional historiography. Shen Yue's biography in the *History of the Liang* (*Liang shu* 13.243) depicts him as the mastermind behind Emperor Wu of the Liang's overthrow of the Qi dynasty, but then alleges that he later came to lose the favor of his erstwhile patron—and that, as an old and ill man, he "died of fright" (*ju sui zu* 懼遂卒) when the Liang emperor sent a representative to scold him for perceived disloyalty. Could the Shen Yue of 487, when he was compiling his *History of the Liu-Song*, have imagined that a quarter century later his antagonists might cast him in this type, and perhaps even on the impetus of his own *History*?

in Wang Zhen'e's biography, and it stops there.[20] He would fulfill his vow. But in the *History of the Northern Wei*'s version of Liu-Song history, Wang, or the historiographical function "Wang Zhen'e" represents here, adds an antagonistic thrust: "But if the Nine Bestowals do not reach His Excellency, then that will be *your* fault!" 而公九錫不至者，亦卿之責矣。[21] Liu Muzhi's death in the Wang Hong biography is simply the denouement of this drama: the client was no longer up to the task.

The most conspicuous realizations of the disempowerment of Liu Muzhi are found in the lives of his progeny, appended to his biography. With few exceptions, these are dismal portraits, proof that whatever interiority Liu Muzhi attained—his spirit tablet was being worshipped in the imperial temple!—he could not simply pass it down to his heirs, and the historiography relates their ignominy with great relish, forgoing any ironic veils. The following story is told of Liu Yong, the grandson who would inherit his fief:

> Wherever he went, Liu Yong liked to eat scabs. He thought they tasted like pickled fish. Once, he paid a visit to Meng Lingxiu. Earlier, Meng had undergone moxibustion treatment and his scabs were falling off onto his couch, so Liu gathered them up and ate them. Meng Lingxiu was shocked. "It is in my nature to like these," Liu replied. Meng peeled off the scabs that had not yet fallen and gave them to Liu to eat. After Liu left, Meng wrote to He Xu: "Liu Yong has been chewing on me and my whole body is bleeding."
>
> 邕所至嗜食瘡痂，以為味似鰒魚。嘗詣孟靈休，靈休先患灸瘡，瘡痂落牀上，因取食之。靈休大驚。答曰：「性之所嗜。」靈休瘡痂未落者，悉褫取以飴邕。邕既去，靈休與何勗書曰：「劉邕向顧見噉，遂舉體流血。」[22]

---

20. *Song shu* 45.1368, where the wording, but not the meaning, is slightly different: 不剋咸陽，誓不復濟江而還也。

21. *Wei shu* 97.2133. The *History of the Southern Dynasties* (comp. 659) records the same, with slight variation, in its biography of Wang Zhen'e; *Nan shi* 16.454–55. The variation might suggest a common source—might it have been Xu Yuan's *History of the Liu-Song*?

22. *Song shu* 42.1308. This story is also found in the *Yiyuan* (*Garden of the Unassimilable*), a mid-fifth-century collection of unverifiable tales. See Wang Genlin et al., eds., *Han Wei Liuchao biji xiaoshuo daguan*, 687. The ennobled sons of Meng Chang 孟昶 (d. 410) and He Wuji, early affiliates of the Founding Ancestor, Meng Lingxiu and He Xu were known for their profligate behavior; see *Song shu* 71.1844–45.

"In his fief state of Nankang," the biography adds, in a variation on the theme, "he had two hundred some clerks. Not caring whether or not they had committed an offense, he would have them whipped in alternation, to regularly use their scabs for his meals" 南康國吏二百許人，不問有罪無罪，遞互與鞭，鞭瘡痂常以給膳. Thus, with figures conveying absolute definition ("wherever," "in my nature," "whether or not," "regularly"), Liu Muzhi's main line is revealed to be—absolutely disgusting. The fief would be revoked from Liu Yong's son in 460, when he attacked his wife with a knife.

Humility was one of Liu Muzhi's honorable traits, and a prime thresholding tactic in the rhetoric of interiority. It is in sharp contrast to this that his second son proved to be absolutely presumptuous about his right to political interiority. While serving as head of the prefectures Xuancheng and Huainan, this Liu Shizhi is said to have engaged in flagrant profiteering, but when the regional governor, none other than Wang Hong, sent men to investigate him, he drove them away with the following remark:

> Go back and tell your governor that Liu Shizhi has done his part for the imperial house, and not a small part at that. What would it matter if I were to steal a few million? Not to say that I have! You will not get a shred of evidence from me—not from my clerks, not from my subjects, not from our government documents.

治所還白使君，劉式之於國家粗有微分，偷數百萬錢何有，況不偷邪！吏民及文書不可得。」[23]

"How brazen is the argumentation of Liu Shizhi!" 劉式之辯如此奔, Wang Hong is reported to have commented.

Both the preceding anecdotes echo, and thus undermine, the biography of the family patriarch, specifically section III-V, in which Liu Muzhi admits his flaws but turns them, via inverse synecdoche, into a symbol of his loyalty. For Liu Muzhi, flawed nature was a prompt toward interiority—but his heirs simply "inherit" his flaws in spades. Liu Shizhi mounts a defense, but it is a lame one, based in a simplistic definition—I am loyal to the throne and that is it, so there is no need to even consider whether I

---

23. *Song shu* 42.1309.

have any flaws. These contrastive echoes sound again in the account of Liu Shizhi's son, Liu Yuu 劉瑀 (d. ca. 458; his name is romanized here as "Liu Yuu" to avoid confusion with the given name of the Founding Ancestor), who is described as "haughty by nature, unwilling to see anyone rise above him" 性陵物護前，不欲人居己上.

Formerly we saw that Liu Muzhi, grounding himself in the higher definition of "honor" (*yi*), was willing to betray the trust of others in order to supply his patron with intelligence. His grandson uses the same value, but in a dishonest fashion, as would follow from his corrupted "nature." The story goes that Liu Yuu was a client of Liu Jun 劉濬 (429–53), the second son of Emperor Wen and a historiographical villain: in 453 he would join his elder brother in rebellion against their father, a cataclysmic event for the Liu-Song imperial house. Also on the staff was a poet named Gu Mai 顧邁, said to be particularly intimate with their patron. The jealous Liu Yuu first acted to gain intimacy with Gu Mai, echoing his grandfather's old ploy. "He unreservedly told him *everything*, including matters regarding the women of his household, pouring out all the things one should never speak about" 深布情款，家內婦女間事，言語所不得至者，莫不倒寫備說. In this way, Gu Mai came to trust him, and when the patron, trusting Gu Mai, told Gu of the private affairs of *his* household, Gu would then innocently relay these back to his good friend. Then, on a day when the two men were together at the archery grounds, Liu Yuu suddenly summoned a clerk. When Gu asked him why, he replied:

> His Excellency has treated you like a family member, sharing all his personal details with you, but you go and spill this information to the outside world, so that now, everyone knows everything. I am an official serving under His Excellency. How could I not report this?
>
> 公以家人待卿，相與言無所隱，而卿於外宣泄，致使人無不知。我是公吏，何得不啟。[24]

The grounds of Liu Yuu's argument are exactly the same as those used by his grandfather: the client's sense of honor and duty. But Liu Yuu is not a noble rhetor. Through his duplicity, he has concocted a situation in

---

24. *Song shu* 42.1309.

which endoxic definition leads, perversely, to unrighteous consequences: incensed, the patron sent Gu Mai off to exile in Guangzhou, while Liu Yuu's own career advanced.

The historiography has still more bad things to say about Liu Muzhi's descendants. A third grandson, for instance, was made a government bondservant for profiteering as a prefect. But one other passage in the account of this Liu Yuu may encapsulate the entire fate of Liu Muzhi's family—and epitomize wisdom and ignorance in Southern Dynasties political culture. In 452, on the eve of his patron's rebellion, Liu Yuu had the foresight to take a posting as governor of far-off Yizhou—modern Sichuan, a rich if treacherous satrapy in this period. After the rebellion had been quieted, he quickly joined the side of the new emperor (Xiaowu, r. 453–64) and returned to court, where he served in a high staff position and then as court Censor (*yushi zhongcheng* 御史中丞), in which capacity he gained renown for his attacks on the high gentry. But this level of achievement was not enough for him. He wanted to be made Attendant in the Palace (*shizhong* 侍中), a title both highly prestigious and, because it entailed physical proximity to the emperor, strongly "interior." The court elite resisted, and Liu Yuu petulantly demanded a return to Sichuan. At this moment, he is recorded as having said:

> In a life of official service, if one does not enter [the capital] one should exit [to the provinces]. How can one forever tarry on the threshold?
>
> 人仕宦，不出當入，不入當出，安能長居戶限上。[25]

Liu Yuu sees only the direct goals of power at court and profit abroad. For the next five years he would hold powerful positions, including head of personnel on the Secretariat, but all while breaking norms and insulting peers and even kinsmen left and right. On his death, he was given the posthumous title "The Recalcitrant" (Gangzi 剛子), and some historian took up his pen to write the account we read today, of a man, and a family, so antipathetic to the art of thresholding.

Were the descendants of Liu Muzhi really so iniquitous? We must again recall that historiography was not primarily a retrospective enterprise, but

---

25. *Song shu* 42.1310.

an accumulation of contemporary materials naturally saturated with bias. Liu Muzhi's loftier competitors saw him as someone who *should* be estranged from their patron and that was written into his biographical record, albeit not directly into his biography proper. As for his progeny, there was nothing to guarantee the interiority they had inherited: where Liu Muzhi played a pivotal role in the dynasty's establishment, his sons and grandsons were, in their political age, neither fish nor fowl, not the high gentry the throne needed to cultivate for its prestige or the talented men of lower status who were of such utilitarian use. They may indeed have had a surfeit of personal failings, but it is likely their failings were drummed up, spread about, and bundled into the historical record by their enemies, happy to push them into the exterior. Handed such material, the "good historian" Shen Yue has "transmitted it" to posterity, as the careful Confucian historian was wont to do. But does their portrayal in this way in his *History* reflect a true historical judgment? Clearly Shen Yue did not reject this depiction outright, but that is not to say he endorsed it, and the perspective the *History of the Liu-Song* took on Liu Muzhi was, we shall see, somewhat different.

The Use of Liu Muzhi

Returning to Liu Muzhi himself, we continue to find, scattered about the *History*, other episodes that show him in a negative light. But is antagonism from his enemies—together with the vagaries of a rhetoric that would, eventually, range into negative territory—the only explanation or even the best explanation for such material? It is true that Liu Muzhi the biographical "subject" loses much of the agency he had worked to accrue in his political life, but this loss signifies something different in the larger concept of dynastic historiography, where the "biography" is a "commentary" (*zhuan*) on the "classic" (*jing*) narrative of an imperial court. In his participation in that loftier historiographical level, Liu Muzhi serves his patron as a kind of "scapegoat," the "cathartic vessel" whose instance facilitates a resolution of the political frictions that accompanied the Founding Ancestor's ascendance.[26]

26. For "scapegoat," a signature device in the rhetorical theory of Kenneth Burke, and "cathartic vessel," see Burke, *Language as Symbolic Action*, 94. It has been suggested

Liu Muzhi and the Founding Ancestor were men of similar standing, from the broad middle and lower gentry of the Southern Dynasties' premier military garrison town, Jingkou. At the capital, a day's journey up the Yangtze River, stood the gentry elite, naturally positioned against them but not unamenable to political cooperation, and indeed the negotiation of some form of cooperation was a necessity, if a stable socio-political regime with the ability to resist invasions from the north was to be maintained. In this negotiation the Founding Ancestor eventually, by means persuasive and lethal, gained the upper hand, securing accommodation with the capital's premier political group. In one sense, Liu Muzhi was his key advisor in this process—witness the virtuoso speech analyzed in chapter 1. At the same time, in his "exteriorized" life, Liu Muzhi is used to *represent* the social gap between the Founding Ancestor and his political competitors, who looked on such men with disdain. For the gentry elite, negative depictions of Liu Muzhi were an outlet for anxiety in the face of a rising power, while for the Founding Ancestor such representations of Liu Muzhi could prompt his own interior progress, encouraging the capital elite's endorsement of the incipient dynasty. Thus, when Liu Muzhi's alleged alienation from his patron and his (historically factual, due to his death) replacement at the Founding Ancestor's side by the capital elite is presented in the Wang Hong biography, he looks weak, "shamed and frightened" in the face of his high gentry competitors, but he is strong in terms of the historiographical function he is serving—as an allegorical sacrifice to compensate for the Founding Ancestor's humble origins.

It is by shedding this symbolic part that the Founding Ancestor gains the acquiescence of Wang Hong, the most esteemed member of the capital elite. Two scrolls later in the *History*, we find Liu Muzhi involved in a very similar scapegoating scene. The member of the elite in question here is Xie Hui 謝晦 (390–426), a young gentryman who became the Founding Ancestor's client before the northern campaign of 416 and would serve as a senior minister after the dynastic founding. His biography speaks of the relationship in strong terms: "The Founding Ancestor showered him with favor and reward beyond anything shown to his other clients" 高祖深加

---

that another kind of scapegoating—the retrospective construction of a villain—can be detected in the biography of the talented but flatfooted Fan Ye 范曄 (398–445); see Sebastian Eicher, "Fan Ye's Biography in the *Song Shu*: Form, Content, and Impact," 63n71–72.

愛賞,羣僚莫及. Could those "other clients" have included Liu Muzhi? The biography continues:

> When Xie followed the Founding Ancestor on campaign in the Luoyang and Chang'an regions, all essential matters, within and without, were entrusted to him. When Liu Muzhi would send an emissary to report on matters in the capital, Xie Hui would frequently raise dissenting opinions. Muzhi was incensed by this: "Is His Excellency coming back or not?"
>
> 從征關、洛,內外要任悉委之。劉穆之遣使陳事,晦往往措異同,穆之怒曰:「公復有還時不?」[27]

The rhetoric of the absolute is granted to Xie Hui, and Liu Muzhi is left at a loss, his flummoxed response a variation on the fated illness that will strike him down upon Wang Hong's return a short time later. If only his patron would return and stand face to face with him, he could regain his interiority! Instead, the Founding Ancestor stands apart, creating a new interior space increasingly stocked with members of the high elite. Xie Hui's biography continues with a second configuration of Liu Muzhi's death and alienation:

> The Founding Ancestor wanted to appoint Xie Hui as his Interior Gentleman Retainer [on his duchy staff], but when he presented this idea to Liu Muzhi, Muzhi was insistent that the post should not be given to him. And for as long as Liu Muzhi was alive, Xie Hui received no promotion. When news of Liu's death reached them in the north, the Founding Ancestor cried inconsolably, but Xie Hui, who happened to be on duty at the moment, was overjoyed, and he went directly into the office to make arrangements for Muzhi's funeral. On that very day, an instruction was sent out to promote Xie Hui to Interior Gentleman Retainer.
>
> 高祖欲以為從事中郎,以訪穆之,堅執不與。終穆之世不遷。穆之喪問至,高祖哭之甚慟。晦時正直,喜甚,自入閤內參審穆之死問。其日教出,轉晦從事中郎。[28]

---

27. *Song shu* 44.1348.

28. *Song shu* 44.1348. This scene is inverted in the life of Liu Muzhi's grandson, the Liu Yuu discussed above: he leaps into the air and shouts with joy when he hears of the death of the elite gentryman who had blocked *his* career.

Anecdotes like these are overdetermined, the product of various motivations and the object of multiple uses. In 426 Xie Hui would be executed as a rebel by Emperor Wen (r. 424–53), brought down by the machinations of a competing elite faction that included Wang Hong. In the eyes of the official Liu-Song *History* he is a flawed figure, if not a bad one, and Liu Muzhi's blocking of his appointment is historiography's way of foreshadowing the fact that Xie is not a man the Founding Ancestor could trust with his enterprise. At the same time, the anecdote allegorizes the Founding Ancestor's reconciliation with the elite, with Liu Muzhi's demise serving as a prompt. Liu Muzhi appears as a defining force, but only to be circumstantialized, and as soon as he dies, a higher member of the gentry takes his place, propelled by the rhetoric of immediacy—Xie Hui "happened to be on duty," the same figure that motivated Liu Muzhi's first meeting with the Founding Ancestor. The topic of contrast intensifies the effect, the joy of Xie Hui—and others of the gentry who might have been eager to take a larger stake in the now almost certain establishment of a new dynasty—rendered in chiaroscuro by the Founding Ancestor's deep sadness.

The same allegory plays out in the biography of Yan Yanzhi 顏延之 (384–456), one of the period's great writers, where the rejection of Liu Muzhi is again a means of facilitating or prompting gentry endorsement of the Founding Ancestor. One of Yan's sisters was married to Liu Muzhi's daughter, but Yan, it is said, refused even to meet him. In the narrower context of Yan's biography, the point made is a moral one: that Yan was a high-minded gentleman living in poverty, and even when he had a chance to be promoted by the power of his day, he refused on principle. The base Liu Muzhi serves as a prompt for the protagonist's display of his lofty morality. Yet again, there is a broader, historiographical prompt being set in motion, facilitating the rise of the Founding Ancestor. The biography continues to see Yan Yanzhi eventually come in to serve under the new dynasty, his rejection of Liu Muzhi having served its purpose.[29]

Elsewhere the Founding Ancestor himself joins Liu Muzhi playing the humble, symbolic foil. In the story of Wang Zhi 王智, like Xie Hui from a famed clan (the Langya Wang) but not of a powerful family, the Founding Ancestor is the voice of functional self-deprecation:

29. *Song shu* 73.1891.

> When the Founding Ancestor was working with Liu Muzhi to plan the campaign against Liu Yi [in the year 412], Wang Zhi was present. A few days later, Muzhi spoke to the Founding Ancestor: "A military campaign is a serious affair. What were you thinking, letting Wang Zhi in on it?" The Founding Ancestor just laughed: "This man is lofty and aloof. How would he pay any mind to discussions among people like us?" Such was the favor Wang Zhi received.
>
> 與劉穆之謀討劉毅,而智在焉。它日,穆之白高祖曰:「伐國,重事也,公云何乃使王智知?」高祖笑曰:「此人高簡,豈聞此輩論議。」其見知如此。[30]

Again, this is not a narrative of historical fact but a historiographical allegory showing how the Founding Ancestor catered to the elite, beginning with, or even to the extent of, lesser lights like Wang Zhi. Deference to the gentry elite is put in Liu Muzhi's own mouth in the following anecdote, from the biography of another member of the slightly lesser elite, Xie Fangming (380–426).

> Liu Muzhi, then Prefect-Martial of Danyang, was the most powerful personage of the time and all those at court and beyond gathered around him, like spokes around a wheel. There were only four men who refused to make Liu's acquaintance: Xie Hun, Xie Fangming, Chi Sengshi (d. 412), and Cai Kuo (379–425). Muzhi found this a matter of deep regret. Later, Fangming and Cai Kuo did come to pay him a visit, and he was overjoyed, saying to the Founding Ancestor: "Xie Fangming is the young colt of a fine family! Just let him go and he will be a Prime Minister, to say nothing of whether he has talent to boot."
>
> 丹陽尹劉穆之權重當時,朝野輻輳,不與穆之相識者,唯有混、方明、郗僧施、蔡廓四人而已,穆之甚以為恨。方明、廓後往造之,大悅,白高祖曰:「謝方明可謂名家駒。直置便自是台鼎人,無論復有才用。」[31]

Liu Muzhi as the hub of a wheel is a figure we have seen in his biography, but whereas there it stands for his (overweening) power, here it is

---

30. *Song shu* 85.2177–78. Wang Zhi's niece would become empress to Emperor Ming; see *Song shu* 41.1295.
31. *Song shu* 53.1523.

manifestly part of a contrastive scheme. His power is ostensibly absolute—but not really, for the best men reject him, and when two of those do condescend to pay their respects to him, he is forced to exteriorize himself from the power of judgment. As his patron did with Wang Zhi, so Liu Muzhi draws a line between the character of these eminent personages and any "discussion" (the echoing trope *lun* 論, here negated as "to say nothing of") he and his patron might have about them. There may be some light irony here—the implication is that the high gentry, despite their tight hold on the upper strata of officialdom, were not necessarily all so talented—but the overall inflection of the allegory is positive, symbolizing the entry of the gentry into the Founding Ancestor's interior space, and it is with them as his advisors—and not with someone like Liu Muzhi—that his dynasty will have a chance to bolt forward like a "young colt."

To what extent was the exteriorization of Liu Muzhi in this kind of anecdote decidedly a strategic facade? Not only did two of the elite gentrymen just named finally come to visit Liu Muzhi, the two who did not, Xie Hun and Chi Sengshi, were executed early in the Founding Ancestor's rise, during the prosecution of Liu Yi in 412. The Founding Ancestor and his prime client rhetorically demurred on their right to engage with the gentry elite, but they were unquestionably doing so in actuality. A passage included in Liu Muzhi's biography in the *History of the Southern Dynasties*—a seventh-century compilation based on the *Song shu* and other dynastic histories but marked by more rumor and less courtesy—but not in Shen Yue's *History* makes this point in periphrastic fashion:

> When the emperor [i.e., the Founding Ancestor] had assumed the Mandate, he was always found recollecting Liu Muzhi with a sigh. "Had Muzhi not died," he would say, "he would be helping me rule the realm. This is what is meant when it is said 'That man, he is lost, / The state shall collapse.'"

及帝受禪，每歎憶之，曰：「穆之不死，當助我理天下。可謂『人之云亡，邦國殄瘁。』」[32]

The couplet invoked by the Founding Ancestor comes from the *Classic of Poetry* (Mao 264), and when the same lines are used, twice, in the *Zuozhuan*

---

32. See *Nan shi* 15.427 for the passages discussed in this paragraph.

(Wen 6, Xiang 26), they are said "to mean that there are no good men to be had" 無善人之謂. That is the meaning intended here, with specific reference to one particular good man. The Founding Ancestor, *always* recalling his loyal advisor, has little faith in the bona fides of the elite who now surround him, trying to guide the change in dynasties in their own favor. To this sentiment, one of those honorable men, a high-ranking court elder, presents a rebuttal:

> To this, Fan Tai (355–428), the Grand Master for Splendid Happiness, replied: "With a sagely sovereign above us and a court below filled with outstanding talents, the success or failure of the dynasty would not necessarily depend on Muzhi, his well-acknowledged deeds in a time of trouble notwithstanding."[33]
>
> 光祿大夫范泰對曰：「聖主在上，英彥滿朝，穆之雖功著艱難，未容便關興毀。」

Fan Tai vouchsafes some (circumstantial) power to Liu Muzhi, but he reserves the real (defining) power of causing the dynasty to succeed, or fail, for the "sagely" Founding Ancestor and the wise advisors who serve him now—that is, Fan Tai and his peers. But the Founding Ancestor insists:

> The emperor just smiled: "Do you not know of the famous steed of antiquity, prized for its ability to run a thousand miles in a single day?"
>
> 帝笑曰：「卿不聞驥騄乎，貴日致千里耳。」

This is to restore Liu Muzhi—a full "steed," not a mere "colt" like Xie Fangming. However grand his current advisors may be, they could not or rather *would not* have brought the Founding Ancestor from anonymity to the throne in little over a decade, "a thousand miles in a single day." Only Liu Muzhi had the talent and the motivation to accomplish that. The historiography reinforces the point by tacking on a variant reply:

---

33. Elsewhere in the *History of the Southern Dynasties* we find Wang Hong himself dismissing Liu Muzhi's importance, speaking in very similar fashion; *Nan shi* 15.541–42.

Later, the emperor again said: "Since Muzhi died, people have not treated me with respect." That is how fondly Liu Muzhi was remembered by him.

帝後復曰：「穆之死，人輕易我。」其見思如此。

This remark affirms Liu Muzhi's interiority, as his patron's acknowledged confidante. But it also confirms the utility of his exteriorization, for the gentry could only be reassured by the emperor's acknowledgment that with Liu Muzhi's death he had lost some of his authority over them.

The strategic effect of historiography and history and patron and client working their rhetoric together comes across directly in the very first appearance of Liu Muzhi in the *History of the Liu-Song*, in scroll one, his patron's imperial annals. He is introduced with the absolute quality familiar to us from his biography:

> The Recorder Adjutant Liu Muzhi was a man of strategic acumen. His Excellency [the Founding Ancestor] took him as his primary advisor, certain to consult him on every single move.

錄事參軍劉穆之，有經略才具，公以為謀主，動止必諮焉。[34]

In the context of the annals of the Founding Ancestor, however, Liu Muzhi's absolute interiority ("certain . . . every move") does not stand on its own. It is put forth in order to be contradicted, serving as a prompt for his patron. The time is the sixth month of 409 and the Founding Ancestor is on campaign in the Shandong peninsula. An emissary of the Qin, a powerful state in the northwest, has come with a threat: Cease your attack on our ally, or we will send our armored cavalry to crush you. The Founding Ancestor sends this messenger off brusquely: Go tell your ruler that after I finish here, I will rest my troops for three years and then come to conquer him. If he wants to deliver himself into my hands now, all the better! But the story continues:

> Liu Muzhi rushed in when he heard that an emissary from the northwest had come, but His Excellency had already sent the man off. When the

---

34. For the quotations in this paragraph, see *Song shu* 1.16–17.

Founding Ancestor relayed the entire exchange, Muzhi castigated him: "You have always been certain to consult with me on everything, no matter how minor. This ought to have been discussed thoroughly—how could you have responded so carelessly? Far from being intimidating, your reply will only serve to anger them! If aid from the northwest should arrive suddenly, while the campaign here proves more difficult than expected, I don't know what we shall do."

穆之聞有羌使,馳入,而公發遣已去。以興所言并答,具語穆之。穆之尤公曰:「常日事無大小,必賜與謀之。此宜善詳之,云何卒爾便答。公所答興言,未能威敵,正足怒彼耳。若燕未可拔,羌救奄至,不審何以待之?」

The need for thorough discussion is a topos Liu Muzhi "will" deploy in the Pi Chen episode in his own biography, a year and a half prior to this event in historical time. There, need for discussion works as Muzhi intends it, prompting his patron's entry into the capital. Here it prompts his patron forward in a different way: allowing him to wave away his advisor's well-intentioned but excessive circumspection and supplant it with a display of battlefield acumen:

With a laugh, His Excellency replied: "This is the art of war. It is beyond your range of knowledge, and that is why I did not speak with you. You see, in war, speed is of the essence. Had they truly been able to rescue their allies, they would certainly have feared my knowing it—how could they have sent an emissary? Rather, they saw how I have come to put down the Yan and, fear already in their hearts, they tried to scare me off with big talk."

公笑曰:「此是兵機,非卿所解,故不語耳。夫兵貴神速,彼若審能遣救,必畏我知,寧容先遣信命。此是其見我伐燕,內已懷懼,自張之辭耳。」

The Founding Ancestor is able to read the minds of his enemies: he knows what they *anticipated*, what they *would have* done, what effect they *hoped to have* on him. And sure enough, he would be proved right: the Qin did not attack. Further, his boastful counter to the Qin would be fulfilled: he would indeed conquer the northwest (albeit briefly, and some seven years later, not three). His control of the historiographical process of dynastic foundation glistens—with the facilitation of his prime client, who again, but in an oblique way, has demonstrated his rhetorical artistry.

Written into History

The early medieval historical actor's life continued after his death, as he became part of a past that was at once retrospectively assessed and shaped according to the needs of the present. The earliest known posthumous historical representation of Liu Muzhi appears as the longest single section of his biography—the memorial the Founding Ancestor submitted to the Jin throne to request imperial honors for him after his death.[35] His portrait in this petition is of course very positive, but what is noteworthy is the artful articulation of the celebration of Liu Muzhi himself, on the one hand, and the Founding Ancestor's unique access to his talents on the other. Again, the historiographical Liu Muzhi is proving his rhetorical use in his patron's rise. The difference after death is only that the historical actor became more openly available as a rhetorical token.

The memorial's introductory section lays the groundwork with two enthymemes. The first is the idea that "the most urgent of the ancient sage kings' teachings is to esteem the worthy and recognize the good" 崇賢旌善，王教所先. This argument is noble, but unremarkable, and a second plank lends it the strength of specificity: "in granting its rewards, the most important principle is for the state to grant *posthumous* rewards" 念功簡勞，義深追遠. The idea is that posthumous rewards will encourage men to serve the state to the fullest of their abilities, up to and including death, but there is also a specifically historiographical dimension here. With its authority over retrospectively awarded honors, the state crafts history, stamping out the pluperfect historiographical patterns that prove the success, or failure, of historical actors within its compass.

The memorial's second section is a straightforward narrative of the deeds of this particular candidate for posthumous honor, but it features a clever turn on the topic of consequence. Liu Muzhi's merit is brought out in absolute terms: he worked in every capacity ("inside" and "outside") and tirelessly, "exhausting body and mind alike." The description culminates in Liu Muzhi's performance in charge of the capital, where he was "a ridgepole of the state," that is, the very one keeping the roof from blowing off the faltering Jin dynasty. Here the author of this eulogy—Fu Liang 傅亮

---

35. For the full text, see the appendix, section V-D.

(374–426), unnamed in the *History* but known to us through the attribution of this piece to him in the *Wen xuan*, the sixth-century literary anthology—lays down a neat rhetorical trick:

> He was promulgating the grand vision of the state, constructing a sage's reign. But just then, his aims and accomplishments not yet finished, [he died, and far] and near all were brought to sadness.
>
> 方宣讚盛猷，緝隆聖世，志績未究，遠邇悼心。(V-D)

In this telling, Liu Muzhi's path of "aims and accomplishments" has been broken off with his untimely death, right on the cusp (*fang*, "just then") of its fruition. The orator then purports to supply a conclusion to the consequential process:

> And in Your Majesty's generosity, you have granted him a favorable account, bestowing him a court position equivalent to the Three Dukes. With this, honor and mourning have both been fulfilled, his spirit shown great favor indeed.
>
> 皇恩褒述，班同三事，榮哀兼備，寵靈已厚。(V-D)

The court has done him his due—has it not? He has already, as recorded in the passage immediately preceding the memorial, been named "Regular Outrider Attendant and Defender General, given rights to establish a staff and ceremonies equivalent to those of the Three Dukes of the realm." In what way has he been left unfulfilled?

This false bottom is in fact the prompt for the essay's argument for further court honors for the Founding Ancestor's right-hand man. First, the speaker ratchets up the absolute quality of Liu Muzhi's deeds:

> And yet, in my humble reckoning: Since the hasty beginnings of the effort to establish this reign of Righteousness Resplendent (i.e., the restoration of the Jin after Huan Xuan's usurpation), difficulties have never ceased to arise. External threats have been severe, even as internal turmoil became more and more intense. The times are awry, our age full of troubles, nary a year of peace. And I, of such meager talents, have had to bear the weight of the empire. In this, I have truly relied on Muzhi's excellent assistance.

臣伏思尋，自義熙草創，艱患未弭，外虞既殷，內難彌結，時屯世故，靡歲暫寧。臣以寡乏，負荷國重，實賴穆之匡翼之益。(V-D)

The scene is reset in hyperbolic terms, Liu Muzhi given a defining role. The restoration, out of an age gone awry, was borne on the shoulders of one man, the Founding Ancestor, but that man could not have done it alone—Liu Muzhi's role was essential. "Were it not for the aid of this man," the Founding Ancestor's voice goes on to aver, "none of this could have been achieved."

What the Founding Ancestor, or his ghostwriter, is doing is shifting to a new, interior audience perspective. Where the opening enthymemes in this memorial to the throne were "focalized" in the court's own perspective—it was in the state's interest to recognize its subject's merits—here the source of recognition is no longer the failing house of Jin but the rising founder of a new dynasty:

And was it only his honest talk and fine plans that have spread to the ears of the masses? For he also offered sincere critique and candid counsel, sharing his hidden thoughts in the privacy of my tent. Speaking truthfully as his knees touched mine, then using crafty words in public—no one could plumb his depths! His deeds, far too numerable to name, were hidden from the view of the court, his achievements unknown to the world.

豈唯讜言嘉謀，溢於民聽；若乃忠規遠畫，潛慮密謀，造膝詭辭，莫見其際。功隱於視聽，事隔於皇朝，不可稱記。(V-D)

As the privileged audience for the *real* deeds, the true contributions of Liu Muzhi, the Founding Ancestor becomes the linchpin of this act of commemoration: only he can relay them fully to the court, so that it may fulfill its duty of recognizing its meritorious ministers.

The focalization of Liu Muzhi's life and its memorialization in the Founding Ancestor returns us to the interplay of interiority and exteriority. Liu Muzhi is granted an extreme degree of interiority here, as the key to his patron's restoration of the political order. The Jin imperial court, meanwhile, has been utterly exteriorized, being reduced to the function of performing enthymematic functions at the Founding Ancestor's behest. Yet having established interior positions for patron and client alike, the memorial ends with well-performed, not to say disingenuous, thresholding displays by both men. First, Liu Muzhi is seen deferring the honors that, in death, he can no longer defer:

> [Yet] he tread the path of humility and dwelled in moderation, becoming more and more steadfast in his resolve. Whenever it was proposed to grant him a fief and emolument, he was always adamantly deferential, to the most extreme degree. This is the reason why, though his merit towered over our age, he was never graced with a fief.
>
> 履謙居寡，守之彌固，每議及封賞，輒深自抑絕。所以勳高當年，而未沾茅社 ... (V-D)

This is strategic humility, preserving himself as the object of the second enthymeme voiced in this petition—the recipient of posthumous honor. But in the context of the memorial, his thresholding is not about his family's reward, about enabling the state to fulfill its enthymematic duty, or even about the illumination of the ascendance of the Founding Ancestor. It gives, at this rhetorical moment, the Founding Ancestor the chance to distinguish himself by enunciating a principle that straddles the boundary of public good and private value. "Thinking over this," the Founding Ancestor intones in the memorial's concluding passage, "I feel an eternal pain in my heart":

> I toiled together with him in good times and bad, observing with him the way things end and the way they begin. Our friendly bond, strong as precious metal and fragrant as the orchid, was deep in principle and full of intimate feeling. Thus have I submitted what is in my heart to the ears of Your Majesty's court. I hereby present this request to the throne, and ask that it be fully deliberated on in the Secretariat.[36]
>
> 臣契闊屯泰，旋觀終始，金蘭之分，義深情密。是以獻其乃懷，布之朝聽。所啟上，合請付外詳議。(V-D)

With his invocation of the "principle" (*yi*, or "honor" or "duty") of sincere friendship, alluded to in the phrase "the way things end and the way they

---

36. The bureaucratic instruction in the concluding sentence appears only in the *Wen xuan* text, but deliberation is a meaningful part of the public-private topos here, as discussed in chapter 5.

begin" (*zhongshi*), from the "Doctrine of the Mean," the speaker elevates his persuasion above the petition for mere material emolument.[37] Trifling reward has become the simple consequence—"thus have I . . ." (*shi yi*)—of the sincere bond of friendship that has such defining purchase over the Founding Ancestor's heart. With this profession of deep feeling, the patron's friendship with his client stands as a microcosm of the loyalty and sincerity the imperial throne needs from its subjects, and it consolidates the reorientation of perspective, symbolizing the Founding Ancestor's acquisition of Jin authority.

Through the remainder of his biographical afterlife, Liu Muzhi continues to play the prompt for the rise of the Founding Ancestor and the consolidation of the dynasty he would establish. When his patron takes the throne, in 420, Liu Muzhi is remembered again in the Founding Ancestor's voice, now directly in an imperial edict, and his family fief increased. This must be juxtaposed with the more likely apocryphal materials included in his *History of the Southern Dynasties* biography, cited above, where the Founding Ancestor resisted elite efforts to efface Liu Muzhi's memory. The edict of 420 pairs him with Wang Zhen'e, the military man who allegedly questioned Liu Muzhi's political capabilities, suggesting he would be unable to arrange the Nine Bestowals for his patron. Thus, with his edict, the Founding Ancestor was sending a message to the court elite: you may be powerful now, but this man—he on whom you have cast your scorn—*does* represent me, and that fact shall be acknowledged by you. A decade later, in 432, under Emperor Wen, Liu Muzhi was put in the imperial ancestral temple—together with Wang Hong. We may interpret this, in the year of Wang Hong's death, as a renewed admonition to the elite, reminding them that imperial sovereignty bound them together with less high-born subjects of the realm. In 448, the same emperor sent an offering to his grave, "to express Our eternal memory of him." This was perhaps to use the imperial memory of him to consolidate the emperor's authority over the court, at that time factionalized and on the cusp of a disastrous campaign against the mighty Northern Wei.

---

37. "Sincerity is the way things end and the way they begin. Without sincerity there is nothing" 誠者, 物之終始。不誠無物 (*Liji zhengyi* 53.405a). Here following the *Wen xuan* reading of the memorial.

It is this symbolic thread—deploying Liu Muzhi to point up the failings of the early fifth-century elite—that Shen Yue picks up in the argument of contrast he presents in the "historian's evaluation" appended to his *History*'s joint Liu Muzhi–Wang Hong biography. This line of argument is already hinted at in the historical materials, including the critical overtones that can be detected in Liu Muzhi's lack of concern for the actual talents of Xie Fangming, above, and less indirectly in the critique of the feckless Eastern Jin elite in the following anecdote:

> [Wang] Jingzhi was treated well (i.e., cultivated) by Liu Muzhi and he approached Muzhi with a request for the [highly honorable] post of Palace Attendant. After he had raised the matter several times, Muzhi responded: "If you hadn't asked, you would have gotten it long ago." And indeed, he never received the appointment.
>
> 靖之為劉穆之所厚，就穆之求侍中，如此非一。穆之曰：「卿若不求，久自得也。」遂不果。[38]

The depiction of Liu Muzhi's progeny, however negative it is, may also be read in part as a critique of their gentry antagonists. Liu Yuu, the grandson discussed at length above, exhibits a boorish character, but also a positive kind of resistance against the elites who sought to hold him back, as when he attacks Wang Sengda 王僧達 (423–58)—the youngest son of Wang Hong: "He relies on his elite pedigree, but his actual talent is unquestionably low grade" 膺籍高華，人品冗末.[39] Even Liu Yuu's posthumous name, Gang, actually has an ambiguous double valence: he is "Recalcitrant" (*gangbi* 剛愎), but in another historiographical sense "Resolute"

---

38. *Song shu* 92.2272. Wang Jingzhi was a grandson of the great Wang Xizhi.
39. *Song shu* 42.1309. Historiographically, this is an inversion of Liu Muzhi's bland endorsement of Xie Fangming's elite status. Another anecdote finds Liu Yuu livid when He Yan 何偃 (413–58, son of He Shangzhi 何尚之 [382–460], who is featured in the debate in chapter 4) claims his appointment to a prime prefecture "sullies the ranks of the esteemed elite" (*sanwu shiwang* 參伍時望). His indignation contrasts directly with the humility voiced by Liu Muzhi in section III-B of his biography, where he hopes his appointment does not cause him to surpass anyone more qualified.

(*gangzheng* 剛正), reflecting his and his kinsmen's position in the imperial house's battle against entrenched upper gentry interests.

Perhaps Shen Yue particularly selected and accentuated such materials when he made his "newly compiled" *History of the Liu-Song* in the 480s. He certainly underscores it in the biography's summary discussion (V-J), which falls into two sections: a lengthy recapitulation of the story of the fall of the Eastern Jin and a more concise tribute to Liu Muzhi's role in the restoration.

The main theme of Shen Yue's reprise of the fall of the Jin is the absolute quality of Jin decadence, and the consequent absolute necessity for a renewal. He bombards the reader with words associated with "order" and its desuetude. The "mainstay lines of Jin authority" (Jin *gang* 晉綱) fell slack. The "foundational laws" (*xianzhang* 憲章) of the Jin court came to be ignored. One minister led the dynasty into "disorder" (*luan* 亂), while another "laid waste to" (*nüe* 虐) the imperial dignity. The "inherited canons" (*yidian* 遺典) of Jin were "scattered like leaves" (*ye san* 葉散), as the "old laws" (*jiuzhang* 舊章) laid out by the dynasty's early meritorious ministers were "broken apart like floes of thawing ice" (*bing li* 冰離). All of value being "ground into the dirt" (*sao di* 掃地), every person in authority interpreted the "canons of state" (*guo dian* 國典) to his own liking, and each powerful family advocated its own variety of "mainstay lines for the court" (*chao gang* 朝綱). The ancient Way of the sage kings was "in danger of extinction, hanging by a thread" 不絕者若綖. Into this exigent breach steps the Founding Ancestor, "emending the disordered laws" (*gai luanzhang* 改亂章), and doing so with immediate efficacy: "No sooner were the authoritative commands of the Founding Ancestor issued, than those at court and abroad observed them" 威令一施，內外從禁.

Turning to Liu Muzhi, Shen Yue's pithy encapsulation of his contribution reads, in its entirety:

And this was—was it not?—all the doing of the All-Encompassing Promulgator Duke [Liu Muzhi]. Was it for nothing that he was recognized as the dynasty's ancestral minister, to be worshipped in the Pure Temple of the Founding Ancestor?

此蓋文宣公之為也。為一代宗臣，配饗清廟，豈徒然哉！(V-J)

The phrase "ancestral minister" echoes the historian Ban Gu's appraisal of Xiao He, the founding minister of the Han.[40] At the basic propositional level, Shen Yue is affirming the essential contribution of Liu Muzhi, that the restoration of "order" was "all his doing," and he is giving the historian's imprimatur to this man's worship in the imperial temple, and his placement at the forefront of the *History*'s biographies. At the same time, however, Shen Yue hedges these statements: "Was it not?" translates the particle *gai*, indicating an opinion of what is probable but not definite. That is, Liu Muzhi's accomplishment is admitted as a fact, but without the full, socially confirmed certainty of endoxa. When he wonders "was it for nothing" (*qi turan*), the reader can only wonder along whether or not it in fact *was* for nothing, either in the sense that Liu Muzhi's descendants could not enjoy his prestige, or because neither his achievements nor his memory could prevent the dynasty from falling victim to elite factionalism and imperial dysfunction.

What explains Shen Yue's reticence is that he is not really talking about Liu Muzhi at all, but using Liu Muzhi as a contrastive foil to talk about the ineptitude of the fifth-century elite. Completely and pointedly left unmentioned in his discussion is the other subject of scroll forty-two, Wang Hong.[41] Although it is true that the "historian's evaluation" sections of the dynastic histories were discretionary, with no expectation to cover all of a chapter's material, Shen Yue's omission of him here resonates with a viewpoint espoused more directly elsewhere in his *History*. In scroll ninety-four, writing on "imperial favorites" (*enxing* 恩倖), the court's employment of low-born men is ascribed to the decadence of the early medieval gentry.[42] In the chapter on recluses, he purposefully takes these high-minded gentlemen down a notch, insisting on "leaving an empty category for true worthy recluses" 虛置賢隱之位.[43] Perhaps most notably, the section of biographies of "filial and dutiful" (*xiao yi* 孝義) subjects is dedicated to what one modern scholar has termed "model commoners,"

---

40. *Han shu* 39.2022. As noted in chapter 1, the biography itself echoes a patron-client theme in Xiao He's "life."

41. As noted by the historical critic Wang Mingsheng (1722–98), *Shiqi shi shangque* 60.468.

42. *Song shu* 94.2301–2.

43. *Song shu* 93.2276.

men of humble birth whose conduct should put the *History*'s gentry readership to shame.[44] When Shen Yue says here that the great reformation brought on by the Founding Ancestor was *probably* due to Liu Muzhi, who *really is* in the imperial temple for good reason, the point he actually makes is: Look at how far the elite had fallen, such that it fell to *this* person to revive imperial state! No man of higher birth could do better? Small wonder the dynasty failed and was replaced by Our Qi (479–502)—and let us pray that we can rise to the task. Liu Muzhi is the prompt that points toward Wang Hong, an unvoiced symbol of elite failure.

⁂

Liu Muzhi was a biological person who lived and did what he did and eventually died. But he and other actors on the stage of early medieval history "lived" in another way as well—rhetorically potent historiographical lives, during their time on Earth and beyond it. Thus Liu Muzhi, the formidable interiority he gained for himself in the performance of his role notwithstanding, was deployed in life by his patron, at his death in an opposite fashion by his enemies, in the afterlife by the throne, and then by the historian on the level of historical interpretation. In all of these uses, Liu Muzhi the person is exteriorized, becoming a component, a "prompt," in the ploys and arguments of others. But in his exteriorization, in playing the fool in his patron's progress or the foil in the historian's judgments, he also attains a thresholded kind of interiority. In his place of prominence in the *History* of his patron's dynasty, Liu Muzhi became the proverbial tortoise enshrined high up in the ancestral hall: a shell, alienated from what he might have been while truly alive, but, fanciful Zhuangzian ideals aside, possessed of a sacred power, a glistening exteriority. Liu Muzhi might hardly have asked for more.

Meanwhile, with subjects like this, the historiography of interiors and exteriors sublates itself into a well-tempered whole of eulogy and irony. Only in a late and lesser sense is this an effect of the historian, apportioning "praise and blame" in order to uphold moral standards and expressing his judgments through purposeful emphases in his text. The historiographical vectors of praise and blame were part of the historical action itself.

44. *Song shu* 91.2241–59, and Keith Knapp, "Exemplary Everymen: Guo Shidao and Guo Yuanping as Confucian Commoners."

THREE

An Essay in Officialdom

> All events are stylized by aid of [a] conventional set of formulas. In order to arrive at the historical facts, one only has to eliminate these formulas.
> —Hans Bielenstein, "The Restoration the Han Dynasty: With Prolegomena on the Historiography of the *Hou Han Shu*"

Large tracts of the dynastic biography are the preserve of the plain record of the protagonist's career, indicating how he climbed up, down, and across the ladders of the state bureaucracy. If these career dossiers are not always completely accurate—when we have other sources at our disposal, such as epigraphy, we often find that they have been abridged, simplified, or corrupted—their apparent purpose is to convey historical fact, devoid of any style or rhetorical disposition. Modern biographers use these accounts to reconstruct individual careers, while broader inquiries mine them for material that shows how official positions functioned and evolved, and how those offices served to accommodate different socio-political groups into the state system.

But no text is devoid of style, and no style devoid of significance. When a modern historian describes officialdom as "a dense pattern of intersecting lines that would perplex even the most avant-garde of modernist painters," this is not only to say that the system was complex, but also that it was a distinctive aesthetic dimension of the early medieval world.[1] We should address officialdom as we might look at an abstract painting—taking its textual representation seriously *as* representation, identifying its parts and showing how they come to form a whole.

---

1. Yan Buke, *Pinwei yu zhiwei: Qin Han Wei Jin Nanbeichao guanjie zhidu yanjiu*, 353.

The Grammar of Officialdom

If the political system of early medieval China was a marriage of the imperial state and the gentry, officialdom was its altar. Official status was a means of ensuring gentry support for the ruling regime, because gentry identity was bound tightly to office-holding both materially, through the emolument of salary, and notionally. A gentryman was granted entry into the system at a level corresponding to the rank achieved by his father or grandfather, and it appears that, as a general rule, that point of entry set a rough limit on the highest rank he might attain. Thus, to the extent that he might enjoy his own status outside the system, a "private life" of retirement had to be pursued with politic caution, not just for his own interests but for the sake of his progeny.[2] At the same time, the work of governance—for no matter how bloated the system became, most offices retained actual responsibilities—was for the gentry a mode of social interaction, a very real aspect of their quotidian experience and the primary sense in which the gentry, notwithstanding all its activity outside officialdom, constituted a social class. If to the modern reader the narration of officialdom seems the most impenetrable element of early medieval dynastic historiography, in the early medieval period it must have offered an evocative sketch of the way members of the gentry made their existence in the world.

The narration of officialdom has a relatively subdued presence in the biography of Liu Muzhi, but some of its essential "grammar" is introduced there. We learn that an earlier patron "made him" (*yi wei* 以為) his chief of staff (II-A). Later, under the Founding Ancestor, he was "promoted" (*qian* 遷) to gentleman in an office in the Secretariat, but then "again" (*fu* 復) was put on his patron's staff, where he "carried" (*ling* 領) a prefectural appointment (III-C). Later, Liu Muzhi "rotated up" (*zhuan* 轉) with his patron, and as his patron established full dominance over the capital, he had the potent post of Prefect-Martial of Danyang "added" (*jia* 加) to his

---

2. For a general introduction to the official system in this period, see Lewis, *China between Empires*, 38–45. For an informative interpretation, see Dennis Grafflin, "Reinventing China: Pseudobureaucracy in the Early Southern Dynasties." On the correlations between family status and bureaucratic standing, see Kawai, *Nanchō kizokusei kenkyū*, chapter 8.

portfolio (III-L), and then a generalship "added" on top of that (III-M). His generalship was "advanced" (*jin* 進) to the top of the ranks (III-N) in 414, and in 415 he was "promoted" (*qian*) to Junior Chief of the Secretariat, with his existing titles confirmed "as before" (*rugu* 如故) (III-P), and then "rotated up" (*zhuan*) to the senior position in the following year (III-Q). Finally, a bevy of titles was "retrospectively awarded" (*zhuizeng* 追贈) to him (V-C, V-E) after his death.

More extensive and more typical representations of officialdom are found in the biographies of Liu Muzhi's higher-born contemporaries. The biography of Xu Xianzhi 徐羨之 (364–426), who would become one of the stewards of the court after the Founding Ancestor's death, provides a good example.[3] The biography opens in standard fashion, naming the protagonist and relaying the highest official positions attained by his grandfather and father. It then presents a compact account of Xu's early career path:

a) In his youth, Xu Xianzhi **was** chief of staff for Wang Ya (334–400) when Wang was Tutor to the Crown Prince, [**and then**] head of the personnel section on the staff of General of Settling the North, Liu Laozhi. [He then was appointed] Gentlemen on the Board of Rites of the Imperial Secretariat, but he **did not bow** [**to take office**]. [Later] he was Adjutant of the Middle Troop section on the staff of General of Soothing Armies, Huan Xiu (d. 404). There, he was on staff together with the Founding Ancestor, and they developed a close bond.

羨之少為王雅太子少傅主簿，劉牢之鎮北功曹，尚書祠部郎，不拜，桓脩撫軍中兵曹參軍。與高祖同府，深相親結。

When the loyalist armies rose [against Huan Xuan, in 404], the Founding Ancestor **appointed him by wood placard** to be Adjutant on his General of Settling Armies staff, and [he was later made] Gentleman on the Supplies Board of the Secretariat, and [later] Senior Officer on [Xie Hun's] General of the Palace Guard staff. Working together with (i.e., under) Xie Hun, Xie came to appreciate him deeply.

義旗建，高祖版為鎮軍參軍，尚書庫部郎，領軍司馬。與謝混共事，混甚知之。

---

3. *Song shu* 43.1329–34.

He was "**patched**" as Adjutant on the Commander-in-Chief staff of the Prince of Langya (Sima Dewen, the future Emperor Gong, 386–421, r. 419–20), and [then was made Sima Dewen's] Senior Western Aide of the Grand Minister of the Masses, and [then] Senior Outrider Aide of the governor of Xuzhou [the Founding Ancestor], and [then] Senior Consulting Adjutant on the [Founding Ancestor's] Grand Commandant staff.

補琅邪王大司馬參軍，司徒左西屬，徐州別駕從事史，太尉諮議參軍。

In the eleventh year of Righteousness Resplendent (415), he was **formally appointed** Hawk Flying General, Prefect of Langya, and **then, without break**, to serve as Senior Outrider Aide of the Commander-in-Chief, with his generalship **as before**. When the Founding Ancestor set out on his northern expedition (416), he **rotated up** to Senior Commanding Officer on the Grand Commandant staff, where he **held charge of** matters in the capital, acting as a second to Liu Muzhi.

義熙十一年，除鷹揚將軍、琅邪內史，仍為大司馬從事中郎，將軍如故。高祖北伐，轉太尉左司馬，掌留任，以副貳劉穆之。

Further narrations of officialdom are interspersed through the later sections of Xu's biography.

b) When the Founding Ancestor took the throne (in 420), he **advanced [Xu's] title** to General of Settling Armies, and **added** [the title of] Ever-Accompanying Imperial Outrider.

高祖踐阼，進號鎮軍將軍，加散騎常侍。(1330)

c) Xianzhi was **promoted** to Director of the Secretariat and Governor of Yangzhou, with Ever-Accompanying Imperial Outrider **added**. His **position was advanced** to Grand Minister of Works, and **Overseer of** Secretariat Affairs, with his titles of Ever-Accompanying [Imperial Outrider] and Governor [of Yangzhou] **as before**.

羨之遷尚書令、揚州刺史，加散騎常侍。進位司空、錄尚書事，常侍、刺史如故。(1331)

d) Xianzhi **had been lifted up / had risen up from** commoner clothing (i.e., the middle gentry), and was furthermore not a man of any particular learning, but, relying solely on the power of his ambitions and his well-tempered character, he found himself suddenly residing in the halls of the palace. Those at court and beyond esteemed him and submitted to his judgment, deeming him worthy of a Prime Minister's regard.

羨之起自布衣，又無術學，直以志力局度，一旦居廊廟，朝野推服，咸謂有宰臣之望。(1331)

e) When the Grand Ancestral Emperor (Wendi, r. 424–53) took the throne, he **advanced** Xianzhi to Grand Minister of the Masses, with all his standing titles **as before**, and **changed** his fief to Duke of Nanping, with the emolument of 4,000 households. Xu **insistently declined** the **addition** to his fief.

太祖即阼，進羨之司徒，餘如故，改封南平郡公，食邑四千戶，固讓加封。(1332)

f) In 425, Xianzhi and Senior Auspicious Grandee Fu Liang together submitted a memorial **returning the powers of governance**, saying: ...

元嘉二年，羨之與左光祿大夫傅亮上表歸政，曰...(1332)

g) Thereupon Xianzhi **retreated from his position**, returning to private quarters. When his nephew Peizhi (d. 426), along with Attendant Cheng Daohui (361–429), Prefect of Wuxing Wang Shaozhi (380–435), and others, said this was not appropriate, and their sincere admonitions were effected with extreme ardor, Xu **again beheld** the imperial edict and **engaged** in his official duties.

羨之仍遜位退還私第，兄子佩之及侍中程道惠、吳興太守王韶之等並謂非宜，敦勸甚苦，復奉詔攝任。(1333)

Historians will naturally add the flesh of a narrative of rise and fall to the bare bones of accounts like this. Xu Xianzhi resisted service in the imperial government when it fell into the hands of Huan Xuan, and although he served Huan Xiu, he did so with the Founding Ancestor, whose cause he joined right from the beginning. Establishing himself as a good and able administrator, he continued in staff positions with the Founding Ancestor, and then as his representative on the staffs of the most prominent member of the court elite, Xie Hun, and the most prominent member of the imperial clan, Sima Dewen. As the biography tells it, Xie, the convener of high court culture in this decade, granted Xu social imprimatur by recognizing his talent. He continued to be a prized aide up to the accession of the Founding Ancestor, when he was given a top generalship and honorary title and then elevated to the top of the imperial bureaucracy, first as head of the Secretariat and governor of the lower Yangtze region, and then in appointments filling two of the hoary "Three Dukes" titles. On the accession of the Grand Ancestor as emperor, which he played a key role in engineering, Xu attempted to retreat to the exterior side of the threshold of power, but his associates pushed him back into interior positions—with assistance from his political enemies, and the emperor himself, who knew that continued interiority would ensure his downfall. He would be expelled and executed a year later.

Yet whatever real socio-political life this kind of account relays, as a historiographical artifact it also has an effect at its level of representation. Let us look not at the kind of career Xu Xianzhi had, nor at how his rise sheds light on the operation of the state in a period of dynastic transition, but rather at the words that were used to stitch together portraits like this one, to predicate offices and titles of historical actors, constituting officialdom in language. These words have qualities, and together they form a semiotic system, the interpretation of which can produce a portrait of officialdom itself.

In the accompanying box is a categorized list of officialdom's key terms of narration, many of which appear in the narrative of Xu Xianzhi's career. The starting point is a non-term: ellipsis. Ellipsis is routine in the capsule biographies of minor personages and relatives of those given a full biography, of which the note on Xu Xianzhi's father is a typical example: "His father, Zuozhi, [was, or rose to] Magistrate of Shangyu" 父祚之,上虞令. But it is also strewn throughout the longer narratives. In the opening passage of the Xu Xianzhi materials given above, for instance, four offices are specified, but any indication of when he held these positions, or how long he spent in each one, is elided. He is "appointed by wood placard" (*ban*, on which see below) to a staff position under the Founding Ancestor, and then a post as a "gentleman" (*lang*) in the Secretariat follows, with no syntactic break. Was this concurrent with the staff position? Probably not: the simple verb *wei* ("[and] was") is implied. The use of ellipsis extends to a general reluctance to elaborate on historical detail. The passage goes on to place Xu as the senior officer under the court's most powerful generalship, the

Officialdom's Terms of Narration

Degree zero terms
  [null] (ellipsis)
  yi wei 以為 (to make someone an official: state-focalized)
  wei 為 (to be: actor-focalized)

Terms of appointment: state-focalized
  bi 辟 (to "open up" an actor's career by appointing him to a staff position)
  chu 出 (to "send out" from the capital for provincial service; to be sent out)
  chu 除 (literally, to bring up the stairs; that is, to promote to a particular office)
  ju 舉 (to "raise up," identifying as a candidate for official service)
  ming 命 (to "command" to take a certain office)
  qing 請 (a patron's "request" for an actor to join his staff)
  shu 署 (to assign to a certain "bureau")
  xuan 選 (to select)
  zhao 召 (to summon to office)
  zheng 徵 (to summon to the capital for official service)

Terms of appointment: actor-focalized
  bai 拜 (to bow to accept an office)
  bubai 不拜 (to refuse to bow)
  bujiu 不就 (to refuse to "proceed to" take up an appointment)
  buqi 不起 (to refuse to be "raised up")
  feng 奉 (to uphold; *fengzhao* 奉詔, to uphold an edict)
  gui 歸 (to return; *guizheng* 歸政, to return power)
  qi 起 (to be "raised up" out of private life and into officialdom)
  qiu 求 (to request an office)
  rang 讓 (to defer, often "insistently" [*gu* 故])
  xun 遜 (to retreat; *xunwei* 遜位, to retreat to a lower position)

Absolute interiority / exteriority
  she 攝 (to uphold; *sheren* 攝任)
  shi 事 (to serve)

weiren 委任 (to entrust completely)
zhang 掌 (to hold charge of)

Terms that maintain space in the system

ban 版 (to appoint directly to a staff position, "by wood placard")
bu 補 (to "patch" into an open position, by order of the imperial personnel authority)
jian 兼 (to hold at the same time)
ling 領 ("to carry" an office in addition to a regular appointment; also dai 帶)
xing 行 (in a provisional capacity; "acting")
yuanwai 員外 (supernumerary position)

Agglutination: continuing previous status and adding to current status

gaifeng 改封 ("to replace an old fief with a new one")
jia 加 ("adding")
jinhao 進號 ("to advance one's title," usually a generalship)
jinwei 進位 ("to advance one's position in the court ranks")
qian 遷 (to raise to a different class of ranks)
rugu 如故 (keeping other titles "as before")
xi 徙 (to transfer [often upward])
zhuan 轉 (to rotate through a given rank, generally in an upward fashion, or laterally along with a patron)

Agglutination: temporal verbs and adverbs

chu 初 (in the beginning)
e 俄 (after a certain time)
fu 復 (to "again" hold an office, at a later date)
ji 及 (when it came to the time when)
lei 累 (to serve in a series of offices "cumulatively")
li 歷 (to pass through a series of offices on the way to a higher one)
reng 仍 (then, in consequence, without a gap)
shi 時 (at the time)
wei 未 (not yet; "before he had")
xun 尋 (after a short time)
zhui zeng 追贈 (to bestow a title in retrospect, i.e., posthumously)

General in Charge of the Armies (*lingjun jiangjun*), and it then describes him "working together with Xie Hun" (*yu* Xie Hun *gong shi*)—when in fact Xie Hun was the very general under whom he was serving, on the arrangement of the Founding Ancestor. Ellipsis may be the most prominent stylistic feature of historiography's narration of officialdom, the light touch necessary to a historiography that must deal courteously, and with a "focalization" in the imperial court, with the politics of power and patronage. Rarely catching itself on the thorns of historical explication, ellipsis facilitates the accumulation, or "agglutination," of a densely knitted but smooth and glossy surface.

One step out from ellipsis we find a representation of the basic polarity that runs through the official system, actually and narratively. *Wei* 為, "to be" or "to become," and *yi wei* 以為, "to make," are "degree zero" types of predication, the former focalized in the actor, the latter in the state. In the very first line of the first Xu Xianzhi passage, he simply "was" or "became" a chief of staff. That a patron appointed him is understood but not part of the narration. *Yi wei* is the complementary expression of this: a patron or some state-empowered agent "taking" (*yi*) the historical actor and predicating him with some official position. That is how Liu Muzhi's initial appointment, by Jiang Ai 江敳 (fl. mid-fourth century?), was narrated in section II-A of Liu's biography. As poles in a system, the state and the individual are mutually constitutive, the state (with its delegated patrons) deriving its interiority from power over its participants, the participants bolstering their power from their status as state-sanctioned actors.

Verbs beyond the zero degree grant further agency to the state and actor poles. One important and frequently occurring pair consists of two metonymic expressions for appointment to office, *chu* 除 and *bai* 拜. In terms of actual usage, it is difficult to discern much distinction between the two. For example, it may be said that an actor was *chu*-ed as a "gentleman," or that he *bai*-ed to that position. Beneath their apparent functional equivalence, however, lies a salient semantic contrast. The basic meaning of *chu* is "palace stairway," so to *chu* someone to a position means to "promote them," as if bringing them up the palace stairs.[4] The focalization and

---

4. "Palace stairway" is the gloss for *chu* in the Eastern Han dictionary *Shuowen*; see *Shuowen jiezi zhu* 14B.736. Ru Shun's gloss of *chu* in his *Han shu* commentary (*Han shu* 5.145) connects usage in the bureaucratic context to another meaning of the word, "to

agency of *chu* lie fully with the state. *Bai* means "to bow." This word applies literally in the context of officialdom, for bowing is what an actor did to receive the seal and ribbon that formally conferred an office upon him.[5] Thus, the agency of *bai* is accorded to the historical actor, the one who does the bowing, whereas the subject of *chu* is always the state or its delegate. This balance, however, is weighted in the direction of the state, because he who bows, bows *to someone*. In fact, *bai* can be used causatively, with the state agent as a subject, causing the historical actor to bow. And if we return to our actor-focalized degree zero verb, *wei*, we see the same hidden weight: the historical actor "is" an official, but the appointment and duties are centered in the state.

A second pair of appointment words, *bi* 辟 and *qi* 起, evinces the same weighted balance of state and actor focalization. These terms are used to refer to an actor's entry (or re-entry, for example after a period of mourning) from private life into official service. This use of *bi* would seem to relate to its basic lexical field, of "opening up," as in the cognate characters *pi* 闢 and *pi* 劈.[6] The state, or the patron vested with the state's authority, "splits open" the actor's private world, bringing him up into the realm of officialdom. *Qi*, which means "to rise up," is its actor-agency counterpart, the actor "rising up" out of his private life. Here we again encounter the ambiguity of actor focalization. Both in principle and in terms of actual usage, the actor is frequently the subject of *qi*. A common instance is the expression *qijia* 起家 (or *qijia wei* 為, or *qi wei*), "he rose up out of family life to hold X post." Such expressions, however, always imply a different subject, some authority doing the "raising," and not infrequently the state-subject is stated outright, as it was for one of Xu Xianzhi's contemporaries: "After some time, the Founding Ancestor, about to campaign against Sima

---

remove": one is removed from an old office and placed in a new one. The implications for agency, however, are the same, and Duan Yucai's note on the *Shuowen* entry explains "remove" as an extension of the basic meaning.

5. For evidence by an interesting counterexample, see the biography of Yin Jingren 殷景仁 (390–440; *Song shu* 63.1682), where twice he accepts positions by having a subordinate bow in his stead, and to a palace emissary sent to him at that.

6. If there is an early gloss adequately explaining the use of *bi* in the context of official appointment, I have overlooked it. The word is used only once in this sense in the *Han shu* (81.3332, biography of Kuang Heng 匡衡), but by the Eastern Han it had become a regular term of officialdom, to judge from its repeated use in the *Hou Han shu*.

Xiuzhi (d. 417), raised (*qi*) Liu Cui [who had been mourning for his mother] up as (*wei*) General Pacifying the North and Prefect of Jingling" 俄而高祖討司馬休之，起[劉]粹為寧朔將軍、竟陵太守.[7] Thus, we again find the actor-agency verb in a liminal "middle voice," residing in the actor as an act (rising up), but frequently in contexts where it is made clear that he rises up passively, held in the orbit of the state.[8] Put in the terms of our rhetorical topics, gentry self-definition is undermined, becoming the consequential effect of another defining power.

The three-word set that places *zheng* 徵, "to summon," up against *ru* 入, "to enter," and *chu* 出, "to leave," again demonstrates this balance. "To summon" is to call a member of the gentry to the capital or into the palace for appointment. Agency resides fully with the imperial court. "To enter" is the actor-focalized counterpart of this, with "to leave" as its corresponding antonym. With "enter" and "leave," agency resides in the actor—on the surface. Thus Wang Hong, for instance, "entered [the palace] to become Prime Minister" 入為相, but the servant of the state does not "enter" the capital region, much less the palace—he is allowed, or commanded, to do so.[9] As with the preceding pairs, the balance is weighted toward the state, *ru* actually meaning "[The throne allowed or commanded] A to enter the capital." The same applies to "to leave": though sometimes officials requested exterior postings—they might "beg" (*qiu* 求) for a magistracy or prefectureship, where they could earn a better salary and engage in small capital enterprises—they were "sent out," often into a kind of "exile," by the state.

That the balance tilts toward the state is not surprising, for officialdom is, after all, the state's system. What is important is that the balance persists, because the pole of the private individual is able to, indeed must, retain some interiority—or rather, to utilize the potency of semiotic surfaces. This counterweight is evident in the prominence of the negated forms of the actor-centered terms in the *chu / bai* and *bi / qi* pairs: *bubai* 不拜, "he did *not* bow to take office," and *buqi* 不起, "he did *not* rise up to take office." It may even be justified to translate the simple negative into something stronger: a refusal. Refusing to bow appears in the first

---

7. *Song shu* 45.1379. For one implicit example, see *Song shu* 42.1310.
8. This concept is formulated in Émile Benveniste, "Active and Middle Voice in the Verb."
9. *Song shu* 60.1626.

paragraph of the Xu Xianzhi materials, when he did *not* take office in the court then under Huan Xuan's sway. "Did not bow" appears in this sense more than fifty times in the biographies of the *History of the Liu-Song*, a verbal emblem of the individual actor's resilience in the system. Even more common, appearing more than seventy times in the biographies, is the related phrase *bujiu* 不就, "did not proceed [to take the office to which he had been appointed]." This term is generally associated with the individual's refusal to have his private life "split open"—over a third of the usages of *bujiu* are collocated with *bi*, the state- or state-agent-centered verb of appointment discussed above. In these negative forms, the historical actor reclaims the middle ground of his verbs. Still in the orbit of the state, he establishes a "gravity" of his own, staking out his integrity—or advancing his public career in a more politically astute fashion. Thus, in Xu Xianzhi's case, which is typical, not bowing to take office is not a refusal but a deferral, and he returns to this move later in his career, "deferring" (*rang* 讓), "returning" (*gui* 歸), and "retreating from" (*xun* 遜) the interior powers that have been (perilously) granted him. Early medieval emperors themselves regularly practiced the same footwork, in their edicts and, most notably, when on the cusp of the establishment of a new dynasty the incoming emperor would make a point of deferring three times before taking the throne. From "did not bow" on out, these are all "thresholding" moves.

The third negative form in this series, *buqi* 不起, "did not rise up," appears but eleven times in our *History*, a relative scarcity that is an indication of its importance: it is a "marked" term, denoting not just an act but the defining essence from which that act could spring, a purposeful refusal to allow the state (or the patron) to intervene in the life of the individual. It is especially significant that seven of the eleven appearances are in the biographies of the "recluses," the ultimate polarity of the gentry side of officialdom and, as the apotheosis of thresholding deference, an essential element of early medieval political culture.[10] One recent study has termed this "the necessity of recluses in a dynasty" in this period, pointing

---

10. The other uses of *bu qi* are in otherwise significant locations: the biographies of the unbridled poet Xie Lingyun (385–433; see *Song shu* 67.1772) and of Shen Yue's grandfather, Shen Linzi (377–422; *Song shu* 100.2452), and (twice) in the story of Wei Xuan quoted below.

especially to Huan Xuan's attempt, as satirized in the historiography, to bolster his legitimacy through the recognition of "stand-in recluses" (*chong yinshi* 充隱士)—men who were instructed to "defer" (*rang*) to his appointments.[11] Another humorous (to us) illustration of the recluse's political significance is the story of an esteemed man named Wei Xuan 韋玄, from the Chang'an region. He determinedly "refused to rise" (*buqi*) for court appointments first under the northern Later Qin dynasty and then from the Founding Ancestor, who conquered the Later Qin in 417. The Founding Ancestor's forces were promptly ejected from Chang'an by Helian Bobo 赫連勃勃 (381–425), who declared himself emperor of a Xia dynasty and once again sought to appoint this Wei Xuan. This time, Wei accepted the offer. Incensed, Helian Bobo had him put to death.[12]

Gentry and imperial acts of deference exercise the thresholding power of self-exteriorization, setting a due distance between oneself and political interiority, and imperial recognition of the recluse—repeatedly honoring him with offers of appointment, awarding him honors in absentia, and, not least of all, enshrining him in the dynastic historiography—is an affirmation of thresholding as the prime rhetorical move of early medieval political culture. Lesser forms of deference in the discourse of officialdom, like refusing to bow, are points on this continuum, and are likewise not perceived as resistance but as regular and necessary kinds of political engagement. It is in this spirit that the *History of the Liu-Song* declares that, over the whole sixty years of the dynasty, there were only two men who "did not contrive to defer [each time they were offered office], but instead bowed to accept as soon as they received an appointment" 宋世惟華與南陽劉湛不為飾讓，得官即拜，以此為常。[13] The two men were Wang Hua 王華 (385–427), cousin of Wang Hong and power behind the throne in Emperor

---

11. See Xiaofei Tian, "Representing Kingship and Imagining Empire in Southern Dynasties Court Poetry," 51n83, and *Jin shu* 99.2593–94.

12. Helian Bobo, a Xiongnu, explains his action as follows: "When Yao Xing and Sir Liu summoned him, he refused to rise (*buqi*) for them both, but when I do, he arrives immediately? Does he think that as a non-Chinese I am incapable of comprehending what it means to be a recluse?" 姚興及劉公相徵召，並不起，我有命即至，當以我殊類，不可理其故耶。See *Song shu* 95.2331; also 92.2277 and, indicating that Wei Xuan's family was a local power, 65.1721.

13. *Song shu* 63.1677. The characterization is only superficially positive.

Wen's rise, and Liu Zhan 劉湛 (392–440), the power behind the wayward prince Liu Yikang 劉義康 (409–51)—that is, men who, in the eyes of history, might rather have shown a little bit of deference.

The prized but volatile bureaucratic obverse of reclusion was the absolute devolution of power from the state or its agent to an individual actor. In the Xu Xianzhi materials, we see this when he is put "in charge of" (*zhang* 掌, "held in his palm") affairs in the capital—an intimation of the concentration of power that would lead to, or be said to lead to, his downfall. Another common term is *weiren* 委任, "to entrust responsibility completely," which appeared in expanded form at the beginning of the career narrative in Liu Muzhi's biography, where the Founding Ancestor "entrusted to him total responsibility for the tasks closest to his heart" 委以腹心之任 (III-A). This is the state or the patron completely emptying itself or himself of interiority, "casting down" (*wei*) all of its own agency into the hands of a lower party. There is danger in accruing such power, but when the good actor takes up such a charge, he responds by emptying himself of all interiority in requital: "And Liu Muzhi, for his part, also exhausted himself in his sincere dedication to his patron, leaving absolutely nothing unattended or concealed" 穆之亦竭節盡誠，無所遺隱. In their fullest degree of political engagement, both parties threshold, absolute trust and absolute loyalty in the patron-client relationship a match for the emperor's honoring the integrity of the recluse who refuses to serve him.

Another bureaucratic commonplace that enabled this kind of thresholding was the "acting" (*xing* 行) official, setting a certain distance between the actor and the office with which he is to be identified. Ranked lower than the generally unmarked regular positions, "acting" introduced space into the system by expanding the number of bureaucratic slots open to gentry service, while its lower bar for appointment and acceptance facilitated the use of offices as currency in the consolidation of patron-client relationships.[14] The conclusion of one modern study, finding a number of examples of individuals moving down to lower, "acting" offices before

---

14. The *History of the Liu-Song* treatise on officialdom (*Song shu* 39.1224) specifies that "adjutants" (*canjun*) were regular when formally appointed by the throne (*chu bai* 除拜) and "acting" (*xing*) when the appointment was made by placard through the patron's office (*fu ban* 府板), but goes on to note that by the Jin this distinction had become muddied, with *chu* and *ban* appointments for both types.

moving back up again, is that the initial higher offices had become starting positions ("rising-out-of-private-life posts" *qijia guan* 起家官), but this practice may be better regarded as a way of moving into positions directly under individual patrons, the precarious nature of patronage, and the pride of high-born gentry, making "acting" positions an enticing way of accomplishing this.[15] For men of lower social status, imperial appointments in "supernumerary" (*yuanwai* 員外) capacity performed a similar function, spreading the real and symbolic funds of officialdom with positions sequestered from the formal system.

Two more words in the appointment lexicon also served to inflate the sphere of officialdom. *Ban* 版 (or 板) refers to the patron's direct appointment of an actor to his staff—the *ban* in question should be the "wood placard" on which the appointment was presented.[16] Though a regularized part of the system in the early medieval period, giving patrons more power of direct appointment, conceptually speaking "appointment by placard" also represented a gap in the association of actor with office. Appointed this way to the Founding Ancestor's staff, Xu Xianzhi was something other than just the Founding Ancestor's subordinate. We also see Xu Xianzhi "patched" (*bu* 補) onto the staff of a Jin prince; Wang Hong, the cream of the elite, first joined the Founding Ancestor in this fashion as well.[17] This is dead metaphor—"patching" was the technical term in the Han appointment process for the probationary appointment to a substantive post of an actor newly introduced to the system. But in the context of the pervasive spacing at work in the medieval system, the roots of the metaphor had been planted in new ground. Practically, the function of "patching" was to allow more gentry to cycle through the available bureaucratic positions, from which they tended to resign rapidly, always eager to keep their distance

---

15. See Wang Zhenglu, *Wei Jin Nanbeichao xuanguan tizhi yanjiu*, 243–50, where at least half of the Southern Dynasties examples involve motion into *xing*-acting offices. See also the discussion in Chao Li-Hsin, "Nanchao zongshi zhengzhi yu shihuan jiegou: yi huangdi huangzi fu canjun wei zhongxin," 78–79, which links these positions to the status of the patrons.

16. The definition of appointment "by courtesy" in Charles O. Hucker, *A Dictionary of Official Titles in Imperial China*, entry 4399, is not accurate with respect to the early medieval period.

17. *Song shu* 42.1312.

while taking up new opportunities. Ideally, "patching" attended both to the dignity of the system—in principle complete, it needed only temporary "patches" from human actors—and that of the actors—the positions were provisional stations on the path to a whole career. Again an ironic application illustrates the connotations of the word: rebelling against Emperor Xiaowu and harboring imperial ambitions of his own, the general Lu Shuang 魯爽 (d. 454) sent out a placard that purported to "patch" the prince Liu Yixuan 劉義宣 (415–54) *onto the imperial throne*.[18] Patching was meant to open space downstream in the system, not up.

The technical term *qing* 請, "to request politely," likewise helped sustain the conceptual space of officialdom. It is often made evident that such requests were actually made to the throne (or the Secretariat) by a senior official (i.e., a patron), petitioning for a certain individual to be placed on his staff. For instance, the future Emperor Xiaowu, while stationed in Xunyang, "wrote a missive to the Grand Ancestor (Emperor Wen) to request [the appointment of Yan Shibo] as Chief of Staff on his Southern Commandant staff, but the Grand Ancestor refused him" 啟太祖請為南中郎府主簿。太祖不許.[19] In its regular use, however, the sense conveyed by *qing* is of a polite request from the patron, on behalf of the state, to the individual who will suffer the burden of the office. This is the sense of the common collocation *qing wei* 請為, "to request [the appointment of someone] as," occurring more than twenty times in the biographies, and it is the sense conveyed in Shen Yue's account of an ancestor who was "requested with full ritual politeness (*li qing*) by governors and prefects" 州郡禮請.[20] The contrastive counterparts to *qing* are the directly state- or patron-focalized terms *yin* 引, "to summon," and, especially, *ming* 命, "to command," the latter utilized in full state-focalization in the biography of Wang Hong, when the Founding Ancestor "commands" him to a staff position—after Wang Hong has fled his prefecture rather than battle attacking rebel forces.[21]

The production of symbolic space in the system occurred in concert with the real historical circumstances of the age. The gentry were able to

18. *Song shu* 74.1926.
19. *Song shu* 77.1992. For another example, 54.1538.
20. *Song shu* 100.2444. Also, *Jin shu* 82.2151.
21. *Song shu* 42.1312. For a good example of *yin*, see *Jin shu* 89.2322, where the historiography lumps it together with *qing*.

expend such effort thresholding, distancing themselves in ways greater and lesser from official position, because they were flooded with opportunities to serve. The numbers are startling. At its height, the Western Jin had had some 173 prefectures, in a full domain comprising north and south. The Eastern Jin was much smaller by geographic size and population, but by the late fourth century it had still established 124 actual and "lodged" (*qiao*) prefectures along the Yangtze. Just half a century later, by the middle of the Liu-Song, this number had increased to 238, and at the end of the fifth century, under the Southern Qi, these lower-Yangtze "empires" would have 395 prefectures—double the Western Jin total.[22] To this quantity add the velocity with which the gentry tended to run through the positions, resigning from this to position themselves for that, accruing honor for themselves and opening up spaces for new appointees, as well as the fact that the increase in prefectures was multiplied by a parallel increase in patronage-ready staff positions under princes, regional governors (*cishi*), and generals. Officialdom was an ever-broadening canvas, upon which the gentryman was encouraged to apply his brush liberally. The representational effect of this loose-money political economy was the phenomenon of "agglutination," through which officialdom became a veneer, a historiographical cloak that covered the historical actor as he ran up, down, and across the "steps" (*jie* 階, another technical word) of the system, his profile flattened under a profusion of offices and terms of appointment.

Returning to officialdom's vectors of semantic interplay, *qian* 遷, "to rise up," or rather, "to be caused to rise up" or simply "promoted," would seem to be the most basic verb of official progress, because in theory this is what one would seek to do in one's career. A better description of the typically brachiated "career" through officialdom, however, is offered by *qian*'s counterpart, *zhuan* 轉, which means "to revolve." *Zhuan* retains associations of promotion, but in smaller degrees, within the same rank class or by "rotating" across offices along with one's rising patron. Where the vertically inclined *qian* definitively entails a change of status, *zhuan*

---

22. See Yen Keng-wang, *Zhongguo difang xingzheng zhidu shi*, II:5, 12–16, and, on the brevity of tenure in office in contrast to regular and "lesser" terms of six and three years, 380.

describes lateral motion over a gentler slope, creating not rupture but a rolling, contiguous surface.

The tendency to accumulate official posts synchronically made a corresponding contribution to the effect of agglutination, thickening the surface of the veneer. The "acting positions" discussed above were actual named positions, but one could also "act" in offices provisionally, holding offices "concurrently" (*jian* 兼), or "carrying" (*ling* 領, or *dai* 帶) an office while holding another (higher or lower, respectively) position.[23] Honorary titles—which came with material rewards—were "added" (*jia* 加), as were substantively powerful generalships. New honorary titles were often referred to as "being advanced [through] the titles" (*jin hao* 進號) or "advanced up through the court ranks" (*jin wei* 進位), phrases that accentuate a step-by-step motion. But perhaps the most emblematic marker of contiguity was the award of a new post with the specification that other postings were to remain "as before" (*rugu* 如故), as in passages (c) and (e) of the Xu Xianzhi materials, and section III-P of the Liu Muzhi biography. This is truly contiguous because it has the actor traveling to a new present with his past securely in tow, and in ideal terms this was exactly what happened: even fully relinquished offices accumulated as a long list on the actor's official dossier, whence, posthumously, they became part of his biography. This temporal contiguity carried on into the afterlife with the regular use of honors "retrospectively presented" (*zhuizeng* 追贈). These posthumous honors were of material benefit to the actor's sons and grandsons, who would be eligible for higher entry-level positions, or might inherit a fief, but their symbolic value was also significant. They furthered the agglutination of the representational surface, the glossy exterior that the actor would live on with in eulogy and historiography.

Words that belong more expressly to the level of historical diegesis add gloss to these surfaces. *Reng* 仍, translated in the Xu Xianzhi passages ([a], last paragraph) as "then, without break," is deployed nearly ninety times in this specific, technical usage in the *History of the Liu-Song* biographies. Perhaps best conceived as a diminished form of *nai* 乃, *reng*

---

23. On *xing*, *ling*, and *dai*, see Yen Keng-wang, *Zhongguo difang xingzheng zhidu shi*, II:375–79. A memorial submitted by a young prince in the early 450s suggests that *dai*-carrying and *jia*-adding were, respectively or perhaps collectively, means of offering a salary supplement and providing extra honors for men of high background; see *Song shu* 72.1859.

means "then" but without the heavy sense of consequentiality. It describes a career seen from a distance, not probed by historical inquiry. The appearance of contiguity is similarly enhanced by words like *lei* 累, used for the loose chronological articulation of offices that were "accumulated," and *li* 歷, referring to offices that the actor "passed through" over a certain period of time; these terms are the flattened diegetic counterpart to the ascension of the stairway (*chu*) and the bowing in the mimetic verbs of appointment. Time words perform a similar agglutinative function: *xun* 尋, "after a short while," connotes immediate contiguity in an official career, while *e* 俄, "after some time," bridges any small gaps. *Fu* 復, "again," follows a break in a career, returning the actor to some previous post or patron, like the stitch of a needle returning to its place in a pattern. Finally, ellipsis is also a rhetorical technique geared to the purposes of agglutination, years-long elisions in narrated time obscuring the reader's perception of historical depth.

The Rhetoric of Officialdom

In political systems of all kinds, individuals are at once themselves subject to the system's mercies while also being able to leverage the system against other individuals. The Southern Dynasties gentryman could hardly extricate himself from the culture of officialdom, but he could use that culture to squeeze his competitors to his own advantage. Or others might use it against him. Moreover, manipulation of a system is a complex and less than fully predictable multiple-move game, such that an apparently strategically advantageous action might later turn to misfortune, as the rhetoric of officialdom worked over its subjects.

The capsule summary of Xu Xianzhi's precipitous rise presented above in passage (d) provides a good demonstration of the unstable rhetorical deployment of officialdom, by the historical actors and in the historiography. The argument of the passage is oriented on the topic of consequence, proceeding on two levels: first in the passage itself, then as the passage is integrated into the biography and the history as a whole. The first stage sets out a chain of consequence and shows Xu altering it—a deployment of the figure of "contrary consequence." Xu, it is said, began his life in the plain clothing of commoners, a hyperbolic trope for the middle gentry. Further, he was "not a man of any particular learning." In the regular course of consequence, humble beginnings and humble talents should lead him to a humble endpoint. But Xu, relying "solely" (*zhi* 直, "directly") on the "power of his ambitions" (*zhi li* 志力) and his "well-tempered character" (*judu* 局度), intervenes to change this course of consequence and rise to the court's highest ranks. At this point the historian projects the view into the future: "Those at court and beyond esteemed him and submitted to his judgment, *deeming him worthy of a Prime Minister's regard.*" The word "regard" (*wang* 望, their "expectation" for his future) captures a historiographical pluperfect, as Xu will indeed meet those expectations, as Prime Minister and the senior member of a triumvirate at the court of the new dynasty.

At the higher level of historical argument, however, the normal course of consequence that Xu has redirected is reverted back to its former state, his intervention standing not as an achievement in his own individual story but as a plot point in the dynastic historical narrative. Xu's time at the head of the court was tumultuous, involving the overthrow of the so-called Young Emperor (Shaodi, r. 422–24), the exile and murder of the next prince in line, and the installation of a new emperor—Emperor Wen—who owed little to Xu and his cohort. In the first month of 426, Xu Xianzhi ended his career as a scapegoat—bearing the blame for the court intrigues of these years, he was executed at the behest of the new emperor and displaced by Wang Hong as the preeminent court power. Thus, he rises high, but ends up lower than where he began, the ordinary course of consequence having been restored, and then some.

To say that a fact in the social or political realm can be used rhetorically means that it can be deployed to positive or negative ends. In Xu Xianzhi's case, the negative side is deployed at the level of historiography, but the same rhetorical manipulations went on in the historical mimesis itself. Take the example of Xu's contemporary Kuai En 蒯恩 (d. 418), a man who won the patronage of Liu Yu through his military prowess. His biography in the *History* records:

> When the Founding Ancestor set out on his northern raid [in 416, to capture the old northern capitals, Luoyang and Chang'an, as proof of his ascendance], he left Kuai En behind to attend upon and protect the heir [the future Shaodi], and he commanded the gentry at court to socialize with

Kuai. Kuai En, however, made himself ever more humble and self-deprecating. When speaking with others, he would always call them by their official position and title, whereas speaking of himself he would use the term "this lowly man."

高祖北伐，留恩侍衛世子，命朝士與之交。恩益自謙損，與人語常呼位、官，而自稱為鄙人。[24]

This embryonic anecdote revolves around a disjunction between the two critical hierarchical systems of the Southern Dynasties—social class and official position. Kuai En is a man of rather low social status, but he has been inserted into positions both substantively important—protecting the heir—and fairly high in official rank: the "Dashing Dragon Generalship" (*longxiang jiangjun* 龍驤將軍) held by Kuai was in the "third class" of official rankings, a class that, despite its number, contained the top ordinary court postings, like Director of the Secretariat, and regularly held prestige titles such as Palace Attendant.[25] It was at the lower end of that class, but the title put Kuai at court audiences physically side by side with men of much higher social station.

The passage plays on this disjunction by interweaving two rhetorical acts. The first is Kuai En's constructive, thresholding use of the situation's exigencies. Speaking of himself in a most deprecatory fashion and addressing his court "peers" with assiduous respect, he circumstantializes himself to leverage the initially inhospitable contrast of hierarchies in his favor, persuading others of his good character by restoring confidence in the hierarchical structure that his patron's command had shaken.[26] At the

---

24. *Song shu* 49.1437. The Zhonghua edition emends *wei guan* (lit., "position and office") to the more common compound *guanwei* ("official position"), but the two words can be distinguished.

25. See *Song shu* 40.1261; Du You, *Tongdian* 37.1003 (Jin), 1007 (Song). The second class was for men of particular power, the first a nearly "empty set" reserved for the highest court honors.

26. This command stands in counterpoint to the records, in scroll 94 of the *Song shu*, of later Liu-Song emperors, who (it is said) were unable to force their low-status aides upon the gentry of the court bureaucracy. Those stories are the flip side of the rhetorical topos, "how much power does an emperor hold over the court elite?"

same time, Kuai En is a piece of a larger rhetorical act—the Founding Ancestor's intervention into the politics of the late Jin court. This scene is occurring at the same time that the soon-to-be emperor has left Liu Muzhi, also a man of less exalted social status, in full charge of the court. Here as there, the Founding Ancestor was intervening in, or re-defining, the hierarchy of the capital gentry, splitting the upper gentry on the blade of officialdom. As with Liu Muzhi, Kuai En serves as a proxy for the Founding Ancestor's own rapid ascent, forced upon the higher-born gentry in the same way that the Founding Ancestor—of higher social status than Kuai, but in no way comparable to the capital elite—is asserting his own primacy at this historical moment.

And who is it that pushes Kuai En into this rhetorical scene? It is Liu Yu, the historical person and political actor, but it is also "the Founding Ancestor," the future founder of the dynasty, a role played by Liu Yu and elaborated in the pages of the dynastic history, where the central historiographical character is flanked by his biographical puppets. As was the case with Liu Muzhi, in many instances we will never be able to distinguish between a historical event engineered through historiographical tropes and historiographical explanation masquerading as an event, that is, between actuality and anecdote. The lesson is that the line between them—between a person and his representation, between role-playing and type-casting, between using symbols and being used as a symbol—was not clearly demarcated in this culture. It makes sense for Liu Yu, an astute politician, to use Kuai and Liu Muzhi in this way. At the same time, history—and our History—is representing the "Founding Ancestor" taking actions that *allegorically* illustrate his rise. We put these two strands together to say that Liu Yu acts in concert with the Founding Ancestor, that Kuai En acts artfully on a biographical scale as does the Founding Ancestor on the annalistic level. Political and historiographical plotting were one, historical fact tuning itself in a pluperfect chord with the historiographical narrative to come.

The deployment of officialdom within the mixed mode of historiography—what happened and what was written, and making things happen as they would be written—complicates our interpretation of historiographical rhetoric even when its purport seems clear. For instance, a judgment inserted in the biography of Yu Bingzhi 庾炳之 (388–450), another of Xu Xianzhi's contemporaries:

> [When, as head of the Secretariat's Personnel Department, Yu Bingzhi] held charge of matters of promotion, he not only refused to take into consideration consensus opinions, but was also quite receptive to bribery.
>
> 領選既不緝眾論，又頗通貨賄。[27]

That good and able men will be promoted to the positions they deserve is a staple enthymeme of discourse on officialdom, for in principle the definition of the individual and the definition of the office *ought to* match up. But the imperative of exigence that underpins all rhetorical acts dictates that enthymemes acquire rhetorical force in the breach, not when they are confirmed, just as hierarchies gain traction when they begin to fall into abeyance. Thus, while good careers in officialdom do serve to warrant the character of good historical actors, in active rhetorical practice careers serve better as foils for character faults and for the delivery of historical irony. Here, Yu Bingzhi is set in contrast with his weighty office—head of appointments being the most important substantive post at the imperial court. The history goes on to describe, at great length, how Yu's contemporaries sought to prosecute him, using his official misconduct as evidence. Again, however, there is to be no easy unraveling of the historical and the historiographical, because the narrative judgment just quoted is not so much a fact as it is the historian's uptake of a rhetorical argument made against Yu by his competitors. We might say that the historian agreed with their judgment, or saw no reason to overturn it, and subsumed it into the historiography—and so into history. But the continuity of history and historiography led, commonly if not inevitably, to this kind of passive historical "judgment," such that a rhetorical site like officialdom, straddling both dimensions, had a double agency, conditioning first the historical event of Yu Bingzhi's prosecution at court, and then, as anticipated and engineered by his antagonists, the historiographical narrative of it.

A final pair of examples from this same period illustrates the intricate historical and historiographical interplay of officialdom. The biography of Zhang Shao 張邵 (d. after 428) relates that:

---

27. *Song shu* 53.1517–18. One of Yu Bingzhi's chief antagonists was He Shangzhi, the representative of the puritanical viewpoint in the debate examined in chapter 4.

[In the second month of 422, the Founding Ancestor] split up the region of Jingzhou to establish Xiangzhou and he made Zhang Shao regional governor. When it came time to appoint his military staff, however, Shao submitted that as Changsha (the capital of the region of Xiangzhou) was located in the interior, it was not a place where warfare would occur, so establishing a military staff would be troublesome, and contravene the essential needs of good governance.

分荊州立湘州，以邵為刺史。將署府，邵以為長沙內地，非用武之國，置署妨人，乖為政要。[28]

Jingzhou, stronghold of the upper-middle Yangtze region, was an alternative power base in the Southern Dynasties; the Founding Ancestor divided it to weaken the threat it posed to his new regime. To assist his patron, Zhang Shao grasps another basic enthymeme associated with officialdom: the perfectly reasonable idea that the structure of governance should match the needs of governance. In demilitarizing this region, he weakens himself, but he does so on behalf of the dynasty, and his self-exteriorization is regarded as a righteous action, for in thresholding himself from power he might otherwise have seized, he uses officialdom as a warrant for his loyal character. The historiography relays his action, as proof of Zhang Shao's positive role in the historiography's root narrative.

The counterpart of this example relates an event from about a decade earlier. Yu Yue 庾悅 (ca. 374–411) was a gentryman who had served on the staff of the Jin princes who ran the court in the 390s and then under the imperial usurper Huan Xuan. Like Zhang Shao, he joined the cause of the Founding Ancestor, and during the rebellion of Lu Xun 盧循 (d. 411) he was given civil and military charge of the mid-Yangtze region of Jiangzhou (modern Jiujiang), in between Jingzhou and the capital. After Lu Xun's defeat, however, Liu Yi, the rival general the Founding Ancestor would vanquish in 412, sought to bring the Jiangzhou region under his own control:

---

28. *Song shu* 46.1394. Though included in our received *Song shu*, this chapter is not from Shen Yue's version, a fact observed by the eleventh-century editors of the first printed edition (*Song shu* 46.1400). See also the annals, at *Song shu* 3.58–59, and 3.57 for the restrictions placed on Jingzhou the year before.

After the defeat of Lu Xun, Liu Yi sought military authority over Jiangzhou, submitting that Jiangzhou was an interior region, where the main concerns were civil governance, and thus that it was not suitable to establish a military staff there. He submitted a memorial explaining his views, reading:

盧循平後，毅求都督江州，以江州內地，治民為職，不宜置軍府，上表陳之曰...²⁹

The document that follows is an elegant rhetorical exposition of both a specific truth—regions that do not need military staffs should not have them—and the general enthymeme from which it proceeds—governance must be done in accordance with what is needed, not what is allowed. This is the very same "topic" Zhang Shao had used to his advantage, and both men speak specifically of "interior regions" (*neidi* 內地), a term that would claim these regions as fully within the compass of the imperial court. Liu Yi, however, is deploying this topic antagonistically, to seize interiority from Yu Yue. After the memorial text, the history continues:

Thereupon, Yu Yue's military authority and generalship were taken away, and [as Liu Yi had advocated] his regional governorship was moved to Yuzhang [up the Gan River from and of less importance than Xunyang, the former seat of governance on the Yangtze]. Liu Yi sent a general close to him, Zhao Hui, to lead 1,000 troops at Xunyang, and the 3,000 civil and military men who had formerly been attached to Yu Yue as staff of his Establishing Awe generalship were all transferred over to Liu Yi's command, where he ordered them about mercilessly and humiliated them at will.

於是解悅都督、將軍官，以刺史移鎮豫章。毅以親將趙恢領千兵守尋陽，建威府文武三千悉入毅府，符攝嚴峻，數相挫辱。³⁰

In a sense, Liu Yi is still using officialdom *positively*, to demonstrate, as had Zhang Shao, his understanding of the proper needs of good governance. But the more direct end here is *negative*—to strip power from a competitor with whom he had a long-standing enmity. Liu Yi succeeded, and history

---

29. *Song shu* 52.1490.

30. *Song shu* 53.1491. Also, in slightly different form, at *Jin shu* 55.2208–9 (biography of Liu Yi).

records that shortly after his demotion, a dispirited Yu Yue developed a tumor on his back and died.

Thus we see the exposition of a neutral, endoxic topic associated with officialdom, followed by its antagonistic exploitation in the political sphere. A rhetoric of interiors and exteriors, however, is by nature a rhetoric of reversals, active and passive. Liu Yi is momentarily successful, but when this anecdote is subsumed in the historiography as an illustration of *his* character, the consequence Liu Yi thought he had established dissolves. The passage ends with Liu's ill enjoyment of the fruits of success, seizing Yu Yue's former troops and abusing them. Although Liu Yi's fate is not explicitly adumbrated there, the reader will know that this man, the primary antagonist in the first stage of the Founding Ancestor's ascendance, would meet his death within a year, and indeed that Liu Yu allowed him to accrue power over Jiangzhou only as a step toward having him declared a traitor by the Jin court, ripe for the Founding Ancestor to eliminate.[31] One endoxic truth is displaced by another, broader one: that officialdom, a symbol of public power, is not meant for bad men pursuing their own private interests. Yu Yue's death is unfortunate, but it has served a greater purpose in the larger historiographical context of the legitimation of the Liu-Song state.

Defending the utility of the dynastic histories as historical source material, Hans Bielenstein observes that in them, "events are stylized by aid of [a] conventional set of formulas," but that such "stylization . . . implies no bias."[32] One simply has to learn to see through history's figures of speech. Running contrary to such an approach, and in light of "the necessarily *suasive* nature of even the most scientific terminology," the aim of this chapter has been to recover the bias that lies hidden in a historiographical element that would appear to have no stylization to it at all—officialdom.[33] Like modern scholars who see the bureaucracy of early medieval China

---

31. On this, see the edict Liu Yu elicits from the Jin Emperor An, at *Jin shu* 55.2209–10.
32. Bielenstein, "The Restoration of the Han Dynasty," 47, 81, evaluating the reliability of the *History of the Later Han* (compiled before 445).
33. The quotation is from Burke, *Language as Symbolic Action*, 45.

performing a mediating function, bridging the distance between gentry society and the state, we have identified a political dynamic in the rhetoric and the very grammar of officialdom.[34] We find that when the individual and the state coordinate in the rhetorical space of officialdom, both have room to threshold, using the "culture" with due artistry to prove their moral bona fides. Yet neither representation was very secure: the individual lived in a system that was fundamentally balanced toward the state, and in a world in which he was to leverage that system against other individuals, and they against him, while the state was balanced first by the gentry agency it could not but accommodate, and then by the judgment history would make upon it after the inevitable (?) lapse of its Mandate. In the present, future, or past as it would come to be written, all players could end up on the exterior.

On the exterior ... yet officialdom *was* an exterior surface, in the costumes that ascended with the ranks or in the shining record of dynastic historiography, accumulating, agglutinating, enveloping the whole world of early medieval China. Perhaps there is a relationship between these two aspects of exteriority: the interplay of praise and blame that featured as risk and opportunity in the practice of officialdom provided the tension that sustained the glistening, lapidary representational surface on which individual "lives" were etched, and beneath which real human beings lived.

---

34. Keiji Nakamura, *Rikuchō seiji shakaishi*, 51–52.

FOUR

Historiographical Self-Fashioning

The Rhetoric of a Court Debate

> It may almost be said of Chinese history that it consists exclusively of primary sources.
> —Charles S. Gardner, *Chinese Traditional Historiography*

The historical actor in early fifth-century China was a historiographical actor, living a life he knew would enter some historical record, and perhaps even be included in an orthodox dynastic history. He sought to shape that record, and the primary avenue for such shaping was the production of (potentially) historical documents. In chapter 1 we saw one example of this: the arrival of the court emissary Pi Chen presented Liu Muzhi with a strategic opportunity to represent himself, and in response he created a fine speech that would advance his career as the Founding Ancestor's most trusted client and, in documentary form, his fame as a man of political perception worthy of a historiographical place of prominence. The biography of Wang Hong, the elite gentryman whose influence eventually displaced that of Liu Muzhi, and whose biography is pointedly paired with Liu's in Shen Yue's *History*, presents us with a more elaborate instance of this kind of historiographical self-fashioning. Wang Hong directs a court debate, casting himself in a winning role in the performance.

Wang Hong was the leading power at Emperor Wen's (r. 424–53) court from the first month of 426 to the first month of 429, and to a lesser extent up until his death in 432. A great-grandson of Wang Dao, founding minister of the Eastern Jin, his father, Wang Xun 王珣 (349–400), was the most honored member of the Jin court in the 390s. Coming of age just as the late Eastern Jin court reached its apogee of chaos, Wang Hong cultivated a high-minded reputation, managing to stay above the fray; he allegedly resisted the authority of Huan Xuan, though the anecdotal evidence for this in his biography may belie political relations better left off his resume.[1] When the Founding Ancestor deposed Huan Xuan in 404, he clearly set out to win over Wang Hong, granting him a fief and appointing him to an interim "patched" position that allowed Wang Hong to serve without any particular commitment to the Founding Ancestor's side. Wang Hong probably continued to keep a distance: in 410, his biography briefly notes his flight from his post during a rebellion, a sign that he was watching the winds. Nonetheless, the Founding Ancestor continued granting him appointments, and in 415 Wang Hong became Senior Aide on his Grand Commandant staff.

As we saw in chapter 2, in 416–17, Wang Hong accompanied the Founding Ancestor on his northern campaign and engineered the presentation of the Nine Bestowals, the signal that the gentry elite were amenable to a change of dynasties. In 418 he led the organization of the shadow cabinet of the Duchy of Song, the fief that served as the Founding Ancestor's stepping stone to the imperial throne. He was then made governor of Jiangzhou, a post he would retain through 426. This was an ideal position for him—right on the threshold of power. Jiangzhou was the pivotal bridge region between the capital area, Yangzhou, and the upriver stronghold of Jingzhou. This middle ground had to be put in the hands of a trusted man. It was also more conducive to the honor of Wang Hong, as the scion of a Jin prime minister, to maintain a polite and politic distance from the transfer of the Mandate of Heaven then taking place in the capital. His politic, not to say cagey, attitude toward the dynastic transition can be gleaned from an anecdote in his biography, from 422, shortly before the Founding Ancestor's death:

> At a banquet for his senior ministers, the Founding Ancestor exclaimed: "When I was just a man dressed in commoner's clothes (*bu yi*), I never could have expected to achieve this." Fu Liang and his sort then all went about drafting essays full of high praise for his virtuous deeds. Wang Hong [by contrast] merely remarked: "This is what is known as the Mandate of

1. *Song shu* 42.1312.

Heaven. It cannot be sought out, nor can it be declined." His contemporaries praised his aloof bearing.

高祖因宴集，謂羣公曰：「我布衣，始望不至此。」傅亮之徒並撰辭欲盛稱功德。弘率爾對曰：「此所謂天命，求之不可得，推之不可去。」時人稱其簡舉。[2]

Wang Hong shifts the stasis, turning the focus from the defining power of the Founding Ancestor to something far greater and beyond question—the workings of Heaven—thus balancing dynastic legitimacy with his own self-sovereign reserve. It is an endorsement from the threshold.

The "Fu Liang and his sort" mentioned in this anecdote—a group headed by Xu Xianzhi, Fu, and Xie Hui—were the rival court faction. These men, elite but lacking Wang Hong's prestige, had truly thrown their weight behind the new dynasty, guiding Liu Yu's rise to the throne and leading his imperial court. After the Founding Ancestor's death, not two years after assuming the Mandate, they served as his hand-picked guardians of the "Young Emperor" (Shaodi, r. 422–24), but these senior ministers turned against their allegedly wayward ward to plot his removal. They also disposed of the next prince in line for the throne, installing instead the eighteen-year-old Liu Yilong (407–53), Emperor Wen, who would go on to rule for three decades. Why this triumvirate made such decisive moves may never be fully known, but at the time the newly founded Liu-Song was facing an imminent threat from the Northern Wei, who saw opportunity in the early death of the Founding Ancestor. It is very possible they acted for the greater good of the dynasty, regarding Liu Yilong as the son most likely to succeed in continuing his father's dynastic enterprise.[3] Perhaps they imagined their own power at

---

2. *Song shu* 42.1313.

3. Note the view of Cai Kuo, the father of Shen Yue's patron Cai Xingzong 蔡興宗 (415–72), that Fu Liang and his cohort were right to install a capable emperor but exposed themselves politically when they killed the former emperor and the next in line to the throne; *Song shu* 57.1572–73. Zhu Zongbin, "Jin Gongdi zhi si he Liu Yu de guming dachen," analyzes the political maneuvering in this period, finding (67) that these men succeeded, albeit tragically, in the mission that had been bequeathed to them, to establish the Liu-Song as a viable dynasty.

court waning gracefully as the young emperor established his sovereignty. If so, they were wrong.

Beginning with the Founding Ancestor's 416 campaign against the north, a different group of advisors had begun to coalesce around the future Emperor Wen. The foremost of these were Wang Tanshou 王曇首 (394–430)—Wang Hong's younger brother—and a distant cousin named Wang Hua.[4] Hence, with Wang Tanshou in the capital with the newly enthroned Emperor Wen, Wang Hong still holding Jiangzhou, and Wang Hua maintaining the emperor's stronghold upriver in Jingzhou, a new power structure took shape at court, right under the noses of Fu Liang and his confederates. Realizing their situation, the court guardians quickly made a show of returning power to the emperor, but they were executed in early 426, whereupon Wang Hong was made Grand Minister of the Masses—*situ*, the hoary title, reserved for the court's highest minister, that had been posthumously granted to Liu Muzhi—and governor of the capital region of Yangzhou, with oversight powers over the Secretariat (*lu shangshu shi*). Wang Hong became Prime Minister.

This state of affairs, in turn, was not to last long. It is likely that the early death of Wang Hua, in 427, greatly weakened Wang Hong's position, and Wang Tanshou, still in his early thirties, would die three years later. In the sixth month of 428, after some external urging and internal debate, Wang Hong relinquished the title of Grand Minister, and in the first month of 429 that honor, and shared oversight of the Secretariat, was given to the emperor's brother Liu Yikang (the King of Pengcheng)—or perhaps to the faction that had gathered around that young man. (It is worth noting that it was only in the third month of that year that Emperor Wen established an heir.) Some semblance of a balance of power persisted for the next three years, up to Wang Hong's death, in his fifty-fourth year, in the fifth month of 432. Liu Yikang would then hold sway over the court for the rest of the 430s, before being ousted, and slowly shepherded to his death, by other powers at court.

The court debate that is the focus of this chapter is not dated in the *History*, but it must have taken place between the first month of 426,

---

4. "Cousin" here is the rather far removed *congzu di* 從祖弟, sharing the same paternal great-grandfather.

when Wang took control of the Secretariat, and the seventh month of 429, when one of the participants, Kong Mozhi 孔默之 (b. after 372), was made governor of Guangzhou. Evaluating the evidence, Masumura Hiroshi (1906–85) placed it in the first half of 426, in which case it would have served as a signal of the ambitions of his administration. This is reasonable, though late 428 to early 429 would also seem to be possible.[5] In the latter case, it would stand as Wang's effort to reassert his political authority in the face of the ascendance of the imperial brother Liu Yikang and his associates.

---

5. Masumura Hiroshi, "Sō sho Ō Kō den no dōgo hanhō no giron," 29–34, allowing that the evidence he assembles is contradictory. The annals record the emperor hearing court cases in both the fifth and sixth months of 426 and the tenth month of 428; the debate would have served well as a precursor to these events, and while the earlier dating seems sensible, the later one cannot be discounted entirely. The most pointed evidence for the possibility that the debate took place in late 428 or early 429 is the closing reference to Wang Hong as Defender General (*wei jun*, for *wei jiangjun* 衛將軍). Wang received this title in the first month of 422 (*Song shu* 3.58) but was advanced to Chariot and Cavalry General (*cheji jiangjun*) in the eighth month of 425 (*Song shu* 5.74). That was the title he held in his time of power, stepping back to Defender General in the sixth month of 428 (*Song shu* 5.77) and retaining the latter title until his death (5.81). Thus, if the debate took place in early 426, the emperor ought to be referring to him by his proper generalship. There are ways to explain this: the reference could be anachronistic, as Wang Hong would die with the title of Defender General attached; the title may have had special connotations, his father having held it as well; or some historian could have summarized the edict and not quoted from it. But a parallel imperial response to a memorial Wang Hong submitted in 429 also refers to him as "Defender General"; see *Song shu* 42.1317. Support for an early 429 date also comes from the *Nan shi* 21.570–71, where the debate is placed between date notations of 429 and 432, and after Wang has begun to share power over the Secretariat, though, as in our *History*, this is chronology determined by editing and cannot be regarded as strong evidence.

The debate's placement at the end of the biography has sometimes been used to date it to the 430s, at the end of Wang's life (e.g., Qiao Wei, ed., *Zhongguo fazhi tongshi [disan juan]: Wei Jin Nanbeichao*, 355, dating it to 431), but that is certainly wrong. Rather, its location suggests that Shen Yue appended it to a biography drafted by earlier hands.

Exigence: Wang Hong Opens the Debate

In the debate, Wang Hong calls for discussion on two questions that go straight to the heart of gentry identity and privilege. The first involves the gentry's proper place in the system of "neighborhood groups" (*fuwu* 符伍, literally "tallies of five"). In this practice, developed under the state of Qin and handed down from the Qin empire to the Han and from the Han onward, households were organized in groups of five, each being held responsible for reporting crimes committed by the others. This was one of the more oppressive tools of the imperial state, though reference to it in the *Rites of Zhou* (*Zhou li*) lent it the imprimatur of Confucianism.[6] The feeble imperial machinery of the Southern Dynasties meant that exceptions and privileged status became regular parts of the system, and it is the issue of gentry privilege that Wang Hong probes with his question.[7]

---

6. *Zhou li zhushu* 159.2a. Recent scholarship has emphasized that the institutionalization of Confucianism and the imperial state of the Qin were complementary developments, not opposing forces, and the *Rites of Zhou* itself may be closely associated with the Qin state; see Benjamin A. Elman and Martin Kern, eds., *Statecraft and Classical Learning: The "Rituals of Zhou" in East Asian History*. For an account of the development of the *fuwu* system, see Tu Cheng-sheng, *Bianhu qimin: chuantong zhengzhi shehui jiegou zhi xingcheng*, 131–39; on the system in this period, see Masumura Hiroshi, "Shin, Namichō no fugosei." Numerous specific cases appear in the *Song shu*, often spotlighting the system's excesses; see *Song shu* 53.1524, 54.1535, 55.1550–51, 64.1704, 74.1931, 85.2172–73, 100.2450.

7. I refer to the following versions of the text:
   (1) Three copies of the earliest extant printed edition of the *Song shu*, the core of which dates to the mid-eleventh century. The Bona 百衲 edition, in the *Sibu congkan*, reproduces the best of these, but with alterations.
   (2) The 1974 typeset edition of the *Song shu* published by Zhonghua shuju, edited by Wang Zhongluo; see *Song shu* 41.1317–21. The re-edited 2018 edition is cited for comparison.
   (3) A Southern Song (1127–1279) printing of the *Cefu yuangui*, compiled in 1013.
   (4) The *Nan shi* (*History of the Southern Dynasties*, comp. Li Yanshou et al., Zhonghua zaizao shanben series, Southern Song printing), where an excerpt includes a passage missing from all other texts. These are edited excerpts of the questions and Wang Hong's (but not the other participants') opinions.

In the words of the historian's introduction to the debate, Wang Hong "was widely knowledgeable in matters of governance and he paid careful attention to all matters. Weighing what ought to be done (*yi*) at any given time, he always came to the fairest decisions. [Once,] he sent the Assistants and Office Chiefs of the Eight Seats [of the Secretariat][8] a communique, reading": 弘博練治體，留心庶事，斟酌時宜，每存優允。與八座丞郎疏曰：

> In the laws regarding "crimes committed by members of one's neighborhood group," there is no sub-statute to absolve the gentry of responsibility; yet whenever punishments are issued, the gentry invariably appeal. If we allow the throne to show its generosity by granting them amnesty, then the law will lose its power. But if we actually prosecute them according to the circumstances, then our subjects will find this too severe.[9] We ought to (*yi*) make a new rule for this, to find the proper mean of indulgence and severity.

---

(5) The very brief excerpt—only the questions, presented as Wang Hong's opinions—in the *Tongdian* (170.4410–11), consulting both the modern collated edition and the photo-reprint of a Northern Song printing held at the Imperial Household Agency Archives in Japan.

All our texts ought to derive from an older *Song shu* no longer extant—even, presumably, the *Nan shi*, which contains some unique material. We are faced, however, with the special circumstance that the *Cefu yuangui* was compiled and printed before the printing of the *Song shu*. Thus, I have taken the *Cefu yuangui* as the base text here, noting where I vary from it, where it differs from the Song printings of the *Song shu*, and significant variation in the other texts.

8. The "Eight Seats" had become a conventional term for the Secretariat offices; they are identified in the *Song shu* (39.1235) as the three directors and the secretaries of five offices. The *Tongdian* synopsis inaccurately paraphrases this introduction, saying that Wang Hong "submitted a communique [to the emperor]" 上疏. This misrepresents the opening positions as his opinions.

9. The balance of the law and sentiment, or *circumstance*, was a standard topos in early medieval jurisprudence. See for example the early fourth-century memorial of one Xiong Yuan 熊遠, quoted in the *Jin shu* treatise on the legal code (20.939).

同伍[10]犯法，無人士[11]不罪之科[12]，然每至詰謫，輒有請訴。若[13]垂恩宥，則法廢不可行[14]；依事糾責，則物以為苦怨。宜[15]更為[16]其制，使得優[17]苦之衷也。

The issue here is a basic contrast between the "natural rights" of the gentry and the power of the state. Gentry interests must be protected—but any

10. The old printings of the *Song shu* read 位, a graphic corruption for 伍.

11. *Cefu yuangui*, *Nan shi*, and *Tongdian* (including the collated version prior to the editor's emendations) read 人士 here and below, except where noted. The *Song shu*, from the earliest printing on down, reads *shiren* 士人. Although these terms can be interchangeable, *shiren* is the regular term for "gentry," while the less common *renshi* can have the more specific meaning of "men serving in office." For an example in which the two terms are used differently, see *Sui shu* 25.699 (treatise on punishments, Liang section); numerous examples of *renshi* appear in the *Shishuo xinyu* (e.g., 6/10), a source contemporary with the material collected in the *Song shu*. This variance foreshadows a potent ambiguity in the "definition" of the topic at debate: the participants regard it as a question of general gentry privilege, but in his summary remarks Wang Hong will pointedly limit the focus to officeholders.

12. In the *Tongdian*, the characters 無 and 之 in this clause have dropped out; that cannot be the meaning intended here, but it would fit with the idea of gentry exception. In the following clause, the graph 詰 is printed 話, and 輒 is printed as 轉—both graphic corruptions.

13. *Nan shi* and *Tongdian* insert 常, "always," here.

14. *Tongdian* reads 即 for 則, and both *Tongdian* and *Nan shi* omit 可. This does not alter the meaning.

15. *Tongdian* inserts 謂 ("I say...") before 宜, and lacks the final graph of the preceding clause, 怨. *Nan shi* inserts 恐 ("I fear..."), which like *Tongdian* scans as a sentence opening, but may be regarded as a graphic corruption of 怨—in which case the *Tongdian* reading may be an "improvement."

16. *Tongdian* lacks this character, as well as the 也 that concludes this sentence. From here, the *Tongdian* continues to the second question, including none of the responses. The *Nan shi* inserts a summary of Wang Hong's response, then proceeds to the first four clauses of the second question, followed by a summary of Wang's opinion on that matter.

17. The Zhonghua *Song shu* says that all *Song shu* texts mistakenly write 憂 (*you*, "worry"), but while the character is obscured in the Beiping library print, it does appear to be 優 (*you*, "indulgence") in the version reprinted in the Zaizao shanben series. The *Cefu yuangui* confirms 優 and Wang Zhongluo follows, noting the change; the 2018 Zhonghua edition, meanwhile, reverts to 憂 and notes no alternative.

guarantee risks impinging on the court's legal sovereignty. The laws of the realm must be enforced—but doing so too thoroughly would alienate the gentry, the court's most important constituency. The debaters are urged to find an ideal balance between the extremes of "indulgence and severity," but Wang Hong weights that balance in a way that sharpens the urgency of the matter: the basic focalization of the issue lies in the state. Exceptions are said to damage (*fei*, "to destroy") the integrity of the law. The gentry are referred to as the state's "subjects" (*wu*, literally "things") and their perspective is presented prejudicially, as "resentment" (*yuan*), the nettling rancor of the nameless objects of state rule. The current balance, an ad hoc practice in which state and gentry negotiate informally, is to be replaced by one that, being enacted through a "sub-statute" (*ke*), will be firmly grounded in the state's perspective.

The sense of exigence is redoubled with the second point raised for discussion, addressing how punishments for theft ought to be applied to the gentry:

> Also: the "great punishment" (of death)[18] is prescribed for officials in charge of an office who would steal five bolts [worth of goods], and for forty bolts in ordinary circumstances.[19] Advocates on this matter have all said that such punishment is too severe, and that we should raise the amounts to ten bolts for a person in charge and fifty in ordinary circumstances, with punishment reduced to conscription in the army for thefts of forty [and ten][20] or less. In

---

18. According to a commentary on the Tang Code, the three death punishments in the Southern Dynasties were beheading and display on a post (*xiaoshou* 梟首), halving at the waist (*zhan* 斬), and execution and display of the body in the market (*qishi* 棄市), mentioned by Jiang Ao below; *Tang lü shuyi*, appendix, 597.

19. Compare *Jin shu* 75.1989 with a record of an Eastern Jin palace clerk sentenced to death for the theft of *thirty* bolts of cloth. Article 283 of the Tang Code also specifies thirty bolts, but refers specifically to "officials in charge of an office" (*zhushou*). From Wang Hong's concluding opinion, it can be inferred that he is here referring to standard official positions, filled by the gentry, while "ordinary theft" (*chang tou*) would appear to cover both theft by commoners serving as clerks and any theft by someone—gentry or commoner—not in government service.

20. From the responses (see especially Kong Mozhi) it is clear that this is to be inferred, but it is interesting that Wang Hong has covered the tip of his spear.

this way, we would make a bit more generous allowance for the people, while still being able to warn them away from wrongdoing.

I would like each of you to speak your mind on these questions.

又主守偷五匹,常偷四十匹,並加大辟,議者咸以為重,宜進至[21]偷十匹、常偷[22]五十匹死,四十匹降以補兵。既得小寬民[23]命,亦足以有懲也[24]。想各言所懷。

This is again presented as a matter of finding the proper measure of "indulgence": the existing law punishes theft at certain amounts with death, so a new law has been mooted to temper those consequences, reducing the penalty to conscription. But Wang Hong has other intentions. In point of fact, conscription is a poison pill for the gentry: stripping away their gentry identity through conscription is a worse consequence than punishment by death. The question is meant to shock, but indirectly, with conscription represented in a diminished mode—said to derive from an anonymous and diffuse group of advocates, it is spoken of as a reduction in penalty and referred to periphrastically (*bu*, "patch"). This circumstantialization of the issue is enhanced by the air of diffidence Wang Hong injects into the debate as he closes, in an echo of the voice of Confucius in the classic conversation piece at *Analects* 5/26, by asking only that his respondents "speak their minds."

21. Other texts have 主 for 至, which appears only in the *Cefu yuangui*. Perhaps the *Cefu yuangui* is a graphic corruption—but it may well be the correct reading, "raise *to*." The *Tongdian* and the *Nan shi* excerpt (which puts this sentence into Wang Hong's concluding response), and both Zhonghua *Song shu*, following later *Song shu* printings, read 主 and insert 守 after it, repeating the full term used in the first clause of this passage.

22. *Tongdian* lacks the preceding four characters. This is likely a copyist's error; it greatly inflates the more generous allowance under proposal.

23. *Tongdian* prints 人 for 民—a Tang taboo substitution. The old *Song shu* printings may reflect another way of handling this, printing *min* in a slightly irregular orthography.

24. For 有懲也, *Tongdian* reads 為懲戒, substituting a substantive synonym for the sentence's final particle.

Exposition: Speakers One and Two Set the Terms

Two initial opinions, presented by the modestly ranked assistants (rank six) who helped the Director run the Secretariat, expose the terms for the debate. They will be followed by a Secretary (rank three), then two "gentlemen" officers (again rank six, but a more prestigious variety), then Wang Hong again, with a long concluding judgment.[25]

Whether for purposes of artful patterning or because the rhetorical force of the idea of conscription was so strong, the first speaker, Jiang Ao, responds to the second question first.[26]

> Assistant of the Left Jiang Ao advocated:
> As regards the gentryman who is guilty of theft, but of an amount below the threshold for execution in the marketplace, when the sentence has been issued,[27] he will, naturally, be considered under the category of "harboring illicit goods and licentiously thieving" and will be subjected to "pure censure" by his peers for the remainder of his life, a censure from which no government amnesty shall ever set him free. Thus, the guilty parties will be sufficiently punished, and those who hear of their fates will be forewarned. If, by contrast, we were to lump the guilty gentry together with petty commoners, conscripting them all into the infantry, *that* in my humble opinion would indeed be rather too severe.

---

25. Gentlemen (*lang*) appear right after the Assistants in the Rank Six lists (Du You, *Tongdian* 37.1007–8), but not all gentleman positions were of the same prestige. Most notably, gentleman in the Office of Personnel (*libu*), the position held here by He Shangzhi, the last speaker, was more prestigious than the senior (Left) Assistant; for contemporary evidence of this, see the career path of Yang Xuanbao 羊玄保 (371–464), *Song shu* 54.1534–35.

26. Not much is known of Jiang Ao. The *History of the Southern Qi* (*Nan Qi shu* 39.682) notes two indictments composed by him.

27. *Jing* seems to be a technical term. For example, in the biography of Xie Zhuang 謝莊 (421–66): "Formerly, after the county magistrate had issued (*jing*) [a sentence] for a prisoner, the prefecture would send a clerk-inspector to review the case, and then the sentence (*xing*) would be carried out" 舊官長竟囚畢，郡遣督郵案驗，仍就施刑 (*Song shu* 85.2173). Also *Jin shu* 43.1230. That is, it does not mean here "when the sentence *is* finished," which would imply that gentry were actually punished according to law.

左丞江奥議：人士犯盜，贓不及棄市者，刑竟[28]，自在贓汙淫盜之目，清議終身，經赦不原。當之者足以塞怨，聞之者足以鑒戒。若復雷同輩小，謫以兵役，愚謂為苦。

Jiang Ao's concern is to preserve the gentry's right to define itself. To counter the threat of conscription, Jiang conjures up a gentry that is fully self-regulating: the need for punishment meted out by the state is obviated by the "pure censure" (*qingyi*) of one's gentry peers, which shall "naturally" (*zi*, which here might be rendered as an emphatic "still") and absolutely (*zhong*, here "to the end of" his life) adhere to him. In fact, this is not entirely true: elsewhere we do find imperial edicts in this period specifically intervening in the "pure censure" that Jiang Ao claims is expressly a peer prerogative.[29] As one would expect of a court bureaucrat, however, Jiang Ao frames his rebuttal with great tact, bookending his affirmation with concessions to the state. He begins by acknowledging the state's power to impose punishments and closes by averring that in his "benighted opinion," conscription would be "rather too severe" (*ku*, echoing Wang Hong's phrasing of the first question) a punishment, the point being that there is no *need* for the state to step into the gentry sphere, for the gentry is quite severe enough on its own.

The integrity of gentry identity is likewise at the center of Jiang's response to the first point of debate:

> [As to the first question,] even if members of neighborhood groups do live right next door to one another, the distinction between gentry and commoner is truly one that is handed down from Heaven, so they cannot share responsibility for the crime of harboring illicit goods.[30] However, slaves and clients do interact with the neighbors, and they would know if a theft were committed. Thus, criminal responsibility can be extended to the

---

28. *Cefu yuangui* has 意, a graphic corruption.

29. See, for example, *Song shu* 3.52, in one of the Founding Ancestor's first acts as emperor. On gentry as a social definition, see Nakamura, *Rikuchō kizokusei kenkyū*, part 1, chapter 2.

30. Jiang means that *gentry* cannot be held responsible for *commoner* crimes. But he does not state this limitation, and the question will be addressed specifically by the other respondents.

slaves and clients, but this is simply because they themselves are actually implicated in the offense. It is not that they are being punished in substitution for their gentlemen masters. Gentry with no slaves should not be held responsible at all.

> 符伍雖比屋鄰居，至於士庶之際，實自天隔，舍藏之罪，無以相關。奴客與符伍交接，有所藏蔽，可以得知。是以罪及[31]奴客，自是客身犯愆，非代郎主受罪也。如其無奴，則不應坐。

Modern scholarship regularly cites Jiang Ao's claim that the difference between gentry and commoner is "handed down from Heaven" as an objective description of the gentry's unquestionable social status in this period, ignoring the fact that an enthymeme is part of an argument, not an unquestioned truth. Perceiving that the assignment of gentry to the neighborhood groups is a threat to this "natural" gentry distinction, Jiang tries to show that the gentry are not *really* a part of the system, "even if" they are nominally included in it.

The linchpin of Jiang's argument turns out to be an element not included in the original formulation of the debate question—the slave (*nu*) or bondservant (*ke*).[32] These are different categories of people, as are the "adopted sons" and "family stewards" spoken of below, but they are lumped together by the debate participants: gentry being naturally distinct, it is rhetorically useful to have a complete contrary to serve as a foil. For what would a social group be without its scapegoats? Unlike the gentry, enslaved and otherwise bonded people are *not* distinct, but naturally base and ignoble. Adamantly asserting this distinction, Jiang rejects the notion that these slaves would be punished in the place of their masters, because that would imply some connection between these two completely different entities. Rather, he insists that these lesser beings are materially involved in criminal actions and so should indeed be punished with the neighborhood groups—this in contrast to the gentry, who of course would *never* associate themselves with the commoners in criminal activity.

---

31. *Cefu yuangui* lacks this character.
32. For an overview of these and other related groups, see Tang Changru, "Clients and Bound Retainers in the Six Dynasties Period."

The Secretariat's junior assistant, Kong Mozhi, continues to defend gentry interests, but in a less absolute fashion:[33]

> The Assistant of the Right Kong Mozhi advocated:
> Given the fact that gentlemen and petty men *are* mixed together in the neighborhood groups, mutual surveillance is a duty they cannot avoid. Although gentry and commoner may indeed be separate, one can only reason that they should know of one another's comings and goings. To make an analogy, it is like the way officials are held responsible for their underlings' offenses, even if they personally had no involvement in them. Thus when a crime occurs, it only stands to reason that they should be held cognizant, and if today we regularly transfer criminal responsibility to their adopted sons and family stewards, we must say it is done on the classical principle of "executing the servant"[in place of the master].[34] [Yet] if it is so, then how could those gentry households that possess no slaves have any peace of mind? Given that the gentry are said to be "restored" [from service and tax obligations], they should be allowed to pay fines instead.

> 右丞孔默之議：君子小人，既雜為符伍，不得不以相檢為義。士庶雖殊，而理有聞察，譬百司居上，所以下不必躬親而後同坐。是故犯違之日，理自相[35]關，今罪其養子、典計者，蓋義存戮僕。如此則無奴之室，豈得宴安？但既云復士，宜令輸贖。

---

33. Kong's older brother, Kong Chunzhi 孔淳之 (372–430), was an affiliate of Xie Lingyun and has a biography in the recluses chapter of the *Song shu* (93.2283–84). Mozhi receives a brief notice there: "a scholar of the classics, he authored a commentary on the *Guliang zhuan*." The Kongs were a northern family, but from Kong Chunzhi's biography it appears they had based themselves in Guiji (modern Shaoxing), in the empire's rich southeast. Other glimpses of Kong Mozhi in the *Song shu* allow us to piece together something of his career. In the fifth month of 426, he was part of a cadre of court officials sent out by the emperor on an inspection tour (*Song shu* 64.1699, 92.2270). There he is identified as "Formerly Assistant of the Right," implying either that the debate took place before that time or that he later resumed his position. In the seventh month of 429, he was made Governor of Guangzhou (*Song shu* 5.78), identified as "Assistant of the Left," a promotion from his position at the time of the debate. In Guangzhou, he was prosecuted for corruption, but protected by Liu Yikang. This is related (*Song shu* 69.1820–21) in the biography of his son, Xixian 孔熙先 (d. 446), who went on to use the family wealth to lure the historian Fan Ye into rebellion, also on the behalf of Liu Yikang.
34. *Zuozhuan* Xiang 3.
35. This character has dropped out of the *Song shu* printings.

Kong Mozhi does defend gentry interests, arriving at the correct end result—gentry indemnification—but he makes significant concessions along the way. His mode of argument is the narrow province of logical consequence (*ji* . . . , "given that"). For him, because gentry (*junzi*, "gentlemen") are in fact included in neighborhood groups, it follows ineluctably (as a "duty," *yi*) that they must have obligations as members of these groups. Conceding that the gentry do not live in a vacuum, he "reasons" (*li*, used twice in this passage) that they must certainly be cognizant of commoner wrongdoing. Throughout, he focalizes his argument in the state, taking its point of view as his standard. It is the state that creates the fact—the factual existence of the neighborhood group—that he takes as his starting point, and the analogy he uses to buttress his argument represents the state as the model for his reasoning: it is just like how the supervisor must be held responsible for the misdeeds of his staff even if he does not participate in any wrongdoing. The natural right of the gentry is identified as one that has been "restored" (*fu*) to them by the state, and if they are indemnified from the penalties they so fear, they still must pay a penalty to the state, in slave holdings or cash.

In addressing the second point of debate, Kong again grants agency to the state, even as he works to secure the general protection of gentry interests:

> [As for the proposal that] for ordinary theft of forty bolts, and theft of five bolts by responsible officials, the punishment should be lowered from the death penalty to conscription in the infantry, although such a measure would demonstrate great magnanimity and kindness, and would ease the lives of the people, nevertheless, from time to time it is to be expected that magistrates and prefects, to say nothing of debased members of the ordinary gentry, might commit such an offense, and though such offenders might indeed deserve to be slaughtered, I fear they simply cannot be conscripted into the infantry.[36] In my opinion, the new regulation might be applied to

---

36. Kong Mozhi echoes the view of the early Han statesman Jia Yi 賈誼 (200–168 BCE), who in a famous memorial said that the emperor could exile or demote or even execute a guilty gentry official and his family, but must not conscript him into society's bound ranks, lest the general populace's reverence for the scholar-official class be sullied, and the state held less in awe by them; see *Han shu* 48.2256.

the petty men (i.e., commoners), with the men who serve in office still ruled by the old law as before.

常盜四十疋，主守五疋，降死補兵，雖大存寬惠，以紓民命，然官長[37]二千石及失節士大夫，時有犯者，罪乃可戮，恐不可以補兵也。謂此制可施小人，人士自還用舊律。

A self-defining gentry may lurk in the background of Kong's defense, but it is eclipsed by the defining powers of the state, which lowers penalties and "eases" (*shu*) its subjects' lives with its offers of "magnanimity and kindness" (*kuan hui*). It is the state that sets the laws that determine gentry prerogative, and the gentry are named from a state perspective, as "men who serve in office" (*renshi*). He voices his defense of gentry interests with ambivalence, speaking at once directly (the particle *ye*) and timidly, as if in "fear" (*kong*). He protects the gentry not by arguing for them, but by locating a scapegoat that excuses them: as he did with the slaves above, here Kong makes a propitiatory offering of their "debased" (*shijie*) members, deserving of "slaughter" (*lu*) by the state.

Gentry Reasoning

The two assistants have set out two lines of argument for the following speakers to respond to or pursue. Jiang Ao presented a determined and decisive affirmation of gentry prerogative. Kong Mozhi generally protects gentry interests, but with significant concessions to the state. The next two speakers will argue fervently for gentry privilege, but in very different ways.

Wang Zhunzhi (378–433), of whom more will be said later, addresses the question of neighborhood groups at length. The first part reads:

---

37. The *Song shu* printings read 及 for 長. This is likely pollution from the same graph four spaces down in the text. As Masumura notes, *guanzhang* is idiomatic for county magistrate—the lowest local appointment made at the court level. If, however, we were to follow the *Song shu*, the phrase reads, "men who reach the office of prefect." Neither of the Zhonghua *Song shu* editions notes or incorporates this difference.

The Secretary[38] Wang Zhunzhi advocated:

In the past, when I was the magistrate of Shanyin, the gentry called their inclusion in neighborhood groups being "pressed onto the tally." When [a commoner] in their group committed an offense, [the gentryman] was absolved of responsibility, but when a man of officialdom committed a crime the [commoners of the] neighborhood group were held responsible for reporting it. This is not to say that there was any separate regulation for gentry and commoners. Rather, everyone was simply given punishment in accord with their guilt. For the fact is that well-bred scions of the gentry are completely cut off from the petty commoners, so it is fair to say that they have no way of surveilling them. But when it comes to gentry of fallen morals, in their affairs these men do come into contact with the masses, and given the fact that they are all together in a neighborhood group, [the commoners] are thus to be held responsible for reporting their offenses. At that time, not a few other places operated under this arrangement.

尚書王准之議：昔為山陰令，人士在伍，謂之押符。同伍有愆，得不及[39]坐；人士有罪，符伍糾之。此非士庶殊制，定[40]使即刑當罪耳。夫束脩之胄，與小人隔絕，防檢無方，宜；[41]及不逞之士，事接群細，既同符伍，故使糾之。于時行[42]此，非惟一處。

Wang Zhunzhi fashions a beautifully asymmetric argument based on circumstance: gentry, being aloof, are not responsible for commoner

---

38. It is curious that the document does not identify which office he served as Secretary of at this time. From his biography we learn that, during the period in question, he headed both the Office of Justice (*duguan* 都官, "[monitoring] the officials of the imperial capital") and the all-important Office of Personnel (*libu*).

39. *Cefu yuangui* reads 反, apparently a graphic corruption.

40. *Song shu* printings and the *Cefu yuangui* use this relatively rarer orthography. At the end of the second sentence of the next passage, however, only the *Cefu yuangui* retains it, the *Song shu* having the more common 實. Probably the encyclopedia better preserves an original feature.

41. The Zhonghua editions punctuate 宜 ("suitable," "it is fair to say") with the following clause. I do not see how that makes sense. Kawai (*Nanchō kizokusei kenkyū*, 102) punctuates as here; Masumura ("Sō sho," 38) has a different interpretation, but also puts *yi* with the first clause.

42. *Cefu yuangui* reads 如此 ("was like this"). The meaning does not change, but 行此 ("operated under this arrangement") seems preferable as the more precise word here, and there is a reasonable degree of graphical similarity.

crimes, but commoners *are* responsible for gentry crimes, because any gentryman who commits a crime could only have done so in cahoots with some commoner. The argumentation is inductive and pragmatic. The innocence of the gentry derives from their having "no way" (*wu fang*) of knowing what commoners are doing, while commoner responsibility is due to their material connection (*shi jie*, "in their affairs . . . come into contact") with the wayward gentry. This understanding of the neighborhood responsibility system is said to derive from his experience as a seasoned local governor, experience he facilely extrapolates to "not a few other places."

Wang then carries this pragmatic, circumstantial approach forward to the problem of slave responsibility, advocating the complete exoneration of slaves by generalizing (*lei duo*, "generally") about the way slaves and servants interact with society, based on "practical reason" (*shi li*) and "looking at the facts of the matter" (*ji shi er qiu*). His argument also offers a glimpse into the actual disposition of slave labor in the lower Yangtze economy.

> The Assistant of the Left holds that slaves and clients interact with their neighborhood group and have the opportunity to monitor their activity. Thus, if a member of the group commits an offense, they should be punished accordingly. [However,] if we look at the facts of the matter, this view is not in accord with practical reason. Slave- and client-holding gentry families generally send their slaves out on business. Scattered east and west, few of them dwell in the family residence, and those that do are personal manservants who are kept at beck and call, seldom venturing out of doors. As for family stewards, not one in ten resides at the family residence. [Thus,] if we hold slaves responsible in the neighborhood group, unnecessarily excessive punishments will unquestionably proliferate, and I fear that this will not be in accord with the intention of "establishing laws to fit the crimes."
>
> 左丞議,奴客與鄰伍[43]相關,可得檢察,符中有犯,使及刑坐。即事而求,有乖定理。有奴客者,類多使役,東西分散,住家者少;其有停者,左右

---

43. *Cefu yuangui* inserts the character 伯. *Wubo* is an established compound, but it does not seem to fit here; it could be the result of pollution from the graphically similar character that follows, 相.

驅馳，動止所須，出門甚寡。典計者，在家十無其一。奴客坐伍，濫刑必眾，恐非立法當罪本旨。

Wang Zhunzhi excels in his artful handling of focalization, bringing about a reconciliation of state and gentry points of view. In the first part of the response, he has already framed his argument with a strong gentry focalization, representing the neighborhood group system with a trope that he attributes directly to the gentry: being "pressed" (*ya*) into this system, the gentry suffer at the hand of the state, "tangled up" (*jiu*, here as "surveil" and "report") in its mechanisms. This empathy with the gentry perspective is consonant with the record of Wang's local service in his biography, which observes that as magistrate of Shanyin he "had a reputation for being able" (*you neng ming* 有能名), which is to say, he negotiated generously with the residents of Shanyin.[44] Here he again starts off with a clear gentry perspective, drawing conclusions from the way gentry perceived their relation to their human assets—distant from them in society, but close at hand at home—but then he subtly changes his stance, embracing a state perspective, though one that is reconciled with gentry interests. Punishing slaves, this experienced administrator observes, will lead to "excess" (*lan*), a quality antithetical to good governance, and thus to the state's "original intent" (*ben zhi*) in making laws. Fashioning himself a mediator, on the threshold of the gentry and the state, Wang conjures up the perspective of a state that, powerful as it may be, is rightly careful not to overstep the bounds of good government.

This mixture of rhetorical attitudes turns to irony in his opinion on the second question:

> The Assistant of the [Left][45] holds that men of officialdom who steal less than the amount prescribed for the "great punishments" of death should

---

44. *Song shu* 60.1624. Compare the laissez-faire approach to the same region of Xie Fangming, who is described with the same turn of phrase (*Song shu* 53.1524).

45. All texts read 右 (Right), but as Masumura ("Sō sho," 38, followed by Kawai) shows, the sense of the passage requires the graphically very similar 左 (Left). Assistant of the Left Jiang Ao has just spoken of conscription of commoners, implying amnesty for gentry, and Xie Yuan, below, refers to Jiang's advocacy of amnesty. Kong Mozhi, Assistant of the Right, has suggested separate laws, not amnesties, and his proposal is dismissed in

receive amnesty from conscription into the army. Although he wishes in this way to show generosity to the gentry, I am afraid it will not do enough to thwart wrongdoing. Act according to reason and you are a gentleman, act against it and you are a petty man.[46] The regulations are stern, and yet people still dare to violate them—if we now supply a provision for amnesty, the violators may well become more numerous than before! For the greatest amnesty to the wayward is this: to make them fear the law and so be reformed in their hearts. [Also,] I cannot agree with [the Assistant of the Right's idea of] having different regulations for gentry and commoner.

(右)[左]丞議，人士犯偷，不及大辟者，宥其[47]補兵。雖欲弘士，懼無以懲邪。乘理則君子，違之則小人，制嚴於上，猶冒犯之，況[48]其宥科，犯者或眾。使畏法革[49]心，乃所以大宥不肖。士[50]庶異制，意所不同。

---

the last sentence of this passage. While it is possible that the content of Kong Mozhi's law for the gentry would have specified amnesty as the remedy, and the phrasing of the final sentence (*qie*, "also," or "moreover") in the *Song shu* may suggest not a change of topic but an additional justification, it is more likely that Masumura is correct, and I have followed his emendation.

46. For an analogous use of "act according to reason" (*cheng li*), see Shen Yue's preface to the "Biographies of the Filial and Righteous" (*Song shu* 91.2241); as noted at Wang Zhongluo, *Song shu jiaokan ji changbian*, 1048.

47. The character 其 is from the *Cefu yuangui*; it is absent in the *Song shu* printings and the Zhonghua editions.

48. The *Song shu* printings read 以 for 況. There is little difference in meaning, but the *Cefu yuangui* diction is more emphatic and more specific—and thus less likely an emendation. In addition, we find that the *Song shu* is very possibly corrupted in three other locations (see the preceding and the following two footnotes) in this short passage. These factors, combined with the relative chronological priority of the *Cefu yuangui*, suggest we should not follow the *Song shu* here.

49. The early *Song shu* printings read 其, a graphic corruption. The Zhonghua *Song shu* make this emendation, but only Wang Zhongluo (correctly) cites the *Cefu yuangui*, the new edition referring to a later *Song shu*.

50. There is damage across five columns in this location in the Beiping library copy, including a three-character lacuna after 宥 and before 庶. The other old printings appear "intact," but given the divergence itself and the infelicities in the readings they present at these locations, it is very possible that they have been repaired, as was the critical opinion of Zhang Yuanji (1867–1959); see *Zhang Yuanji guji shumu xuba huibian*, 62–63. Following those later printings, the Zhonghua editions and Masumura and Kawai all read 也且士 for 不肖士; that is, using *ye* to end the preceding sentence without

On the surface, Wang Zhunzhi wholly endorses the state's perspective. The state is "generous" (*hong*), and Wang makes a show of deferentially declining that beneficence, on the grounds that the gentry do not deserve it. Applying a tautologically simple litmus test—if he does good deeds, then he is a (good) gentleman, if he does ill, he is a (bad) petty man—Wang hypothetically excoriates those gentrymen who would breach the stern regulations of the state and take advantage of its policy of amnesty. In a perverse redefinition of amnesty—the process by which the state acquiesces to gentry perspective—he locates "the greatest amnesty" in the state's *punishment* of bad gentrymen, for fear of the laws of the state will cause the wayward subjects "to be reformed in their hearts" (*ge xin*). This marks a remarkable transition in the quality of gentry focalization in Wang's speech, from being "pressed" (*ya*), which connotes begrudging acquiescence to undue state intervention, to being "reformed" (*ge*, literally the "dehairing" of an animal skin as it is tanned into leather), which entails wholesome and necessary, and not at all gentle, state intervention into the gentry domain.

The catch is that Wang Zhunzhi does not play this abject perspective at face value. He speaks in grand tones, but in substance he is really arguing for the preservation of the status quo, according to which indicted gentry may petition the court for leniency. The tautological test he advocates—good is good, bad is bad—effectively retains the path of petitions to the throne, which would presumably indemnify any member of the gentry of any particular wrongdoing on the basis that, as a good "gentleman," he would not have done what he is accused of. Rejecting the position of Kong Mozhi, who would have gentry rights defined legally, he bolsters the more

---

specifying "the wayward" and beginning the final sentence with "moreover" (*qie*). While it is not impossible, given the similarity of 肖 and 且, that the *Cefu yuangui* reading is a graphic corruption, its reading is more likely correct, for two reasons. The *Song shu* is the "easier reading," while "the wayward" would make an unlikely conjecture; moreover, the contrast of "worthy" and "wayward" has a classical antecedent—see *Guliang zhuan*, Zhao 4, "use the worthy to govern the wayward" 用賢治不肖. The new Zhonghua edition notes this repair to their base text—the old edition silently changes it—but claims—perhaps following the note in Wang Zhongluo, *Song shu jiaokan ji changbian*, 1048—that the *Cefu yuangui* also has *ye qie shi*, which is not the case for the more reliable Song printing of that work.

flexible relationship of state-gentry negotiation, a relationship that had served the gentry well over the past century. He openly eulogizes the state's perspective, declining its benevolent inclinations and even prodding the state to be harsher in its treatment of bad gentry, but only to side-step any real change in the gentry's "natural" rights.

Speaker Four: A More Perfect Gentry Casuistry

Listening to Secretary Wang state his case, Xie Yuan (d. after 444) must have felt uneasy—or glimpsed an opportunity.[51] To be sure, Wang ended well, with his paean to the state, and his specific arguments had a certain grace, but overall it was, as Wang himself stated, an exercise in "practical reason." It was an argument from circumstance, and Xie Yuan, who a decade later would be appointed head of an imperial school of "rhetoric" (*wen xue* 文學, "literary learning"), knew himself capable of much finer dialectic than that. He begins by redefining the first debate question in analytical terms of his own devising:

The Gentleman of Palace Affairs Xie Yuan advocated:

Only by correctly determining the "root" of a matter can one properly address the "branches" that spring forth from it. In the case of "pressing" gentry into the neighborhood groups, then, does the root of the matter lie in having them surveil the petty commoners? Or does it lie in having the gentry be surveilled by the petty commoners?

---

51. Xie Yuan has a brief biographical note in the *Song shu* biography of He Chengtian (64.1710–11), who prosecuted Xie for corruption in 444, resulting in his banishment from official service; Xie Yuan, meanwhile, ensured that He Chengtian was demoted for illicit business dealings. The note specifies that he was "known for his talents" and that he was a distant cousin (they shared a great-grandfather) of Xie Lingyun. From the treatise on ritual (*Song shu* 17.463) we learn that Xie was "Gentleman of Palace Affairs, Carrying Charge of the Office of Ritual" in the fourth month of 430—that is, he kept the position he held in the debate for some time. His appointment as head of the school of rhetoric came in 438 (*Song shu* 93.2293–94) or 439 (*Nan shi* 2.46).

殿中郎謝元議謂：事必先正[52]其本，然後其末可言[53]。本所以押[54]士大夫於符伍者，將[55]以檢小人邪？為[56]使受檢於小人邪？

Xie starts his argument with an enthymeme beloved by fundamentalists the world over: that what *really* matters is the "root" definition of the matter. With this in hand, he contrasts two potential roots of the law's intent, echoing Wang's trope of the gentry "pressed" onto the tallies but invoking a much more precise sense of intention. In fact, it will become apparent that he has little interest in digging down to the first "root"—the idea that gentry might be intended to surveil commoners. His argument rests entirely on the second alternative, that gentry are to be surveilled by commoners. Xie Yuan's analytical division is less functional than symbolic, the neat division instantiating the theme of his argument—distinction.

> I note that the Assistant of the Left has stated that gentry and commoner are naturally distinct, and consequently there is no way gentry could be

52. There is a four-character lacuna in the Beiping *Song shu*, after 謂 and before 其. Other printings here insert three (not four) characters: 宜先正, "one ought first to." This was likely a conjectural insertion. Wang Zhongluo's Zhonghua edition incorporates the *Cefu yuangui* reading adopted here, noting the reading in the other *Song shu*. The new Zhonghua edition notes the *Cefu* but gives preference to the later *Song shu*.

53. The Beiping copy has a lacuna at the graph 言, which is the reading of the Song printing of the *Cefu yuangui*. The other versions of the *Song shu* substitute 理 ("sorted out," "rationalized")—which does fit well with Xie Yuan's style of argumentation.

54. The *Song shu* printings have *tan* 探 for *ya* 押, likely a graphic corruption, as suggested by the introduction of this trope by Wang Zhunzhi above, and its repetition again below. Wang Zhongluo emends on the basis of the *Cefu yuangui*; the new Zhonghua edition retains *tan*, noting the alternative.

55. There is a lacuna in the Beiping Library *Song shu*, after 符 and before 以. The other printings insert 而末所 ("and the branch is to"). This is a purely formal conjecture, to parallel the 本所以 that has just appeared, and despite attempts to make sense of it (Masumura, "Sō sho," 40; Kawai, *Nanchō kizokusei kenkyū*, 116n9, omits this and the following clauses entirely, regarding them as corrupt), it makes no sense at all. Wang Zhongluo again rightly emends with the *Cefu yuangui*, while the new Zhonghua edition again injudiciously supplies readings from later *Song shu* texts, putting the *Cefu yuangui* in the notes.

56. There is a one-graph lacuna in the Beiping copy. The others insert 可 ("can it be that") to in place of 為 ("is it for"), roughly producing the right sense. Again, Wang emends, while the new Zhonghua prefers the later *Song shu*.

expected to report offenses committed by commoners. If they are pressed onto the tallies despite their ignorance of commoner activity, then it must be so that they can be surveilled by the common people.

案：左丞稱[57]士庶天隔，則士無(弘)[糾][58]庶之由。以不知而押之於伍，則是受檢於小人也。

Building his case on statements in evidence, he restates Jiang Ao's enthymeme—that the gentry are "naturally distinct"—and builds a deductive chain from the second "root" of his analysis: they are distinct, thus they have no way of knowing what the commoners do, thus they could not be expected to surveil the commoners, thus the purpose of the rule must be for commoners to surveil the gentry. He goes on:

> If this is so, then when a commoner is guilty, the gentryman is free from guilt. But if that is so, in what sense could his servants and bondsmen be held guilty and prosecuted [in place of the master, as advocated by Kong Mozhi]? As to the view [of Jiang Ao] that slaves are materially involved in the activities of the neighborhood group, and that as such they can be expected to report on the commoners, in my opinion this is groundless.

然則小人有罪，士人[59]無罪[60]，僕隸何罪而令坐之？若以實相交關，責[61]其聞察，則意有未因。

57. The Beiping copy has a four-character gap up to 士. The other *Song shu* insert five characters, to read 士犯坐奴，是, "When the gentryman commit and offense, his slave is prosecuted; this [is because]. . . ." That is, an editor has made a guess. The *Cefu yuangui* is correct, and Wang Zhongluo correctly incorporates it. Yet the new Zhonghua edition once again inadvisedly follows the later *Song shu* editions.

58. All texts read *hong* 弘 ("to show mercy to"), but the correct character must be the graphically similar *jiu* 糾 ("to report on the offenses of").

59. Here and in the rest of Xie Yuan's response, *Cefu yuangui* accords with other texts in reading 士人, not 人士. This makes a better parallel for 小人, Xie Yuan's rhetorical object of contrast.

60. The *Song shu* texts have 事 ("issue") for 罪 ("guilt"). This may be correct: it is stylistically preferable, as *zui* is used above and below, and the adjacent usages could have led to a copyist's mistake. There is no significant difference in the meaning, however.

61. The *Song shu* prints 貴 ("it is valued that they") for 責 ("they are expected to," or "held responsible for"), a graphical error. Both Zhonghua editions correct on the basis of the *Cefu yuangui*.

Historiographical Self-Fashioning 141

From the same rule, he further deduces that Kong Mozhi's argument was faulty: if gentry are truly not cognizant, then why should they have to forfeit slaves? But some new reasoning will be required to rebut Jiang Ao's idea that slaves are materially involved in wrongdoing and therefore may be prosecuted. Stepping into this breach with a rhetorical question, Xie Yuan prompts himself to a full display of his powers of casuistry, beginning anew with a new enthymeme:

> And why might that be? [Different] names and substances require different articles of governance, and public and private must have different statutes.
>
> 何者？名實殊章，公私異令。

In short, different things must be considered differently. He then follows the consequences of this enthymeme:

> The slave is not himself [officially] "pressed" onto the tally, for he does not have a "name" in the public realm. As the property of a citizen, he belongs to the private and the base. If we were to allow a person who belongs to the private and base and has no "name" to become involved in the substantive affairs of public governance, we would be muddying the distinction between public and private, and establishing improper connections between names and substances. Based on this line of thought, it is my opinion that slaves should not be held responsible, and that the matter should be traced back to their masters, as deemed appropriate in each individual case.[62] Such a guideline will not concern gentry who do not own slaves.

---

62. A record from 479 shows masters being held responsible for the malfeasance of their slaves; see *Nan Qi shu* 39.681. Xie clearly thinks that will never happen, and the nub of the 479 case is indeed that a gentry official was *not* prosecuted.

奴不押符，是無名也。民之[63]資財，是私賤也。以私賤無名之人，豫令[64]公家有實之任，公私混淆，名實非允。由此而言，謂不宜坐，還從其主，於事為宜。無奴之士，不在此例。

Xie Yuan's formulation of the "specific topic" of the slave must be considered in light of the preceding speakers' formulations. For the first two speakers, the slave played the role of scapegoat, albeit in different ways. In Jiang Ao's more ambitious defense of gentry rights, the slave is a base entity entirely contrary to the noble nature of the gentry. The slave might mix with the commoners, but with the gentry? Certainly not, and Jiang insists that the slave may not be punished as a "substitute" (*dai*) for his master. But that is exactly how the slave is regarded by Kong Mozhi, as he concedes the state's power over the gentry: where Jiang used the slave as the bulwark of a "natural" gap between the gentry and the state, Kong deploys him to bridge that distance in a mutually acceptable fashion. Wang Zhunzhi, meanwhile, uses the slave to present an entirely different point of view. Whatever privileges Jiang Ao and Kong Mozhi carved out for the gentry, they both allowed the basic assumption that the state controls society. Wang, by contrast, channels a view in which society extends well beyond the state's ability to conceive and control it. In the true world in which the

---

63. *Cefu yuangui* and the old *Song shu* printings both read *zhi* 之, and as Masumura ("Sō sho," 42; also Kawai, *Nanchō kizokusei kenkyū*, 116n10) observes, this must be correct. Note also the commentary to the Tang Code, "given that slaves are the same as property" 奴婢既同資材 (*Tang lü shuyi*, 14.271). Uncharacteristically, Wang Zhongluo's 1974 Zhonghua edition follows the later *Song shu* to read *fa* 乏 ("to lack," thus "the people do not own property"). There is no note, but Wang's full collation notes specify that the change should be made silently (*Song shu jiaokan ji changbian*, 1049–50). No explanation is added, but an ideological one suggests itself: surely the "people" (*min*) do not own slaves, but are, rather, poor. This ideological attitude is manifest in the original editorial preface, which was toned down for later printings. The new Zhonghua edition, for its part, follows Wang Zhongluo, with no note—despite the fact that its supposed base text, the Bona 百衲 edition (23b), really and correctly reads *zhi*. The root of this latter problem is that the new edition has both a declared base text and the task (see editorial principle four) of adhering to the old version as much as possible.

64. The *Song shu* lacks the character 令. Its presence could be an error in the *Cefu yuangui*—the graph resembles the immediately following 公, and has also appeared just three sentences earlier.

gentry of the Southern Dynasties dwelled, the society into which they dispatched their slaves, neighborhood groups were an artificial anachronism, the imposition of a northern imperial system onto the very different political economy of the Yangtze River. "Scattered east and west," the slave is a practical instance of the real disjunction between (gentry) society and the imperial state.

Xie Yuan's innovation is to raise Wang Zhunzhi's practical, *circumstantial* invocation of the slave to the level of a conceptual, *defining* difference. His slave is not an instance but a symbol, standing for the realm of the private (*si*), the absolute contrary of the public (*gong*) realm of the state. As an "object" (literally, a "property," *zicai*), the slave has no place in laws that concern the state's "subjects." To apply laws to them would, Xie Yuan argues, be to "muddy" (*hunyao*) the distinction upon which the state's legitimacy rests. Thus, where Wang Zhunzhi could only point vaguely to the "original intent" of the law in question, Xie Yuan is able to marshal an argument that fully explicates what that intention was—a "public" value, instantiated and maintained by the glorious imperial state, against which the base slave stands as foil.

Dealing perfunctorily with the second potential "root" of the matter, Xie Yuan simply puts Kong Mozhi's argument in his own logical framework:

> If [on the other hand] the root of the matter lies in having gentrymen surveil the commoners, then when a commoner commits an offense the gentrymen should also be considered guilty, and in this case the slave will be subject to the principle of "punishing the servant" [as the Assistant of the Right proposed]. But if so, those gentry who do not own slaves will lack peace of mind, and allowing them to pay a fine is not an unreasonable way of handling the matter.

> 若士人本檢小人，則小人有過，已[65]應獲罪，而其奴則義歸戮僕。然則無奴之士，未合宴安。使之輸贖，於事非謬。

---

65. The old *Song shu* and the *Cefu yuangui* print this graph as 巳. It can only be 己, as it is given in both the Zhonghua *Song shu*. This in itself is not significant, but provides evidence for the mixing of the graphs 己, 已, and 巳, at issue in the text of Wang Hong's concluding opinion.

He then recapitulates, with some polite hedging, his preference for the "root" on which he has scored his points:

> The two sub-statutes [proposed by the Assistants of the Left and Right] depend on what the root of the issue is. Here I have simply explicated the two possible roots, hoping to straighten out the proper logic behind each one. As for my uninformed opinion on the issue, I believe we should follow the former proposal, which, by distinguishing sharply between gentry and commoner, is the more perfect in principle.

> 二科所附，惟制之本耳。此自是辯章二本，欲使各從其分。至於求之管見，宜附前科，區別士庶，於義為美。

This is to reformulate the key enthymeme, that gentry and commoner ought to be held distinct. Substantively, he has preserved both gentry and slave. But with this final rhetorical flourish, Xie shifts the stasis of the debate, not resting his case on anything substantive. The airy spirit of his logical argument concludes in sublimity, with a "principle" (*yi*) that is "perfect," or literally "beautiful" (*mei*). The true "root" of his argument is aesthetic, a sublimation of the issue at debate and a thresholded step apart from his more mundane colleagues at court.

Having made his point, Xie Yuan addresses the second debate question only briefly. Graciously accepting the state's offer of amnesty, humbly insisting that the state "need not" allow the gentry to be governed by separate laws, he succinctly preserves the gentry's power of self-definition:

> As regards the regulations on theft, I note the opinion of the Assistant of the Left, that the gentry can never, in the end, don armor to become soldiers, and [so] they should have the good fortune of sharing the beneficence of imperial amnesty. There is no need to follow the old law [as Kong Mozhi advocated]. This is the most appropriate response to what "advocates on this matter have all said."[66]

---

66. Taking *yi xian* as a reference to those exact words, and the proposal they refer to, at the end of Wang Hong's opening speech. There are, however, two other possibilities, one or the other of which is as likely as the reading given by all extant witnesses. If *xian* 咸 were a graphic error for *wei* 為, then we should find a version of the standard formula . . . *yi wei yun* 議為允 "[someone's] opinion is the best," as used, for example, in the

盜制，案左丞議，士人既終不為兵革，幸可同寬宥之惠，不必依其[67]舊律，於議咸允。

The Righteous Contrarian

The next speaker surprises us. All four of the respondents thus far have argued, in their different ways, for gentry prerogative, and now suddenly and forcefully the momentum of the debate is reversed. He Shangzhi was from a respectable but "poor" family—a fact that either informs or is meant to historiographically echo the position he takes in this debate.[68] Addressing only the question of gentry responsibility in the neighborhood groups, his speech begins with a recapitulation of Kong Mozhi's argument:

> The Gentleman of the Ministry of Personnel He Shangzhi advocated:
> I note: Assistant of the Right Kong holds that when someone in a gentryman's neighborhood group commits an offense, the gentryman's slave should be held responsible if he owns slaves, and if he owns no slaves then he should pay a fine.

---

imperial response that punctuates the present debate document. Meanwhile, the conclusion of a similarly reasoned policy memorial elsewhere in the *Song shu* (64.1696) reads "this is more appropriate *in principle*" (*yu yi wei yun* 於義為允). That alternative coheres with the abstraction that distinguishes Xie's argument and is directly parallel with the way he has just concluded his opinion on the other debate question: *yu yi wei mei* 於義為美.

67. The *Song shu* lacks 其, the demonstrative pronoun in "*the* old law."

68. Biography at *Song shu* 66.1732–38. "Poor" (*pin*) means his family was not wealthy. His father, He Shu, served in the Secretariat in the early 400s, where the *History* records him delivering a magnanimous opinion on a legal case; none other than Wang Hong would praise him for being "pure in his conduct" 清身潔己. He Shangzhi joined the Founding Ancestor in 413. In the 440s he headed the Secretariat, and he held lofty honorary titles throughout the 450s, up to his death at the ripe age of seventy-nine. For a study of the He family, see Wang Yongping, *Dong Jin Nanchao jiazu wenhua shi luncong*, 131–95.

吏部郎[69]何尚之議：案孔右丞議，人士坐符伍為罪，有奴罪奴，無奴輸贖。

He then follows the consequences of Jiang Ao's argument, rejecting gentry responsibility, and by extension—though this remains unstated—the necessity of substituting slaves and fines for gentry guilt:

> [However,] if we agree that gentry and commoner are separated by a tremendous gulf, then it would indeed be almost impossible for a gentryman to know of a commoner's affairs. It is inadvisable (*bu yi*) to insist on a law that would require the gentryman to be cognizant of matters that it is nearly impossible for him to know of.

既許士庶緬隔，則聞察自難，不宜以難知之事，定以必知之法。

Thus, the gentry are to be indemnified. But all of this is only by way of introduction, and he begins his real argument with a peculiarly crabbed enthymeme:

> Now, a slave-owning gentryman may be no good, but a non-slave-owning gentryman is not necessarily no good.

夫有奴不賢，無奴不必不[70]賢。

He Shangzhi, who would later be made head of the imperial school of "philosophy" (*xuan xue*, "dark learning"), is not afraid of tendentious argument. In the translation above, "may be" has been inserted into the first clause, but his statement can be interpreted flatly as "those with slaves are not good." In the manner of "begging the question," the second clause uses a double negative to refute a suggestion that does not exist—that people who do not own slaves are not good. The whole statement borders on the

---

69. The *Cefu yuangui* text has dropped the character 郎, "Gentleman." The position is confirmed in He's biography.

70. The above thirteen characters have dropped out of *Cefu yuangui*. This appears to be a copyist's eyeskip error, but the sentence still makes sense, that is, "require the gentleman to be worthy" 必賢 takes the place of "a law that would require the gentleman to be cognizant" 必知之法.

ludicrous, but the deliberately involuted syntax covers, or reveals, a plainer enthymeme of great power: the meek are morally superior to the mighty. He continues:

> Today, those with bevies of slave boys trample heedlessly over the laws of the empire, while those who have no servants at all are forced into dire straits by contemporary regulations. In this way, [great families with the riches of] Cheng and Zhuo always receive the grace of succor,[71] while [pure and impoverished scholars of the likes of] Yan and Yuan are certain to be subjected to the law.[72] When I give this my unworthy consideration, I dare to feel unsatisfied with such a state of affairs.
>   Gentleman of Palace Affairs Xie says that if we subject slaves to the law, that is not in accord with their status [as the private property of their masters], and his point does indeed have its logic. But the truth of the matter is that slaves and servants do interact with the neighborhood commoners, and I fear we will be remiss if we completely fail to prosecute them. I am in agreement with the proposal of the Assistant of the Left.
>
> 今多僮者傲然於王憲，無僕者怵迫於時網。是為恩之所霑，恆[73]在程、卓，法之所設，必加顏、原。求之鄙懷，竊所未愜。謝殿中謂奴不隨主，於名分不明，誠是有理，然奴僕實與閭里相關，今都不問，恐有所失。意同左[74]丞議。

Again it is the rhetorical slave that produces the most trenchant arguments, but where Xie Yuan had used the slave as a symbol for gentry indemnification, He Shangzhi uses it as a sign of gentry guilt. Where the symbol stood for the concept of gentry distinction, the sign points to the existence of a whole class of thing—the wantonly rich gentry. Where the symbol lent intellectual grandeur to a delicate argument, the sign gives the argument a broad sweep, and practical effect, allowing He Shangzhi

---

71. The Cheng and the Zhuo were wealthy Sichuan merchant families of the Western Han, noted together by Sima Qian (*Shiji* 129.3277–78), who describes the Zhuo as "so wealthy that they owned a thousand slaves."

72. Yan Hui and Yuan Xian were impoverished and favored disciples of Confucius; see *Shiji* 67.2187–88 and 67.2207–8, where the noble poverty of both men is emphasized.

73. The *Cefu yuangui* reads 常 for 恆. This is a taboo substitution, avoiding the given name of Song emperor Zhenzong (r. 997–1022).

74. *Cefu yuangui* incorrectly writes 右.

to repartition or *redefine* the matter at hand, making it no longer a contrast of gentry and commoner, but of the dominating rich and bad gentry against the more numerous noble and poor variety. The need for this remedy is emphasized with a topic of contrary consequence: the state shows favor to the bad gentry (who by rights ought to be targeted) while inadvertently discriminating against the good (who ought to be protected). In hyperbolically, absolutely wrong fashion, the state's beneficence has "always" (*chang*) gone to those who least deserve it, while it has been "certain" (*bi*) to prosecute these latter-day disciples of Confucius. Adopting the perspective of the noble poor, the speaker watches helplessly as the rich "trample heedlessly" (*aoran*) over the state's laws. His mission is to set this course of consequence aright.

Technically, He Shangzhi is joining the opinion of Jiang Ao, who has said that slaves, insofar as they do have material interaction with commoners, may be prosecuted. But in spirit his argument is altogether different. For Jiang Ao, slaves are bad, and being bad they are absolutely separate from the gentry, who are, by their own definition, good. For He Shangzhi, slaves are bad insofar as they are a constituent property of a certain kind of (bad) gentry—and so they stand for their masters. The slave as sign allows him to distinguish rich from poor, false from real, and Jiang Ao's position is repurposed for the energetic prosecution of slaves, and thus of their masters.

He Shangzhi has no recorded opinion on the second question. Having made his point, he yielded the stage to Wang Hong, returning to deliver his long summary opinion.

The Orchestrator Returns

The debaters argue individually, but in concert: a defense of gentry prerogative (Jiang Ao); then some concessions to the state (Kong Mozhi, the only speaker to respond somewhat positively to the question of conscription); a full-throated renewal of the defense of gentry interests (Wang Zhunzhi, rejecting any concession on the slaves); a purification of that pro-gentry argument (Xie Yuan, purging Wang Zhunzhi's circumstantial tendencies); and then a sudden counterpoint, asserting the need for a vigorously righteous state to regulate a distinction *within* gentry society—the eternal problem of rich versus poor (He Shangzhi). Picking up the theme of that counterpoint, Wang Hong begins his judgment with a reformulation of the first debate question—and a direct attack on Wang Zhunzhi:

> Wang Hong advocated:
> If we examine the laws and statutes, they make no distinction between gentry and commoner. Likewise, there is no place in which we do not find cases of gentrymen being punished with their neighborhood groups, but because most of them receive the grace of timely pardon, not all of them personally suffer the punishment. Recently, in Wu and Yixing there were individuals from the Xu and Lu families who were brought up on charges[75] together with their neighborhood groups, but the prefects at the time submitted the vermilion judgment of guilt [for imperial judgment],[76] and in the end, it was put to rest. And some gentry from Guiji have said that ten or so years ago members of the "four [powerful] clans" were also found culpable according to this process, though they were able to rely on imperial grace to obtain reprieve.[77] Nevertheless, Secretary Wang claims that in the past there was no gentry responsibility—this I fail to understand. Might it be because he did not encounter this matter during his time in office?
>
> [Now,] with a sagely presence governing the age, the gentry truly need not worry about being treated too severely. The problem is rather that it creates a good deal of trouble to have everything presented to the Emperor for decision on a case-by-case basis. It would be best if we could arrive at a substatute for this, one that strikes a balance between the heavy and the light.

---

75. The phrase *he ji* does appear in at least one legal context (*Tang lü shuyi* 16.311), but its precise meaning here is unclear to me, and the similarity of characters presents the likeness of a textual problem. Yet it must mean something like this, as Kawai (*Nanchō kizokusei kenkyū*, 105) construes it.

76. The term "vermilion judgment of guilt" (*danshu*, literally "vermilion document"), is from the *Zuozhuan* (Xiang 23); compare Lu Ji at *Wen xuan* 37.1699, who speaks of the emperor "erasing his guilt from the vermilion document."

77. *Shishuo xinyu* 8/85 (cited by Kawai, *Nanchō kizokusei kenkyū*, 117n20) uses the same term, "four clans" (*si zu*), and identifies them as the Shen 沈, Wei 魏, Yu 虞, and Xie 謝. An instance of the prosecution of powerful Guiji families in 411 is noted in the *Song shu* annals (2.27), with reference to similar events after 405.

弘議曰：尋律令，既不分別士庶，又人士坐同伍糾謫者，無處無之，多為時恩所宥，故不盡親謫耳。吳及義興適有許、陸之徒，以同符合給，二千石論啟丹書，已、未問[78]。會稽人士云，十數年前，亦有四族坐比[79]被責，以恃[80]恩獲停。而王尚書云[81]舊無同伍坐，所未之解。恐茌任之日，偶不值此事故耶？聖明御世，人(亡識)[士誠][82]不憂至苦，然要須臨事論通，上干天聽，徒[83]為紛擾，不如近與[84]定科，使輕重有節也。

78. The *Song shu* printings and the *Cefu yuangui* print these characters as 已未問. The 1974 Zhonghua edition instead reads 己未間, connecting it to the following clause, thus: "Sometime around the *jiwei* year, that is, around 419. This possibly makes sense, but there is no explanation in the edition or in the full collation notes. The reading of our two earliest texts makes good sense if we take *si* 巳 as *yi* 已 and punctuate with the following clause, as does Kawai (*Nanchō kizokusei kenkyū*, 105). The new Zhonghua edition, meanwhile, and with no note, punctuates with the older edition but prints 己未問. This is not what their claimed base text has, and it is not clear what sense it makes.

79. Here following the *Song shu*. The *Cefu yuangui* has *ci* 此 for *bi* 比, and Wang Zhongluo (*Song shu jiaokan ji changbian*, 1050, specifying a silent change) emends his *Song shu*. The new Zhonghua edition retains *bi*. Kawai (*Nanchō kizokusei kenkyū*, 104) has *ci*, but Masumura ("Sō sho," 46) reads *bi* and provides textual evidence from a similar context (*Song shu* 54.1524, "culpability in a neighbor group" *biwu zhi zuo* 比伍之坐). The more technical *bi* may have degraded into the more common and graphically similar *ci*.

80. Both the Beiping Library *Song shu* and the *Cefu yuangui* read 恃, but the later printings of this edition have recut blocks here, dated 1531, and show a graph that resembles 時, which is taken up in later editions. The Zhonghua edition silently follows this later reading (as specified at Wang Zhongluo, *Song shu jiaokanji changbian*, 1050, which does not note that the *Cefu yuangui* testifies against it). This produces the same term, "timely grace," that appears several clauses above. This could be right, but there is weak textual basis for it, and the rhetorical flavor of "relying on grace" better suits Wang's argument. Masumura and Kawai read 時, as does the new Zhonghua edition.

81. All *Song shu* insert *ren* 人, "people," here. This word could have dropped out of the *Cefu yuangui*—or, given all the other appearances of *ren* in the surrounding text, its insertion could be a copyist's error.

82. All *Song shu* have *shiren cheng* 士人誠, but I believe the *Cefu yuangui* reading, 人亡識, contains an indication of what the text originally said: the correct reading is likely *renshi cheng* 人士誠, the latter two characters having corrupted to the graphically similar 亡 and 識. Thus, the text continues to prefer the less common collocation *renshi*.

83. Only the *Cefu yuangui* preserves this character. Wang Zhongluo notes this in his full collation notes (1050–51) but does not emend or add a note to his text.

84. All *Song shu* have 為 for 與. There is little to choose between the two readings, but note the appearance of 為 six characters above.

This broadside against Wang Zhunzhi reveals an important element in court rhetoric, and of the documentary record more generally: its use as a weapon in political battle. There was a history of personal enmity between these two men. Wang Zhunzhi was born a year before Wang Hong, to a different branch of the famed Langya Wang clan.[85] In his mid-twenties he served on the cabinet of the ill-fated Huan Xuan, and—perhaps eager to erase that error—he was an early adherent to the Founding Ancestor's cause. The background to this particular interchange goes to 418, when he was made "censor" in the Founding Ancestor's Duchy of Song; a position charged with maintaining discipline in the official ranks, his father and grandfather had held this post under the Jin. Shortly thereafter, the poet-aristocrat Xie Lingyun extra-legally executed one of his servants, and Xie was duly prosecuted and removed from office—but not at the direction of Wang Zhunzhi. Wang Zhunzhi had let the offense slide, and it was Wang Hong himself, as Director (*puye*) of the Founding Ancestor's shadow cabinet, who sought the punishment, and when he did so he also insisted on a reprimand for Wang Zhunzhi for dereliction of duty.[86] Wang Zhunzhi was dismissed from his position, though he would return to court upon the Founding Ancestor's accession to the throne, in the sixth month of 420.

As we follow the careers of the two Wangs through the 420s, we find them on opposing court factions. Wang Zhunzhi served as Senior Aide under Xu Xianzhi in 424, before Xu's downfall, and he later affiliated himself with Liu Yikang, the prince who would replace Wang Hong as the preeminent power at court. His biography features an anecdote in which the newly ascendant Liu Yikang expresses confidence that "with two or three men just like Wang Zhunzhi, the empire will be ruled well," while

---

85. See Wang Zhunzhi's biography, *Song shu* 60.1623–25. The difference between these two men serves as a reminder that the basic unit of social and political organization in early medieval China was the family, clustered around the agnatic grandfather-father-son trunk, not the clan. Whatever cachet membership in the "Langya Wang" gave him, Wang Hong's advantages were primarily derived from the political prominence of his father, Wang Xun.

86. *Song shu* 60.1624, 42.1313. Wang Hong's accusation is itself an excellent specimen of documentary rhetoric: he proposes harsh punishments, giving the Founding Ancestor the opportunity to demonstrate his beneficence by way of a lighter judgment.

Wang Hong, just around the time of our debate, is shown flatly informing Wang Zhunzhi that a competitor for his cabinet post was superior to him.[87] This was factional strife, but beneath it may also lie real differences of political position. There is ample evidence, beyond the present debate, that Wang Zhunzhi was a defender of gentry privilege. Favorable reports from his local postings, duly noted in his biography, indicate soft handling of the local elites, an approach that also explains his willingness to overlook Xie Lingyun's crime. In 420, he lobbied the new emperor for state recognition of the mourning period customary among the gentry, twenty-seven months, instead of the officially regulated term of twenty-five (or twenty-six) months, a symbolic difference that, with the emperor's approval, represented a state concession to gentry self-definition.[88] Wang Hong, by contrast, appears to have believed that the gentry had grown slack in its moral purpose, and that the remedy for this condition was the firm hand of the state.[89] Wang Zhunzhi was just the sort of gentryman Wang Hong could do without.

Wang Hong marshals two topics in his repudiation of Wang Zhunzhi. The first is Wang Zhunzhi's own—circumstance. Grasping the bull

87. In adherence to the annals-biography form, the positive comment is in his biography (*Song shu* 60.1624), the negative appraisal in the biography of the court competitor (*Song shu* 54.1535, Yang Xuanbao) who is praised by Wang Hong.

88. Wang Zhunzhi's biography puts this in 421, quoting a memorial presented by Wang (*zou* 奏, a "submission" to the throne) that specifies twenty-five months as the old official term; *Song shu* 60.1624. Without mention of Wang's role, the annals (*Song shu* 3.56) record the change but place it in the tenth month of 420 and put the old term at twenty-six months. The treatise on ritual, meanwhile, places the change in 420 and quotes, with attribution, an abridged version of Wang Zhunzhi's opinion (*yi* 議, "discussion"), the specification of twenty-five months being one of the deleted phrases (*Song shu* 15.392–93).

89. In the interpretation of Kawai Yasushi, the elite (or the "aristocracy," a misnomer) had reached the peak of its power in the early fifth century, but to maintain that power a renewal of vigor was necessary, and that was the question underlying this debate. This view is a refinement of the more functional approach of earlier scholars, who read the debate either as confirmation of the state's indulgence of gentry prerogative or, to the contrary, as evidence of the imperial court's attempt to assert greater authority over the gentry. See Kawai, *Nanchō kizokusei kenkyū*, 99–100, 114.

by the horns, Wang Hong turns to a more absolute form of circumstance, finding that the problem is not that Wang Zhunzhi's knowledge is circumstantial, but that his knowledge of circumstance is so insufficient. "There is no place in which we do not find cases of gentrymen being punished," Wang Hong declares absolutely, going on to dispense with him with arch sarcasm: "Might [his ignorance of what is demonstrably true] be because he did not encounter this matter during his time in office?"

As he rejects Wang Zhunzhi, Wang Hong shifts the ground to a higher form of argument from definition: the law, where he looks but does not find an adequate definition of gentry prerogative.[90] Keeping his focus on the law, Wang Hong identifies a specific lack of gentry distinction in regulations governing the crucial matter at hand, neighborhood groups:

> Furthermore, if we examine the regulations on neighborhood groups, they simply say that government servants, being absolved of regular service obligations, will not be registered on the tallies;[91] assistants and clerks, likewise exempt from service requirements, are also treated this way.[92] [Members of the groups] mutually "press" and control one another. If one person does wrong then another must report him, and this holds for everyone, with absolutely no regard for distinctions of status. It is not true that gentry are exempt from the neighborhood groups.

90. The early fourth-century memorial in the *Jin shu* legal treatise (20.939) cited above enjoins participants in legal discussions to cite specific laws and precedents. Wang Hong makes a point of outdoing the other debaters in this regard.

91. The sub-commentary to Article 33 of the Tang Code quotes a statute (*ling*) to this effect; *Tang lü shuyi* 4.91.

92. See the entry on these "assistants and clerks" (*lingshi*) at Du You, *Tongdian* 22.608–10. One story there indicates that these clerks often came from socially low but rich and powerful families, and as such came into conflict with the more orthodox gentry. See also *Song shu* 39.1237, which suggests there were several hundred such clerks in the Secretariat at this time.

又尋甲符制，蠲士人[93]不傳[94]符耳。令史復除，亦得如之。共相押領，有違糾列，了無等衰，非許人士閭里之外也。

The previous speakers have all subscribed unquestioningly to the belief that gentry are "naturally distinct." Wang Hong dismantles this definition, or at least its relevance, with a new distinction—between men serving the state at a given moment and men who are not. It is these men—whether they were proper gentry officials or "assistants and clerks" from the lower social echelon—who were freed from neighborhood groups, as a perquisite and, presumably, because they could surveil one another quite well enough at the office. This is indeed a precise definition of the word most conventionally associated with the "gentry"—*shi* 士, literally "to serve." Wielding this correct and legally pertinent definition, Wang Hong declares plainly and absolutely that the gentry lack legal indemnity. This is "simply" (the sentence-ending particle *er*) what the law says, and gentry exception categorically does not exist (the construction *fei . . . ye*). In the eyes of the law, he determines, there are "absolutely no distinctions at all" (*liao wu dengshuai*).

Wang Hong continues with a high-handed demonstration of the defective consequences that follow from the definition he has rejected, expounding upon how we know that the gentry are *not* naturally distinct:

> If, according to the various proposals, there is an absolute distinction between gentry and commoner, such that they cannot have knowledge of each other's actions, then when a gentryman commits an offense, the commoner should be free of responsibility. For if we require the commoner to be cognizant of the gentry, how could we absolve the gentry of responsibility for knowing about the commoner? It is not as if the commoners dwell in lofty seclusion, aloof from the dusts and husks of the mundane world! They are right there next door, and the gentry will always be able to hear of their every little action, regardless of whether or not they interact on a daily basis. The

---

93. Here *Cefu yuangui* does read 士人, but this is an exception, because 蠲士人 is a bound phrase, "men who are absolved due to service."

94. Masumura ("Sō sho," 46, followed by Kawai) observes that this character should probably be the graphically similar *fu* 傅. This was a standard term for "attaching" names to a neighborhood group tally.

Assistant of the Right's words about officials [knowing what their subordinates are doing] had roughly the right idea of the matter.

諸議云,士庶緬絕,不相參知,則人士犯法,庶民得不知。若[95]庶民不許不知,何許人士不知?小民自非超然簡獨永絕塵甈者。比門接棟,小以為意,終自聞知,不必須日夕[96]來往也。右丞百司之言,粗是其況。

Skilled semiotician that he is, Wang Hong sees that social separation is not a property that would belong to the gentry, but a relational quality that could describe the commoners equally well—and thus produce the preposterous consequence of commoners freed from the responsibility system. Again wresting the topic of circumstance from Wang Zhunzhi, he shows that the allegedly natural distinction has no real pragmatic value either. What is absolute (*zhong zi*, "will always," or "in the end, they will naturally") is not gentry distinction, but the reality of gentry-commoner interaction in their bustling lower Yangtze world. He accentuates this point with a sardonic application of a stock description of the lofty gentry eremite to a hypothetical commoner, pictured as a quiet recluse, aloof from the "mundane world."

In the next segment of his speech, Wang Hong uses two salient problem cases to further interrogate natural gentry privilege:

> As for gentry of fallen station, they actually do live right there [with the commoners] in the hamlets and lanes. In their knowledge of what happens there, they may as well be considered "commoners in gentry garb." If today we call them "men of officialdom," then [under your proposals] they would be absolved of responsibility for the commoners [with whom they dwell], while if we class them as commoners, they would be punished for offenses committed by other gentry. Whether we consider the legal basis or the facts of the matter, would this not be imbalanced?
>
> The chief clerks, on the other hand, are not considered members of the gentry, for the gentry regard them with scorn. Thus they belong to the petty commoners—but if today we make them liable for offenses [of commoner

---

95. *Cefu yuangui* has dropped the above six characters. Apparently, a copyist skipped the first clause beginning with 庶民.

96. Here following the *Song shu*. *Cefu yuangui* prints the graphically similar 多 (perhaps, "much daily interaction").

和 gentry alike], we will create much discord in the ranks. That is hardly the point of the neighborhood group system, which was intended to prevent [disorder].

如袁[97]陵人士[98]，實與里巷關接[99]，相知情狀，乃當於冠帶小民。今謂之人士，[100]便無[101]小人[102]之坐，署為小民，輒受人士之罰，於情於法，[103]不其頗歟？且[104]都令不及士流，士流（何）[105]為輕，則小人。今[106]使徵預其罰，便事至相糾，閭伍之防，亦為不同。

97. *Cefu yuangui* prints 裏, a graphic error.
98. Here once more the *Song shu* read *shiren* for *renshi*, as again in the following sentence.
99. The character *jie* 接 is a lacuna in the Beiping Library *Song shu*; the other old printings, which in this location have blocks recut in 1491, supply *tong* 通. This is certainly a conjectural emendation. Wang Zhongluo follows *Cefu yuangui*, with a note. Again, the new Zhonghua edition reverses Wang's choice, noting the *Cefu yuangui* and adopting the conjecture of the repaired *Song shu*.
100. The *Nan shi* excerpt of this opinion begins with this clause, minus the opening 今. Excerpting in this fashion twists Wang Hong's point from a specific one about a borderline group (from whom one may draw broader conclusions) to a general one about legal requirements on the gentry. Note that the *Nan shi* supports the *Cefu yuangui* reading of *renshi*, as opposed to *shiren* in the *Song shu* printings.
101. Here following the *Song shu*. *Cefu yuangui* reads the graphically similar 與, "join," but Wang Hong's meaning is that if they are classified as gentry then they will *not* be "joined" into commoner offenses. The *Song shu* reading is supported by the *Nan shi* excerpt.
102. *Nan shi* reads 庶人 here, and again for 小民 in the following clause. The latter would appear to be a taboo substitution.
103. *Nan shi* omits this clause, retains the final clause of this sentence, and omits the following section on "chief clerks."
104. *Cefu yuangui* prints this character with a 入, similar to 具.
105. The *Song shu* lacks the character 何. It does not make good sense, but perhaps it is a corruption of something else—for instance, 以 would make sense and produce smooth syntax for this passage.
106. The character *jin* 今 is clear in *Cefu yuangui*, but all *Song shu* texts have *ling* 令. The Zhonghua editions punctuate *ling shi* 令使 with *xiaoren* 小人 above it and through the end of the clause: 則小人令使徵預其罰. It is not clear to me what viable meaning such a phrase can produce, but Kawai (*Nanchō kizokusei kenkyū*, 106) adopts this punctuation and produces the right sense in his paraphrase. Masamura retains *ling shi* but punctuates and interprets as I do here. That is better, but the best solution is to follow the earliest witness—the sense of *jin shi* ("if today," or simply "if") in the *Cefu yuangui* is salient.

An absolute distinction entails an absolute absence of middle ground, so the existence of these two middle-ground cases points to a fault in the ideal of gentry self-definition. Referring to actual social facts that were certainly known to the other speakers, but painstakingly avoided by them, "gentry of fallen station"—perhaps a euphemism for gentry without prospect for an official career—"actually" (*shi*) dwelled among the commoners. Conversely, commoners in powerful positions in the sub-bureaucracy regularly interacted with the gentry proper, and in some sense belonged to the gentry broadly conceived as a historical class, however much the "real" gentry looked down on them.[107] The idea of gentry distinction cannot, Wang shows, be applied fairly to either of these very significant social groups. The perspective advanced here is neither pro- nor anti-gentry, but assertively public and impartial, arguing that only a strictly legal approach can avoid "imbalance" (*po*) and "discord" (*xiang jiu*). The gentry's defining powers are not so much abrogated as rendered irretrievably biased, and gentry self-regulation cannot but be supplemented, or supplanted, by Wang Hong the Definer and the imperial authority for which he stands.

Wang Hong's final judgment on this question follows:

> In my view, it is true that gentry cannot be punished with their neighborhood groups. [But] what harm could there be in punishing their slaves and clients in their stead? Those without slaves or clients can be punished with fines. And if there are persons who, while dwelling in ordinary society, have dedicated themselves to study and self-cultivation, and proved themselves truly distinct from the petty masses, or if there are persons whose slave holdings are not publicly known,[108] then [in these two situations] the

---

107. This disdain is famously illustrated in the biography of Tao Yuanming, who (it is said) quits his magistracy rather than bow to the lowly folk serving as local inspectors (*Song shu* 93.2287, and compare 92.2268).

108. Here I construe this phrase as a complement to the one that, in the *Nan shi*, precedes it: officials are to report (for another example of *lie shang* in this same context, see *Song shu* 5.80) poor gentlemen, on the one hand, and people with concealed wealth, on the other. Another possibility seems to be "in cases of people who have no slaves, and are particularly esteemed (*ming*) by the masses ..."; the punctuation in the Zhonghua *Nan shi* 或無奴僮，為眾所明者 may suggest such a reading. Perhaps better still, Masamura ("Sō sho," 45–47) interprets it as "when it is clearly known (*ming*) to the public that a person has no slaves," and Kawai (*Nanchō kizokusei kenkyū*, 106), construing it differently

magistrates and the prefects ought to personally carry out an investigation and submit the results to the court, where decisions will be made according to the case.

謂人士可不受同伍之謫耳[109]。罪其奴客，庸何傷邪？無奴客，可令輸贖。[有修身閭閻，與羣小實隔，][110] 又或無奴僅為眾所明者，官長二千石便當親臨列上，依事遣判。[111]

Wang endorses the solution advocated by Kong Mozhi, whose analogy ("had roughly the right idea," *cu shi*) he approved of above: gentry may use slaves and fines in lieu of punishment. The insouciant tone of his endorsement, however, implies a different objective. He allows gentry indemnity as a "mere" fact (the final particle *er* again). By putting his judgment in the form of a rhetorical question ("what harm could there be . . ."), he suggests that only the misguided—like Wang Zhunzhi—could have thought the gentry could be let off the hook entirely. Moreover, he adds two specific clauses, granting the state the agency to expand and contract the gentry ranks. In this, he joins the interventionist spirit of He Shangzhi.

Turning to the second question, Wang Hong continues to project this critical edge, the ethos of the imperial minister, from the gentry but not of it, reorganizing society for the greater public (imperial) good:

> As for thefts of five and forty bolts, respectively, it had been my opinion that the punishments should be ameliorated. This was truly because petty clerks, in their ignorance, may find themselves overcome by greed when handling items of value, or they may find themselves guilty of a severe crime simply

---

but with similar effect, "when people are able to testify to the fact that a person clearly (*ming*) does not have slaves." Regardless, Wang Hong is following the line of He Shangzhi, distinguishing pure gentry from the bad ones with large holdings of slaves and bondsmen. Compare *Shishuo xinyu* 3/4, which recounts a third-century magistrate flushing illicit bondservants out of the estates of the southeastern high gentry.

109. For the final *er* 耳, *Nan shi* reads *qu* 取 ("take"). This seems to be a corruption, but the modern edition punctuates it with the following clause.

110. These two clauses are only found in the *Nan shi*. As it seems unlikely that the *Nan shi* would have invented this out of whole cloth, I regard it as integral, but it is curious that it should have dropped out of the *Song shu* as a whole, and prior to the compilation of the *Cefu yuangui*.

111. *Nan shi*'s treatment of question one ends here.

because they acted carelessly. Pondering this in my heart, I have often felt it a pity, and thus I wished to raise the amounts somewhat and make their lives less precarious. When it comes to the magistrates and above (i.e., appointments staffed by the gentry proper), however, they receive great honor and emolument and have been entrusted with the management of a bureau of the government. They should rectify their conduct and illuminate the laws of the empire, monitoring their subordinates and preventing wrongdoing. Yet some of them would personally violate the laws and statutes, obscuring the law in reckless pursuit of profit. For these, five bolts is sufficient allowance indeed! And no gentrymen out of office would have reason to conspire to steal forty bolts [and thus be subject to conscription]! If they did, it would doubtlessly be appropriate to have them punished according to the law. What pity would be due to them? Still, this kind of gentryman can be killed but cannot be punished, just as you have said.

偷五疋四十疋謂應見優量者，實以小吏無知，臨財易昧，或由疎慢，事蹈重科，[112]求之於心，常有可愍，故欲[113]小進疋數，寬其性命耳。至於官長以上，荷蒙祿榮，[114]付以局任，當正己明憲，檢下防非，而親犯科律，亂法冒利，五疋乃已為弘矣。士人[115]無私[116]相偷四十疋理。就[117]使至此，致

112. The *Nan shi* omits the following four clauses, substituting for them a sentence drawn from the original proposition: "we should raise the amounts to ten bolts for a person in charge and fifty in ordinary circumstances, with punishment reduced to conscription in the army for thefts of forty or less" 宜進主守偷十疋，常偷五十疋死，四十疋降以補兵.

113. The *Cefu yuangui* has dropped this character.

114. The *Nan shi* omits the following four clauses, breaking the fifth clause in half and putting it with the end of the sentence: "[to allow them to] recklessly pursue the profit of five bolts is already sufficient" 冒利五疋，乃已為弘.

115. The Beiping Library copy misprints 七人 for 士人; this is corrected in the 1531 recut blocks, on which see also the following note. Here *Cefu yuangui* reads *shiren*, not *renshi*. This makes some sense, because Wang Hong is referring to strictures on the gentry as a social class, but the *Cefu yuangui* reverts to *renshi* three sentences below.

116. The Beiping Library copy and the *Cefu yuangui* print *hong* 弘, which has just appeared five spots above, for *si* 私. This is very likely a graphic corruption—their common base text must have had this error. The *Nan shi* has the correct graph, and when this *Song shu* page was recut in 1531, a correction was made. The "Bona" edition produces the Beiping Library block here but with this and the preceding error (七人) silently corrected.

117. *Cefu yuangui* lacks this character.

以明罰，固其宜耳。並何容復加哀矜？且此輩人士[118]可殺不可讁，有如諸論。[119]

Re-defining the point at issue, Wang Hong tells the court that what he "really" (*shi*) meant with this proposal was to show lenience to the lesser members of the bureaucratic ranks, whether they committed offenses in supervisory or subordinate positions. It was *not* to show lenience to the gentry proper, be they in office or out, for the true gentryman has no "reason" to steal anything. To him, existing legislation is already sufficiently "generous" (*hong*).

Here Wang Hong's audience will certainly come to ask: if he never intended the new rule to apply to the gentry, why did he not say so from the beginning? Wang's answer, and the real answer his answer conceals, is given in the final words of his speech:

> But this was not my original intention. I heard talk of this in the street the other day and it occurred to me that we might discuss it, not anticipating that the matter would prove so complex. Given that the various opinions are irreconcilable, it seems best to put the matter to rest. If, on the other hand, we are not willing to do so, I say we should gather together our opinions and submit them to the throne, allowing the Sagely Emperor to make the decision.

> 本意自不在此也。近聞之道路，聊欲共論，不呼乃爾難精。既眾議糾紛，將不如其已。若呼不應停寢，謂宜集議奏聞，決之聖旨。

This is a classic thresholding move. He has raised a provocative, even disturbing issue, one that concerns the privileges of the early medieval political order's protected social class. This is not something a Prime Minister does lightly, and yet that is how he frames the debate, as a subject he raised

---

118. Following *Cefu yuangui*, supported by *Nan shi*. The *Song shu* texts continue to read *shiren*.

119. The *Nan shi* stitches the final sentence together as follows: 士人至此，何容復加哀矜。且此輩人士可殺不可讁. It then misleadingly appends clauses from Wang Hong's closing statement: "I say we should submit [these cases] to the throne, allowing the Sagely Emperor to make the decision" 謂宜奏聞，決之聖旨. But Wang Hong is submitting their debate record to throne.

without any particular motive. "This was not my original intention"—then what was? I heard it "in the street"—and brought roadway gossip into court?[120] The matter has proved "so complex"—because the original question was so poisonous? Perhaps we should "put the matter to rest"—and what was the point of the discussion? Distancing himself from the question, exteriorizing himself from it, *circumstantializing* the whole affair, he paradoxically revives and enhances the rhetorical exigence he ostensibly puts to rest. Were Wang Hong to speak plainly, he would say: Representatives of the empire's gentry, I am simply rattling your cage. You must now see my "original intention." Are you not ashamed, to be apologizing so fervently for the private interests of your social class, or its none too worthy members? Do you not now see how a true gentryman, as a "man of officialdom," should speak? Do you not see the firm hand the state will apply to you—or not, by its own beneficence? Whatever definitions his interlocutors have established, whatever consequences they have produced—all that was substantive about the debate has been swept aside. What remains, and what is exalted by the other participants' diminution, is the authority of Wang Hong and the state he represents. When the questions were posed, "ought" (*yi*) was materially transitive—the debate was about taking action. Now, the debate over, that "ought," the nucleus of exigence, is revealed to be truly rhetorical, not about taking action, but demonstrating the ethos of the debate's convener.

Finally, the discussion is turned into a written document and presented to an audience far above Wang Hong's court interlocutors—the emperor, who affirms his rhetorical performance.

> The Grand Ancestor Emperor [Emperor Wen] issued an edict:
> The Defender General's opinion is the appropriate one.[121]

太祖詔：衛軍議為允。

---

120. "I heard talk of this in the street" is again a light evocation of the voice of Confucius, who, at *Analects* 17/9, warns that it is not virtuous to participate in such talk.

121. *Nan shi* and *Tongdian* paraphrase the conclusion in ways that read more resolutely. The former says that "Emperor Wen followed Wang Hong's proposal" 文帝從弘議; the latter, which quotes Wang Hong's two debate questions as his opinions, that "these were followed" 從之.

Into the Historical Frame

In the early months of his reign, the Founding Ancestor issued a flurry of short edicts. He granted fiefs and promulgated amnesties, he lowered taxes and raised salaries, he sent delegates out to inspect conditions in the provinces, he increased the state-sanctioned mourning period by 4 percent. One of these edicts introduced a minor institutional adjustment that may have had a direct effect on the debate we have examined here: noting that discussions of policy issues were often abridged and synthesized and presented in a collective form, he commanded that henceforth opinions should be presented individually, with their authors' names attached.[122] The effect of that order was to turn discussion into speech and questions of governance into matters of political representation.

Not that debate necessarily required such an intervention to be recognized as an authored genre. If not quite a fully fledged literary form, Liu Xie 劉勰 (d. ca. 522) does treat "discussions" (*yi* 議)—the genre label used in this document—in his great treatise on literary writing, defining it as the realm of "ought" (*yi* 宜), and debate was a hallowed structural device in fictional literature, notably the rhyme-prose (*fu*).[123] The discussions that come down to us in Wang's biography are like short literary works, representing the aims and temperaments of the individual speakers, and as an articulated whole orchestrated by Wang Hong, it serves as his own well-wrought ethos presentation, the main purpose of many a literary composition. Thus, leveraging the literary and political qualities of court discussion, Wang Hong, with his underlings acting as his foils, wrote himself into history as the stalwart minister of his age.

Or did he? For historiographical representation started but did not end with the actor. It is true that Wang Hong's court nemesis, the prince Liu Yikang, would first be reduced to the status of a commoner and then executed, while Wang himself would be on the right side of history, nominated, with Liu Muzhi, for inclusion in the imperial temple, and arrayed, likewise with Liu Muzhi, at the forefront of the Liu-Song *History*. The

---

122. *Song shu* 3.56, in the eighth month of 420.
123. Liu Xie, *Wenxin diaolong zhushi* 24.265.

debate opponent toward whom he directs his scorn, Wang Zhunzhi, would also receive a decidedly checkered historiographical account, damned with faint praise by Shen Yue: "full of talent, but lacking in wisdom—what a shame!" 蓋由才有餘而智未足也，惜矣哉.[124] Most importantly, Shen Yue's inclusion of this debate in the *History of the Liu-Song* was at least in part due to his agreement with the critical points made here by Wang Hong: Shen also believed that the early Liu-Song gentry deserved little leniency, and he himself, on several occasions, encouraged the state to intervene in gentry affairs in ways that would have put fear into Wang Zhunzhi.[125]

Nevertheless, Wang Hong was a part of that Liu-Song gentry, no matter how he might present himself. We recall from chapter 2 Shen Yue's historian's judgment in scroll 42: there was no mention there of Wang Hong. This might be explained away as a question of emphasis, not judgment. It might also be a reflection of the historian's cautious reticence, for Wang Hong was the great-uncle of a founding minister of the Qi, Wang Jian 王儉 (452–89).[126] But it is also an expression of doubt, in the historiographical mode of "subtle words" (*wei yan*). This is the more ambivalent historiographical appraisal of Wang Hong that is suggested in the *History*'s treatment of his heir, who "rode a high horse."[127] And it appears in Wang Hong's biography as well, where he is qualified as an all too human creature:

---

124. *Song shu* 60.1629. As noted earlier, Wang Zhunzhi's biography says that he was much appreciated in Shanyin, and the same is said of his later term as prefect of Liyang. But with the rise of Wang Hong, his biography changes tack, twice declaring that Wang Zhunzhi was *not* held in high regard by the gentry elite. See *Song shu* 60.1624.

125. Notably, his rejection of a marriage agreement struck by a gentryman with a commoner (*Wen xuan* j. 40) and his discussion of falsified household registrations (Du You, *Tongdian* 3.59–61), both of which postdate the compilation of the *Song shu*. For a discussion of Shen Yue's political philosophy, see Yoshikawa Tadao, *Rikuchō seishinshi kenkyū*, chapter 7.

126. Wang Jian was the grandson of Wang Tanshou, the younger brother who played a key role Wang Hong's political group.

127. For his heir, Wang Xi 王錫, see *Song shu* 42.1323, describing him as *gao zi wei yu* 高自位遇.

And yet, he was rash and could act in an undignified way, and by nature he was irritable and intolerant. Whenever someone offended him, he would curse them to their face.

而輕率少威儀，性又褊隘，人忤意者，輒面加責辱。

This characterization is followed by an acid anecdote that serves as the historiographical punctuation to Wang Hong's "life." It is nothing short of an indirect riposte to the very image Wang crafts in his debate document:

> In his youth, he had sometimes gambled at the lodgings of [a certain] Gongcheng Ziye. Later, when he had reached a position of power, someone came to him to beg for appointment as a county magistrate. He was most insistent. As it happens, this person had once been brought up on charges for gambling, so Wang Hong berated him: "You can gamble for money, can't you? What need have you of an official salary?"
>
> To this the man replied: "I wonder where I might find Gongcheng Ziye..." And Wang Hong fell silent.

少時嘗摴蒲公城子野舍，及後當權，有人就弘求縣，辭訴頗切。此人嘗以蒲戲得罪，弘詰之曰：「君得錢會戲，何用祿為！」答曰：「不審公城子野何在？」弘默然。

Wang Hong, or the historical character "Wang Hong," falls silent, and the historian is not inclined to speak on his behalf.

※

In the end, Wang Hong is granted "interiority" by virtue of his location in the *History*, and in his overall presentation there, including the moral ground he is allowed to stake out with his debate document. At the same time, to some degree the historian has exteriorized him from the authoritative image he projected in his life and documents, by leaving him in the less stable realm of anecdote and by withholding the confirmation of a positive historical judgment. As was the case with Liu Muzhi, however, we are left to wonder how vitiating such an ambivalent outcome was. As Liu Muzhi played the prompt in his patron's rise, Wang Hong too left himself on the threshold of interiority, a naturally imperfect statesman contributing partially to the historical accomplishments of the dynasty he served. The political actors of Southern Dynasties China flicker on the historical horizon, now apparent in their own agency, now obscured, just as they might have envisaged, given the historiographical rhetoric they participated in but could hardly control—the production of "primary sources" and their subsumption into history.

FIVE

The Historical Process

> The expansion of the bureaucratic structure of the state in the Han and later, and the replacement of paper for bamboo and silk, resulted in an ever-expanding amount of archival material.
> —Albert E. Dien, "Historiography of the Six Dynasties Period"

Liu Muzhi is identified at the beginning of his biography as a historian type:

> As a young man, he was fond of reading books and their associated commentaries and notes.[1] He read widely and knew much, and his talents were recognized by Jiang Ai of Jiyang.
>
> 少好書、傳，博覽多通，為濟陽江斅所知。(II-A)

Being well versed in the documentation that was behind or would become historiography is how he got his start in life, and exercising control over the flow of documents is how he would spend his last years, both in his capacity as head of the imperial bureaucracy and in a more specifically historiographical way:

---

1. *Shu zhuan* ("books / documents and commentaries / biographies") commonly appears in biographies to refer to fondness for "book learning." An Eastern Han source, the *Dongguan Han ji*, testifies to a fuller form that suggests the translation used here: "the many books and their associated commentaries and notes" (*zhong shu zhuanji* 眾書傳記; cited at *Hou Han shu* 34.1175).

When he found the time, he would copy out books in his own hand, browsing through writings of all sorts and editing documents into publishable form.

裁有閒暇，自手寫書，尋覽篇章，校定墳籍。(III-U)

Together, these passages support the notion that Liu Muzhi led a historiographically informed existence, playing the role of Xun Yu. Yet as we have seen, whatever control of the historiographical record Liu Muzhi possessed was tenuous: other forces contributed, often negatively, to the formation of his image. Put generally, the process of historiography overwhelmed the agency of its individual participants. This chapter identifies three major functions within that process: the flourishing of documentation, the tension between historiography as a public and a private value, and the exigence of an ever-incomplete historical record.

The Documentary Motive

The historiographical act in early medieval China began not with the activities of evaluation, editing, and publication that we conventionally associate with historiography, but with the production of "historical" documents.

One index to the signal importance of the document is the very title of our chief source, the *Song shu*. There is no one single fitting translation of the word. On the analogy of Ban Gu's *History of the Han* (*Han shu*), we have rendered it simply as the "History" of the Liu-Song. The use of *shu* in the title of Ban Gu's work, however, was itself ambiguous.[2] In the narrow sense, it was meant to be the "book," or history, *of the Han*. This at once follows from and stands in contrast to the use of the word in the original title of the historical work authored by Sima Qian and his father, known to us as the *Shiji*, "Records of the Grand Scribe," but called by Sima Qian "The Book (*shu*) of His Excellency [my father] the Grand Scribe" ("Taishigong shu" 太史公書).[3] Thus, *shu* is indeed a book of history, Ban Gu's work being narrower in scope and expressly state-oriented. In a grander sense,

---

2. See *Han shu* 100B.4235, 100B.4271.
3. *Shiji* 130.3319–20.

however, the *Han shu* drew on another aspect of the word's history, alluding back to one of the Confucian Classics: the *Shang shu* 尚書, or "Hallowed Documents." Ban Gu's *Han shu* was meant to provide for the Han what the *Shang shu* did for antiquity: a documentary history. It was this aspect a mid-twentieth-century scholar insisted on when he translated *Han shu* as the "Han Documents," and *not* as "History of the Han," and at least one recent writer has endorsed the suggestion that the purpose of the *Han shu* was more to preserve documents than to present a historical account of its own.[4]

We need not adopt *Documents of the Liu-Song* as the translation for our history, but we should follow through on this insight. What we so readily call "history" was in early medieval China a matter of documents: their production, collection and editing, and the creation of whole works—"books"—in which documentation was adequately contextualized. If the *Song shu* in particular has been criticized for carrying this documentary tendency too far, a look at any of our medieval histories will show that they are, in great part, composed of edited documents.[5] The imperial annals (*ji*) are heavily edited court diaries (*qiju zhu*). The treatises (*zhi*) are based on records held in the state archives, and the efforts of scholars to supplement and edit such records. The biographies (*zhuan* 傳), "commentaries" to the "canon" of history relayed in the annals, are also strongly rooted in documentary materials, drawing from genealogies (*pudie* 譜牒), household registrations (*buji* 簿籍) and other records of official service, posthumously compiled "records of conduct" (*xingzhuang* 行狀), and non-orthodox

---

4. Clyde B. Sargent, "Subsidized History: Pan Ku and the Historical Records of the Former Han Dynasty," esp. 119, 120, 141. For the endorsement, see Stephen W. Durrant, "The Han Histories," 494. For different reasons, Enno Giele, *Imperial Decision-making and Communication in Early China: A Study of Cai Yong's "Duduan,"* 6–9, also proposes that translation of the titles of these histories should adhere to the most basic meaning of the word *shu*, "writings" or "documents."

5. For a notable early criticism, see Liu Zhiji, *Shitong tongshi* 5.113–20 ("Zai wen"). See also Zhao Yi, *Nianer shi zhaji jiaozheng* 10.204. These later critics repeatedly assail early medieval dynastic historiography for this tendency, with Shen Yue's work as the most egregious instance. But by the Tang, the proportion of documentation in a finished history was on the decline, so readers like Liu Zhiji were not engaging this period of Chinese historiography on its own terms.

biographical accounts such as the *biezhuan* 別傳, biographies circulating "separately" (*bie*), not or *not yet* properly edited for inclusion in the "array" (*lie*) of biographies in a dynastic history. Last but not least, as we have seen, actual documents have a place of prominence in the biographies, regularly being quoted at length, and even shorter forms of quotation, marked simply by the word *yue* 曰, "he said," can be understood as a minor mode of the quotidian documentary praxis of the biographical subject. The anecdotes, likewise, which one might be inclined to consider embellishments of orally circulated historical accounts, entered the documentary record at an early stage and circulated in that form.

The point is not to say that historiography was "only" the collecting and editing of documents, or, conversely, to place emphasis on the art of how the documents were selected and presented. Such were the terms of debate when scholars in the mid-twentieth century sought to address the nature of Chinese historiography, to declare it "scissors and paste" or not.[6] Rather, we should turn the perspective around, asking not to what extent historiography was the collection of documents, but to what extent the production of documents was the production of historiography. It is not a coincidence that this culture should have produced both documents and historiography in prodigious quantities, for the two were aspects of the same phenomenon.

The highest level of documentation as historiographical act was the documentary build-up to a transfer of Heaven's Mandate from one

---

6. See Sargent, "Subsidized History"; Homer H. Dubs, "The Reliability of Chinese Histories"; Bielenstein, "The Restoration of the Han Dynasty," 21–40; and Dien, "Historiography of the Six Dynasties Period," 509–11. On the whole, Sargent is polemical and writes too broadly, but he makes important points about the limitations of these "histories"; Dubs, rebutting Sargent, is more precise and deploys textual evidence, but he contributes little to our judgment of the quality of the sources, which is the main point of Sargent's critique. It is also worth noting the different standpoints from which these two scholars approached their material. Dubs had primarily used the "History of the Han" to tell the history of the Han, translating a significant portion of the original work. Sargent wrote his critique after an attempt to use the same source to tell the history of Wang Mang's (r. 9–23) Xin ("New") Dynasty, an important historical epoch excoriated in the *Han shu* as a period of usurpation.

dynastic house to another.[7] This was a political and a ritual process, but it was also a fundamentally documentary one, creating a historical change by laying the foundation for a historiographical account of the rise of a new dynasty. The Founding Ancestor's establishment of the Liu-Song proceeds in this fashion—"causing" the death of Liu Muzhi along the way—but the mechanisms are particularly well illustrated by the negative example of Huan Xuan, the ephemeral emperor of 403–4. Having established himself as a dominant power in the middle Yangtze region, we see him "repeatedly submitting [records of] auspicious sightings, as good omens on his behalf" 屢上禎祥以為己瑞.[8] Note that these are not really omens per se but *records* of omens, documents that warrant his rise. Taking control of the capital, he goes on to choreograph a series of what his biography—in the *History of the Jin*, the "book" of the royal house he overthrew—labels false memorials and forged edicts. This is a typical example, with the historian's narrative contextualization:

> Huan Xuan submitted a false memorial requesting to go back to his fief [in Jiangling], but then himself authored the [responding] edict, commanding him to remain in the capital. When an imperial emissary was sent forth to read this edict, Xuan submitted a second memorial, insisting on his initial request, but quietly sent word to the Son of Heaven that He should issue another edict, in his own handwriting, insisting on retaining Huan in the capital. This was how Huan Xuan acted, always sullying the documents of the state with his false words.
>
> 玄偽上表求歸藩，又自作詔留之，遣使宣旨，玄又上表固請，又諷天子作手詔固留焉。玄好逞偽辭，塵穢簡牘，皆此類也。[9]

---

7. For overviews of this practice, which began with Wang Mang and was an important step in dynastic transitions throughout the early medieval period, see Miyakawa Hisayuki, *Rikuchō shi kenkyū: seiji shakai hen*, chapter 2; Zhao Yi, *Nianer shi zhaji jiaozheng* 7.143–46, 148–49; and Liu Zhiji, *Shitong tongshi* 18.470. For analyses of the process based on a "file," contained in Pei Songzhi's commentary to the *Records of the Three Kingdoms*, of forty-two documents from the Han-Wei dynastic transfer, see Carl Leban, "Managing Heaven's Mandate: Coded Communication in the Accession of Ts'ao P'ei, A.D. 220"; and David R. Knechtges, "The Rhetoric of Imperial Abdication and Accession in a Third-Century Chinese Court: The Case of Cao Pi's Accession as Emperor of the Wei Dynasty."

8. *Jin shu* 99.2590.

9. *Jin shu* 99.2593.

By producing "documents of state" (*jiandu*, literally the "bamboo slips and wood boards" on which official records had traditionally been kept), Huan Xuan creates a historical record that prompts him toward the interior. Later, chased from the capital, he continued with such efforts to shape the documentary record in his favor:

> While abroad, Huan Xuan made a court diary (*qiju zhu*), recounting how he resisted the loyalist forces.[10] In his telling, his direction of his troops was flawless. The generals had disobeyed their orders, and this, not poor strategy, had led to defeat. And thereupon he became so obsessed with telling this version of the story, and promulgating it near and far, that he had no time to consult with his advisors.
>
> 玄於道作起居注，敘其距義軍之事，自謂經略指授，算無遺策，諸將違節度，以致虧喪，非戰之罪。於是不遑與羣下謀議，唯耽思誦述，宣示遠近。[11]

In the end—or the end as told, with relish, in the *History of the Jin*—Huan's subordinates came to refer to him not as "Emperor" but as "Huan, the issuer of edicts" 桓詔.[12] His documentary prowess fully ironized, Huan's historiographical self-fashioning did not in the least carry through to the next stages of the historiographical process.

Wang Hong's debate document shows the documentary process at work on a less exalted level, as does the portrayal of the editing of documents in Liu Muzhi's biography. A more thorough example is provided by one of their contemporaries, Wang Shaozhi. Wang authored a chronicle of the late Eastern Jin, and for this he is known to us as a historian, but extant sources also amply demonstrate the more diffuse role he played in the production of historiography's materials. He was one of a handful of men in charge of drafting documents during Liu Yu's rise to the throne, and after the establishment of the dynasty he was again "given charge of the documents of the Song" (*zhang Song shu* 掌宋書), a true precursor, in the sense discussed here, of the later *Song shu*. Later he would compose a

---

10. "Loyalist forces" (*yijun*) represents the perspective of those forces, who would restore the Jin, and of the *History of the Jin*. It is not the term Huan Xuan would have used.
11. *Jin shu* 99.2599.
12. *Jin shu* 99.2599.

set of song lyrics for performance in the imperial temple, a historiographical genre of its own and one destined for inclusion in the dynastic history.[13] We also find him submitting notice of an omen, of sweet dew, creating a historiographical pluperfect for the rising imperial aspirant.[14] We know that as Prefect of Wuxing he composed a eulogy for a deceased local worthy, and also a long four-syllable poem for two local scholars on their way to the court.[15] These compositions had a social existence—the poem was presented to the two men as a sort of reference letter—but they were equally historiographical acts, duly entered (the eulogy is mentioned, the poem quoted in full) into our *Song shu*, the "history" or "documents of Song," where they testify to the goodness of the recipients, to the wisdom of Wang Shaozhi, and to the sagacity of the newly empowered Emperor Wen, on whose behalf Wang served.

But none of these was to be Wang Shaozhi's greatest historiographical contribution. The *History of the Jin* closes the annals of Emperor An (r. 397–418) with the following pluperfect construction:

> In the beginning, a prophecy claimed that "After Changming (Emperor Xiaowu, r. 372–96) there will be two more emperors." When Liu Yu was ready to engineer the transfer of the Mandate to his new dynasty, he secretly sent Wang Shaozhi to strangle the emperor and establish Emperor Gong (r. 419–20), so that the prophecy could be fulfilled.
>
> 初識云「昌明之後有二帝」，劉裕將為禪代，故密使王韶之縊帝而立恭帝，以應二帝云。[16]

---

13. *Song shu* 60.1625, 20.579–80.
14. *Song shu* 28.818.
15. *Song shu* 54.1539, 91.2248–49.
16. *Jin shu* 10.267. Wang's biography in the *Song shu* is a little gentler: it leaves out the prophecy and has him merely poisoning the emperor, and that with the aid of others in the palace; see *Song shu* 60.1625, which also records his appointment as Jin historiographer. Shen Yue, meanwhile, would, in several likely apocryphal tellings, play a similar role in the establishment of the Liang dynasty in 502, engineering the death of the last Qi emperor; see *Nan shi* 5.160 and *Zizhi tongjian* 145.4518 with a story set around 502, and its cognate, pluperfect counterpart from 513 in Shen's biography at *Liang shu* 13.243.

In 413, the Jin court had appointed Wang Shaozhi Assistant Gentleman of Composition, tasking him with compiling the dynasty's history. In 419, he truly did his best to finish the work.

If *shu*, "document," is the general phenomenon, a more particular period term well encapsulates the vital significance of documentation: *lu* 錄, the plainest word for both the verb and noun senses of "record." A standard example, from the biography of one of the Founding Ancestor's early adherents, Kuai En: "The Founding Ancestor *put* Kuai's successive achievements *into the official record*" 高祖錄其前後功勞.[17] On this basis, Kuai En received a fief of 500 households. Thus, being put into the record was a pivotal event in the actor's life—and then in his afterlife, when his descendants prospered on the fruit of his historiographical fame. This aspect is pointedly conveyed in the biography of Yu Bingzhi, who, as recounted in chapter 3, was removed from office late in his career for corrupt conduct and died without any official position. Despite that unfortunate end to his mortal career, after his demise Emperor Wen elected to "put his longstanding sincerity into the official record (*lu*), and [on this basis] posthumously restore his original offices" 太祖錄其宿誠，追復本官.[18]

The semantic range of the word *lu* sheds light on the full import of documentation. First, the word's most material sense, meaning "to preserve," brings out the significance of making a record. The ten-year-old Zhang Fu 張敷 (fl. ca. 430), for instance, seeks out the former belongings of his mother, who died during his birth. "Finding only a fan, he sealed it up and preserved (*lu*) it, and whenever he came to think of her, he would open the box and weep" 唯得一扇，乃緘錄之。每至感思，輒開笥流涕.[19] The placement of men's names and actions into the official record was a metaphorical version of this "preservation," with the historian as curator. Meanwhile, a darker side of "preservation" exposes a different aspect of the historical record. *Lu* is commonly used, either alone or in combination with other words, to mean "arrest." Of one figure, for instance, it is said that "every time he broke the law, the prefecture and county sent out orders to arrest (*lu*) him. But he would always leap over the walls of the house,

---

17. *Song shu* 49.1437.
18. *Song shu* 53.1522.
19. *Song shu* 46.1395.

and no one could seize him" 每犯法，為郡縣所錄，輒越屋踰牆，莫之能禽.[20] Elsewhere, the Founding Ancestor, incensed at a general's failure to advance into battle, "ordered his aides to seize (*lu*) him, and was going to have him beheaded" 命左右錄來，欲斬之.[21] The immediate sense is physical arrest, but the documentary associations remain, insofar as official arrest means to have one's name and unlawful actions put down on record, and thence into the historical record. But the historical record is a complex thing, filled with potential turning points, and for the general who would have been beheaded, the exigence of arrest serves as a prompt to turn negative documentation into positive. Seizing the moment, he reinvigorates himself and leads the charge into battle, leaving history to remember him in a good way.

The positive and negative valences of the "record" are comprehended in a third application of the word *lu* in early medieval historiography. Used to indicate a function in the bureaucratic apparatus, to *lu* is not to record but to have oversight over the records of a given office. The most prominent example is the full oversight over decisions of the imperial court, bestowed regularly to the most powerful minister, as the "overseer (*lu*) of the affairs of the Secretariat" 錄尚書事, but the function extended to the lower rungs of government, where we regularly find, for instance, locally appointed advisors (*canjun*, "adjutants") given overseer privileges.[22] The scope of this right is made clear in an incidental note in our *Song shu*: the overseer would review and actually cosign the documents issued by that office.[23] Oversight, then, entailed control over the documentary culture of early medieval China, but such power in turn entailed responsibility, and the political history of this period shows us how precarious control over documents was. The mocking of Huan Xuan as "Huan the issuer of

20. *Song shu* 50.1447.
21. *Song shu* 50.1444.
22. That is, the "adjutant with oversight" (*lushi canjun* 錄事參軍); but also other titles indicating documentary control, for example, including *jishi* 記室 (adjutant [in charge of] the record room) and *zhubu* 主簿 (master of records). On the office or role of the "overseer" of the Secretariat, see Wang Zhenglu, *Wei Jin Nanbeichao xuanguan tizhi yanjiu*, 286–88.
23. *Song shu* 57.1572, in which Cai Kuo, before the downfall of Xu Xianzhi, who was at that time the Overseer of the Secretariat, presciently refuses to serve in a position in which he would have to sign documents with Xu.

edicts" is one example, confirming that an individual's sedulous attempts to control historiographical documents could all too easily come to naught when they were contextualized at a later point in the historical process. One interesting response to this volatility was to seek a particular kind of threshold position—by destroying the documents one had received or written. The statesman Xie Shu 謝述 (390–435) is an example of the former: he makes a point of distancing himself from documentary power when he has his son burn a handwritten imperial edict agreeing to Shu's proposal for an amnesty. Xie feared that preserving the edict would look like an act of self-aggrandizement.[24] On the authors' end, we find Yang Hu 羊祜 (221–78), a powerful official in the Western Jin, famously burning the documentary record of his contributions to his court.[25] Xun Yu, the doppelgänger of Liu Muzhi, is also said to have destroyed the written record of his time as head of the Han government.[26] Incineration is to take a record and turn it into a meta-record that transcends the documentary process.

In sum, participation in the establishment and maintenance of the historical record was unavoidable, and with it came power, but also danger. Little wonder, then, that to the befuddlement or irritation of later readers, historians in this period preferred to preserve documentation—the most potent political actor of all—in such overwhelming quantity.

Historiography as Public and Private Interest

Putting things into the record means putting them into the *public* record. Thus, charged with upholding and regulating the public sphere, History with a capital "H" was a kind of ethical value, its lessons standards to be lived up to, the histories that presented these standards aptly referred to as "good histories" (*liang shi*, a term that also refers to the editors of the

---

24. *Song shu* 52.1496.
25. *Jin shu* 34.1019–20.
26. *Sanguo zhi* 10.317, Pei commentary, quoting the "separately circulating biography," where this lack of a record serves to prompt a highly eulogistic account of Xun's contributions. This may be a topos, echoing across various biographies.

histories, "good historians").[27] Yet neither the historiographical act nor ethical values in general can be classified simply as "public." Rather, an ethical value is the point of intersection for the interactive domains we conveniently distinguish as "public" and "private," and in practice public action regularly takes the form of private initiative.

A remark in the biography of Wang Tanshou, Wang Hong's youngest brother, epitomizes the nature of historiography, as the melding of public standards and private voices. Emperor Wen wishes to award him a fief for his role in the ouster of Xie Hui et al., but Wang declines:

> Though I appreciate the personal (*si*, "private") show of favor, how would an honest historian (*zhi shi*) look upon this?

陛下雖欲私臣，當如直史何。[28]

Artfully invoking the contrast between public and private, Wang Tanzhi refers to the ideal of the historian as impartial arbiter of our personal conduct. And yet, ideals are put to individual rhetorical uses. Using the ideal of historiography as a prompt, Wang strategically distinguishes himself as a deferent man in the eyes of history, and this thresholding move serves as a plot point in the longer story told in his biography. As the youngest brother of the court's preeminent power, Wang Tanshou has no interest in self-aggrandizement, which would expose their family enterprise to the same forces of destruction brought to bear on their court predecessors. Declining the fief at this point, when its acquisition would have been unnecessary and even counterproductive, proves to be a side-step on another path toward interiority, for he does receive the fief at a more useful point in his life—posthumously, for the benefit of his heirs. The public value of historiography served to buoy private interests.

Of course, public and private are not always so easily reconciled, a problem again well illustrated by counter-example. The poet Xie Lingyun is known to us for his literary achievement, but his biography also

---

27. For example, *Jin shu* 82.2184 (Sun Sheng) and 82.2150 (Gan Bao); the "Histories and biographies" chapter of the *Wenxin diaolong*; and related terms like *jiashi* 佳史 ("fine history"), used to describe Wang Shaozhi's Jin history in a passage discussed below.

28. *Song shu* 63.1679–80.

emphasizes the breadth of his learning, noting how "in his youth he was fond of study, reading widely across the many books" 靈運少好學，博覽群書.[29] His erudition is evident in his literary works, but more directly it also qualified him for work on state documents. His biography relates that in the mid-420s:

> [Emperor Wen] commissioned him to put the documents (*shu*) of the palace archive in order, filling in whatever material might be missing. Moreover, finding that there was no one history for the entire Jin, the emperor ordered Lingyun to compile a *History* (*shu*) *of the Jin*. He was able to set out the broad outlines of the work, but in the end the book (*shu*) remained unfinished. After some time, he was promoted to Palace Attendant, and the emperor received him at all hours of the day and night, bestowing great favor upon him. Lingyun's poetry and calligraphy (*shu*) were both skillful beyond compare, and whenever he finished a composition, he would copy it out in his own hand. Emperor Wen called them "twin treasures."
>
> [But] Lingyun believed that a person of his social status and his talent ought to be involved in imperial decisions, and that is what he expected when he was called to court. In fact, the emperor only consulted him on cultural and philosophical generalities, and every time he attended the emperor, all they did was engage in sophisticated conversation. Meanwhile, Wang Tanshou, Wang Hua, Yin Jingren, and others, men who in reputation and rank had always stood below Lingyun, were all entrusted with serious matters. Unable to accept this, Lingyun professed illness and excused himself from his court duties.
>
> 使整理祕閣書，補足遺闕。又以晉氏一代，自始至終，竟無一家之史，令靈運撰晉書，粗立條流。書竟不就。尋遷侍中，日夕見引，賞遇甚厚。靈運詩書皆兼獨絕，每文竟，手自寫之，文帝稱為二寶。既自以名輩，才能應參時政，初被召，便以此自許，既至，文帝唯以文義見接，每侍上宴，談賞而已。王曇首、王華、殷景仁等，名位素不踰之，並見任遇，靈運意不平，多稱疾不朝直。[30]

---

29. *Song shu* 67.1743.

30. *Song shu* 67.1772. The *Song shu* regularly refers to emperors by their temple names and here "Emperor Wen" should be "the Grand Ancestor" (Taizu). Wang Zhongluo's collation notes ascribe this to copying in from the *Nan shi*. Since early printings of the *Song shu* have a lacuna here, however, it remains possible that the anecdote itself was integral to Shen Yue's work.

What this passage—in which our key word *shu* appears in the four distinct senses of "document," "history," "book," and "calligraphy"—describes is an individual's inability to capture a public good. Xie Lingyun clearly has the talent of a historian, as recognized by the imperial commission to compile a history of the Jin. This recognition turns ironic when he is not allowed to actualize his knowledge of historical events through counsel to Emperor Wen's court. He is granted the task of the good historian but not his identity.

Another example of how the authority of the historian could be at once granted and withheld involves Xu Yuan, the compiler of the main predecessor of Shen Yue's *History of the Liu-Song*. That later *History* relegates Xu Yuan's "life" to its highly unsympathetic "imperial favorites" (*en xing* 恩倖) chapter. Therein, his contribution *to* historiography is undermined by his treatment *in* historiography:

> Xu Yuan was a lackey, skilled in the art of flattery, well able to read the subtle signals of his masters. He had browsed through quite a range of historical books, and he was particularly familiar with court ritual. He came to wait upon the emperor early in the era of Prime Excellence (424–53), participating in court decisions. He knew how to pander to his audience, and he was able to finish his arguments with decoration from the classical writings— and so the Grand Ancestor (Emperor Wen) favored him.

> 爰便僻善事人，能得人主微旨。頗涉書傳，尤悉朝儀。元嘉初便入侍左右，預參顧問。既長於附會，又飾以典文，故為太祖所任遇。[31]

Unlike Xie Lingyun, Xu was able to leverage his historical learning to exercise influence at the imperial court, in a career that spanned five decades. The socio-political reasons for this discrepancy are clear enough: Xie was a remnant nobleman of the previous dynasty, while Xu was the kind of talented but ordinary man who would be very useful to an emperor seeking to enact his will over various gentry and princely factions. But historiography gives and historiography takes away: the "honest historian" of the future, revising the very work Xu Yuan had himself compiled, tars him as a sycophant and diminishes his knowledge of the historical tradition as

---

31. *Song shu* 93.2310.

mere (the sardonic "quite" of the adverb *po*) browsing. Elsewhere, Xu's biography describes him as "arbitrary (*zhuan duan*) and preposterous" 專斷乖謬, using a related epithet to describe his historical work: "He drew from the work of his predecessors, but Xu Yuan single-mindedly (*zhuan*) made a book of his own" 爰雖因前作，而專為一家之書.[32]

Another historian-manqué was Wu Xi 吳喜 (427–71), who won the favor of Emperor Xiaowu (r. 453–64) and held great sway at court through the 460s. In 471, however, the throne, fearing his power had grown too great, "granted him suicide." A long edict was issued, dismissing him as a deceitful slanderer and opportunistic flatterer, and even going so far as to suggest that he had planned to usurp the throne.[33] An earlier anecdote, true or not, provides the pluperfect backing to that documentary denouement:

> Wu Xi began as an unofficially appointed clerk on the staff of the Leading Army general. He came to understand documents (*shu*) somewhat, so this General of the Leading Army, Shen Yanzhi (397–449), had him copy the office diary. When he finished copying a passage, he was pretty much able to recite it from memory. Once, Shen Yanzhi composed a memorial deferring an appointment, but the manuscript was lost before he had submitted it to the throne. Wu Xi had seen it once and was able to write out a copy on the spot, without a single omission. And so Shen Yanzhi came to "understand him" deeply (i.e., act as his patron).
>
> Thereupon, Wu Xi began to browse through the *Records of the Grand Historian* and the *History of the Han*, achieving quite some familiarity with past and present affairs. When one of Shen Yanzhi's adherents, Zhu Zhongmin, entered the palace to serve as Head Scribe, he recommended Xi as a scribe-clerk, and [later] Wu Xi was promoted to Clerk of Imperial Charts. But when Emperor Wen called for a certain document, Wu Xi opened the scroll up and presented it to him backward, whereupon the emperor, incensed, had him ejected from the court.

---

32. *Song shu* 93.2308.

33. Granting him suicide allowed his son to inherit the fief, and was likely a conciliatory gesture toward Wu Xi's many supporters in his armed retinue and in the southeastern region from which he hailed. The edict, one of the longest in the *Song shu*, offers a view on the circulation of power outside the imperial family and their upper gentry affiliates.

初出身為領軍府白衣史。少知書,領軍將軍沈演之使寫起居注,所寫既
畢,闇誦略皆上口。演之嘗作讓表,未奏,失本,喜經一見,即便寫赴,無
所漏脫,演之甚知之。因此涉獵史、漢,頗見古今。演之門生朱重民入為
主書,薦喜為主書書吏,進為主圖令史。太祖嘗求圖書,喜開卷倒進之,太
祖怒,遣出。[34]

The deep knowledge of a true historian is given a sardonic twist, as a man who barely knows the documentary tradition acquires an uncanny familiarity with it by serving as a copyist. The narrative then enfigures this as Wu Xi losing favor with the Grand Ancestor for presenting a book *backward*, a literal inversion of the intended direction and spirit of historiography.

The imprimatur of history as an ethical value was denied to Xie Lingyun, Xu Yuan, and Wu Xi. Returning now to Wang Shaozhi, we see a positive example, but one that reveals a fine line between those historiography favors and those to whom it denies its honors. Wang's biography relates this account of his historical work:

> Shaozhi's family was poor, and [so] when his father served as magistrate of Wucheng, the family settled there. Fond of histories, Shaozhi browsed widely and came to know many things, and he began his career as acting adjutant on the staff of the Defender General Xie Yan (d. 400). In his youth, [his father] Weizhi had been a man of ambitions and ideals, and he made copies of all the edicts and memorials of the day, collecting and recording (*lu*) all sorts of documents, great and small, from the Grand Prime (376–96) and Esteeming Peace (397–401) reign eras. Building on his father's work, Shaozhi privately compiled an "Annalistic History of the Reign of the [Jin] Emperor An" (Andi, r. 397–418). When it was finished, his contemporaries all said that he ought to serve in a historian's office, and so he was formally appointed Assistant Gentleman of Composition, from which position he was ordered to update his work, bringing it up to the ninth year of Righteousness Resplendent (413). His prose fluent, his opinions well-turned, his work is "a fine history" (*jiashi*, or "fine historian") of a latter age.

韶之家貧,父為烏程令,因居縣境。好史籍,博涉多聞。初為衛將軍謝琰
行參軍。偉之少有志尚,當世詔命表奏,輒自書寫,太元、隆安時事,小

---

34. *Song shu* 83.2114, 83.2117n5.

大悉撰錄之，詔之因此私撰晉安帝陽秋。既成，時人謂宜居史職，即除著作佐郎，使續後事，訖義熙九年。善敍事，辭論可觀，為後代佳史。[35]

This narrative revolves around three important historiographical motifs. The first is poverty—noble poverty, not the abject sort. (The family is relocating from the more prestigious capital area, the southern base of the Langye clan, to a prosperous southeastern region that likely afforded an easier path to material comfort.) Poverty is a common if not necessary trait of historians of this period: of the figures to be discussed below, Wang Yin 王隱 (ca. 284–ca. 354), Gan Bao 干寶 (fl. early fourth century), and He Fasheng 何法盛 (fl. mid-fifth century) are also examples.[36] What is significant is not poverty itself, but the way poverty interposes a certain distance between the individual and the political and social world in which he exists. Implicitly building on the enthymeme deployed in the opinion of He Shangzhi in the debate in chapter 4—that the impoverished gentryman is a good gentryman—poverty serves as an ethos warrant for the good character of the historian.

A related motif is ambition, ascribed to both Wang Shaozhi and his father. This is in some sense the consequence of poverty, insofar as poverty prompts the need to better one's condition. As a youth, his father Wang Weizhi had "ambitions and ideals" (*zhi shang*); his historiographical enterprise was a form of political action, in the fallen age in which he found himself. The son is likewise "fond of" (*hao*) histories, a personality characteristic that identifies him as an aspiring contributor in the political sphere. The connection between ambition and historical interests is made explicit in the biographies of two of Shaozhi's rough contemporaries. Of one Mao Xiuzhi 毛脩之 (375–446), a native of the Sichuan basin, it is said: "An ambitious youth, Xiuzhi read quite a few histories" 脩之有大志，頗

---

35. *Song shu* 60.1625. Note the polite ellipsis of Wang Shaozhi's career during the reign of Huan Xuan.

36. See, respectively, *Jin shu* 82.2142, 82.2149, and *Nan shi* 33.859. Wang Tanshou, though certainly not poor, makes a special point of his relative impoverishment, refusing all of his inheritance except the family books.

讀史籍.³⁷ And Yin Jingren, who would dominate the Liu-Song court in the early 430s, is described thus:

> He was not interested in adding literary polish to his learning, but he was a sensitive and nimble thinker, and although he did not discourse on abstract philosophical questions, he had a deep understanding of the principle of things. When it came to state documents, court protocol, and historical statutes, as well as the notes and documents associated with them, he never failed to gather and copy (*lu*) them. Discerning men could see that he harbored worldly ambitions.
>
> 景仁學不為文，敏有思致，口不談義，深達理體，至於國典朝儀，舊章記注，莫不撰錄，識者知其有當世之志也。³⁸

As with genteel poverty, ambition finds its meaning in the way it integrates private experience into the public realm. The knowledge of statecraft that the study of history affords is personal and practical, but history also imbues his ambitions with an abstract quality: the ethical imprimatur of the "good historian," acknowledged legislator of the world.

The third significant motif here is the notion of historical scholarship as a family enterprise.³⁹ The great models of early medieval historiography, the *Shiji* and the *Han shu*, were family undertakings. In the more recent past, the case of Wang Yin, who fled to the south as a teenager during the fall of the north, mirrors that of Wang Shaozhi:

> His father, Wang Quan, served as Magistrate of Liyang. Fond of study as a youth, he had ambitions of writing something, and he always privately (*si*) made records of (*lu*) dynastic events and the draft biographies of meritorious ministers. But he died before completing his work. Wang Yin, in turn, lived

---

37. *Song shu* 48.1426. Mao Xiuzhi spent the last quarter of his life in the Northern Wei, where, his biography in the *History of the Liu-Song* tells us, he instructed the Toba rulers in "the ritual system of the Central States" 中國禮制, incurring the wrath of the Liu-Song emperor.

38. *Song shu* 66.1681.

39. See also Xiaofei Tian, *Beacon Fire and Shooting Star: The Literary Culture of the Liang (502–557)*, 121–22, mentioning family-compiled histories and describing literary writing as a "family business."

a quiet life of study, seeking no patronage from the powerful. With broad learning and wide-ranging attention to worldly happenings, he took up the enterprise (*ye*) inherited from his father, becoming quite well informed on events at the Western (i.e., Northern) court.

父銓,歷陽令,少好學,有著述之志,每私錄晉事及功臣行狀,未就而卒。隱以儒素自守,不交勢援,博學多聞,受父遺業,西都舊事多所諳究。[40]

The point is not only that fathers and sons worked together on historical projects but that such projects were privately held family "enterprises" (*ye*), stores of "cultural capital" as valuable as and more stable than any business venture. Observing the profitability of these historiographical ventures does not cheapen the ideal, or dilute the seriousness with which these scholarly families approached their work, or diminish the contribution of these works to historical inquiry. It is simply to stress that the private pursuit of a publicly convertible value—historiography—was literally a valuable enterprise. Witness Wang Biaozhi 王彪之 (305–77), great-grandfather of Wang Zhunzhi of the debate in chapter 4:

> Wang Biaozhi's learning was broad and he knew many things. He was particularly well-versed in court ritual, for knowledge of this had been passed down for generations in his family, and he also knew all about the affairs of the previous Eastern Jin courts. He kept these materials sealed in a blue box, and his contemporaries called this "the blue box learning of the Wang family."

彪之博聞多識,練悉朝儀,自是家世相傳,並諳江左舊事,緘之青箱,世人謂之「王氏青箱學」。[41]

---

40. *Jin shu* 82.2142.

41. *Song shu* 60.1623–24. There is a funny inversion of the "blue box learning" (*qingxiang xue*) trope in the *Nan Qi shu*: Wang Jian, a scion of the Langya Wang clan who by other accounts was a very learned man, seeks to bolster his allegedly deficient knowledge of court precedent by offering prizes to his underlings if they can supply him with good examples. The bounty he set out included a desk, assorted clothing, and (in?) a "cloth-wrapped box" (*jin xiang* 巾箱). See *Nan Qi shu* 39.685 (biography of Lu Cheng 陸澄, 425–94), and compare the neutralized version in Wang Jian's own biography, at 23.436.

Wang Biaozhi's family learning is not historiography in its finished state but the protean documentary knowledge that historical actors will draw on to make history, and that later stages of historiography will organize into historical narrative. The value of this material is analogous to that of historiography proper: privately held public knowledge that will provide "capital" for the family members' success in the realm of officialdom—though Wang Zhunzhi does not seem to have profited by it.

These three motifs play positive roles in the construction of Wang Shaozhi as a good historian: poverty is a prompt toward sanctioned interiority and ambition is his motive to accomplish a socially validated deed, while the success of his family enterprise is both the fruit of his labor and a worthy contribution to the public weal. Yet there is also an ambivalence to them, a sense that for each the balance may tip untowardly toward the private. The socio-political distance represented by noble poverty may turn into disaffection and estrangement. Ambition—to make a mark in the public sphere—can be regarded solely as a matter of private gain. Historiography produced as a family enterprise can be interpreted as advocacy of a partial—biased or simply insufficient—view of history. Communing with the ideal of the "good historian" can smooth over these tensions, but it does not resolve them.

The most prominent profile of the public-private relationship in historiography is the standard but misleading characterization of dynastic historiography in the early medieval period as the work of private individuals, in contrast to the bureaucratic commissions in the Tang and later.[42] This view does not hold up because the public mandate applied regardless of whether historiography was produced "privately" or by imperial commission, because, in the characterization of Liang Qichao (1873–1929), by the early medieval period history "had become the public property of society" 已漸為社會所公有.[43] For example, when Emperor Wen desired, in 443, to perform the new year's plowing ritual and ordered He Chengtian to compile a ritual protocol, it was found that Shan Qianzhi 山謙之 "had

---

42. A notable early example in modern scholarship is Jin Yufu, *Zhongguo shixue shi*, chapter 4. For a good comprehensive discussion, see Hao Runhua, *Liuchao shiji yu shixue*, 153–60, which also emphasizes historiography's connection to family prestige.

43. Liang Qichao, *Zhongguo lishi yanjiufa*, 16 (chapter 2).

already privately (*si*) gathered the materials, and so these were submitted to the throne" 已私鳩集，因以奏聞.[44] Private historiography done right was the anticipated fulfillment of a public need.

A good illustration of the public envelope around private activity is the privately erected funeral stele, a practice that began in the late second century and was twice proscribed in the third century before becoming common again under the enervated southern court of the fourth.[45] The historical accounts inscribed on these monuments—unreservedly eulogistic biographies—spoke to the advantage of the decedent's family and their political allies, narrow interest groups that, in the view of the imperial proscription of 278, "issued partisan (*si*, "private") praise and embellishment, creating and spreading empty and false narratives" 既私褒美，興長虛偽.[46] But outright proscription was only one, ineffectual way of dealing with partisan historiography. Around 413—just as Liu Muzhi was reviewing documents at court—the historian Pei Songzhi submitted a memorial on the subject to the newly ascendant Founding Ancestor. His argument concludes not by calling for a proscription per se, but by shifting the stasis to the greater issue of the assertion of public values:

> In my view, all those desiring to erect steles should be required to report their intentions to the court, which will allow them to proceed only after court discussion (*chao yi*) has approved it. In this way, we aim to prevent spurious narratives, while promoting those that are splendidly well-evidenced, so that a hundred generations from now people will know them to be true. Thus will the Righteousness (*yi*, "Honor") of our age, and our conformance with the Way, be known and revered in future ages.
>
> 以為諸欲立碑者，宜悉令言上，為朝議所許，然後聽之。庶可以防過無徵，顯彰茂實，使百世之下，知其不虛，則義信於仰止，道孚於來葉。[47]

---

44. *Song shu* 14.353.

45. For an overview of this practice and the restrictions that were placed on it, see Liu Tao, "Wei Jin Nanchao de jin bei yu li bei." From the late fifth century, the epitaph inscription (*muzhiming*), a related genre, became increasingly commonplace.

46. *Song shu* 15.407.

47. *Song shu* 64.1699.

Public oversight over historiography meant reconciling conflict among individual historiographical undertakings, whether they were deemed public or private.

The "court discussion" (*chao yi*) spoken of by Pei Songzhi is related to the debate in chapter 4: a record, for the judgment of posterity, of publicly held positions. The task of historiography proper was to proceed *as if* through such a "court discussion," rendering historical narratives and judgments endoxic, or coherent with the good judgment of the public sphere. In the case of the commemorative steles, the problem is not just that a family could present a biased account but that its relation to other accounts, serving other biases, needed to be adjudicated. A similar problem existed for dynastic histories, as evident in the following pair of narratives regarding the relation of Shen Yue's *History of the Liu-Song* to a competing work by a younger contemporary, Pei Ziye 裴子野 (469–530), the great-grandson of Pei Songzhi. According to Pei's biography in the *History of the Liang* (*Liang shu*, compiled 636):

> During the era of Prime Auspices (Yuanjia, 424–53), Pei's great-grandfather, Pei Songzhi, had been commanded to continue work on the history of Song begun by He Chengtian. Pei died before he was able to bring his work to a state of completion (*cheng*), and Pei Ziye had always desired to carry his forebear's enterprise on to completion (*ji cheng xian ye*). When, toward the end of the era of Eternal Brightness (Yongming, 483–93), Shen Yue's *History of the Liu-Song* came into circulation, Ziye picked up the task, culling and editing it[48] into the *Brief History of the Liu-Song*, in twenty scrolls. There was much excellence both in his narrations and in his judgments, and when Shen Yue saw it, he exclaimed: "I am no match for this!" Xiao Chen

---

48. The "it" here (there is no object pronoun in the Chinese) is the draft he had inherited from his grandfather—Pei was not "culling" Shen Yue's work, though he must have drawn extensively from it. See Tang Xiejun, *Shijia xingji yu shishu gouzao*, 113, citing Zhang Xuecheng's 章學誠 (1738–1801) observation on the meaning of "abridgment" (*lüe*). Pei's work is not extant, but references to it show that Pei's facts differed from Shen's in a number of instances, indicating reference to other materials—that is, Pei Songzhi's work, supplemented with more recent documents collected by Pei Ziye himself. Discussions of Pei's history include Qiu Min, *Liuchao shixue*, 135–39; and Tang Xiejun, *Shijia xingji yu shishu gouzao*, chapters 5 and 6, which discuss and compare it with the *Song shu*, and appendix three, for a collection of possible fragments.

(480–531) of Lanling, Fu Zhao (454–528) of Beidi, and Zhou She (464–529) of Runan all held it in high regard.

初,子野曾祖松之,宋元嘉中受詔續修何承天宋史,未及成而卒,子野常欲繼成先業。及齊永明末,沈約所撰宋書既行,子野更刪撰為宋略二十卷。其敘事評論多善,約見而歎曰:「吾弗逮也。」蘭陵蕭琛、北地傅昭、汝南周捨咸稱重之。[49]

This is a classic example of historiography as family-held cultural capital: Pei Ziye, then a very young man, utilizes his patrimony to make his name in the world, and to make this name he places himself in direct competition with a historian a generation senior, presenting his work as superior to the one in circulation and winning the admiration of his contemporaries. In this *History of the Liang* account, the competitive motif is played down, covered over with a courtly grace: Shen Yue plays the gentleman, acknowledging the young man's talents. The balance is different in the account in the less courteous retelling in the *History of the Southern Dynasties* (*Nan shi*, compiled 659, with the key differences underlined):

> During the era of Prime Auspices, Pei's great-grandfather, Pei Songzhi, had been commanded to continue work on the history of the Song begun by He Chengtian. Pei died before he was able to bring his work to a state of completion, and Pei Ziye had always desired to carry his forebear's enterprise on to completion. Then, at the end of the era of Eternal Brightness, <u>Shen Yue's *History of the Song* said that "after Pei Songzhi, nothing was heard [of Pei's history]."</u>[50] Ziye picked up the task, editing [Pei Songzhi's work] into the *Brief History of the Song*, in twenty scrolls. There was much excellence both in his narrations and in his judgments—and <u>it said "[Emperor Xiaowu] executed Prefect of Huainan Shen Pu (i.e., Shen Yue's father), because he</u>

---

49. *Liang shu* 30.442.
50. Or of Pei's family? The current text of Shen Yue's work says something much simpler: "He continued He Chengtian's history of the dynasty, but he died in 451, age 80 *sui*, before he was able to compile (*zhuan shu*) anything.... Songzhi's essays and his *Annals of the Jin* are in circulation, along with [his son] Pei Yin's commentary on Sima Qian's *Records of the Grand Historian*" 續何承天國史,未及撰述,二十八年,卒,時年八十。...松之所著文論及晉紀,駰注司馬遷史記,並行於世 (*Song shu* 64.1701). According to the story told here, this would be the revised version. More likely, the story is a caustic invention on the commonplace of biased history.

did not join with the righteous defenders of the throne."⁵¹ Horrified (*ju*), Shen Yue went barefoot to pay his respects to Pei, begging to mutually put the matter to rest. "I am no match for you!" he exclaimed of Pei's *opus*.

初，子野曾祖松之，宋元嘉中受詔續修何承天宋史，未及成而卒，子野常欲繼成先業。及齊永明末，沈約所撰宋書稱「松之已後無聞焉」。子野更撰為宋略二十卷，其敘事評論多善，而云「戮淮南太守沈璞，以其不從義師故也」。約懼，徒跣謝之，請兩釋焉。歎其述作曰：「吾弗逮也。」⁵²

Here no graceful veil covers the private acrimony, and the public value of historiography offers no reconciliation. In the *History of the Liang* version, the elder man affirms his historiographical judgment by fairly recognizing the talents of a rising member of the younger generation. They are mutually defining. In the *History of the Southern Dynasties* narrative, the selfsame exclamation—"I am no match for this / you!"—signals instead Shen Yue's humiliation at finding himself on the weaker end of a private historiographical battle. Its looser hold on historical fact aside—there is little reason to think Shen Yue originally shortchanged the Pei family—it is on account of this kind of narrative that the *History of the Southern Dynasties* has a besmirched historiographical status; it is less "orthodox" than the true dynastic histories because it lacks their restraint, their courtly surface, their obeisance to the Confucian dictum of "holding one's tongue when speaking of the worthies." The eulogistic tenor of the biography in an orthodox dynastic history brings a public-mindedness that sets things in good order, its public authority not a judgment that voids private perspectives, but an assured comprehension of them.⁵³

---

51. In the postface to his *Song shu*, Shen Yue tells his family history. There, his father is slow in joining the forces of the Filial and Martial Emperor because he is too devoted to his family, who would be endangered in his absence from the capital, and he is executed because an old enemy calumnies him to the new emperor. See *Song shu* 100.2464–65; Mather, *The Poet Shen Yüeh*, 7–12, claims that this traumatic event caused Shen to be especially circumspect throughout his political career.

52. *Nan shi* 33.866.

53. Along these lines, Tang Xiejun has argued that Shen Yue's commission to compile a new history of the Liu-Song was a response to the appearance of a very partisan version compiled by one Liu Xiang 劉祥—a hot-blooded great-grandson of Liu Muzhi; see Tang Xiejun, *Shijia xingji yu shishu gouzao*, chapter 4, and *Nan Qi shu* 36.639–43.

Returning to the case of Wang Shaozhi, strangler-historian, we find another example of historiography's public-private tension at work in this way:

> In his history of the Jin, Wang Shaozhi had written of the [illicit] business activities of Wang Xun and the rebellious political activity of Wang Xin. Wang Xun's son Wang Hong and Wang Xin's son Wang Hua were both men of great fame, and Shaozhi, fearing they would do harm to him, tightly allied himself with Xu Xianzhi, Fu Liang, and their clique.
>
> When the Youthful Emperor (Shaodi, r. 422–24) took the throne, Shaozhi rose to Imperial Attendant, and Outrider as before. In the first year of the Reflection of Stability era (423), he was sent out as Prefect of Wuxing [a desirable posting in the rich southeast]. [Then,] when Xu Xianzhi was executed [in 426], Wang Hong became Prime Minister, with charge over Yangzhou [the region in which Wuxing was located]. Although Wang Hong himself did not cut off relations with Shaozhi, his brothers and cousins, who did not know Shaozhi, ostracized him. Meanwhile, Shaozhi, ever fearful that Wang Hong would prosecute him for some offense, toiled hard night and day in his prefectural posting. He produced an excellent administrative record there, and Wang Hong suppressed his private (*si*) grudge. Emperor Wen praised them both.
>
> 韶之為晉史，序王珣貨殖，王廞作亂。珣子弘，廞子華，並貴顯，韶之懼為所陷，深結徐羨之、傅亮等。少帝即位，遷侍中，驍騎如故。景平元年，出為吳興太守。羨之被誅，王弘入為相，領揚州刺史。弘雖與韶之不絕，諸弟未相識者，皆不復往來。韶之在郡，常慮為弘所繩，夙夜勤厲，政績甚美，弘亦抑其私憾。太祖兩嘉之。[54]

This passage braids the historiographical and the political into a single narrative. With his history, Wang Shaozhi had established a reputation as a "good historian" by placing the public interest first, narrating the excesses of the late Jin court and the failings of its elite guardians, and thus endangering his own private interests. Ostensibly in response to this danger, he tied himself to the ill-fated faction of Xu Xianzhi, Fu Liang, and Xie Hui. Both his written work and this political disalignment serve as "prompts," setting up an exigence from which politics and historiography can redeem

---

54. *Song shu* 60.1626–27.

him, as Wang Hong is unable to bring himself to harm a "good historian"—particularly not one who has also validated his historical acumen through able performance of the duties of an administrator, and is thus himself a worthy subject for future historians. As a public value, the guarantor of endoxa, historiography brings together two servants of the state who otherwise, privately, would have fallen into irreparable discord. When the emperor praises them as a pair (*liang*, "both"), he is endorsing the power of orthodox historiography to comprise the narrow interests of its individual participants, resting on the threshold of judgment one way or another.

The Exigence of Incompletion

An antinomy of completion and incompletion runs through our values: we expect them to be whole but we know that they are not, and that lack provides their exigence. So it is for historiography.

One specific storyline in our early medieval sources provides an illustration that is both substantive and symbolic: the commonplace of historiography as the object of theft and plagiarism. Shen Yue himself reports an instance of this in the memorial he submits with his *Song shu*. Writing this history of the Liu-Song, he explains to his imperial audience, was not his original interest:

> For a long while I wondered why there was still no complete history of the Jin, and in my early twenties I had the idea that I might compile and "relay" such a work. Early in the Greatest Beginning reign period (465–71), Cai Xingzong, the General Campaigning West, made a request on my behalf to Emperor Ming (r. 465–72), who issued an imperial response granting me permission, and from that day up until recently, for more than twenty years, I worked to compile such a history, in 120 scrolls. But though I had established a full outline, some materials still awaited collection, and early in the reign of Eternal Brightness (483–93), a thief stole the fifth case of scrolls.
>
> 常以晉氏一代，竟無全書，年二十許，便有撰述之意。泰始初，征西將軍蔡興宗為啟明帝，有勅賜許，自此迄今，年逾二十，所撰之書，凡一百二十卷。條流雖舉，而採摭未周，永明初，遇盜失第五帙。[55]

---

55. *Song shu* 100.2466.

His true interest, he claims, was a history of the more distant Jin, not the Song, but after twenty years his work was still incomplete—and what was near completion was made incomplete again at the hands of some thief.

What kind of thief would have stolen Shen Yue's intellectual property? Earlier stories have some answers:

> At that time [early in the Liu-Song], there was a Chi Shao of Gaoping who was also writing a *History of the Revival of the Jin*,[56] and he showed it to He Fasheng a number of times. Scheming to obtain the book, Fasheng said to him: "You are famous and have a prosperous career—you have no need of a history to advance your reputation with. But I am an impoverished scholar, unknown in society. I, like Yuan Hong and Gan Bao before me, can only rely on writing a history to make my name known to posterity. Make a gift of it to me!" But Chi Shao would not give it to him. When the work was finished, it was placed in a cabinet in Chi Shao's study. Fasheng paid a visit. Chi Shao was not there—so he broke into the study and stole the book. When Chi Shao returned, his work was lost, and he had no other copy. And thereupon such a work circulated under He Fasheng's name.
>
> 時有高平郗紹亦作晉中興書，數以示何法盛。法盛有意圖之，謂紹曰：「卿名位貴達，不復俟此延譽。我寒士，無聞於時，如袁宏、干寶之徒，賴有著述，流聲於後。宜以為惠。」紹不與。至書成，在齋內廚中，法盛詣紹，紹不在，直入竊書。紹還失之，無復兼本，於是遂行何書。[57]

The topos of the pure historian living in poverty is ironized here, as He Fasheng, the "impoverished scholar" (*han shi*, "scholar from a cold [socially low] family"), turns to brazen thievery after his plea for pity is ignored. But it is not that only the poor would steal from the rich, as a related tale in the *History of Jin* account of Wang Yin shows. Born to noble poverty (*hansu* 寒素, "cold but pure"), as we have seen, Wang Yin established a reputation by continuing the "enterprise" he "inherited" from his father,

---

56. This work is, as the anecdote suggests, lost, if it indeed existed, and we know little of this Chi Shao, though the Chi clan of Gaoping was, as the anecdote relates, part of the Eastern Jin upper elite. "Also" in this sentence refers back to the work of Xu Guang, after whose biography this anecdote is inserted.

57. *Nan shi* 33.859. For a discussion of He Fasheng's history, casting doubt on the veracity of this anecdote, see Qiu Min, *Liuchao shixue*, 78–80.

who had "privately" begun collecting materials for a history of the Jin. After the flight south, Wang Yin had even received an imperial (i.e., "public") commission to continue his work. But then:

> At that time (in the 320s), Gentleman of Composition Yu Yu was privately (*si*) compiling a *History of the Jin*. As a native of the southeast, he was not familiar with the affairs of the central (i.e., Western Jin) court, so he paid a number of visits to Wang Yin, and even borrowed his work and secretly copied from it. Thus, his range of material grew larger. Afterward, he came to despise Wang Yin, making no pretense to conceal it. Yu Yu was from a wantonly powerful family (*haozu*) and pursued alliances and factions with other rich and powerful men. He slandered Wang Yin, and eventually Wang lost his post and returned home in disgrace.
>
> 時著作郎虞預私撰晉書,而生長東南,不知中朝事,數訪於隱,并借隱所著書竊寫之,所聞漸廣。是後更疾隱,形於言色。預既豪族,交結權貴,共為朋黨,以斥隱,竟以謗免,黜歸于家。[58]

Here the endoxic hierarchy of bad-rich versus noble-poor is back in its proper order, the poor scholar suffering at the hands of the rich one. Indeed, Wang Yin later finds a new patron and is able to finish his work. But in a bitter historiographical twist, he is alienated from his achievement once again, as the Tang-era *History of Jin* in which his biography appears—a work that drew on Wang Yin's history—ruthlessly denigrates his work:

> Wang Yin was an avid writer, but his prose was clumsy and disordered. When the narrative is properly told in his work, it is invariably from his father's compilations (*zhuan*); when it is sloppy and barely comprehensible, it is Wang Yin's own writing (*zuo*).
>
> 隱雖好著述,而文辭鄙拙,蕪舛不倫。其書次第可觀者,皆其父所撰;文體混漫義不可解者,隱之作也。[59]

At least Wang Yin is allowed to play a filial foil for his good father.

---

58. *Jin shu* 82.2142.
59. Proving that the course of historiography is never complete, modern scholars have attempted to rehabilitate Wang Yin's reputation. See Qiu Min, *Liuchao shixue*, 74–76.

Anecdotes like these show how historiography was literally valuable, as a family's substantive cultural capital, but they also make a more rhetorical point: the history as physical object is stolen because it is a thing of great value, but because theft is an immoral action contrary to the ideal of historiography, the thief therefore loses as he gains, while the one who loses his historical work collects the energy of exigence. Thus, although Chi Shao and Wang Yin are very different types of people, these two anecdotes both frame them positively. Wang's noble poverty is increased by the loss suffered at the hands of a power-hungry courtier. Chi's loss may not be historically accurate—nowhere else is the work in question attributed to anyone but He Fasheng—but in the anecdote he comes off as the righteously aggrieved, and whatever actual deficiencies are found in that history were certain to be attributed to the thief. Shen Yue, meanwhile, could present himself as a good historian of the Jin, without having to present a work for others to find fault with, and testifying about his lost Jin history was also a means of politely distancing himself from any controversy his *History of the Liu-Song*—an assigned task, versus a labor of love—might arouse, a predicament developed in the paired Pei Ziye anecdotes discussed above.

The push and pull of completion and incompletion, and the insistence of the latter, also manifests itself in the standard tropes that narrated the work of historiography. On the one hand, the complete naturally has a place of prominence. Value is granted to the creation of whole works, which are "erected" (*zhu* 著, a standard word for literary "composition" in general) or "brought to completion" (*cheng* 成). The history produced by "a single family" (*yi jia* 一家, or "lineage of thought") indicates a coherent, recognizable, and transmissible entity, and the strongest word for authorship, *shuzuo* 述作, "to relay the old (*shu*) but also create something new (*zuo*)," marks the work as an integral whole.[60] But what is "complete" is easily rendered incomplete, and the partial nature of the "family" runs counter to the public task of historiography—it is *merely* the accomplishment of

---

60. This term is applied to historiography in the biography of Wang Yin (*Jin shu* 82.2142) and in the *History of the Southern Dynasties* version of the Pei Ziye–Shen Yue anecdote. It overwrites the *contrast* famously made by Confucius: "I relay *but do not* create" (*Analects* 7/1).

one particular family, and the creation of something new is an accomplishment of individual ambition, and thus inherently "partial."

The motif of incompletion is reflected directly in the vocabulary associated with the actual process of assembling a history. The first step was the "gathering" (*ji* 集) of materials, an activity rendered most evocatively in the trope *jiuji* 鳩集, "to gather like doves," as in the description of Shan Qianzhi's "private" work quoted above. Like small birds, materials float in from beyond the historian's direct control, and may yet take flight despite being caged in a book. The historiographical work is one that, through its various stages and in its ostensible completion, can always be contracted or expanded, future historians "editing" (*shan* 刪, "culling") or "channeling it into a stream [of explication and further documentation]" (*zhu* 注, generally referred to as "commentary"). The most common verb applied to historiographical work, *zhuan* 撰, to "compile," is cognate with "select" (*xuan* 選) and strongly implies that compilation includes both the gathering and the appropriate winnowing of the available documentary record. A key step in producing a complete history in early medieval China came when the historian developed an unfinished outline vision of what the whole work might look like, "roughly establishing its [main] branches and streams" (*cu li tiaoliu*), as Xie Lingyun's work on a Jin history was described.[61] Drawn to completion, it may be said that the work was "harnessed" (*le* 勒), a word that acknowledges that "completion" is an artificial constraint from which history has a propensity to break free.[62] Nearer to the finished product, "rough drafts" (*cao* 草) are made, which is to say, incomplete wholes.

The complementary relationship of the complete and the incomplete is a key locus of any rhetorical impulse: to have rhetorical exigence, something must be in abeyance, but there must also exist a vision of a whole—a goal, a direction for action. On the private end of the historiographical spectrum, incompletion is a prompt for individual distinction, be it through replacing a stolen work, as Wang Yin did, or by finishing a family enterprise, like Pei Ziye. For higher purposes, incompletion is a prompt toward greater, public ends: a fully ethical vision of the world from which human judgment and action always stand at some distance, in some condition of imperfection, always leaving it to a future actor to determine or

---

61. *Song shu* 67.1772. See also Shen Yue's account of his *History of Jin*, above.
62. For example, Shen Yue's account of Xu Yuan's work, at *Song shu* 100.2467.

re-determine. In short, good histories are possible because good histories do not exist. That is the rhetorical essence conveyed in an early Eastern Jin missive to the throne by Wang Dao, the leading statesman of the newly established southern court:

> It is a general truth that the actions of emperors and kings must be written down, put into fine books, and handed down to infinite posterity. The Promulgating Emperor (Xuandi, i.e., the pre-dynastic ancestor Sima Yi 司馬懿, 179–251) established order to the borders of land and sea, and the Martial Emperor (Wudi, r. 265–90) received the Mandate from the Wei. Their virtue was of the greatest sort, their deeds grand, they were peers to the high sages of antiquity—and yet, their annals and the [associated] biographies [of the men who helped them] are not to be found in our imperial archives, nor have songs of their virtue been set to the music of winds and strings [in temple songs]. Now, Your Majesty, sagacious and perspicacious, standing at a moment of great revival, ought (*yi*) to establish a state historian, to gather and compile the imperial annals, from the shining accomplishments of the ancestors down to the deeds of those who aided the establishment of the Mandate. All effort shall be made to make the record true, that it may serve as a standard for future generations, satisfying the desire of the empire's subjects, pleasing the hearts of mortals and spirits alike. Truly, thus would you realize the utmost beauty of a broadly shared harmony, and make the great base of an imperial enterprise. A full complement of official historians ought (*yi*) to be established, with Gan Bao, Assistant Gentleman of Composition, and others commissioned to work on this compilation.
>
> 夫帝王之迹,莫不必書,著為令典,垂之無窮。宣皇帝廓定四海,武皇帝受禪於魏,至德大勳,等蹤上聖,而紀傳不存於王府,德音未被乎管絃。陛下聖明,當中興之盛,宜建立國史,撰集帝紀,上敘祖宗之烈,下紀佐命之勳,務以實錄,為後代之準,厭率土之望,悅人神之心,斯誠雍熙之至美,王者之弘基也。宜備史官,敕佐著作郎干寶等漸就撰集。[63]

Wang Dao presents a simple syllogistic argument, with appropriate embellishments. A defining norm is established—that great deeds must be recorded in history, as a model for posterity—and it is affirmed that the deeds of the Jin emperor's forebears were indeed great. What animates this

---

63. *Jin shu* 82.2149.

normative vision is the gap between the enthymeme and the reality—the rhetoric of "what ought to be done" (*yi*, appearing twice here). The need allows the fulfillment, through the promotion of worthy talents, of both private and public interests.

The same rhetorical opportunity is shown in a more institutional perspective in a note from the treatise on officialdom in the *History of the Liu-Song*:

> Under the Jin system, when an Assistant Gentleman of Composition took up his position, he was required to compile a biographical account of a renowned servant of the state. In the early Song, however, the court was newly established and there were no men suited for such biographical treatment, and so this system fell into abeyance.
>
> 晉制，著作佐郎始到職，必撰名臣傳一人。宋氏初，國朝始建，未有合撰者，此制遂替矣。[64]

These words were possibly written in the 420s, when the Liu-Song was just consolidating its own array of distinguished men. For the Liu-Song state, the lapse of routine historiographical work since the fall of the Jin furnished an exigence of the incomplete. The absence of raw material—the stalwart state servants deserving of biographical treatment—gave the dynasty's statesmen, like Wang Hong, an opportunity for distinction, and the state could buttress itself by filling out the memory of those who had worked toward its establishment, like Liu Muzhi. As these men acted, as the court gradually stepped into the breach, so rose the historians to transcribe their historiographical actions, beginning with He Chengtian and continuing through Shen Yue. The memorial with which Shen Yue submitted his hundred-scroll work to the throne picks up this thread in its closing passage, the final words of our *History*:

> Shamed by the Southern Scribe and Dong Hu of antiquity,[65] and with apologies to the more recent Sima Qian and Ban Gu, your servant has, with the

---

64. *Song shu* 40.1246.
65. The Southern Scribe and Dong Hu appear in the *Zuozhuan* (Xiang 25 and Xuan 2) as paradigms of the honest historian. Discussions of these legends include Pulleyblank,

small talents of an ordinary villager, relayed the splendid canons of an entire era, aiming, in the prose of my narratives and in my arrangement of events, for the model of antiquity, but fearing that I have fallen short of the truly worthy, and for this I bow into deep contortion, the sweat of shame pouring willy-nilly down my face. The imperial annals [which form the root] and the biographies [which array from the base as if they were its commentaries] have been produced in a clean copy, making seventy scrolls, in seven volumes, and your servant hereby scrupulously announces the presentation of these; the treatises that I am compiling will be submitted when they are complete (*cheng*). Having scrupulously drawn up a table of contents, I visit the palace office and kneel down with this memorial, to present the book to the attention of the Emperor. Your servant, Shen Yue, truly in fright and in fear, bangs his head on the ground once and again, [acknowledging] the mortal gravity of his offenses.

臣遠愧南、董,近謝遷、固,以閭閻小才,述一代盛典,屬辭比事,望古慚良,鞠躬跼蹐,靦汗亡厝。本紀列傳,繕寫已畢,合七帙七十卷,臣今謹奏呈。所撰諸志,須成續上。謹條目錄,詣省拜表奉書以聞。臣約誠惶誠恐,頓首頓首,死罪死罪。[66]

Going beyond the self-flagellating display of deference customary to memorials to the throne, Shen Yue declares the presentation of something complete, an integral whole comprising "the splendid canons of an entire era" (*yidai shengdian*), but at the same time insists that it is incomplete—notionally in relation to its historiographical forbears, and literally in that the physical book he is submitting with the memorial is unfinished, lacking the treatises.[67]

Settling into the historiographical pluperfect, his good history would indeed be deemed deficient—in one version of the clash with Pei Ziye detailed above, and later and verifiably by the great Tang dynasty historical critic Liu Zhiji, who would harshly criticize his work for having included too much documentation and detail. But how might Shen Yue have taken

---

"The Historiographical Tradition," 144–45, Schaberg, *A Patterned Past*, 262–64, and Wai-yee Li, "Pre-Qin Annals," 436–38.

66. *Song shu* 100.2468.

67. A recent study has drawn on encyclopedia evidence to suggest that Shen Yue's treatises may have circulated separately and in a more detailed version than is found in the current *Song shu*; see Chen Shuang, "*Taiping yulan* suo yin *Song shu* kao," 92–98.

such criticism—or "exteriorization?" In one historiographical world, at least, he handled Pei Ziye's with aplomb. More than that, for the historiographically astute Shen Yue, Liu Zhiji's implicit expectation—that he should produce a work that, in a shining state of completion, would "shame" the ancients, that he would presume to insert himself into the interiority of the historical record, by crafting it into a concise and sensible whole—is more foil than foe. Far better to "relay" a work replete with documentation and for that reason fully ensconced in the rhetoric of incompletion, a lightly edited work awaiting the interpretation of later readers. The critical, not to say polemical, approaches to historiography of the likes of Liu Zhiji cannot adequately acknowledge the wisdom of the threshold position of presenting history "as it was"—replete with raw material.

Fires of documentation blazed in the hearths of the early medieval Chinese gentry and the state they served, sparked by a historiographical culture of self-representation and fueled by paper. If only we could still feel its living warmth: to see the missives sent by the Founding Ancestor in the hand guided by Liu Muzhi, to read the documents selected and copied by Liu himself, to behold the writ of abdication of the last Jin emperor—written out, at the usurper's insistence, in his own calligraphy.[68] In the flotsam remains of early medieval manuscripts we may catch a physical glimpse of what it was like, but never much of one: mostly we face the documentation in the cold generic font of the historical compilation.

Yet the embers still glow, because historiography is a continuum. The historical actor, already articulated as he is by the historiographical forms he lived with, is the starting point of the historiographical process, performing with the consciousness of what was to come—that his or her private productions might be selected for and ironed into a glossy public-minded historical mimesis—ideally that of the "annals and biographies" form in which the individual life resonated most fully. Now we stand on the other side of this intertemporal relation. Are we persuaded by their historiographical representations? Do we accept their biases? Do we believe

---

68. *Song shu* 12.46. See also *Song shu* 57.1582, where the authority of a document in the imperial hand is contrasted with an order issued normally from the palace office.

their *Documents?* To some extent we must, if we are to engage with these materials on fair ground.

With these materials, and with these historical actors. The dead cannot hear the arguments we make in return, but they knew the historical process to be incomplete and uncertain. They knew that the pluperfect game of having future people or events affirm them could not be played without the possibility of a negative response. They can ask only that the negative response be formulated using a language or a logic that they might be able to understand. Our comprehension of this historical culture, wrapped tight in its distinctive shrouds, must take shape as a motion between interiors and exteriors, with an appreciation for historical judgments that linger on the threshold.

CONCLUSION

Epideictic History

> Galloping forth with its praises, its criticisms duly tailored, history shakes the souls of myriad generations of readers.
> —Liu Xie, from the encomium to the "Histories and Biographies" chapter of the *Wenxin diaolong*

Etymology offers a rough way of enunciating what makes Chinese historiography distinctive. The Greek and Latin roots of the English word "history" associate it with the epistemological acts of investigation and study. In contrast, the Chinese word *shi* 史 originally meant "scribe," implying more an activity and an institution than an enterprise of inquiry. It is true that etymology only takes us so far in trying to understand what culturally significant words like this really meant. One recent discussion of *shi* observes that "scribe" is not capable of conveying the complexities of historical recordkeeping in pre-imperial China.[1] In the early medieval period, meanwhile, when *shi* became a category term for "history," it did so in every meaningful sense of that word, from the assessment of evidence to its arrangement in a narrative form, from a deep interest in the workings of the human world to an adherence to principles of objectivity, responsibility, and generosity of judgment. *Shi* does indeed mean "history." But the question is what specific properties defined this particular realization of a common endeavor—and scribal origins point us in the right direction.

From the idea that history developed out of the activity of scribes proceeds one of the main points of this book—that the production and

---

1. See Stephen Durrant, "From 'Scribe' to 'History': The Keyword *shi* 史," 85, 89; see also, for a novel interpretation that links the "scribes" to (rhetorical) speech, David Schaberg, "Functionary Speech: On the Work of *Shi* 使 and *Shi* 史."

then reproduction of documents constituted the core of Chinese historiographical practice. The next step is to recognize that the making of a historical document was itself a form of historical action. This is implicit in the stories about the "good historians" of antiquity, who made their mark on the historical record by making their mark on the historical record. Yet this kind of historiographical action was in no way limited to historians: historical actors in general came to act with a historiographical consciousness, crafting a documentary record for the use of historians proper in the future. In this way, biography literally became a kind of "life writing"—writing done by the living, in the form of documents written and published and anecdotes enacted and recorded, negotiating their interests in the view of a future judgment upon them. This phenomenon received full expression in the paper-fueled culture of the early medieval period, and it is reinforced in works like the *History of the Liu-Song*, which was compiled when much of the relevant documentation was still extant, preserving prodigious amounts of it.

Thus, the early medieval art of history was a form of verbal action, which is to say that it was a form of rhetoric. All historiography, the world over, has a rhetorical dimension to it. Convincing stories must be forged out of sources, persuasive judgments drawn from and attached to historical events. Yet the relevance of rhetoric to a highly contemporary historiography like this one is of a different nature, for the push and pull of the "interior-exterior dynamic" was not a retrospective battle over interpretation but a here-and-now attempt to plot the course of historical events as they would be recorded. This historiography, evolved from the scribal tradition, was less a kind of inquiry than a species of politics, and in politics, rhetoric is a first-order element.

At the same time that the reality of rhetoric pulses through the histories, rhetoric makes a fruitful point of entry to early medieval historiography for nearly opposite reasons: not because historiography was so deeply informed by it, but because history was considered to hold truths that transcend mere rhetoric, and for that matter, because rhetorical analysis in the sense it is used in this book was completely alien to the historians of early medieval China. Rhetoric is an outside, "etic" approach, repartitioning the subject matter and allowing us to peer around the dignified pate of the "good historian." One advantage of this approach is that rhetoric places the issues of politics and bias squarely in the foreground, issues that are acknowledged in the traditional "good historian" framework but expressly as bugbears. Thus Liu Xie, the author of the literary treatise *Wenxin diaolong* and younger contemporary of Shen Yue, frets that "the historian carries responsibility for an entire age, bears a duty for the whole world—and for all that he finds himself entangled in criticism" 然史之為任，乃彌綸一代，負海內之責，而贏是非之尤.[2] Not even an exemplar like Ban Gu can avoid this fate, he laments, much less the more ordinary historian, whose pen might accidentally veer into poor judgment. In this view, the only proper safeguard is a stability of moral purpose. From the rhetorical point of view, however, Liu Xie is simply describing the normal state of affairs for creators and compilers of historical material, who do so within the fray of the mundane world, never apart from it. While morality may guide the historiographical enterprise, giving it a "public" gravitas, it is these "private" interests that give historiography its momentum.

Similarly, on the question of bias, Liu Xie excoriates the historian who would bow to established interests, "dressing the middling men of lofty families up in fullest honors, while throwing scorn on virtuous men of lower station, blowing cold frost on one while puffing sweet dew on the other, fame and forgetting all at the mercy of his pen" 勳榮之家，雖庸夫而盡飾；屯敗之士，雖令德而螢埋，吹霜煦露，寒暑筆端. Again, he purports to condemn a flaw, but in doing so provides a description of a certain characteristic of historical writing in his time: the reader taking a rhetorical view is better prepared to acknowledge bias as a feature of the art. It was a challenge the good historian could manage, by understanding the biases in his sources and being circumspect with those created in his own work—or it was a challenge that was impossible to manage, the welter of biases contained in historical sources forever threatening to overwhelm the historian who worked mainly through the selection of received materials.

The idea that a historian might not have been able to extricate himself from the rhetoric of the documents, anecdotes, and draft histories that reached his hands points to the broader problem of rhetoric's "active" and "passive" aspects. Making active use of the rhetorical resources at their disposal, human beings pursuing their purposes in life seek to persuade others. At the same time, they become tokens in a rhetorical economy, in the service of the persuasions of others and, more than that, in thrall to the

---

2. Liu Xie, *Wenxin diaolong zhushi* 16.172.

self-propelling rhetorical culture itself—for to speak of a "culture" is to identify a set of ways in which people dwell in an already persuaded state of being, immersed in certain kinds of arguments and tropes. In this passive sense, human actors are the means of existence for historiographical forms—documents, anecdotes, official careers—creating arguments and narratives but in the weak sense of filling the vacuums of textual and aural space in a churning discursive economy. No longer the rhetorically crafted denotation of historical event, this kind of historiography was a trans-historical presence, using the human actor to realize itself in a series of permutations, and attending to this process puts us at the center of the combined peril and opportunity early medieval historical sources confront us with: the historical record is grounded in its own processes of recording as much as it is in historical events. That event and record are two sides of one coin turns out to be one of the most crucial historical factors for us to grasp.

It is also instructive to think about which of the traditional genres of rhetoric we might best ascribe historiography to—acknowledging, of course, that it is a kind of its own. The three conventional branches or genres of rhetoric are the "forensic"—judging past events—the "deliberative"—deciding a course of future action—and the "epideictic"—a rhetorical display in the present moment. In this mapping of rhetoric onto the three basic categories of time, historiography clearly pertains to the first, because the writing of history involves discerning narratives in or fitting narrative models onto artifacts of the past and making arguments based on those reconstructions. Deliberation on future action, meanwhile, has provided one major way of expressing the distinction of the Chinese tradition, in which "history functioned as the very explanation of the relevance of the past to the present," a didactic "mirror" held up by the good historian.[3]

---

3. On-cho Ng and Q. Edward Wang, *Mirroring the Past: The Writing and Use of History in Imperial China*, 259. See also Watson, *Ssu-ma Ch'ien*, 135–43, observing the impact of the instrumental use of historical example for rhetorical ends in early China; and Vincent S. Leung, *The Politics of the Past in Early China*, which reviews and extends recent scholarship that moves beyond "mere moralistic didacticism" (12) as a characterization of historical thought in the early period, focusing instead on how the past was deployed in political argument. Needless to say, didacticism was a regular motive for historiography in many cultures; for example, Daniel Woolf, *A Global History of History*, 44–46, on the emphasis on example in Roman historiography.

It is dynastic historiography's inherent connection to the epideictic branch, however, that proves to be the most informative rhetorical perspective. Historiography is a demonstrative art of (mostly) praise and (to a lesser extent) blame. This is a familiar characterization in a new light. "Praise and blame" (*baobian* 褒贬) was a core concern of traditional Chinese historiography, but it is invariably framed as a judgment on the past or a lesson for the future. The epideictic perspective unmoors praise and blame from its transitive objects, making history not about something but an art of presentation that is an effect in its own right. "It is the function of the historian," as Burton Watson writes, but altering his emphasis, "to prolong the memory of goodness by preserving its record for all ages *to see*."[4] To adopt an expansive characterization of epideictic oratory in the Western world, we may say that the greater purpose of historiography was not to represent the past but to use past events in a presentation of "the shining and unanimous face of the society's universal understanding."[5]

As such characterizations indicate, the primary color of the epideictic, and of an epideictic historiography, is praise, not blame. In the Western tradition, praise was favored because it "promoted social cohesion and aimed at literary beauty," while "the rhetorical theory of the epideictic speech of blame remained underdeveloped, and the corresponding practice scarcely ventured beyond the schoolroom."[6] The natural beauty of praise was likewise the most important aspect of Chinese historiography. Again the pithy if broad summation of Burton Watson: "For the Chinese, the immortality of history was the great goal of life."[7] More broadly still, Liang Qichao: "For the most part, traditional historiography was written for the dead."[8] Under this conception, what was expected of historiography, and especially biography, was immortal fame, not infamy: "The purpose of biography was essentially commemorative, born from a desire to provide a record of the deceased's achievements and personality for his surviving descendants,

4. Watson, *Ssu-ma Ch'ien*, vii, emphasis added.
5. Laurent Pernot, *Epideictic Rhetoric: Questioning the Stakes of Ancient Praise*, 99.
6. Pernot, *Epideictic Rhetoric*, 65. See also Cristina Pepe, "(Re)discovering a Rhetorical Genre: Epideictic in Greek and Roman Antiquity," which outlines the ways epideictic discourse was delimited.
7. Watson, *Ssu-ma Ch'ien*, 157.
8. Liang Qichao, *Zhongguo lishi yanjiufa*, 31 (chapter 3).

relatives, and associates."⁹ "The most coveted eventual destination for a biographical text is not the grave of its subject, or a collection of biographies, but the dynastic history itself."¹⁰ And there are many inductive reasons to place praise first in an evaluation of this historiography. Court annals (of good emperors) naturally showed their sovereigns in a favorable light. The preponderance of lives incorporated in any given dynastic history were of men who had conducted themselves (more or less) admirably. In the written documents that formed the historiographical backbone, praise was a main point of leverage, and indeed a great many documents seem to exist for little reason other than the presentation of praise.

The predominance of praise raises the question of what role blame played as a constituent part of epideictic rhetoric, and epideictic historiography in particular. One answer is that it served as a foil: when blame appears, it is to bolster the prestige of the unblamed or to render praiseworthy deeds all the more salient. But blame also had a more subtle function. Praise is inherently problematic because it runs too close to flattery. It needs the tempering of blame, its gentle "circumstantialization," to persist as a public value worthy of epideictic display. Returning to Liu Xie's discussion of historiography:

> Truly, "honoring the worthy and concealing their shortcomings" is the sagely instruction established by Confucius, as slight flaws do nothing to detract from fine pieces of jade. [However,] to deliver stern warnings to those who might do evil wanton acts—that is the true purpose for the historian's honest, upright pen, just as the farmer who sees a weed will be certain to hoe it to the ground. Indeed, this sub-statute sets the standard for all historians, past and present.
>
> 若乃尊賢隱諱，固尼父之聖旨，蓋纖瑕不能玷瑾瑜也；奸慝懲戒，實良史之直筆，農夫見莠，其必鋤也。若斯之科，亦萬代一準焉。¹¹

Liu Xie starts by acknowledging that Confucius has established praise as historiography's founding principle—enjoining the historian to gloss over the foibles of good men, storing their lesser moments away in anecdote,

9. Twitchett, "Problems in Chinese Biography," 29.
10. David McMullen, *State and Scholars in T'ang China*, 193.
11. Liu Xie, *Wenxin diaolong zhushi* 16.172.

burying them elsewhere in the history, or eliding them altogether. The memorialization of good men was truly history's most important task. At the same time, troubled by the potential consequences of a full endorsement of the principle of praise, he chooses to emphasize the importance of adhering to a "sub-statute" that requires the historian to exercise fully his powers of honest and objective blame.

As with their attempts to defuse bias rather than accept it as a part of the historical art, critics like Liu Xie tend to stress the importance of blame and cast aspersions on the emptiness of praise. For this reason, readers may be likely to conclude that Liu Xie "stresses the role of the historian as moralist and his heavy responsibility to tell the truth without fear or favour."[12] Yet what is really at issue is not a binary choice between judgments of praise or blame, nor between historical approaches that would prefer one aspect over the other, but a mutually defining relationship at the heart of an epideictic "praise and blame" historiography. In the end, Liu Xie sustains that weighted balance, conveying it aptly and succinctly in his chapter's rhymed summary verses: "Galloping forth with its praises, its criticisms duly tailored, history shakes the souls of myriad generations of readers" 騰褒裁貶，萬古魂動. His mixed metaphor elevates praise, which "gallops" (teng) forward with the force of a stallion, and accords blame the necessary but resolutely complementary function of "tailoring" (cai) its accounts down to due measure.

This returns us, finally, to the interior-exterior political dynamic in which historiography participated. The basis of that dynamic is a simple relationship of interior power to exterior weakness, but it is more complex than that: the exterior has a power of its own, as a threat to interiority, as a prompt toward its constitution, or in the persistence of exterior surfaces like historiographical representation. Historiography, for its part, also operates simply, in accordance with its eulogistic bent, issuing praise that reflects interior worth and casting blame on that which was, or should have been, exteriorized. But eulogy contains the seeds of irony. Historiography's glossy exterior is the mask that conceals, and holds the power to reveal, interiors that are not what they appear to be, and it is the medium through which blameworthy appearances can redeem themselves, as functions in greater historiographical acts. Reversing the polarity of definition and

---

12. Pulleyblank, "The Historiographical Tradition," 153.

circumstance, the ironic capability of epideictic historiography is a power, but one that is all the more precious for its fragility, because its ironies can only persist while left intact. For the historical actor, the historian, and the reader of history, the only constant position is the threshold, where interior and exterior join, preserving by not fully engaging the integrity of both.

It is my view that there is nothing more important in the study of early medieval China than coming to an understanding of historical writing in that era. It drove the culture and it shapes our perception of it. There is nothing more important—or more challenging, and even more vexing, and it is a problem that must be addressed not once, and certainly not through one single case study, but on every excursion into the field. What the present study offers is a record of one such excursion and its lessons learned. Some of those lessons might even have a general import, to the study of premodern China and beyond.

When reading a historical source, what is the first question we should ask of it? I think we ought to ask what biases we can detect in it. Naturally, this includes the perspective of the source's author or, more often in our case, its compiler, but it is a great mistake to dwell too long on that moment: the point of view of Shen Yue, or, to take a more famous case, of the Tang historiographers who compiled the histories of the Jin and the Northern and Southern Dynasties, is only a small part of the picture, and it is only occasionally recoverable. The bias that should most concern us lurks in the words, the sentences, the paragraphs, and the whole components of the historical text, vectors that represent interests or the distillations of some conflict of interests. I believe biases at this level are too often overlooked. Perhaps this is because working through them is not easy, and sometimes not possible: in the historiography that has been compiled and handed down to us, private interests are frequently jumbled together and smoothed over, while public values are leveraged in various ways by various historical actors, and anyway are themselves hardly univocal. The melodies have disappeared into the medley.

Underscoring bias, however distorted it may have become, amounts to saying that historical writing is a venue for and a representation of political action—the "interior-exterior" dynamic posited at the outset of this study.

In premodern China, politics was a very potent element of historiography, as history was tied up with the state's presentation of itself and of its core issue, the negotiation of a viable state-gentry polity; but surely all historical writing is to some degree political in this sense, as a forum for the airing of biases and an attempt, not always successful or even genuine, to reconcile them. What is crucial—certainly in early medieval Chinese historiography, and probably beyond—is the fact that political actors and historians alike lack full agency in this historiographical politics. Everyone is caught up in its web of bias. Actively controlled rhetorical vectors often matter less than the energy, or rhetorical "exigence," in the system itself, impelling its human agents to produce the biases that are in its nature.

Motivated by this rhetoric, historical actors create historiographical surfaces. What has here been described as a unity or concert or confusion of historical action and historiographical representation is, I suggest, an essential quality—*the* essential quality—of early medieval Chinese culture, but its relevance is broader than that: historical writing of all kinds communicates both with its content and with its representational effect, with the message conveyed and with the impact of the message's outer form on specific audiences. In premodern China, these representational surfaces had wide currency. The role / type complex—the emulation of historical models by historical actors, and the definition of historical actors with reference to those models—was one kind of surface. The sculpting in time of an official career was another. These animated representations circulated in textual form, and the most generalized historical form was expressly textual: the document, the primary model for which may be identified as the *shi* poem. Canonically known as the exterior representation of interior intent, it is the exterior dimension that should be emphasized. These actor-created surfaces made the patchwork that would be stitched together to constitute the realm of history.

The inherently biased surfaces of historiography came together with a certain disposition—the epideictic mode described earlier in this conclusion. That is, the basic bias produced in historiographical action was positive, or eulogistic. For biographical writing, we may trace this tendency back to the pens of the decedents' friends and affiliates, or more deeply into the realm of ancestor worship, and for the annals, to the brushes of court historiographers who, honest as they might (often) have been, were tasked with presenting to posterity the noble visage of a house entrusted with the Mandate of Heaven. That is how it was in early medieval or simply premodern China, but perhaps, again, we should not find such a praise-oriented historiography so strange. If it is alien to the scholarly, "reflective" conception of history, there is something universal to the epideictic mode—for it is readily apparent that many readers and users of history prefer to view their past in an attractive garb, and reject the kind of history that does not so present it.

Praise is the dominant orientation of epideictic rhetoric, but blame is its integral counterpart. In historiography, blame can include explicit excoriation and condemnation by historical actors and then historians, but more importantly it is a part of the system's weighted disposition: historiography's epideictic charge primarily produces positive representations, but then, with a reversal of current, the positive becomes negative. The two states are sometimes separated into different texts, or they may appear as a mixture—or one of them was never realized at all, but its murmuring is faintly audible if we listen carefully for it.

What, then, are readers of this epideictic kind of history to do with it? First, they must never get too caught up in its lines of bias, whether those pull toward praise or toward blame. At least, one should be keenly aware of the bias—that what appears as event or perspective on event is often part of some rhetorical performance, and that these "primary sources" mix up the biases as they relay them. Second, readers must relax, if never quite relinquish, the expectation that historiography can be drafted into the service of ordinary acts of historical scholarship, peeling back the representation to uncover some real world that lies beneath. There is no beneath, for the reality was interwoven with its representation. Though it is truly not an easy thing to treat history in this way, like the historical actors we study, we can only stand on the threshold, occasionally accessing the interior space but spending more time exploring historiography's exterior surface, seeking to understand not what the symbol-using and -misusing animal meant by its symbols, but how those symbols furnished and drove the expansion of its universe. To attend to the significance of representation itself—that is a challenge crucial to the study of early medieval China, if by no means unique to it.

APPENDIX

The Song shu *Biography of Liu Muzhi* (360–417)

I.

Liu Muzhi: public name Daohe, minor public name Daomin; native of Ju county, Dongguan prefecture;[1] a descendant of Fei, the Han dynasty prince of Qi posthumously known as Daohui.[2] His family had lived in Jingkou for generations.[3]

劉穆之,字道和,小字道民,東莞莒人,漢齊悼惠王肥後也。世居京口。

II

A

As a young man, he was fond of reading books and their associated commentaries and notes.[4] He read widely and knew much, and his talents were recognized by Jiang Ai of Jiyang.[5] When Jiang became Establishing the Martial General and Fief-Prefect of Langya,[6] he made Liu Muzhi his chief of staff.[7]

少好書、傳,博覽多通,為濟陽江敳所知。敳為建武將軍、琅邪內史,以為府主簿。

B

In the beginning, Liu had once dreamed that he was boating on the sea with the Founding Ancestor. A great wind suddenly arose, frightening him, but when he looked down from the boat he found two white dragons escorting them on either side. Then they came to a mountain, its peaks towering beautifully, its shrubbery growing dense. He found it most delightful.[8]

Then, upon the conquest of Jingkou,[9] the Founding Ancestor spoke to He Wuji:[10] "I urgently require a chief of staff. Where shall I look for one?" Wuji replied: "There is none better than Liu Daomin."[11] "Ah, I too know him," said the Founding Ancestor, and immediately he rushed a messenger off to summon him.

At that time, Liu Muzhi heard a ruckus coming from within Jingkou. At dawn, he arose and went out to the field-path [to see what was happening], and at that moment he happened to meet up with the messenger. Liu Muzhi stared at him for a long while, saying nothing. Then he returned to his house, where he tore his cloth skirt apart to make a pair of [warrior's] pants[12] and set out to see the Founding Ancestor.

The Founding Ancestor spoke to him: "My uprising to defend the grand righteousness of the empire has just begun and right now I face many difficulties. I urgently require an officer for my army—would you, sir, know anyone up to the task?"

"As your esteemed generalship has just been established,"[13] Liu Muzhi replied, "a talented officer is indeed needed. In this immediate moment, perhaps my abilities will not be surpassed by those of another?"[14]

Smiling at this, the Founding Ancestor replied: "If you can condescend yourself to do it, then the success of my enterprise is certain."

And immediately at that sitting, Liu Muzhi accepted the appointment.

初，穆之嘗夢與高祖俱泛海，忽值大風，驚懼。俯視船下，見有二白龍夾舫。既而至一山，峯崿聳秀，林樹繁密，意甚悅之。及高祖克京城，問何無忌曰：「急須一府主簿，何由得之？」無忌曰：「無過劉道民。」高祖曰：「吾亦識之。」即馳信召焉。時穆之聞京城有叫譟之聲，晨起出陌頭，屬與信會。穆之直[15]視不言者久之。既而反室，壞布裳為袴，往見高祖。高祖謂之曰：「我始舉大義，方造艱難，須一軍吏甚急，卿謂誰堪其選？」穆之曰：「貴府始建，軍吏實須其才，倉卒之際，當略無見踰者。」高祖笑曰：「卿能自屈，吾事濟矣。」即於坐受署。

III

A

He joined in the capture of the capital [in the third month of 404]. When the Founding Ancestor first took the city, the major decisions were all made, in the immediate moment, on the initiative of Liu Muzhi. Thereupon, the Founding Ancestor entrusted to him total responsibility for the tasks closest to his heart, and was certain to consult him on every single move. And Liu Muzhi, for his part, also exhausted himself in his sincere dedication to his patron, leaving absolutely nothing unattended or concealed.

從平京邑，高祖始至[16]，諸大處分，皆倉卒立定，並穆之所建也。遂委以腹心之任，動止咨焉。穆之亦竭節盡誠，無所遺隱。

B

At that time, the rule of the Jin court had grown lax, its awe and authority no longer heeded. Powerful clans and men of illicit riches wielded their power with no compunctions, while the common folk suffered in extreme poverty, with no place even to stand their feet. More than that, the edicts issued under [the prime minister] Sima Yuanxian had been full of error, while the regulations promulgated by [the usurper] Huan Xuan had been too overbearing.[17] [Responding to this,] Muzhi gave careful consideration to the needs of the times and set things straight using proper methods. And in not ten days, the customs of the realm were completely reformed.[18]

時晉綱寬弛，威禁不行，盛族豪右，負勢陵縱，小民窮蹙，自立無所。重以司馬元顯政令違舛，桓玄科條繁密。穆之斟酌時宜，隨方矯正，不盈旬日，風俗頓改。

C

Muzhi was promoted to Gentleman on the Board of Sacrifices of the Secretariat,[19] and then again made chief of the Founding Ancestor's staff,[20] and [then] Record-Keeper-Adjutant, and [then] Overseer-Adjutant,[21] holding in addition the office of Prefect of Tangyi.[22] For merit in the suppression of Huan Xuan,[23] he was enfeoffed as Five Degrees Viscount of the County of Xihua.[24]

遷尚書祠部郎,復為府主簿,記室、錄事參軍,領堂邑太守。以平桓玄功,封西華縣五等子。

D

In the third year of the reign of Righteousness Resplendent [407],[25] Wang Mi, Governor of Yangzhou, died.[26] In the regular order of things, the Founding Ancestor should have entered the capital region to assist [i.e., assert control over] the court, but Liu Yi and the other powers did not want the Founding Ancestor to do so, so they proposed appointing Xie Hun, General of the Interior Armies, as Governor of Yangzhou.[27] Others wanted to grant the governorship to the Founding Ancestor but have him hold it in Dantu [i.e., Jingkou], turning control of the court over to the Director of the Secretariat, Meng Chang.[28] They sent the Second Assistant to the Secretariat, Pi Chen, to confer with the Founding Ancestor on these two plans.[29]

Pi Chen was first received by Muzhi, to whom he explained the views of the men at court. Pretending to excuse himself for a trip to the toilet, Muzhi sent off a secret communique to the Founding Ancestor. It said:

Pi Chen has just arrived. Do not agree to anything he says.

When the Founding Ancestor received Pi Chen, he sent him to wait outside and called for Muzhi. "What did you mean when you said not to agree to anything proposed by Pi Chen?"

義熙三年[30],揚州刺史王謐薨,高祖次應入輔,劉毅等不欲高祖入,議以中領軍謝混為揚州。或欲令高祖於丹徒領州,以內事付尚書僕射孟昶。遣尚書右丞皮沈以二議咨高祖。沈先見穆之,具說朝議。穆之偽起如廁,即密疏白高祖曰:「皮沈始至,其言不可從。」高祖既見沈,且令出外,呼穆之,問曰:「卿云沈言不可從,其意何也?」

E

To which Liu Muzhi replied:

In the [not so distant] past, the rule of the Jin court went awry, and it has been so for not just a single day. On top of this, Huan Xuan usurped the throne—the Mandate of Heaven had already begun to shift. [But now] Your Excellency has revived the imperial fortunes, and for this your merit shall tower over ten thousand antiquities.

Having accomplished great deeds, you have attained a position of great prominence.[31] [But] a great position and towering merit cannot be maintained for a long time. Given Your Excellency's current situation, how could you possibly make yourself humble and weak, remaining a mere general in charge of a border region?

Liu [Yi], Meng [Chang], and the other Excellencies rose up from ordinary life together with Your Excellency, standing up with you on the side of great Righteousness [i.e., the revival of the Jin house]. At root, their desire has simply been to use the merit they acquired in the restoration of the monarch to acquire riches and nobility. [But] every enterprise has its necessary sequence, and so they have momentarily deferred their claims to great deeds [awaiting the better time to assert them].[32] It is not that they have sincerely submitted to anyone's authority, or truly resigned themselves to being subjects to any master. Balanced in power and circumstances, they will eventually devour one another.[33]

The root of imperial power is bound to [the capital region] Yangzhou. [As such,] it cannot be granted to anyone else, and that in recent years it was assigned to Wang Mi was a matter of expedience. Should a great strategy, one destined for success, necessarily follow this course of action? If today you again grant this region to another man, then by all reckoning you shall find yourself under the command of others. And once you have lost your grip on the handle of power, it cannot be regained.

Furthermore, with your towering deeds and weighty merit, Your Excellency is not easily disposed of. Their fears of you and their suspicions will intermingle, and malevolent intentions will arise from all sides. How could you fail to consider the dangers that lie in the future?

Today, the opinion of the court is such as it is and you must respond to it, but were you to insist that the appointment go to you, that would be a difficult argument to make. Rather, you should say:

> The divine province [of Yangzhou] is the root of governance, and the Prime Minister [who commands it] is a man of lofty importance. This is the "stairway" for revival or for disaster, and as such it should be a matter for careful selection. Given the great importance of this matter, it is not to be discussed in the abstract, so I will provisionally enter the court to discuss the alternatives exhaustively together with you.

When Your Excellency reaches the capital, it is a clear certainty that they will not dare to pass over Your Excellency in favor of some other person.

The Founding Ancestor followed his advice, and thus he came to enter the capital to assist the court.[34]

穆之曰:「昔晉朝失政,非復一日,加以桓玄簒奪,天命已移。公興復皇胙[35],勳高萬古。既有大功,便有大位。位大勳高,非可持久。公今日形勢,豈得居謙自弱,遂為守藩之將邪?劉、孟諸公,與公俱起布衣,共立大義,本欲匡主成勳,以取富貴耳。事有前後,故一時推功,非為委體心服、宿定臣主之分也。力敵勢均,終相吞咀。揚州根本所係,不可假人。前者以授王謐,事出權道,豈是始終大計必宜若此而已哉。今若復以他授,便應受制於人。一失權柄,無由可得。而公功高勳重,不可直置,疑畏[36]交構,異端互起,將來之危難,可不熟念。今朝議如此,宜相酬答,必云在我,厝辭又難。唯應云『神州治本,宰輔崇要,興喪所階,宜加詳擇。此事既大,非可懸論,便暫入朝,共盡同異』。公至京,彼必不敢越公更授餘人明矣。」高祖從其言,由是入輔。

F

Muzhi joined in the northern campaign on Guanggu [in 409–10][37] and returned south to quell Lu Xun [in 410].[38] He was always in the commander's tent helping devise strategy, making resolute decisions on all sundry affairs. Liu Yi and the others resented the favor shown to Muzhi, and at every opportunity they casually insinuated that his power had grown too great. But the Founding Ancestor only trusted him more and more.

從征廣固,還拒盧循,常居慎中畫策,決斷眾事。劉毅等疾穆之見親,每從容言其權重,高祖愈信仗之。

G

Whatever Muzhi heard from outsiders, whether great or small, he never failed to certainly relay on, without omitting anything, even the gossip and invective of the wards and villages, or minor happenings on the roadsides. The Founding Ancestor always made a show of knowing every little thing there was to know about the comings and goings of the common people—and all this knowledge came from Muzhi.

穆之外所聞見，莫不大小必白，雖復閭里言謔，塗陌細事，皆一二以聞。高祖每得民間委密消息以示聰明，皆由穆之也。

H

Also:[39] Muzhi was fond of social gatherings, his receptions always full of guests. [In this way] he spread about people to serve as eyes and ears, so he was certain to know everything about people's opinions at court and beyond, and he would submit all of these to the Founding Ancestor's attention without concealing anything, even the peccadilloes of his intimate associates. For this someone once criticized him. "With His Excellency's perspicacity,"[40] he responded, "he would surely come to know of it anyway. And having received His favor, Honor forbids me from concealing anything: that is why Zhang Liao reported on Guan Yu when the latter was about to rebel."[41]

又愛好賓遊，坐客恆滿，布耳目以為視聽，故朝野同異，穆之莫不必知。雖復親暱短長，皆陳奏無隱。人或譏之，穆之曰：「以公之明，將來會自聞達。我蒙公恩，義無隱諱，此張遼所以告關羽欲叛也。」

I

Muzhi established the protocol for all of the Founding Ancestor's activities. [For instance,] the Founding Ancestor's calligraphy was naturally clumsy, so Muzhi said to him: "This may be a minor matter, but you are sending your handwriting far into the four directions. I beseech Your Excellency to pay a bit of attention to it." But the Founding Ancestor was not able to put his mind to it, and at any rate his natural abilities limited him, so Muzhi took a different approach: "Just write your characters large, letting your brush go as it will. Even if your characters are a foot across, it is no cause for worry. For, being large, they will show an accommodating nature, and the display of natural propensity will be quite beautiful." Following his counsel, the Founding Ancestor would fill up a sheet of paper with just six or seven characters.[42]

高祖舉止施為，穆之皆下節度。高祖書素拙，穆之曰：「此雖小事，然宣彼四遠，願公小復留意。」高祖既不能厝意，又稟分有在。穆之乃曰：「但縱筆為大字,一字徑尺,無嫌。大既足有所包,且其勢亦美。[43]」高祖從之,一紙不過六七字便滿。

J

When Muzhi sought to promote someone, he would stop at nothing.[44] "Though I may not promote the worthy as well as the Gentleman Director Xun (Xun Yu) did," he would regularly remark, "I do not promote the *not worthy*."[45]

凡所薦達,不進[46]不止,常云:「我雖不及荀令君之舉善,然不舉不善。」

K

Muzhi and Zhu Lingshi were both skilled in official correspondence.[47] Once, he and Lingshi were responding to letters in the presence of the Founding Ancestor. From dawn to noon, Muzhi sent out a hundred replies to Lingshi's eighty—and was able to keep up the conversation all the while.

穆之與朱齡石竝便尺牘,嘗[48]於高祖坐與齡石答書。自旦至日中,穆之得百函,齡石得八十函,而穆之應對無廢也。

L

Muzhi rotated up to [General of the] Central Army's and [then] the Grand Commandant's Officer-in-Charge.[49] In year eight of the era of Righteousness Resplendent (412), Prefect-Martial of Danyang (the capital city) was added to his portfolio.[50]

轉中軍、太尉司馬。八年,加丹陽尹。

M

When the Founding Ancestor campaigned west against Liu Yi [in the ninth month of 412], he made Zhuge Zhangmin overseer of the [Grand Commandant's] home office, in charge of all matters in the rear guard.[51] [However,] suspicious of Zhangmin's loyalties, he left Muzhi to assist him, adding the Establishing Awe generalship to his titles, granting him a staff and assigning troops under his command. And indeed, Zhangmin did have disloyal intentions—but he hesitated, unable to bring himself to action. Sending everyone away, he addressed Muzhi:

> All the rumors have it that the Grand Commandant [i.e., the Founding Ancestor] and I are not on good terms. How has it come to this?

Muzhi replied:

> His Excellency has gone upriver on a distant campaign and he has entrusted his elderly mother and young children under your banner. If his trust in you were anything less than fully complete, how could he have done such a thing?[52]

And so Zhangmin's mind was somewhat put at ease. When the Founding Ancestor returned, Zhangmin was put to death.[53]

高祖西討劉毅，以諸葛長民監留府，揔攝後事。高祖疑長民難獨任，留穆之以輔之。加建威將軍，置佐吏，配給實力。長民果有異謀，而猶豫不能發，乃屏人謂穆之曰：「悠悠之言，皆云太尉與我不平，何以至此？」穆之曰：「公泝流遠伐，而以老母稚子委節下，若一毫不盡，豈容如此邪？」意乃小安[54]。高祖還，長民伏誅。

N

In the tenth year (414), [the Founding Ancestor] promoted Muzhi to General of the Front,[55] supplied with ten thousand bolts of cloth and three million cash per year.

十年，進穆之前將軍，給前軍府年布万匹，錢三百万。

O

In the eleventh year (415), the Founding Ancestor campaigned west against Sima Xiuzhi.[56] Liu Daolian (368–422), General of the Central Army, was put in charge of the [Grand Commandant's] home office, but each and every matter, whether major or minor, was in fact decided by Muzhi.[57]

十一年，高祖西伐司馬休之，中軍將軍道憐知留任，而事無大小，一決穆之。

P

Muzhi was promoted to Junior Chief of the Secretariat, carrying charge of personnel matters.[58] His generalship and prefecture remained as before.

遷尚書右僕射,領選,將軍、尹如故。

Q

In year twelve (416),[59] the Founding Ancestor undertook his northern campaign, leaving his heir behind as General of the Central Army, overseeing the Grand Commandant's home office. Muzhi rotated up to Senior Chief of the Secretariat, carrying charge of the Overseeing and Central Armies,[60] his generalship, prefectureship, and control of personnel matters all remaining as before. He was given an armed guard of fifty men.[61] And he entered to take up residence in the Eastern Fort.[62]

十二年,高祖北伐,留世子為中軍將軍,監太尉留府;轉穆之左僕射,領監軍、中軍二府軍司,將軍[63]、尹、領選如故。甲仗五十人。入居東城。

R

On the inside, Muzhi took control of the imperial court; on the outside, he made provisions for the armies abroad. He decided administrative matters with a river-like flow, obstructed in no matter.

穆之內揔朝政,外供軍旅,決斷如流,事無擁滯。

S

Guests gathered like spokes around the hub of a wheel,[64] petitioning him for all kinds of favors, and the requests he faced, in the court and outside, stacked up on his stairways and filled his rooms. But Muzhi's eyes no sooner glanced over submissions of testimony than his hand wrote out the administrative rejoinders, and as his ears took in the requests so responses were issued from his mouth. No confusion resulted, and each and every matter was properly handled.

賓客輻輳，求訴百端，內外諸稟，盈堦滿室，目覽辭訟，手答牋書，耳行聽受，口竝酬應，不相參涉，皆悉贍舉。

T

Also: he often gave banquets for his favored guests, carrying on his conversation and appreciative laughter for hours on end, never growing weary.

又數客瞕賓，言談賞笑，引日亘時，未嘗倦苦。

U

When he found the time, he would copy out books in his own hand, browsing through writings of all sorts and editing documents into publishable form.[65]

裁有閑暇，自手寫書，尋覽篇章，校定墳籍。

V

By nature he was wantonly extravagant, certain to demand a full banquet for every meal.[66] Even his breakfasts were invariably made for ten men. Fond of entertaining, Muzhi never dined alone, and whenever mealtime drew near he would regularly gather ten or so guests to dine in his quarters. Such was his regular habit. Once, he sought to explain himself to the Founding Ancestor:

> I, Muzhi, come from a poor and lowly family that often struggled even to get by. Since gaining your favor, I have always tried hard to be frugal, but my daily needs have indeed been rather excessive. Yet apart from this, I have never let you down in the slightest way.

性奢豪，食必方丈，旦輒為十人饌。穆之既好賓客，未嘗獨餐，每至食時，客止十人以還者，帳下依常下食，以此為常。嘗白高祖曰：「穆之家本貧賤，贍生多闕。自叨忝以來，雖每存約損，而朝夕所須，微為過豐。自此以外，一毫不以負公。」

IV

In the thirteenth year (417), his illness became severe. By imperial edict, a standing Doctor of the Yellow Gate was sent to treat him. In the eleventh month, he died, in his fifty-eighth year.

十三年,疾篤,詔遣正直黃門郎問疾。十一月卒,時年五十八。

V

A

The Founding Ancestor was in Chang'an at that time, and when he heard the death announcement he was startled and spent several days in grief. Originally he had intended to remain there some time, and to go on to raid the areas northeast of the Yellow River, but with Muzhi dead the capital was now entrusted to no one, so he rushed back to Pengcheng, where he put Xu Xianzhi provisionally in charge of the home office. The court affairs that formerly had been always decided by Muzhi were all to be passed north for consultation with the Founding Ancestor.[67]

高祖在長安,聞問驚慟,哀惋者數日。本欲頓駕關中,經略趙、魏。穆之既卒,京邑任虛,乃馳還彭城,以司馬徐羨之代管留任,而朝廷大事常決穆之者,並悉北諮。

B

Of the twenty thousand armed and civilian men that Muzhi had had charge of on his staff of the Front Army, three thousand were assigned to the staff of Xu Xianzhi's Establishing Awe generalship, the remainder to the Central Army generalship held by the Founding Ancestor's heir.[68]

穆之前軍府文武二萬人,以三千配羨之建威府,餘悉配世子中軍府。

C

Muzhi was posthumously granted the titles Regular Outrider Attendant and Defender General, and given rights to establish a staff and ceremonies equivalent to those of the Three Dukes of the realm.

追贈穆之散騎常侍、衛將軍、開府儀同三司。

D

Additionally, the Founding Ancestor submitted a memorial to the throne, as follows:[69]

高祖又表天子曰：

> Your servant has heard it said that the most urgent of the ancient sage kings' teachings is to esteem the worthy and recognize the good; and that in considering merit and selecting contributions [for commemoration], the awarding of posthumous honors is a matter of gravest principle. Thus, the Master of Merit of old held the bamboo tablets, duly recording all examples of unflagging effort, and the shining virtue of good men grew only brighter after their deaths.[70]

> 「臣聞崇賢旌善，王教[71]所先；念功簡勞，義深追遠。故司勳秉策，在勤必記[72]；德之休明，沒而彌著。

> The deceased Senior Chief of the Secretariat and General of the Front (Army)[73] Liu Muzhi rose out of commoner clothes to assist in the righteous renewal of the imperial house. On the inside, he brought forth all the fine plans there were to find. On the outside, he busied himself with all the many tasks of governance.[74] Tireless in his service in civil and military matters, he exhausted mind and body alike. When he was promoted to head the court, and to govern the capital region, he set forth good instruction as the head of the many offices, and protected and renewed the grand plan of the state.[75] And when, in recent years, the chariots of war were on distant campaign, he resided in the capital as protector, and truly those at court and beyond were well pleased with his meritorious ways of pacification. With such a well-formed sense of judgment, he was indeed a ridgepole of the state, and a pillar.

> 故尚書左僕射、前軍將軍臣穆之，爰自布衣，協佐義始，內竭謀獻，[76] 外勤庶政，密勿軍國，心力俱盡。及登庸朝右，尹司京畿，敷讚百揆，翼新大猷。[77] 頃戎車遠役，居中作扞[78]，撫寧之勳，[79] 實洽朝野。識量局致，棟幹之器也。[80]

He was promulgating the grand vision of the state, constructing a sage's reign. But just then, his aims and accomplishments not yet finished, [he died, and] far and near all were brought to sadness. And in Your Majesty's generosity, you have granted him a favorable account, bestowing him a court position equivalent to the Three Dukes.[81] With this, honor and mourning have both been fulfilled, and his spirit has already been shown a favor all too great.[82]

方宣讚盛化,[83] 緝隆聖世,[84] 志績未究,[85] 遠邇悼心。皇恩褒述,班同三事,榮哀既備,寵靈已泰。[86]

And yet, in my humble reckoning: Since the hasty beginnings of the effort to establish this reign of Righteousness Resplendent, difficulties have never ceased to arise. External threats have been severe, even as internal turmoil became more and more intense. The times are awry, our age full of troubles, nary a year of peace. And I, of such meager talents, have had to bear the weight of the empire. In this, I have truly relied on Muzhi's meritorious assistance.

臣伏思尋,自義熙草創,艱患未弭,外虞既殷,內難亦荐[87],時屯世故,靡有寧歲[88]。臣以寡乏[89],負荷國重,實賴穆之匡翼之勳[90]。

And was it only his honest talk and fine plans, which have spread to the ears of the masses? For he also offered sincere critique and candid counsel, sharing his hidden thoughts in the privacy of my tent. Speaking truthfully as his knees touched mine, then using crafty words in public—no one could plumb his depths![91] His deeds, far too numerable to name, were hidden from the view of the court, his achievements unknown to the world. That after toiling for a cycle of twelve years my enterprise has found success, that in going out on campaign and in assisting the court in the capital I have been fortunate enough not to have sullied the charge I have received from Your Majesty—were it not for the aid of this man, none of this could have been achieved.[92]

豈唯讜言嘉謀,溢于民聽;若乃忠規密謨,潛慮帷幕[93],造膝詭辭,莫見其際。事隔於皇朝,功隱於視聽者,不可勝記。[94] 所以陳力一紀,遂克有成,[95] 出征入輔[96],幸不辱命,微夫人之左右,未有寧濟其事者矣。[97]

[Yet] he tread the path of humility and dwelled in moderation, becoming more and more steadfast in his resolve. Whenever it was proposed to grant him a noble's fief, he was always adamantly deferential, to the most extreme degree. This is the reason why, though his merit towered over our age, no fief was ever extended to him. Thinking over this, I brood upon him eternally. How could this be ignored? [Thus,] I propose that he should additionally be made a full Duke, and that a fief domain should be given posthumously. In doing so, Your Highness will ensure that the glory of a loyal and impartial servant will live on after his death, grand rewards forever making their way to good men.

履謙居寡，守之彌固，每議及封爵[98]，輒深自抑絕。所以勳高當年，而茅土弗及[99]，撫事永念[100]，胡寧可昧。謂宜加贈正司，追甄土宇，俾忠貞之烈，不泯於身後，大賁所及，永秩於善人[101]。

I toiled together with him in good times and bad, observing with him the way things end and the way they begin. Our friendly bond, strong as precious metal and fragrant as the orchid, was deep in principle and resonant with intimate feeling.[102] Thus have I submitted what is in my heart to the ears of Your Majesty's court. (I hereby present this request to the throne and ask that it be fully deliberated on in the Secretariat.)[103]

臣契闊屯夷[104]，旋觀終始[105]，金蘭之分，義深情感[106]。是以獻其乃懷，布之朝聽。所啟上，（合請付外詳議。）」

E

Thereupon, Muzhi was further granted the titles of Attendant in the Palace and Duke of the Masses, and enfeoffed as Marquis of Nanchang county, supplied with the income of 1,500 households.[107]

於是重贈侍中、司徒，封南昌縣侯，食邑千五百戶。

F

When the Founding Ancestor received the imperial throne [in 420], he recalled Muzhi's essential contribution to his reception of Heaven's Mandate, issuing an edict:

> The deceased Attendant in the Palace, Duke of the Masses, and Marquis of Nanchang, Liu Muzhi, with his deeply considered counsel and far-reaching plans, began the foundation of Our imperial undertaking, his meritorious deeds helping to create Our great enterprise. Verily, truly, this was a selfless contribution befitting a true kingly minister.[108]
>
> Now, the course of nature has been renewed [with the establishment of Our dynasty] and guardian ministers have been established. At such a moment, I remember this man, and verily I mourn him deeply. Let him be advanced to Duke of Nankang prefecture, with a fief of 3,000 households.[109]

The deceased General of the Left and Governor of Qingzhou, Wang Zhen'e, decimated the rebel leaders in Our victory in the regions of Jing and Ying, and was as important as the Zhou general Fang Shu in Our campaigns to the north.[110] Remembering his tireless efforts and recalling his achievements, I have never forgotten what was in his heart. Let him be advanced to Marquis of Longyang county, with his fief increased to 1,500 households.[111]

高祖受禪,思佐命元勳[112],詔曰:「故侍中、司徒南昌侯劉穆之,深謀遠猷,肇基王跡,勳造大業,誠實匪躬。今理運惟新,蕃屏竝肇,感事懷人,寔深悽悼。可進南康郡公,邑三千戶。故左將軍、青州刺史王鎮惡,荊、郢之捷,剋剪放命,北伐之勳,參跡方叔。念勤惟績,無忘厥心。可進龍陽縣侯,增邑千五百戶。」

G

Muzhi was given the posthumous title of "Duke All-Encompassing Promulgator."[113]

謚穆之曰文宣公。

H

In the ninth year of Prime Goodness [432] of the reign of the Grand Ancestor [Wendi, r. 424–53], [Muzhi's spirit tablet] was granted an accompanying place in the sacrifices at the Founding Ancestor's temple.[114]

太祖元嘉九年,配食高祖廟庭。

I

In the fourth month of the twenty-fifth year [448], the imperial carriage passed by Muzhi's tomb while on a visit to Jiangning.[115] An edict was issued, saying:

> The deceased Palace Attendant, Grand Minister of Public Works, and Duke of Nankang, Liu Muzhi, brought his moral virtue to the assistance of the establishment of the mandate of Our dynasty, protecting and glorifying Our towering enterprise. His advice was far-reaching, his primal merit

flourishing, and so his name and deeds have been engraved on Our sacrificial implements, his righteous acts glowing in Our archival records. Thus, We have already established him as heir to the goodness of the wise men of old, promulgating his spirit to later generations. Now, on an outing, We come to gaze from afar upon his burial grounds, and we lament, like the lords of old, at the sight of a great minister's tomb.[116] Let an offering be made at the gravesite, to express Our eternal memory of him.

二十五年四月,車駕行幸江寧,經穆之墓,詔曰:「故侍中、司徒、南康文宣公穆之,秉德佐命,翼亮景業,謀猷經遠,元勳克茂,功銘鼎彞,義彰典策,故已嗣徽前哲,宣風後代者矣。近因遊踐,瞻其塋域,九原之想,情深悼歎。可致祭墓所,以申永懷。」

J

Muzhi had three sons. The eldest, Zilü, was the heir...[117]

[The text continues with his sons and their progeny—all of whom are portrayed as venal personalities. The biography of Wang Hong follows. Shen Yue then appends the following appraisal to this scroll.]

Your subject the Historian comments:

史臣曰:

The gradual disintegration of the mainstay lines of Jin authority had its reasons. The Filial and Martial Emperor (Xiaowu, r. 372–96) ruled decorously but passively, so his good graces did not reach those below him. Meanwhile, Sima Daozi (364–403) sat atop the imperial clan but lacked virtue, so the foundational laws of the state collapsed. Then Wang Guobao (d. 397) initiated disorder, and Sima Yuanxian laid waste to the court. In this way, the canons bequeathed by the Jin ancestors and the old laws of the Jin's former stewards were as if ground into the dirt, scattered like fallen leaves, broken apart like floes of thawing ice.

晉綱弛紊,其漸有由,孝武守文於上,化不下及,道子昏德居宗,憲章墜矣。重之以國寶[118]啟亂,加之以元顯嗣虐,而[119]祖宗之遺典,羣公之舊章,莫不葉散冰離,掃地盡矣。

[At that time,] the authority of the ruler was not properly established and the ministers did as they wished. Each interpreted the canons of the state to his own will, and different families held to different versions of court protocol. The fate of the taxpaying commoners fell entirely into the hands of the powerful families, and the stores of the empire became their private hoards.

主威不樹，臣道專行，國典人殊，朝綱家異，編戶之命，竭於豪門，王府之蓄，變為私藏。

Thereupon, disaster rose up with a demon in the East (i.e., the Sun En uprising, 399–402), and difficulties befell the entire realm [with the usurpation of Huan Xuan in 403]. As if washed off in a flood, the Way of the sage kings was in danger of extinction, hanging by a mere thread. Then, in a single morning, the Founding Ancestor initiated the righteous restoration, and in that precarious moment, like in the midst of a flood, the bad laws were reversed, fair ways promulgated in their place, and, even while still mounted for battle, whip in his hand, the righteous order of esteemed sovereign and subservient ministers was reestablished. No sooner were the authoritative commands [of the Founding Ancestor] issued than those at court and abroad observed them, and so the decadent customs of the Great Beginning and Esteeming Peace reign periods [i.e., the period from 376 to 401] were exchanged for the glorious ones of the eras of Establishing Martial Authority and Eternal Peace [i.e., the first reigns of the Eastern Han, 25–75 CE]. And this was—was it not?—all the doing of the All-Encompassing Promulgator Duke [Liu Muzhi]. Was it for nothing that he was recognized as the dynasty's ancestral minister, to be worshipped in the Pure Temple of the Founding Ancestor?[120]

由是禍基東妖，難結天下，蕩蕩然王道不絕者若綖。高祖一朝創義，事屬橫流，改亂章，布平道，尊主卑臣之義，定於馬棰之間。威令一施，內外從禁，以建武、永平之風，變太元、隆安之俗，此蓋文宣公之為也。為一代宗臣，配饗清廟，豈徒然哉！

Notes

1. Dongguan was a northern prefecture, located in modern Shandong. According to Hu Axiang, *Liuchao jiangyu yu zhengqu yanjiu*, 438, the "lodged" (*qiao* 僑) Dongguan in the south was not in Jingkou itself (modern Zhenjiang) but between there and Lake Tai, in modern Wujin.

   It is noteworthy that Ju county of Dongguan prefecture was also the native region of the Founding Ancestor's first wife. She died before his rise to power, but her brothers, Zang Tao 臧燾 (353–422) and Zang Xi 臧熹, were critical participants, and Zang Xi's son, Zang Zhi 臧質 (400–454), would be powerful enough to lead a rebellion in 454.

The *Yiwen leiju*, the seventh-century encyclopedia, preserves a "Stele for the Minister of the Masses Liu Muzhi" ("Situ Liu Muzhi bei" 司徒劉穆之碑), ascribed to Fu Liang, who is the author of the Founding Ancestor's memorial in section V-D of this biography; see *Yiwen leiju* 47.836. The stele inscription calls Liu Muzhi a native of Pengcheng (modern Xuzhou, well south of Dongguan but also lodged in the Jingkou area). This discrepancy might suggest that, at Liu Muzhi's death, Fu Liang simply associated him with the Founding Ancestor, whose Liu family did indeed hail from Pengcheng. At the same time, however, the stele text's account focuses on Liu Muzhi's martial accomplishments, a perspective at odds with the biography. While this, too, could be attributed to differences in "historical memory," I suspect otherwise. Though it cannot be proved conclusively, the *Yiwen leiju* extract is likely not about Liu Muzhi at all, but a stele for a contemporary who was also posthumously awarded the title *situ*—the Founding Ancestor's younger half-brother Liu Daogui 劉道規 (370–412; biography at *Song shu* 51.1470–75). The stele narrative fits Liu Daogui's experience exactly, as does, naturally, the identification of its subject's native place. One textual clue also hints at a problem here: the Song dynasty printing of the *Yiwen leiju* has blotted out the "public name" (*zi*), likely an index of confusion between the similar names of Liu Daogui (*zi* Daoze 道則) and Liu Muzhi (*zi* Daohe 道和).

2. Liu Fei was a son of the founding emperor of the Han; see *Shiji* 52.1999. Such a distant kinship relation was almost meaningless, but not necessarily untrue, and it lent Liu Muzhi some prestige, as advisor to a future emperor. In the context of Liu Muzhi's relatively low social status, there may be some symbolism in the fact that "Liu Fei's mother was an unrecognized wife of the Founder of the Han from the time when he was still an unknown" 其母高祖微時外婦也 (*Han shu* 38.1987).

3. Career summaries for a biographical subject's grandfather and father regularly appear here. Though they may have served in low local positions deemed unworthy of mention in the official biography of a man worshipped in the imperial temple, their absence here likely means that Liu Muzhi's grandfather and father held no office. That would technically make Liu Muzhi a "commoner"—but hardly one lacking socio-political competence, and the biography of Liu Xiuzhi 劉秀之 (397–464; *Song shu* 81.2073–76), the son of one his cousins, shows that Liu Muzhi had relatives who were county magistrates (*ling*) and had served in the Secretariat.

4. It seems possible to interpret *shu zhuan* ("books / documents and commentaries / biographies") as "historical documents." Compare *Song shu* 94.2310 (Xu Yuan) and 96.2371 (Xianbei tuyuhun), where knowledge of ritual precedent is implied.

5. "Recognized" (*zhi*, "known") is standard terminology in dynastic historiography's treatment of patronage. On Jiang Ai see the brief note appended to the fuller biographies of his erudite and upstanding grandfather (Jiang Tong 江統) and father (Jiang Bin 江彪) at *Jin shu* 56.1539, and with more detail the commentary at *Shishuo xinyu* 5/63, where he is portrayed as a proud gentleman rejecting the advances of Wang Gong 王恭 (d. 398), ally of Huan Xuan and antagonist of Jiang Ai's patron—see the following note—Sima Daozi.

In the biography's discussion of Liu Muzhi's descendants (*Song shu* 42.1311, not translated here), we learn that his daughter married a man from Jiyang, Cai You 蔡祐.

Moreover, from an anecdote (see note 113, below) in Liu Muzhi's *Nan shi* biography (15.427), not included in the *Song shu*, we learn that Liu's wife was the daughter of one Jiang Si 江嗣, presumably a member of the Jiang of Jiyang. The *Nan shi* anecdote has Liu begging for food from his Jiang in-laws, suggesting that she came from a more established family. Finally, in the *Song shu* chapter on "good officials" (92.2269–70) we find one Jiang Bingzhi 江秉之 (381–440) beginning his career on Liu Muzhi's staff. Thus it appears Liu Muzhi had developed close ties with prominent families of Jiyang. The northern prefecture of Jiyang (near modern Kaifeng) was far from Dongguan, but the two were lodged in the same area in the south—between Jingkou and Lake Tai (Hu, *Liuchao jiangyu*, 435). In other words, northern choronyms aside, these families were already localized in Jingkou.

6. "Establishing the Martial" (*jianwu*) was in the middle of the second tier of generalships, a respectable post. Prefects of prefectures located in fiefdoms were called *neishi*, here rendered as "fief-prefect." The Langya fief was an especially prestigious one, having been held by the founding emperor of the Eastern Jin. From 374 to 392, it was held by Sima Daozi, brother of Emperor Xiaowu (r. 372–96) and the preeminent court power from the mid-380s; see *Jin shu* 64.1731, 1372. We know that Jiang Ai served under Sima Daozi because the *Jin shu* (56.1539) places him as consultant-advisor (*ziyi canjun*; see *Jin shu* 56.1539) on the Rushing Mount general's (*piaoji jiangjun*) staff—a generalship then held by Sima Daozi. From this we can conclude that Liu Muzhi began his career between 387 and 392, near the age of thirty, by taking a significant staff position in the service of a man—perhaps related to him by marriage—who was in the patronage of the most powerful imperial clansman of the time.

The *Nan shi* (15.423) edits this down as "he began as chief of staff on [the generalship based in] Langya" 初為瑯邪府主簿, wrongly implying that he was chief of staff to the generalship.

7. The "chief of staff" (*zhubu*) was a critical if humble position; see Yen Keng-wang, *Zhongguo difang xingzheng zhidu shi*, II:183 and (citing passage II-B here) 212–13.

8. The *Taiping guangji* (comp. 978) preserves two other dreams in which Liu Muzhi foresees his rise to power on the coattails of the Founding Ancestor; see *Taiping guangji* 276.2184, citing the *Yiyuan* 異苑 and the *Xu yiji* 續異記. The *Yiyuan* dream contains a Freudian reading: "Once, on an overnight trip to the other side of the Yangtze, he dreamed of two boats coming together to form one double-boat. A florid canopy was placed atop it, and the decorations reflected the highest protocols of etiquette. With this boat, he rose into the heavens" 嘗渡揚子江宿，夢合兩船為舫，上施華蓋，儀飾甚盛，以升天.

9. In the second month of 404; see *Song shu* 1.6. In the annals' narration of the Founding Ancestor's rise, Liu Muzhi does not appear until the campaign on the Shandong peninsula, in mid-409; see section III-F.

10. He Wuji was a nephew of Liu Laozhi, the preeminent general of the late 390s and early 400s. The Founding Ancestor served under Laozhi, and He Wuji became his earliest confederate in the rising against Huan Xuan. He died in battle with Lu Xun (section III-F) in 410. See his biography at *Jin shu* 85.2214–16, and the narrative in *juan* 1 of the *Song shu*.

11. The use of the "minor public name" in the dialog here explains its otherwise unnecessary inclusion in the biography's opening paragraph.
12. For the association of wearing "pants" with joining into battle, see *Song shu* 59.1606, where Zhang Chang 張暢 (408–57) is shown changing from mourning robes to "brown leather pants" to put down a rebellion. It may also allude to Gai Kuanrao 蓋寬饒 (d. 60 BCE), the redoubtable Western Han official feared by the elite of his day, who cut his robes short when taking charge of a palace guard; see *Han shu* 77.3244.
13. Presumably this refers to the elevation of the Founding Ancestor as leader of the uprising against Huan Xuan, just after the taking of Jingkou; see *Song shu* 1.7–8. Made "Establishing the Martial" (*jianwu*) general in the eighth month of 401, during the rebellion of Sun En, he does not appear to have received any new generalship at this time.
14. Perhaps this response was a standard expression of client humility, or a historiographical topos for which; a similar phrase is used in a like context by the early Eastern Jin figure Zhou Guang 周光 (*Jin shu* 58.1585), receiving an appointment from the imminently rebellious Wang Dun 王敦 (266–324). But that parallel could point to an irony buried in our narrative.
15. 直 has dropped out of the old printing of the *Song shu*. It is present in both the *Nan shi* and the excerpt in the *Cefu yuangui* (900.5b).
16. The old printing has these two characters reversed—an apparent error.
17. Sima Yuanxian was the son of Sima Daozi, brother of Emperor Xiaowu and uncle of Emperor An. Daozi led the weak Jin court in the 390s, and in 399 the young Yuanxian took over prime ministerial powers; see *Jin shu* 64.1732–40. This led directly to the uprising of Huan Xuan, who took the throne in the twelfth month of 403 but was driven from the capital by the Founding Ancestor just four months later.
18. In the *Song shu* annals (1.9), it is also said that the "customs of the realm were completely reformed"—but there the effect is attributed to the Founding Ancestor's example of probity in the face of the shame felt by the court ministers who had given their allegiance to Huan Xuan, and the change is said to take only "two or three days," not ten.
19. A brief posting in the Secretariat (sixth rank; see Du You, *Tongdian* 37.1004) gave Liu Muzhi a regular official footing, from which he could return to lower but more substantive directly appointed positions on his patron's staff.
20. This likely refers to the Lord Over the Army (*zhenjun*; see *Song shu* 1.9, accepting the correction—confirmed in many of the biographies—noted at 1.24) generalship the Founding Ancestor received from the Jin emperor on his restoration in the third month of 404.
21. Generalships were staffed with "adjutants" (*canjun*, literally "advising on military matters"); "record-keeper" (*jishi*), in charge of drafting documents, was the second-highest of these advisors and "overseer" (*lushi*) was the highest, "copied" (*lu*) on the activities of the whole staff. See Yen Keng-wang, *Zhongguo defang xingzheng zhidu shi*, II:198–201. When Liu Muzhi first appears in the annals, in the seventh month of 409, he is identified as "overseer adjutant."

It was at this time that Wang Hong—Liu Muzhi's historiographical adversary—was "patched" (*bu* 補) onto the staff as a "consulting advisor" (*ziyi canjun* 諮議參軍), a prestige posting above the substantive ones granted to Muzhi; see Yan Keng-wang, *Zhongguo defang xingzheng zhidu shi*, II:192–93.

22. Prefect was a rank five appointment, frequently held concurrently by staff advisors. Two Tangyi coexisted at this time. The original one was north of the Yangtze, near modern Luhe 六合; see Hu, *Liuchao jiangyu*, 66, and *Song shu* 45.1373 (Xiang Jing 向靖) and 51.1474 (Liu Daogui) for postings there. The second was the lodged version near the capital; see *Song shu* 51.1462 (Liu Daolian). Two points might suggest that Liu Muzhi was given the more unstable northern one: Liu Daolian, the Founding Ancestor's brother, had been made prefect of the southern Tangyi, and the award to Liu Muzhi may have coincided with the Shandong campaign of 409, warranting a prefectureship north of the Yangtze. Zhou Yiliang suspects that this and others like it were appointments "on paper," referring to the northern Tangyi because Liu Yu's generalship at that time included military control over the region of Yuzhou 豫州; see Zhou Yiliang, *Wei Jin Nanbeichao shi zhaji*, 153–54.

23. As indicated in note 1, I do not trust the authenticity of the Fu Liang stele inscription. Insofar as it is an ostensible source, however, the stele has "Liu Muzhi" going up the Yangtze to campaign against Huan Xuan in 404. This stands in contrast to the biography, which emphasizes his role in controlling the imperial capital. The relevant section of the stele reads: "At that time, the Prime Culprit [Huan Xuan] had fled the capital like a rodent, fortifying himself in Jingzhou, and the imperial carriage (i.e., the emperor, hijacked by Huan) was abroad, loping about the Nine Rivers region (i.e., Xunyang). His Excellency personally led the assembled vassals, striking like lightning from the river's banks, exhorting those who simply wished to return home and stoking the ambitions of those soldiers who longed to make their mark" 時元兇竄遁, 擁據荊沔。乘輿播幸, 越蹈九江。公率先羣后, 電發川湄, 獎懷本之眾, 勵思奮之士。The stele text—as we have it, excerpts being the regular practice of the *Yiwen leiju*—then jumps forward to a second Yangtze campaign, of 410.

24. The investiture likely took place in the tenth month of 406, when the Founding Ancestor petitioned the Jin court for honors and rewards for a full 1,848 of his comrades; see *Song shu* 1.13.

The "five degrees" fief was, from the Eastern Jin to the Liang, a lower order, below the regular fiefs that the Western Jin had previously referred to with this term; see the discussion at Wang Antai, *Zai zao fengjian: Wei Jin Nanbeichao de juezhi yu zhengzhi zhixu*, 140–71. It is thought that these "five degrees" fiefs provided no emolument, but only a measure of prestige (see Wang Antai, *Zai zao fengjian*, 159–60), and that the Founding Ancestor made special use of them to acquire honor for the members of the lower gentry in his following.

"Viscount" (*zi*), the rank awarded Muzhi, was the second lowest of the five ranks of nobility. By contrast, Wang Hong, Liu Muzhi's counterpart in this chapter of the *Song shu*, was made "five degrees marquis" of Huarong 華容 county; *hou* was the second noble rank but the top one in the "five degrees," *wudeng*. Wang had at that point performed no real service for the Founding Ancestor.

Xihua was in Chen prefecture, of which there were again two. The original lay north of the Huai river and well beyond the compass of Eastern Jin sovereignty. The southern one was north of the Yangtze—Hu Axiang, *Liuchao zhengqu*, 99, puts it in the vicinity of modern Hefei—in the same unstable borderland as the prefecture of Tangyi. Although there may not have been a substantive connection between the viscount and his fief, the contrast with Wang Hong is again worth noting: Wang's Huarong, just outside of the seat of Jingzhou (modern Changsha), was a rich and well-positioned spot along the Yangtze River axis.

25. The reign title, adopted after the ouster of Huan Xuan, refers to the "resplendent" (*xi*) success of the Founding Ancestor and his group's "righteous" (*yi*, or "loyal," "dutiful") restoration of the Jin emperor. It is not clear, however, how many of the actors in this restoration actually believed the Jin could be revived. The Founding Ancestor's aspirations should have become fairly clear at his entry into the capital in early 408, if not even earlier—when he quickly produced three potential heirs, born in 406 and 407.

26. According to the annals, this was the twelfth month of 407. In the first month of 408 the Founding Ancestor took his post in the capital; *Song shu* 1.14. Wang Mi (biography at *Jin shu* 65.1758–59) was a grandson of Wang Dao, the founding minister of the Eastern Jin, and he had inherited Wang Dao's fief. He joined Huan Xuan and led his short-lived imperial court, a role he continued to play, as a figurehead, after the restoration.

27. Liu Yi (biography at *Jin shu* 85.2205–11) was the Founding Ancestor's key military competitor, said to have been the favored choice of the gentry elite. Xie Hun (brief biography in *Jin shu* 79.2079), a grandson of the great Xie An, was at the top of the court elite in the early fifth century. Both men would be killed in the Founding Ancestor's purge of 412.

28. Meng Chang was a powerful general who held the office from the fall of Huan Xuan to 410, when he is said to have committed suicide in the face of pending dishonor (*Song shu* 1.19). Meng Chang is historiographically "lost": Shen Yue (*Song shu* 100.2467) expressly relegated his biography to a history of the Jin, but our current *Jin shu*, compiled in the early Tang, mentions him only in passing, though it does feature his wife (*Jin shu* 96.2518) in its chapter on outstanding women.

29. Pi Chen is otherwise unknown.

30. In the old printing, these two characters have corrupted to 王季.

31. In the tenth month of 406, the Founding Ancestor had been made duke (*gong*) of Yuzhang prefecture, with the staff of his generalship increased to "one degree below that [the preeminent force of the 380s] Xie An had possessed" (*Song shu* 1.13). This is apparently the "position of great prominence" Liu Muzhi refers to, although he may also intend positions that his patron has hitherto declined but will accept on his entry to the capital.

32. Using the same wording, Liu Yi himself ruefully assesses the situation this way in his biography, in an episode from 410, just before the disastrous defeat in battle that would precipitate his downfall; see *Jin shu* 85.2208.

33. Taking *xiang* 相 as a direct object marker, this statement might be interpreted more directly, as "they will eventually devour *you*."

34. Xun Yu, the apparent historiographical paradigm for Liu Muzhi (see section III-J, and chapter 2), also makes a key speech propelling his patron, Cao Cao, to seize the moment and take control of imperial authority, in that case custody of the emperor himself; see *Sanguo zhi* 10.310. That passage concludes: "And so the Great Ancestor [Cao Cao] went to Luoyang and 'welcomed' the emperor, establishing the [provisional] capital at Xu" 太祖遂至洛陽，奉迎天子都許. Xun Yu took charge of the Secretariat—as would Liu Muzhi, in somewhat delayed fashion, in 415–16.
35. The Zhonghua edition prints 柞.
36. The *Nan shi* excerpt, misparsing the text, reads 直置疑畏 as a phrase.
37. Guanggu (near modern Linzi) was the capital of the prosperous Shandong peninsula region, controlled by the "Southern Yan" state and retaken by the Founding Ancestor in 410.
38. Lu Xun was a brother-in-law of Sun En, leader of the uprising in 399 which provided the start of the Founding Ancestor's rise to prominence. After Sun's defeat, Lu Xun and his confederates retreated to modern Guangzhou, where they were tolerated by an empire incapable of confronting them. When the Founding Ancestor set off to raid the Shandong peninsula in 409, Lu Xun's confederate and brother-in-law Xu Daofu 徐道覆 convinced him to take the opportunity to raise an attack on the capital. They were at first successful—killing He Wuji, the general in II-B, in battle and inflicting a disastrous defeat on Liu Yi. The defeat of Liu Yi was a mixed blessing for the Founding Ancestor, who rushed back to the capital and organized a counterattack, exterminating Lu and Xu in 411 and disposing of Liu Yi in 412.

The questionable stele inscription (see notes 1 and 23, above) features this event at length. Xu Daofu is named instead of Lu Xun, and Huan Qian 桓謙, cousin of Huan Xuan, is also specified. After Huan Xuan's fall, Huan Qian had fled to the north and then to the Sichuan region, where in 410 he joined with the regional leader Qiao Zong 譙縱 (d. 413) and led an attack down the Yangtze, to be killed at Jingzhou by Liu Daogui—that is, very likely the real subject of this stele inscription. The stele's account is vivid:

> Then, with Huan Qian, who relied on the [social, political, economic] capital his family had accumulated, and Xu [Dao]fu, who shamelessly took advantage of the spear tip of his fortuitous victories, the followers of disorder rose up like the spikes on a porcupine. On the interior [i.e., at the capital] the root of the empire was endangered, while on the exterior [the enemies] had the momentum of head and tail working in concert. [But] His Excellency, wielding his unique and numinous prowess in war, his stratagems odd yet crystal clear, marshalled the troops and regarded the dangers with total equanimity. Flying off like a run of clouds, west up the river, the leviathan was sundered in the water; driving his carriages again toward the east, the long snake was put to death on the land. [And so] the situation that had been so precarious, like chess pieces stacked up high, was transformed into the stronghold of a solid mountain. His munificent merit and fulsome deeds were known in full measure at the imperial court, and his pure influence and good example were forever to be remembered in the middle Yangtze region.

桓謙籍累葉之資，徐羨忸驟勝之鋒，習亂之徒，若蝟毛而起，內懷根本之虞，外通首尾之勢。公靈武獨運，奇謨內湛，鞠旅陳眾，視險若夷；飛雲西汜，則水截鯨鯢，乘轅東指，則陸殫長虵。迴累卵之危，成維山之固；豐功茂勳，大造於王室。淳風懿化，永結於荊南。

39. "Also" (*you*) often introduces an anecdote that is a variation of the preceding one, a common feature of early medieval historiography.

40. A slight variation of this phrase, "With his Excellency's perspicacity," is used in a remark by Xun Yu regarding his patron, Cao Cao, in Xun Yu's *Sanguo zhi* biography (10.313).

41. The account of Zhang Liao and Guan Yu in the latter's *Sanguo zhi* biography (36.939–40) is rather different in tone. Having been captured by Cao Cao in the year 200, Guan Yu continued to fight valiantly under him, while his allegiance to Liu Bei, his true patron, remained unmoved. Sensing this, Cao Cao is said to have sent Zhang Liao to investigate, whereupon Guan Yu confessed his ambivalence, while insisting he would do something to repay Cao's good will before leaving. However, Pei Songzhi's commentary—submitted to the throne in 429, and thus a potential influence on Liu Muzhi's biography—cites a passage from the *Fuzi* 傅子, a mid-third-century work, that is closer to the sense here: having divined Guan Yu's intentions, Zhang Liao hesitates, wondering whether he should protect a "brother" or report to a "father." He chooses the latter path. For another Liu-Song era use of this allusion, see *Song shu* 53.1519.

42. This anecdote may be read as an allegory of the Founding Ancestor's rise: he remains uncultivated, but that clumsiness acquires different definition as the gentry elite are forced to accept it.

43. The *Song shu* texts uniformly read not "the display of natural propensity (*shi*) will be quite beautiful" but "[your] reputation (*ming*) will be quite beautiful," with one alternative witness introducing a third variant: "the display of natural propensity will be awe-inspiring (*wei*)." The evidence:

- Old *Song shu* printing: 且其名亦美
- *Nan shi* version of Liu Muzhi's biography (15.425): 其勢亦美
- *Cefu yuangui* (190.8b; Song printing 190.8b): 且其名亦美
- *Cefu yuangui* (722.4b; Song printing not extant): 且其勢亦偉

One way to address the *ming* / *shi* variant is to stick to the base text, the oldest printing of the *Song shu*. That "reputation" (*ming*) is not a printer's error is ensured by the same reading in one location in the *Cefu yuangui*, which was compiled before the *Song shu* was printed. At the same time, it is possible to prefer the *Nan shi*, which was compiled in the seventh century, presumably on the basis of the *Song shu* biography. Thus, citing the *Nan shi* and the other *Cefu yuangui* instance (722.4b, which, as the Ming printing, could very well itself have been emended), Wang Zhongluo's Zhonghua edition emends the text. I believe that evidence of extant texts alone supports *ming*, but that the emendation to *shi* is nevertheless likely correct. The phenomenon of graphic corruption through cursive script provides support for this choice: the more complex 勢 could be reduced to the simpler 名, but the reverse is much less likely. Moreover, and perhaps of most importance, "reputation" makes weak sense with the specific topic of discussion, calligraphy, whereas "natural propensity" is an established critical term in discourse on calligraphy. As for the second variant location, *wei / mei*, judgment is hampered by the absence of a Song dynasty printing of the *Cefu yuangu* for this location, but the preponderance of evidence supports *mei*, "beautiful."

44. As discussed in chapter 2, the same phrasing is used in a description, attributed to Cao Cao in the third-century *Fuzi* 傅子, of Xun Yu's promotion of worthy talents: "The Gentleman Director Xun stops at nothing in his promotion of worthy men" 荀令君之進善，不進不休; see the commentary at *Sanguo zhi* 10.325; also *Jin shu* 39.1157, which reads, as in our text, 不進不止. In the same passage, Cao Cao calls Xun Yu and his nephew "the two gentlemen directors" (*er lingjun*), the same epithet used in the next sentence in our passage; see also Cao's edict, quoted at *Sanguo zhi* 22.647 (Wei Zhen), and discussion in the same terms in the "separately circulating biography" (*bie zhuan*) of Xun Yu cited at *Sanguo zhi* 10.317.

45. The key primary sources on Xun Yu are his *Sanguo zhi* biography (10.307–19) (comp. late third century), with additional material cited in Pei Songzhi's commentary (compiled 429), and the biography in Fan Ye's *Hou Han shu* (comp. mid-fifth century; 70.2280–93). For discussions of Xun and his historiographical representation, see Zhao Yi, *Nianershi zhaji jiaozheng* 6.129–30; Guo Shuo, "'Han chen' yihou 'Wei chen'"; and de Crespigny, "A Question of Loyalty." Xun was from a politically prominent Han family and was generally regarded as a Han minister, not a subject of the Wei. He played a clear and pivotal role in the rise to power of Cao Cao, founder of the Wei dynasty, but he also, apparently, had reservations about Cao's displacing the Han dynasty. In this regard the humble Liu Muzhi, who had no ties to the Jin court, could not have been more different.

It is noteworthy that Wang Dao, the founding minister of the Eastern Jin, is also recorded comparing himself to Xun Yu; see *Jin shu* 65.1746. As discussed in chapter 2, this could be a "role" Wang and then Liu took on, or a "type" in which Liu and even Wang Dao were cast. At the least, it is conceivable Liu Muzhi could have seen his control of appointments in this way—but with Liu Muzhi's death as it is related in the biography of Wang Hong, the analogy to Xun Yu becomes an ironic one, of two men (allegedly) alienated from their patrons.

46. The *Nan shi* reads 納, "to be accepted," for 進, "advanced." This may be a change to make the meaning of the passage come across more clearly.

47. Zhu Lingshi (biography at *Song shu* 48.1421–24) was a military man with a solid political background: his grandfather, father, and two elder uncles had all held prefectureships. His family was closely associated with that of Huan Xuan, the usurper. He nominally joined the Founding Ancestor's cause in 404, but it seems to have been 408 (when the Founding Ancestor took charge of the capital) before he, along with his brother Zhu Chaoshi 朱超石, did so wholeheartedly. Their biographies pointedly record the sense of duty they maintained toward the Huan, but they likely possessed substantive military powers, so the Founding Ancestor would have cultivated them. Distinguishing himself in campaigns of 410 and 412, in 413 Lingshi was charged with the conquest of Sichuan, for which he was enfeoffed as a one-thousand-household marquis. He returned to high staff positions with his new patron, but in

418, entrusted with the protection of the Founding Ancestor's son in Chang'an, he and his brother were killed by northern armies.

Zhu was posted in the capital in 416, when the Founding Ancestor began his northern expedition, and his biography says that Liu Muzhi trusted him implicitly, consulting him on all matters. How is this anecdote to be interpreted? We might note that in 409–10, the time frame in which this biography seems to place the anecdote, Zhu Lingshi's position was quite marginal. He was even dismissed from the staff during the Shandong campaign. Thus, this is a less "interior" person, to contrast with the more interior—in position and in talent—Liu Muzhi. Alternatively, the anecdote must be viewed against a larger segment of the lives of these men. In this view, Zhu has a stronger family background (though he was still not a member of the capital elite—see the anecdote at *Song shu* 48.1423–24), and will rise to a strong position. Thus, the scene would depict Liu Muzhi outstripping his political peers, which is indeed the main theme of his biography.

Against these specific interpretations, Zhu Lingshi might be read as a "foil character," simply there to illustrate Liu Muzhi's administrative prowess. This generic reading may be supported by the appearance of a cognate anecdote below, in section III-S.

48. The *Song shu* reads "regularly" (常, or "always"); however, in the *Nan shi* and at three locations in the *Cefu yuangui* it is the more sensible "once" (*chang* 嘗), and Wang Zhongluo emends the text accordingly. This unremarkable confusion may reflect the function of this anecdote, and even the anecdote at large—to reveal the protagonist's character. "Always" quicker and more nimble in the task, Muzhi's talents were absolutely superior to those of his competitors.

49. Ding Fulin correctly inserts a punctuation mark between *zhongjun* and *taiwei*; see *Song shu jiaoyi* (Shanghai: Shanghai guji, 2002), 170. The Founding Ancestor took these positions in 408 and 410, respectively. Thus, technically speaking, the first of these appointments appears to precede the narrative of III-F, which notes events from 409 to 411.

Sima, "Officer in Charge," was the second highest staff position, in charge of military affairs and often more powerful than the "senior aide" (*zhangshi*) who ostensibly headed the staff; see Yen Keng-wang, *Zhongguo difang xingzheng zhidu shi*, II:190–91. This position was on a higher tier than the chief of staff and adjutant positions Muzhi had previously held.

50. This line quietly relates a momentous advance in Liu Muzhi's career. Danyang was the capital region, hence the empire's premier prefectureship. It was held from 404 to 410 by Meng Chang. He was briefly succeeded by two members of the capital elite, Yuan Bao 袁豹 and Chi Sengshi, both associated with Liu Yi, the Founding Ancestor's competitor; see *Song shu* 52.1500, 1.28. With Liu Muzhi the office shifted definitely to the Founding Ancestor's control. Thus the appointment symbolizes both Muzhi's ascendancy and that of his patron, who in 412 eliminated Liu Yi and all associated with him. Liu held Danyang until his death in 417, when he was succeeded by Xu Xianzhi, his bête-noir and more elite competitor for the Founding Ancestor's favor.

238 *Appendix*

In an impolite anecdote in Liu Muzhi's *Nan shi* biography but not present in the *Song shu*, translated in note 113, below, this career advance is used as a symbol of his rise to formidable prominence.

51. Zhuge Zhangmin is accorded a very negative biography in the *Jin shu* (85.2212–13), where he is described as base, greedy, harsh, and simply bad. "When he was executed," it is said, "all men, gentry and commoner alike, rejoiced as if freed from shackles, regretting only that it had taken so long for justice to be served" 諸葛氏之誅也，士庶咸恨正刑之晚，若釋桎梏焉. Objectively speaking, however, he appears to have been a formidable military power. This is reflected in the large fief—a county-level duchy of 2,500 households—he received after helping expel Huan Xuan.

52. The *Jin shu* biography of Zhuge Zhangmin tells an abbreviated version of this anecdote but carries this particular point into the scene of his execution. Upon returning to the capital, the Founding Ancestor summoned him and, contrary to Zhuge's expectations, poured out his heart to him. As Zhuge relaxed, a steward grabbed him from behind and killed him.

53. This anecdote is part of a curious historiographical chain of verbal echoes, connected at different points to two different but related versions. First, in the biography of He Chengtian, it is Liu Muzhi who, worried about Zhuge Zhangmin's intentions, calls He Chengtian for a private audience. After receiving He's advice, he pronounces himself grateful: "Were it not for you, I never would have thought of a solution. I might not even have had the chance to return to Dantu as a commoner! (i.e., I might have died)" 非君不聞此言。頃日顧丹徒劉郎，恐不復可得也; see *Song shu* 64.1702. Meanwhile, in the *Nan shi* biography of Liu Muzhi, Zhuge himself uses almost the same words just before he falls into the Founding Ancestor's trap: "Those of low station will desire to be high, while those of high station will find themselves in danger. If today I wished to return to Dantu as a commoner, I would not be so lucky" 貧賤常思富貴，富貴必踐危機。今日思為丹徒布衣，不可得也; see *Nan shi* 15.425; *Jin shu* 85.2213.

54. The *Nan shi* concludes this sentence with "and Liu Muzhi made preparations to resist him" 穆之亦厚為之備. As far as I can determine, this is attested nowhere else; it may have dropped from the *Song shu* at an early date, or it might be the *Nan shi* "clarification" of a bald narrative. The *Nan shi* goes on to insert a quotation from Zhu Lingshi, found in his biography in our current *Jin shu*, but elsewhere put into Liu Muzhi's mouth: see the preceding note.

55. A "General of the Front" (*qian jiangjun*) is named in the tenth tier, slightly better than the middle, of generalship titles listed in the *Song shu* treatise on officialdom (39.1226). There is a risk of confusion, as this could be an abbreviation of the more substantive "General of the Front Army" (*qianjun jiangjun*; see *Song shu* 39.1248). Fu Liang's memorial, in section V-D, uses the latter title, and section V-B refers ambiguously to "the staff of his Front army / generalship" (*qian jun fu*), but reference here to "General of the Front" is most likely correct. Recent holders of the *qian jiangjun* title had included Wang Xun, court power in the 390s, Liu Laozhi, the most powerful general in the lead-up to Huan Xuan's usurpation, and Zhuge Zhangmin, the general Liu Muzhi artfully displaces in section III-M.

56. Sima Xiuzhi (biography at *Jin shu* 37.1109–11) was a member of the Jin imperial clan who resisted, or was an obstacle to, Liu Yu's imperial rise.

57. Liu Daolian, younger brother of the Founding Ancestor. Compare his biography, which simply records that Daolian was left in charge of the home office (*Song shu* 51.1462). This reticence is routine in this historiography, though in the passages that follow in Daolian's biography he is depicted in a very negative light, which is faintly reflected here. Liu Daolian's title, "General of the Central Army," appears three classes above Liu Muzhi's, "General of the Front," in the *Song shu* treatise on officialdom; *Song shu* 39.1225–26.

58. Charge of personnel matters was the most consequential authority one could hold on the secretariat. Liu Muzhi's activity in this capacity might be illustrated in the specimen of his calligraphy preserved in the famous Chunhua Pavilion collection of stele rubbings. The piece is a short missive, apparently addressed to someone who has been appointed to office but has tried to beg off on account of a death in the family. It was written when the Founding Ancestor was on campaign—perhaps up the Yangtze against Sima Xiuzhi in 415 or to the north in 416. A tentative translation reads:

> Indeed, sir, I have heard of the hardship that has fallen on your family (?). A most sudden misfortune. [But] official promotions have been made and must be carried out. And the matter has already been decreed by the Emperor—what recourse might I have to alter it? Sir, for the moment you should proceed to take up the position. When His Excellency (i.e., the Founding Ancestor) returns, he may consider changing the regulations, upon (?) reporting on the situation of the armies. Yours plainly, Liu Muzhi.

所欲足下家弊耳。倉卒無祿。官推遷，不得不相用。事已御出，寧復吾所得迴復。足下且當就之。公還，當思更律，啟申師情事也。劉穆之白。

See Morino Shigeo and Toshiyuki Satō, *Junka kaku chō*, 1:138–39, 2:73–74. In this interpretation, the tone and rhetorical stance fit well with what we learn of Liu Muzhi in the biography: he is humble, his addressee apparently a man of higher status, but he makes strategic use of this "exterior" position, placing himself outside the power of those—his patron, the emperor—with authority to accommodate the request.

59. The annals specify the eighth month of 416.

60. Although there was apparently an Overseeing the Army generalship (see the *Song shu* ritual treatise, 18.508), here oversight over the troops under the Grand Commandant's banner should be intended; compare the bestowal of this duty on Zhuge Zhangmin in 412 (64.1702).

61. Here the *Nan shi* adds the two characters *ru dian* 入殿, meaning "and was permitted entry into the imperial palace." Wang Zhongluo emends on this basis. It is true that palace entry is regularly associated with the granting of an armed guard—for example, *Song shu* 51.1462 (Liu Daolian). However, the citation of this passage (in his annotation to the Fu Liang memorial, section IV) in Li Shan's *Wen xuan* commentary—submitted in 658, one year before the *Nan shi* was authorized by the Tang court—lacks mention of "entry into the imperial palace." The *Cefu yuangui* citation (*Songben*, 458.11a) also reads with the *Song shu*. Thus, while it remains possible that the *Song shu* was simply corrupted at an early date, the more solid conclusion is that the *Nan shi*, and following it our Zhonghua punctuated edition, is guilty of falling too easily in line with the rhetoric of this biography. Liu Muzhi's ascendance is portrayed as rapid

and absolute—but perhaps he was not actually granted armed access to the imperial court.

62. The annals, which date this to the eighth month of 416, add that Liu Muzhi "comprehensively administered everything, inside the court and without" 總攝內外 (*Song shu* 1.36). The biography, as "commentary" to the classic, unfolds that characterization into section III-R, amplifying it with the anecdotes in sections S, T, U, and V.

The "Eastern Fort" (*dongcheng*) refers to the "Eastern Office" 東府, placed by the thirteenth-century scholar Hu Sanxing (*Zizhi tongjian* 104.3284) east of the palace. The annals record the Founding Ancestor fortifying this office in 414 (*Song shu* 2.31).

63. This character is not in the old printing of the *Song shu*.

64. The figure of "spokes around a wheel" is also used to describe Liu Muzhi's power in the biography of Xie Fangming; see *Song shu* 53.1523. There a compound point is made: it is said that four members of the capital elite (Xie Hun, Xie Fangming, Chi Sengshi, and Cai Kuo) resisted joining into Liu Muzhi's banquets—but that two of those (Fangming and Cai Kuo) later relented. The two who did not relent were noted affiliates of Liu Yi. See the discussion in chapter 2.

Note that the presence of Xie Hun in the other use of this phrase indicates a date before Xie's execution in 412. That is, it would be somewhere *before* the events narrated in section III-L here—for instance, together with the cognate anecdote at III-K. In the context of this biography, however, this passage is intended to reflect the teetering height of Liu Muzhi's career.

65. This echoes section II-B, which noted his youthful interest in historical writing, and it may be a record of something that was simply true. It also has something of a parallel in advice that Xun Yu, the historiographical paradigm for Liu Muzhi, offered to Cao Cao. Noting Cao's military accomplishments on behalf of the Han dynasty, Xun Yu advised his patron to take care of the dynasty's scholarship as well, "putting commentaries and notes in publishable form" (*kanding zhuanji* 刊定傳記); see *Sanguo zhi* 10.317–18, commentary, quoting a "separately circulating biography" (*biezhuan*). The hidden implication here could be that Liu Muzhi would have been working on Jin court documents and writings, failing, like Xun Yu, to keep track of his patron's new alliances.

66. For "full banquet" (*fang zhang*) as a figure of excess, compare *Song shu* 76.1972.

67. Note the error in the *Song shu* annals (2.43), where the misprint of *yi* 以 for *bei* 北 ("north") implies that all powers were suddenly delegated to Xu Xianzhi. That was not the case, either from the perspective of the Founding Ancestor, still wary of the capital elite, or from the point of view of those gentryman who, like Wang Hong, were in competition with Xu Xianzhi. The following passage, in which less than a sixth of Muzhi's forces are transferred to Xu's command, confirms this.

68. That is, Xu Xianzhi ascended, but the Founding Ancestor's power, which Liu Muzhi had done so much to fortify, remained closely held.

69. This text is included in the *Wen xuan* (j. 38), the early sixth-century literary anthology, as the work of Fu Liang, the Founding Ancestor's primary speechwriter and one of the advisors who would oversee the throne after the Founding Ancestor's death in 422, up to Emperor Wen's purge in 426. The title there is: "On Behalf of

the Duke of Song, A Memorial Seeking the Addition of Bestowed Honors for Liu [General] of the Front" 為宋公求加贈劉前軍表.

As the *Wen xuan* seems to be the better-preserved text, I have, with some reservations, essentially substituted it for what appears in the *Song shu*, with all variations noted. This seems better than blindly following the *Song shu* as it looked when it was put into print in the mid-eleventh century, as it appears that the *Song shu* text has been emended. However, while some of the variations in the *Song shu* appear due to textual transmission, others suggest conscious editing. The possibility cannot be excluded that some of the discrepancies are the result of editing by Shen Yue or someone else involved in copying archival materials out into the *Song shu*. It is also possible that two versions were in circulation: a public, archive version and a revised author's version, the latter being taken up into the *Wen xuan* and other later works; this is the speculation of Chen Jingyun 陳景雲 (1670–1724), cited at *Wen xuan jiuzhu jicun* 12:7615. In both cases, it would be wrong to follow the *Wen xuan* in a study of "a *Song shu* biography," even if the *Wen xuan* more accurately reflects the author's text. Yet it is odd that the text in the *Nan shi*, which was based on the *Song shu*, generally reads with the *Wen xuan*.

The *Wen xuan* is consulted here in six editions: the early manuscript once in the collection of Yang Shoujing and the Kujō 九条 manuscript; the early eleventh-century state school (*guozijian*) printing; the Korean reprint of the 1094 Xiuzhou Six Ministers edition; the Shanghai guji punctuated Hu Kejia edition; and the *Wen xuan jiu zhu jicun*, the recently published variorum edition.

70. "Considering merit" (*nian gong*) is what the sage king Yu is urged to do in the *Shang shu*; see James Legge, *The Shoo King*, 57–58. "Posthumous honors" is literally "chasing back into the distant past," a reference to the worship of the ancestors at *Analects* 1/9. The "Master of Merit" is an office listed in the *Rites of Zhou* (*Zhou li zhushu* 30.203–4).

71. The "Five Ministers" *Wen xuan* has *hua* 化 for 教. The *Song shu* and all other sources, including the Li Shan *Wen xuan*, read *jiao*.

72. All *Wen xuan* texts read *ji* 記, as does the excerpt from the memorial in the *Nan shi*, but the *Song shu* has *shu* 書. *Bishu* is much the more common collocation, including in the *Zhou li* passage cited here by Li Shan. But that is another reason for preferring the *Wen xuan* / *Nan shi* reading, which is not unattested (e.g., *Wen xuan* 56.2418) in this context: *shu* is likely a divination.

73. Wang Zhongluo, following the Qing dynasty scholar Sun Bin 孫彪, emends *qian jun jiangjun* to *qian jiangjun* 前將軍. This is the reading in the *Nan shi*, it appears in the Japanese Kujō manuscript (see *Wen xuan jiuzhu jicun* 12:9617), and it conforms with section III-O and elsewhere, including the annals in the *Song shu* (2.43) and *Jin shu* (10.266). The likely cause of the problem, which manifests itself in a variety of ways in the extant *Wen xuan* texts, is that an extra *jun* slipped into the phrase *qian jiangjun*. It is possible, however, that our historical sources are incomplete, and that he was given both the *qian jiangjun* title and substantive command of the *qianjun* troops. See also note 55, above.

74. "Fine plans" (*mou you*) and "many tasks of governance" (*shu zheng*) are drawn from the *Shang shu*; see Legge, *The Shoo King*, 540 and 525–26.

75. This line refers to Liu Muzhi's promotion to Prefect of Danyang in 412, and then to head of the Secretariat in 415 and 416; see sections III-L, III-P, and III-Q. The narrative here muddies the sequence, forcing Li Shan to cite the biography out of order.

    For "promoted to head the court" (*deng yong*, "raised up and put to use"), see Legge, *The Shoo King*, 23. For "set forth good reports" (*fuzan*), see Legge, *The Shoo King*, 37 (as *fuzou* 奏); that is, he governed well. For "head of the many offices" (*baikui*), Legge, *The Shoo King*, 31, where Legge renders it as an office ("Grand Regulator") analogous to Prime Minister; it could also mean simply "the many offices." For "the grand plan of the throne" (*dayou*), Li Shan cites the *Shijing* (Mao 195, st. 4, where the present text reads 猶), but the better reference is the opening of the "Officers of Zhou" ("Zhou guan") chapter of the *Shang shu*: "The king said: 'It was the grand method [*da you*] of former times to regulate the government while there was no confusion, and to secure the country while there was no danger'" (Legge, *The Shoo King*, 525; the term *baikui* is used in the following sentence). This was what Liu Muzhi was, in an age of confusion, "renewing." The Five Ministers commentary is far too direct in claiming that he was "facilitating the great Way of a new lord" 輔新君之大道.

76. Following the *Wen xuan*, and the *Nan shi*; the *Song shu* has 端 for 竭. This is likely a graphic corruption.

77. Following the *Wen xuan* and the *Nan shi*. The *Song shu* has the preceding two clauses reversed, along with the variant "moral power of the throne" 王化 in place of "the grand plan" 大猷. Thus: 翼新王化，敷讚百揆. What could have given rise to this divergence? Note that the word 猷 has just appeared—it is possible that an editor did not think Fu Liang would repeat himself. That motivation seems to explain the 猷 / 化 crux seven sentences below in the text. But why would the clauses have been switched? Stylistically there is a subtle difference, and the *Wen xuan* and *Nan shi* version adopted here seems better: what he did followed by its grand effect, as opposed to the effect supplemented by a more specific action.

78. This is the orthography of the old *Song shu* printing. The printed *Wen xuan* texts have this as 捍, but the Yang Shoujing manuscript has the same orthography as the *Song shu*.

79. Following the *Wen xuan* text, also the *Nan shi*, for *ning* 寧, for which the *Song shu* has *ji* 寄. The *Song shu* version might be rendered, "his meritorious handling of what had been entrusted (*ji*) him." Wang Zhongluo comments that "both make sense." *Ji* seems a likely graphic corruption of *ning*—but, perhaps by coincidence, the Kujō manuscript also reads *ji*, with a note that the Li Shan *Wen xuan* read *ning*, and with *ning* entered again in the text margin. This makes a puzzle.

80. These two clauses are absent from the *Song shu*, but appear in both the *Wen xuan* and in the *Nan shi*. The omission of an intact clause is not well explained as copyist error, so this is either an abridgement or an addition—likely the former.

81. The term used for "Three Dukes" is an archaism; see Legge, *The Shoo King*, 534 (Officers of Zhou). The reference is to the bestowal of honors in section V-C.

82. "Honor and mourning" appear as a pair at *Analects* 19/25: "Honored in life, mourned in death." "Great favor" is sourced in the *Zuozhuan* (Zhao 7), but had currency in early medieval formal discourse (e.g., *Song shu* 43.1344).

83. Where the *Wen xuan* and the *Nan shi* read *hua* 化 ("teachings," "transformation"), the *Song shu* has *you* 猷 ("plans"). Seven lines above, this variation was reversed, the *Song shu* having a phrase with *hua* and the *Wen xuan* and *Nan shi* with *you*. This suggests editing for style and to avoid repetition, but on which side of the textual ledger did the editing occur?
84. The Yang Shoujing and Kujō manuscripts have 代 for 世. This may be a taboo substitution indicating Tang provenance for those manuscripts, or their faithfully transmitted base texts. However, the taboo is not maintained consistently: the phrase 時屯世故, below, appears intact. Later editors might have corrected a presumed taboo.
85. The *Nan shi* alone reads *zhong ji* 忠績 ("loyal accomplishments") for *zhi ji* 志績 ("aims and accomplishments"). This is likely a graphic corruption—but it makes good sense in the context. Note that the *Nan shi* version elsewhere also shows signs of graphic corruption, for example, above, printing 念切 rather than 念功 (*Zhonghua zaizao shanben* ed. 4b; corrected in the modern Zhonghua edition).
86. Where all *Wen xuan* texts and the *Nan shi* read 榮哀既備，寵靈已泰, the *Song shu* has 榮哀兼備，寵靈已厚 "Honor and mourning have *each* been fulfilled, his spirit shown *grand* favor indeed." That is, 兼 replaces 既, and 厚 replaces 泰. Graphic corruption does not seem a good explanation for the first, though it could apply to the second. In the former case, stylistically the *Song shu* is more sophisticated in distinguishing "honor" and "mourning"—but perhaps by way of textual accident. In the latter, though we find precedents for both words collocated with the phrase "favor for the spirit" (e.g., *Sanguo zhi* 52.1221 for *hou* and *Jin shu* 66.1777 for *tai*), the contrastive emphasis is stronger in the *Wen xuan* reading: grant these additional honors, even if more than enough has been done for him already.
87. The *Song shu* reads 彌結 ("internal troubles *are woven thicker and thicker*") for *yi jian* 亦荐. The *Wen xuan* and *Nan shi* reading has a rarer word, and that word, *jian*, has good classical precedent: it is used in the very sense of an onslaught of troubles in the *Zuozhuan* (Xiang 22). Curiously, though, Li Shan does not gloss this phrase.
88. The *Song shu* reads 靡歲暫寧, "not a single year has seen a moment of peace." Li Shan cites classical precedent for the *Wen xuan* and *Nan shi* reading, and if it remains hard to say how the *Song shu* text arose, or to declare it wrong, emendation of a damaged manuscript is a good possibility.
89. The *Song shu* opens this clause with the rhetorical question marker *qi* 豈; it is absent from the *Wen xuan* and *Nan shi*, the passage reads better without it, and, crucially, the word appears in the following sentence. Printed editions of the *Wen xuan* (but not the *Nan shi*) read *lie* 劣 ("faulty") for *fa* 乏 ("lacking," "meager talents"). This is certainly a graphic corruption—the Yang Shoujing manuscript reads the same as the *Song shu* and *Nan shi*. But the gloss of *lie* in the Five Ministers' commentary shows that this error was already present in their text, in the early eighth century, and the Kujō manuscript cites a textual note from a no-longer-extant portion of the *Wen xuan jizhu*, confirming that the Five Ministers edition (and not others) read *lie*.
90. The *Song shu* prints *yi* 益 ("excellence") for *xun* 勳 ("merit," "deeds").
91. As cited by Li Shan, the *Guliang zhuan* (Wen 6) is the source of this contrastive figure—sincere private speech versus strategic dissemblance in public. This description and that below of Liu Muzhi resolutely declining honors find echoes in the

Jin shu biography of Yang Hu, a key advisor to the founder of the Jin; see *Jin shu* 34.1019–20.

92. The phrase "Without the aid of that man..." is borrowed from the *Zuozhuan* (Xi 30). Although the context is entirely different, the speaker there is Duke Wen of Jin, stating his adherence to the value of "benevolence" (*ren* 仁). Thus, while not an "allusion," it does borrow from the classic to enhance the ethos of the current speaker, the Founding Ancestor.

    The sentiment and the use of the word *ji* 濟 ("achieved") constitute a small gesture to the "life" of Xun Yu. Cao Cao, in a memorial that generally resembles this one, requests a fief for Xun Yu, attributing to his client his own success sustaining the Han court, for example, "It is through the deeds of Xun Yu that I have achieved this success" 或之功業，臣由以濟 (*Sanguo zhi* 10.315, commentary, from the "separately circulating biography" of Xun Yu; also a second memorial, quoted from the same source, at 10.317).

93. For these two clauses the *Song shu* alone has 忠規遠畫，潛慮密謨 ("For he also gave sincere critiques and far-reaching counsel, sharing his hidden thoughts and stealthy counsel"). More generic, the *Song shu* version appears to be an editorial repair.

94. For this sentence, the *Song shu* alone has: 功隱於視聽，事隔於皇朝，不可稱記. That is, the first two clauses are reversed, the (optional) nominalizing particle *zhe* 者 is absent, and *cheng ji* ("spoken of and put onto the record") replaces *sheng ji* ("be counted on the record"). The *Wen xuan* taxis seems better: from specific (the knowledge of the court) to general (the knowledge of people in general). But does editorial emendation explain the reversal of clauses in the *Song shu*?

95. The *Song shu* reverses the characters 遂克.

96. The Five Ministers commentary says this phrase refers to Liu Muzhi himself. The memorial does deliberately mix Liu Muzhi's accomplishments with those of his patron, but the real subject here must be the Founding Ancestor, as indicated by the modal word *xing* 幸 ("by good fortune") in the following clause, and by the meaning of the sentence in its entirety.

97. The Five Ministers text lacks the final character, 矣. The margin of the Kujō manuscript, meanwhile, notes, via the editor of the *Wen xuan jizhu*, that the *Wen xuan* text of Lu Shanjing 陸善經 (fl. eighth century) lacked the last four-character phrase entirely. There is nothing to be done with this information, but it runs parallel to the *Song shu* text's earlier excision of the nine-character phrase 識量局致，棟幹之器也.

98. The *Song shu* alone reads 賞 ("emolument") for *jue* 爵 ("fief")—a sensible change that may in fact strengthen the rhetorical point, but also more general and hence suggestive of a repair.

99. The *Song shu* reads 而未沾茅社 ("he was never graced with a fief"). Note that the *Song shu* has the rarer term here (*maoshe*, vs. *maotu*); that again, the syntax is changed, such that it is not a simple matter of one text repairing or emending a certain location; and that the *Song shu* formulation, with "never" and "graced," is rhetorically stronger. However, both 土 and 及 appear in the text several lines below—a possible reason for avoiding those characters here—and the *Song shu* differs from all other texts, including the two *Wen xuan* manuscripts.

100. For 念 ("brood upon," "remember"), the *Song shu* reads 傷 ("feel pain for"). The *Song shu* seems rhetorically stronger, but again a repair or emendation is suspected—"feel pain for" is generic in a memorial of lament.
101. The *Song shu* has these same four clauses, but with the sequence of the pairs reversed: 俾大賚所及，永秩於善人，忠正之烈，不泯於身後 ("You will ensure [bi] that grand rewards shall forever make their way to good men, and that the glory of a loyal and impartial servant will live on after his death"). One character also varies, *zheng* 正 ("impartial") for the semantically and phonetically close *zhen* 貞 ("sincere"). Could this be the record of a court declamation, later fixed and revised by its author? What problem in the *Song shu* text would have led to an emendation that kept two full clauses mainly intact, simply reversing their positions under the word "ensure" (*bi*)? The *Song shu* reading is superficially sensible, placing the living ("good men") before the dead. But of course Liu Muzhi is already dead, and the global sense of the *Wen xuan* taxis is superior: as a general, transcendent category, "good men" and their proper rewards belong after the simple fact of the awards being made posthumously. As Li Shan notes, "rewards to good men" derives from *Analects* 20/1: "The Zhou gives great rewards, and the good men are enriched." The less intuitive *Wen xuan* seems better.
102. "Metal and orchid" (or "metal and eupatorium") was a common kenning for friendship, attributed to Confucius in the "Attached Commentary" to the *Book of Changes*; see Richard John Lynn, *The Classic of Changes: A New Translation of the I Ching, as Interpreted by Wang Bi*, 58–59.
103. The bureaucratic metadiscourse of the final sentence appears only in the *Wen xuan*—here the *Nan shi* stays with the *Song shu*.
104. For 夷 ("level," or "good times"), the *Song shu* has 泰 ("peaceful times"). This could be a graphic error.
105. The *Song shu* reverses these two characters, as *shi zhong* 始終. The superficial meaning is the same—but only *zhongshi* appears in the Classics (e.g., the *Book of Changes*, hexagram 1), and thus is the choice of refined diction. Furthermore, in the discursive context here, an allusion to a line in the Doctrine of the Mean may be intended: "Sincerity is the beginning and the end of things" 誠者，物之終始. Here as elsewhere, the *Song shu* differs from the *Nan shi* and from all *Wen xuan* texts, including the early manuscripts.
106. The *Song shu* alone reads *mi* 密 for *gan* 感, thus "thick with feeling," which would be naturally parallel with the paired phrase "deep in principle" (*yi shen*). While neither *qing gan* nor *qing mi* seems common, the former is hapax legomenon in pre-Tang texts collected in the Scripta Sinica database. This makes graphic corruption a possibility, but the early manuscripts confirm that the *Wen xuan* text is not, at least, a late corruption, and the smoothness of the parallel makes "thick" more likely an editor's guess.
107. Nanchang (modern Nanchang, Jiangxi) was in Jiangzhou, up the Gan River from Pengli Lake.
108. The last phrase translates *feigong*, a stock term derived from hexagram 39 (line 2) in the *Book of Changes*.

109. Nankang was also in Jiangzhou, but at the head of the Gan River, at modern Ganzhou, far south of Nanchang, his former fief.
110. Wang Zhen'e (biography at *Song shu* 45.1365–71) was from a northern military family that had served the "Qin" empire of Fu Jian 苻堅 (337–85). After the fall of that state, the thirteen-year-old Zhen'e came south with his family, settling in Jingzhou. He did not join the Founding Ancestor until the latter's northern campaign of 409, but upon doing so he became one of the rising power's most important generals, up to his death in a chaotic factional dispute that followed the Founding Ancestor's conquest of Chang'an. Wang Zhen'e's biography notes that he was, like Liu Muzhi, given a place of worship in the Founding Ancestor's personal temple. The general Fang Shu alluded to here was the subject of a *Shijing* paean (Mao 178 采芑). The fief named below, Longyang county, was on the southwest edge of Lake Dongting, in Jingzhou; it is smaller than Liu Muzhi's.
111. The *Nan shi* notes the elevation of Liu Muzhi's fief at the founding of the Liu-Song, but substitutes an anecdote for this edict. The passage, in which Liu Muzhi's contributions are doubted by the minister Fan Tai and reaffirmed by the Founding Ancestor, is translated and discussed in chapter 2.
112. The old printing misprints 勛 as 動.
113. Here the *Nan shi* inserts a second humorous anecdote:

When Muzhi was young, his family was poor, and he never stood on ceremony. He drank and ate to his heart's content, with no attention to the refinement of his personal character. He especially enjoyed going to visit his wife's family, where he would beg for food, and suffer disgrace for it, though he took no shame in that at all. His wife, a daughter of Jiang Si, knew the ways of the world, so she forbade him from going to visit the Jiangs. Later there was a feast, and Muzhi was expressly told not to go, but go he did, and when he had eaten his fill, he even asked for betel nut. The Jiang brothers toyed with him: "Betel nut is for digestion! But you're *always* hungry, what do you want that for?" [Then (this may be a variation on the same anecdote, compounded into a biographical narrative)] his wife sold her hair to pay for a full table of food for her brothers to provide for Muzhi, and from that day she would not "face Muzhi in private." Later, when Muzhi rose to Prefect of Danyang, he planned to summon his wife and her brothers [for a banquet]. Thereupon, his wife bowed her head to the ground, weeping and begging his forgiveness. "I've never harbored any grudges," he replied, "so you've no need to worry." When everyone was full and drunk, Muzhi had his kitchen staff present them with a golden bowl filled with a whole bushel of betel nut.

穆之少時，家貧誕節，嗜酒食，不修拘檢。好往妻兄家乞食，多見辱，不以為恥。其妻江嗣女，甚明識，每禁不令往江氏。後有慶會，屬令勿來。穆之猶往，食畢求檳榔。江氏兄弟戲之曰：「檳榔消食，君乃常飢，何忽須此？」妻復截髮市肴饌，為其兄弟以餉穆之，自此不對穆之梳沐。及穆之為丹陽尹，將召妻兄弟，妻泣而稽顙以致謝。穆之曰：「本不匿怨，無所致憂。」及至醉飽，穆之乃令廚人以金柈貯檳榔一斛以進之。

The lack of abstemiousness thematized here is the same quality leveraged by Liu Muzhi himself, or his historiographical avatar, in section III-V.

The kernel of this story—the man mistreated when lowly, yet magnanimous after his rise—was a generic topos. See for instance *Song shu* 76.1972, and—the biography of Shen Yue himself—*Liang shu* 13.242.

114. It seems possible that the death of Wang Hong, in the fifth month of this year (*Song shu* 5.81), allowed Liu Muzhi's ascension. Liu Muzhi's addition to the temple is not recorded in the annals.
115. The ritual treatise (17.486), specifying the *bingchen* day, records the presentation of this sacrifice. Jiangning was southwest of the capital. The larger context was perhaps the ongoing effort to consolidate the body politic in anticipation of war with the Northern Wei; three consecutive entries in the *Song shu* annals (5.95–96) show Emperor Wen readying his armed forces.
116. Literally "with the imagination of the Nine Plains [the burial ground for senior ministers, upon which Viscount Wen of Jin gazed and felt sorrow], I sighed in lamentation, my feelings deep." For the allusion, see *Guoyu* (Jin yu) 14.471.
117. As mentioned in note 5, a daughter was married to the Cai family of Jiyang, but efforts were also made to marry into the capital elite: one son was married to a younger sister of the famed literatus Yan Yanzhi (*Song shu* 73.1891). His nephew Liu Xiuzhi, whose family history helps us fill out Liu Muzhi's socio-political background, was married to a daughter of He Chengtian (*Song shu* 41.2073).
118. The old printing reverses these two characters, to 寶國.
119. The old printing has 兀 for 而. This must be a graphic corruption.
120. The phrase "ancestral minister" echoes the historian Ban Gu's appraisal of Xiao He, a founding minister of the Han; see *Han shu* 39.2022, and compare the more functional appraisal at *Shiji* 130.3311. "Pure Temple" is the title of a Zhou hymn in the *Classic of Poetry* (Mao 266), a poem for the sacrifice to King Wen, the Zhou founder.

Works Cited

The *Song shu*

The essential reference point for the *Song shu* is the typeset edition published by Zhonghua shuju in 1974, edited by Wang Zhongluo 王仲犖 (1913–86), with the assistance of Fu Xuancong 傅璇琮 (1933–2016). I have primarily referred to the sixth printing (1996). This is a composite text, collated by an expert in the history of this period; Wang Zhongluo, *Song shu jiaokan ji changbian* provides fuller explanation for its editorial decisions, specifies its (many) silent emendations, and supplies relevant material from other sources. In 2018, Zhonghua shuju published a newly re-edited edition of the *Song shu*, but it will be an unfortunate result if this were to replace the older one. True, recent scholarship (see especially Zhen Dacheng, *Zhonggu shishu jiaozheng*, 38–104) has demonstrated that Wang Zhongluo sometimes emended his text more than he might have. Nevertheless, his is a work of conscientious restoration, where the new edition elects instead, and with no particular editorial acumen, to roll Wang's edition back toward the old *Sibu congkan* "Bona" 百衲 text, which served our scholarly grandfathers so well.

The *Song shu* we read today descends from a printed edition commissioned by the emperor in 1061 and produced sometime after that. That edition is no longer extant, but it was reprinted in the twelfth century and the latter edition survives in a number of copies, in different states and conditions of repair. Here three copies have been consulted selectively: (a) the copy formerly in the Beiping Library collection, shipped to the Library of Congress and now held at the Palace Museum in Taipei, available on microfilm, and reproduced, in retouched and therefore less preferred form, as the Bona edition; (b) a photo-reprint of a version held in the National Library of China, reproduced in the *Zhonghua zaizao shanben* 中華再造善本 series; (c) a photo-reprint in the *Yuwai Hanji zhenben wenku* 域外漢籍珍本文庫 (fifth series) of a copy held in the National Archives of Japan. These are referred to collectively as the "old printings" of the *Song shu* and are differentiated where necessary.

When the standard histories were put into print in the eleventh century, some 600 years after Shen Yue compiled his *Song shu*, editors were naturally working with imperfectly transmitted texts. They passed on some of these imperfections, while undoubtedly smoothing over others in their effort to produce a printable text, and as reprints and new editions were made in the following centuries, new imperfections and emendations came into being. That is what makes Wang Zhongluo's work so great: knowing that the *Song shu* we have today is irrecoverably imperfect in many ways, he actually tried to identify its problems and solve them.

(For a good, brief appraisal of the textual history of the *Song shu* and Wang Zhongluo's contribution to it, see Du Zexun and Sun Qi, "Du Wang Zhongluo *Song shu jiaokan ji changbian*.") It should go without saying that, as with any modern critical edition, someone willing to reinspect the sources might see things in a different light and even make new discoveries.

The best glimpses we have of the *Song shu* from behind the curtain of print—and that curtain presents a rather uniform appearance, the scope of variation among the printed editions not being great—are from the encyclopedia tradition, and two very large tenth-century compilations in particular. Wang Zhongluo draws extensively on the *Cefu yuangui*, which was compiled in 1013, half a century before the *Song shu* was put into print. This is a very important corrective, even if the researches of Zhen Dacheng, cited above, show that the Ming reprint of this work must be handled with care. Compiled even earlier, in 983, the *Taiping yulan* also contains traces of a *Song shu* (but sometimes a *Song shu* other than Shen Yue's) that differed from the one that we have now; this topic is explored to great effect in Chen Shuang, "*Taiping yulan* suo yin *Song shu* kao." Beyond this, there are briefer excerpts in Tang encyclopedias and commentaries, and comparison can be made with the *Nan shi* (History of the Southern Dynasties, compiled 659), which drew heavily on the *Song shu*; a recent study by He Zhaofeng, "*Song shu* Xuan guifei zhuan liuchuan ji yiwen kao," shows how these materials can be put to use.

Other Premodern Chinese Sources

Cefu yuangui 冊府元龜. Compiled in 1013 by Wang Qinruo 王欽若 et al. (1) Ming printing, reprint Beijing: Zhonghua shuju, 1960, 1982. (2) *Songben Cefu yuangui* 宋本冊府元龜. Reprint Beijing: Zhonghua shuju, 1989.

Chunqiu Guliang zhuan zhushu 春秋穀梁傳注疏 (*Guliang zhuan*). *Shisanjing zhushu* edition.

Chunqiu Zuozhuan zhu 春秋左傳注 (*Zuozhuan*). Edited by Yang Bojun 楊伯峻. Bejing: Zhonghua shuju, 1990, 2005.

Du You 杜佑 (734–812). *Tongdian* 通典. Edited by Wang Wenjin 王文錦 et al. Beijing: Zhonghua shuju, 1988.

Guoyu 國語. Edited by Shanghai shifan daxue guji zhengli yanjiusuo. Shanghai: Shanghai guji chubanshe, 1978.

Hou Han shu 後漢書. Compiled by Fan Ye 范曄 (398–445). Beijing: Zhonghua shuju, 1965, 2001.

Jin shu 晉書. Compiled in 648 by Fang Xuanling 房玄齡 (579–648) et al. Beijing: Zhonghua shuju, 1974, 2003.

Jiujia jiu Jin shu jiben 九家舊晉書輯本. Compiled by Tang Qiu 湯球 (1804–1881). Edited by Yang Zhaoming 楊朝明. Zhengzhou: Zhongzhou guji chubanshe, 1991.
Liang shu 梁書. Compiled in 636 by Yao Silian 姚思廉 (557–637) et al. Beijing: Zhonghua shuju, 1973, 1987.
Liji zhengyi 禮記正義. *Shisanjing zhushu* edition.
Liu Xie 劉勰 (d. ca. 522). *Wenxin diaolong zhushi* 文心雕龍注釋. Edited by Zhou Zhenfu 周振甫. Beijing: Renmin wenxue chubanshe, 1981, 2002.
Liu Zhiji 劉知幾 (661–721). *Shitong tongshi* 史通通釋. Edited by Pu Qilong 浦起龍 (1679–1762). Shanghai: Shanghai guji chubanshe, 1978.
Lunyu yizhu 論語譯注 (*The Analects*). Edited by Yang Bojun 楊伯峻. Bejing: Zhonghua shuju, 1980, 2000.
Nan Qi shu. Compiled by Xiao Zixian 蕭子顯 (489–537). Beijing: Zhonghua shuju, 1972, 1997.
Nan shi 南史. Compiled in 659 by Li Yanshou 李延壽 et al. (1) Beijing: Zhonghua shuju, 1975, 1987. (2) *Zhonghua zaizao shanben* 中華再造善本 series, vol. 104. Beijing: Beijing tushuguan chubanshe, 2003.
Sanguo zhi 三國志. Compiled late third century by Chen Shou 陳壽 (233–297), commentary by Pei Songzhi 裴松之 (372–451). Beijing: Zhonghua shuju, 1959, 1990.
Scripta Sinica. Database maintained by the Institute of History and Philology, Academia Sinica. http://hanchi.ihp.sinica.edu.tw.
Shijing 詩經 (*Classic of Poetry*). (1) *Mao shi zhengyi* 毛詩正義. *Shisanjing zhushu* edition. (2) *A Concordance to the Shih Ching*. Harvard-Yenching Institute Sinological Index Series, Supplement no. 9. Revised edition. Tokyo: Toyo Bunko, 1962.
Shisanjing zhushu 十三經注疏. Edited by Ruan Yuan 阮元 (1764–1849). Beijing: Zhonghua shuju, 1980, 1996.
Shishuo xinyu jianshu 世說新語箋疏. Compiled by Liu Yiqing 劉義慶 (403–444). Annotated by Liu Xiaobiao 劉孝標 (462–521). Edited by Yu Jiaxi 余嘉錫 (1884–1955). Revised edition. Shanghai: Shanghai guji, 1993.
Shuowen jiezi zhu 說文解字注. Compiled by Xu Shen 許慎 (ca. 55–ca. 149). Annotated by Duan Yucai 段玉裁 (1735–1815). Hangzhou: Zhejiang guji chubanshe, 1998.
Sui shu 隋書. Compiled in 636 by Wei Zheng 魏徵 (580–643) et al. Beijing: Zhonghua shuju, 1973, 2002.
Taiping guangji 太平廣記. Compiled in 978 by Li Fang 李昉 et al. Beijing: Zhonghua shuju, 1961.
Taiping yulan 太平御覽. Compiled in 984 by Li Fang et al. Taipei: Taiwan Shangwu chubanshe, 1967, 1992.

Tang lü shuyi 唐律疏議. Compiled in 653 by Zhangsun Wuji 長孫無忌 (594–659) et al. Taipei: Hongwenguan chubanshe, 1986.

Wang Genlin 王根林 et al., eds. *Han Wei liuchao biji xiaoshuo daguan* 漢魏六朝筆記小說大觀. Shanghai: Shanghai guji chubanshe, 1999.

Wang Mingsheng 王鳴盛 (1722–1798). *Shiqi shi shangque* 十七史商榷. Edited by Huang Shuhui 黃曙輝. Shanghai: Shanghai shudian, 2005.

Wei shu 魏書. Compiled in 554 by Wei Shou 魏收 et al. Beijing: Zhonghua shuju, 1974, 1987.

Wen xuan. Compiled by Xiao Tong 蕭統 (501–531). (1) You Mao 尤袤 1181 edition. Photoreprint. Zhonghua zaizao shanben series, vol. 402. Beijing: Beijing tushuguan chubanshe, 2004. (2) You Mao, edited by Hu Kejia 胡克家 et al. Typeset reprint. Shanghai: Shanghai guji, 1986. (3) Xiuzhou 秀州 ("Kyujanggak" 奎章閣) edition. Reprint of a 1428 Korean printing of an edition produced at Xiuzhou in 1094. Institute of Oriental Culture, University of Tokyo, shelf mark 貴重-39. http://kanseki.ioc.u-tokyo.ac.jp. (4) *Tang chao Wen xuan jizhu huicun* 唐鈔文選集註彙存. Edited by Zhou Xunchu 周勛初. Shanghai: Shanghai guji chubanshe, 2000. (5) Photocopies of Japanese manuscripts once held in the collection of Yang Shoujing 楊守敬 (1839–1915), now at the National Palace Museum, and the Kujō 九条 manuscript. (6) Liu Yuejin 劉躍進 and Xu Hua 徐華, eds., *Wen xuan jiuzhu jicun* 文選舊註輯存. 20 volumes. Nanjing: Fenghuang chubanshe, 2017.

Yiwen leiju 藝文類聚. Compiled in 624 by Ouyang Xun 歐陽詢, et al. (1) Typeset reprint, edited by Wang Shaoying 汪紹楹. Revised edition. Shanghai: Shanghai guji chubanshe, 1999. (2) *Songben Yiwen leiju* 宋本藝文類聚. Shanghai: Shanghai guji chabanshe, 2013.

Zhao Yi 趙翼 (1727–1814). *Nianer shi zhaji jiaozheng* 廿二史劄記校證. Edited by Wang Shumin 王樹民. Beijing: Zhonghua shuju, 2013.

Zhou li zhushu 周禮注疏. *Shisanjing zhushu* edition.

Zizhi tongjian 資治通鑑. Compiled in 1084 by Sima Guang 司馬光 (1019–86). Commentary by Hu Sanxing 胡三省 (1230–1302). Punctuated edition. Beijing: Zhonghua shuju, 1956, 1996.

Secondary Scholarship

Asselin, Mark Laurent. *A Significant Season: Cai Yong (ca. 133–192) and His Contemporaries*. New Haven, CT: American Oriental Society, 2010.

Balazs, Etienne. "History as a Guide to Bureaucratic Practice." In Etienne Balazs, *Chinese Civilization and Bureaucracy*, edited by Arthur F. Wright and translated by H. M. Wright, 129–49. New Haven, CT: Yale University Press, 1964 (first published in French in 1961).

Benveniste, Émile. "Active and Middle Voice in the Verb." In *Émile Benveniste, Problems in General Linguistics*, 145–51. Translated by Mary Elizabeth Meek. Coral Gables, FL: University of Miami Press, 1971.

Bielenstein, Hans. "The Census of China during the Period 2–742 A.D." *Bulletin of the Museum of Far Eastern Antiquities* 19 (1947): 125–63.

———. "The Restoration of the Han Dynasty: With Prolegomena on the Historiography of the *Hou Han Shu*." *Bulletin of the Museum of Far Eastern Antiquities* 26 (1954): 1–209.

Bilsky, Manuel, McCrea Hazlett, Robert E. Streeter, and Richard M. Weaver. "Looking for an Argument." *College English* 14, no. 4 (1953): 210–16.

Bird, Otto. "The Tradition of the Logical Topics: Aristotle to Ockham." *Journal of the History of Ideas* 23, no. 3 (1962): 307–23.

Bitzer, Lloyd F. "The Rhetorical Situation." *Philosophy and Rhetoric* 1, no. 1 (1968): 1–14.

Blinn, Sharon Bracci, and Mary Garrett. "Aristotelian *Topoi* as a Cross-Cultural Analytical Tool." *Philosophy and Rhetoric* 26, no. 2 (1993): 93–112.

Burke, Kenneth. *Language as Symbolic Action: Essays on Life, Literature, and Method*. Berkeley: University of California Press, 1966.

Campany, Robert Ford. *Making Transcendents: Ascetics and Social Memory in Early Medieval China*. Honolulu: University of Hawai'i Press, 2009.

Chao Li-Hsin 趙立新. "Nanchao zongshi zhengzhi yu shihuan jiegou: yi huangdi huangzi fu canjun wei zhongxin" 南朝宗室政治與仕宦結構: 以皇弟皇子府參軍為中心. Ph.D. diss., National Taiwan University, 2010.

Chen Shuang 陳爽. "*Taiping yulan* suo yin *Song shu* kao" 《太平御覽》所引《宋書》考. *Wen shi* 113 (2015): 79–98.

Chen, Jack W., and David Schaberg, eds. *Idle Talk: Gossip and Anecdote in Traditional China*. Berkeley: University of California Press, 2014.

Chen, Shih-Hsiang. "An Innovation in Chinese Biographical Writing" [Review of Zhu Dongrun 朱東潤, *Zhang Juzheng dazhuan* 張居正大傳]. *Far Eastern Quarterly* 13, no. 1 (1953): 49–62.

Chittick, Andrew. *The Jiankang Empire in Chinese and World History*. New York: Oxford University Press, 2020.

———. *Patronage and Community in Medieval China: The Xiangyang Garrison, 400–600 CE*. Albany: State University of New York Press, 2009.

———. "The Southern Dynasties." In *The Cambridge History of China: Volume 2, The Six Dynasties, 220–589*, edited by Albert E. Dien and Keith N. Knapp, 237–72. Cambridge: Cambridge University Press, 2020.

Crowley, Sharon. "When Ideology Motivates Theory: The Case of the Man from Weaverville." *Rhetoric Review* 20, no. 1–2 (2001): 66–93.

Curtius, Ernst Robert. *European Literature and the Latin Middle Ages*. Translated by Willard R. Trask. Princeton, NJ: Princeton University Press, 1953.

de Crespigny, Rafe. "A Question of Loyalty: Xun Yu, Cao Cao and Sima Guang." In *Sino-Asiatica: Papers Dedicated to Professor Liu Ts'un-yan on the Occasion of His Eighty-Fifth Birthday*, edited by Wang Gungwu, Rafe de Crespigny, and Igor de Rachewiltz, 30–59. Canberra: Australian National University, 2002.

Dien, Albert E. "The Disputation at Pengcheng: Accounts from the *Wei shu* and the *Song shu*." In *Early Medieval China: A Sourcebook*, edited by Wendy Swartz, Robert Ford Campany, Yang Lu, and Jessey J. C. Choo, 32–59. New York: Columbia University Press, 2014.

———. "Historiography of the Six Dynasties Period (220–581)." In Feldherr and Hardy, eds., *The Oxford History of Historical Writing*, 509–34.

Dien, Albert E., ed. *State and Society in Early Medieval China*. Stanford, CA: Stanford University Press, 1990.

Ding Fulin 丁福林. *Song shu jiao yi* 宋書校議. Shanghai: Shanghai guji chubanshe, 2002.

Du Bois, W. E. B. "Is Man Free?" [Review of Richard M. Weaver, *Ideas Have Consequences*]. *Scientific Monthly* 66, no. 5 (1948): 432–33.

Du Zexun 杜澤遜 and Sun Qi 孫齊. "Du Wang Zhongluo xiansheng *Song shu jiaokan ji changbian*" 讀王仲犖先生《宋書校勘記長編》. *Shupin* 4 (2010): 3–12.

Dubs, Homer H. "The Reliability of Chinese Histories." *Far Eastern Quarterly* 6, no. 1 (1946): 23–43.

Durrant, Stephen W. "From 'Scribe' to 'History': The Keyword *shi* 史." In *Keywords in Chinese Culture*, edited by Wai-yee Li and Yuri Pines, 85–119. Hong Kong: Chinese University of Hong Kong Press, 2020.

———. "The Han Histories." In Feldherr and Hardy, eds., *The Oxford History of Historical Writing*, 485–508.

Eberhard, Wolfram. *A History of China*. Fourth edition. Berkeley: University of California Press, 1977.

Eicher, Sebastian. "Fan Ye's Biography in the *Song Shu*: Form, Content, and Impact." *Early Medieval China* 22 (2016): 45–64.

Elman, Benjamin A., and Martin Kern, eds. *Statecraft and Classical Learning: The "Rituals of Zhou" in East Asian History*. Leiden: Brill, 2010.

Feldherr, Andrew, and Grant Hardy, eds. *The Oxford History of Historical Writing: Volume 1: Beginnings to AD 600*. Oxford: Oxford University Press, 2011.

Franke, Herbert. "Some Remarks on the Interpretation of Chinese Dynastic Histories." *Oriens* 3, no. 1 (1950): 113–22.
Froeyman, Anton. "Concepts of Causation in Historiography." *Historical Methods: A Journal of Quantitative and Interdisciplinary History* 42, no. 3 (2009): 116–28.
Gardner, Charles S. *Chinese Traditional Historiography*. Cambridge, MA: Harvard University Press, 1961 (1938).
Ge Jianxiong 葛劍雄, ed. *Zhongguo renkou shi* 中國人口史. 6 volumes. Shanghai: Fudan daxue chubanshe, 2000.
Gentz, Joachim, and Dirk Meyer, eds. *Literary Forms of Argument in Early China*. Leiden: Brill, 2015.
Giele, Enno. *Imperial Decision-Making and Communication in Early China: A Study of Cai Yong's "Duduan."* Wiesbaden: Harrassowitz, 2006.
Graff, Richard. "Topics/Topoi." In *Rhetoric and Stylistics: An International Handbook of Historical and Systematic Research*, edited by Ulla Fix, Andreas Gardt, and Joachim Knape, 717–28. Berlin: Walter de Gruyter, 2008.
Grafflin, Dennis. "Reinventing China: Pseudobureaucracy in the Early Southern Dynasties." In Dien, ed., *State and Society in Early Medieval China*, 139–70.
Grethlein, Jonas, and Christopher B. Krebs, eds. *Time and Narrative in Ancient Historiography: The "Plupast" from Herodotus to Appian*. Cambridge and New York: Cambridge University Press, 2012.
Guo Shuo 郭碩. "'Han chen' yi huo 'Wei chen': shijia bixia Xun Yu shenfen de liubian" 漢臣抑或魏臣：史家筆下荀彧身份的流變. *Anhui shifan daxue xuebao (renwen shehui kexue ban)* 44, no. 1 (2016): 61–67.
Hao Runhua 郝潤華. *Liuchao shiji yu shixue* 六朝史籍與史學. Beijing: Zhonghua shuju, 2005.
Hardy, Grant. *Worlds of Bronze and Bamboo: Sima Qian's Conquest of History*. New York: Columbia University Press, 1999.
Hartwell, Robert M. "Historical Analogism, Public Policy, and Social Science in Eleventh- and Twelfth-Century China." *American Historical Review* 76, no. 3 (1971): 690–727.
He Zhaofeng 赫兆豐. "*Song shu* Xuan guifei zhuan liuchuan ji yiwen kao: jian kao jinben Song shu Liu Ziluan zhuan de cuoye" 《宋書》宣貴妃傳流傳及佚文考——兼考今本《宋書》劉子鸞傳的錯頁. *Wei Jin Nanbeichao Sui Tang shi ziliao* 38, no. 2 (2018): 70–82.
Hegel, G. W. F. *Lectures on the Philosophy of World History, Volume 1: Manuscripts of the Introduction and the Lectures of 1822–23*. Edited and translated by Robert F. Brown and Peter C. Hodgson, with William G. Geuss. Oxford: Clarendon Press, 2011.

Holcombe, Charles. *In the Shadow of the Han: Literati Thought and Society at the Beginning of the Southern Dynasties*. Honolulu: University of Hawai'i Press, 1994.

Hu Axiang 胡阿祥. *Liuchao jiangyu yu zhengqu yanjiu* 六朝疆域與政區研究. Rev. ed. Beijing: Xueyuan chubanshe, 2005.

Hucker, Charles O. *A Dictionary of Official Titles in Imperial China*. Stanford, CA: Stanford University Press, 1985.

Jin Yufu 金毓黻 (1887–1962). *Zhongguo shixue shi* 中國史學史. Shanghai: Shanghai guji chubanshe, 2014.

Jullien, François. *The Propensity of Things: Toward a History of Efficacy in China*. Translated by Janet Lloyd. New York: Zone, 1999.

Kawai Yasushi 川合安. *Nanchō kizokusei kenkyū* 南朝貴族制研究. Tokyo: Kyuko shoin, 2015.

Kawakatsu Yoshio 川勝義雄. *Rikuchō kizokusei shakai no kenkyū* 六朝貴族制社会の研究. Tokyo: Iwanami shoten, 1982.

Kennedy, George A. *Aristotle: On Rhetoric; A Theory of Civic Discourse*. New York: Oxford University Press, 1991.

Knapp, Keith. "Exemplary Everymen: Guo Shidao and Guo Yuanping as Confucian Commoners." *Asia Major*, Third Series, 23, no. 1 (2010): 87–125.

Knechtges, David R. "The Rhetoric of Imperial Abdication and Accession in a Third-Century Chinese Court: The Case of Cao Pi's Accession as Emperor of the Wei Dynasty." In *Rhetoric and the Discourses of Power in Court Culture: China, Europe, and Japan*, edited by David R. Knechtges and Eugene Vance, 3–35. Seattle: University of Washington Press, 2005.

Kou, Lu. "The Epistolary Self and Psychological Warfare: Tuoba Tao's (408–452, r. 423–452) Letters and His Southern Audience." *Journal of Chinese Literature and Culture* 7, no. 1 (April 2020): 34–59.

Leban, Carl. "Managing Heaven's Mandate: Coded Communication in the Accession of Ts'ao P'ei, A.D. 220." In *Ancient China: Studies in Early Civilization*, edited by David T. Roy and Tsuen-hsuin Tsien, 315–42. Hong Kong: Chinese University Press, 1978.

Legge, James (1815–1897). *The Shoo King*. Taipei: Southern Materials Center, 1991 (1865).

Leung, Vincent S. *The Politics of the Past in Early China*. Cambridge: Cambridge University Press, 2019.

Lewis, Mark Edward. *China between Empires: The Northern and Southern Dynasties*. Cambridge, MA: Belknap Press of Harvard University Press, 2011.

———. *The Construction of Space in Early China*. Albany: State University of New York Press, 2006.

———. *Writing and Authority in Early China*. Albany: State University of New York Press, 1999.

Li Jutian 李菊田. "*Song shu* zuanxiu shimo kao" 《宋書》纂修始末攷. *Shuowen yuekan* 3, no. 8 (1943): 76–88.

Li, Wai-yee. "The Idea of Authority in the *Shih chi* (*Records of the Historian*)." *Harvard Journal of Asiatic Studies* 54, no. 2 (1994): 345–405.

———. "Pre-Qin Annals." In Feldherr and Hardy, eds., *The Oxford History of Historical Writing*, 415–39.

Liang Qichao 梁啟超 (1873–1929). *Zhongguo lishi yanjiufa* 中國歷史研究法. 1922. New edition, edited by Tang Zhijun 湯志鈞. Shanghai: Shanghai guji chubanshe, 1998.

Liu Tao 劉濤. "Wei Jin Nanchao de jin bei yu li bei" 魏晉南朝的禁碑與立碑. *Gugong boyuyuan yuankan* 95, no. 3 (2001): 4–11.

Lynn, Richard John, trans. *The Classic of Changes: A New Translation of the I Ching, as Interpreted by Wang Bi*. New York: Columbia University Press, 2010.

Mansvelt Beck, B. J. *The Treatises of Later Han: Their Author, Sources, Contents, and Place in Chinese Historiography*. Leiden: Brill, 1990.

Masumura Hiroshi 曾村宏. "Shin, Namichō no fugosei" 晉、南朝の符伍制. *Kagoshima daigaku shigaku* 4 (1956): 1–32.

———. "Sō sho Ō Kō den no dōgo hanhō no giron" 《宋書》王弘傳の同伍犯法の議論. *Kagoshima daigaku bunka hōkō* 4: *shigaku hen* 1 (1955): 22–47.

Mather, Richard B. *The Poet Shen Yüeh (441–513): The Reticent Marquis*. Princeton, NJ: Princeton University Press, 1988.

McMullen, David. *State and Scholars in T'ang China*. Cambridge: Cambridge University Press, 1988.

Miyakawa Hisayuki 宮川尚志. *Rikuchō shi kenkyū: seiji, shakai hen* 六朝史研究：政治．社会篇. Tokyo: Nihon gakujutsu shinkōkai, 1967.

Moloughney, Brian. "From Biographical History to Historical Biography: A Transformation in Chinese Historical Writing." *East Asian History* 4 (1992): 1–30.

Morino Shigeo 森野繁夫 and Toshiyuki Satō 佐藤利行, eds. *Junka kaku chō* 淳化閣帖. Tokyo: Hakuteisha, 1988.

Nakamura Keiji 中村圭爾. *Rikuchō kizokusei kenkyū* 六朝政治社会史研究. Kyoto: Kyuko shoyin, 2013.

Ng, On-cho, and Q. Edward Wang. *Mirroring the Past: The Writing and Use of History in Imperial China*. Honolulu: University of Hawai'i Press, 2005.

Olberding, Garret P. S., ed. *Facing the Monarch: Modes of Advice in the Early Chinese Court*. Cambridge, MA: Harvard University Asia Center, 2013.

Olbricht, Peter. "Die Biographie in China." *Saeculum* 8 (1957): 224–35.

Owen, Stephen. *Readings in Chinese Literary Thought*. Cambridge, MA: Council on East Asian Studies, Harvard University, 1992.
Pearce, Scott, Audrey Spiro, and Patricia Ebrey, eds. *Culture and Power in the Reconstitution of the Chinese Realm: 200–600*. Cambridge, MA: Harvard University Asia Center, 2001.
Pepe, Cristina. "(Re)discovering a Rhetorical Genre: Epideictic in Greek and Roman Antiquity." *Res Rhetorica* 1 (2017): 17–31.
Perelman, Chaïm, and Lucie Olbrechts-Tyteca. *The New Rhetoric: A Treatise on Argumentation*. Translated by John Wilkinson and Purcell Weaver. Notre Dame, IN: University of Notre Dame Press, 1969.
Pernot, Laurent. *Epideictic Rhetoric: Questioning the Stakes of Ancient Praise*. Austin: University of Texas Press, 2015.
Pines, Yuri. "Zhou History and Historiography: Introducing the Bamboo Manuscript *Xinian*." *T'oung Pao* 100, nos. 4–5 (2014): 287–324.
———. *Zhou History Unearthed: The Bamboo Manuscript "Xinian" and Early Chinese Historiography*. New York: Columbia University Press, 2020.
Pulleyblank, E. G. "The Historiographical Tradition." In *The Legacy of China*, edited by Raymond Dawson, 143–64. Oxford: Clarendon Press, 1964.
Qiao Wei 喬偉 et al., eds. *Zhongguo fazhi tongshi (disan juan): Wei Jin Nanbeichao* 中國法制通史（第三卷）：魏晉南北朝. Beijing: Falü chubanshe, 1999.
Qiu Min 邱敏. *Liuchao shixue* 六朝史學. Nanjing: Nanjing chubanshe, 2003.
Rapp, Christof. "Aristotle's Rhetoric." In *The Stanford Encyclopedia of Philosophy*, edited by Edward N. Zalta. Metaphysics Research Lab, Stanford University, 2022. https://plato.stanford.edu/archives/spr2022/entries/aristotle-rhetoric.
Sargent, Clyde B. "Subsidized History: Pan Ku and the Historical Records of the Former Han Dynasty." *Far Eastern Quarterly* 3, no. 2 (1944): 119–43.
Schaberg, David. "Functionary Speech: On the Work of *Shi* 使 and *Shi* 史." In Olberding, ed., *Facing the Monarch*, 19–41.
———. *A Patterned Past: Form and Thought in Early Chinese Historiography*. Cambridge, MA: Harvard University Asia Center, 2001.
Skinner, Quentin. *Reason and Rhetoric in the Philosophy of Hobbes*. New York: Cambridge University Press, 1996.
Tang Changru 唐長孺 (1911–94). "Clients and Bound Retainers in the Six Dynasties Period." In Dien, ed., *State and Society in Early Medieval China*, 111–38.
———. "Wei Jin Nanbeichao shiji juyao" 魏晉南北朝史籍舉要. In Tang Changru, *Wei Jin Nanbeichao Sui Tang shi jiangyi* 魏晉南北朝隋唐史講義. Beijing: Zhonghua shuju, 2012.
Tang Xiejun 唐燮軍. *Shijia xingji yu shishu gouzao: yi Wei Jin Nanbeichao yishi wei zhongxin de kaocha* 史家行跡與史書構造——以魏晉南北朝佚史為中心的考察. Hangzhou: Zhejiang daxue chubanshe, 2014.

Tian, Xiaofei. *Beacon Fire and Shooting Star: The Literary Culture of the Liang (502–557)*. Cambridge, MA: Harvard University Asia Center, 2007.

———. "Representing Kingship and Imagining Empire in Southern Dynasties Court Poetry." *T'oung Pao* 102, nos. 1–3 (2016): 18–73.

Tu Cheng-sheng 杜正勝. *Bianhu qimin: chuantong zhengzhi shehui jiegou zhi xingcheng* 編戶齊民：傳統政治社會結構之形成. Taipei: Linking Publishing, 1990.

Twitchett, Denis C. "Chinese Biographical Writing." In *Historians of China and Japan*, edited by W. G. Beasley and E. G. Pulleyblank, 95–114. London: Oxford University Press, 1961.

———. "Problems of Chinese Biography." In *Confucian Personalities*, edited by Arthur F. Wright and Denis Twitchett, 65–83. Stanford, CA: Stanford University Press, 1962.

van Els, Paul, and Sarah A. Queen, eds. *Between History and Philosophy: Anecdotes in Early China*. Albany: State University of New York Press, 2017.

Wan Shengnan 萬繩楠, ed. *Chen Yinke Wei Jin Nanbeichao shi jiangyan lu* 陳寅恪魏晉南北朝史講演錄. Guiyang: Guizhou renmin chubanshe, 2012.

Wang Antai 王安泰. *Zai zao fengjian: Wei Jin Nanbeichao de juezhi yu zhengzhi zhixu* 再造封建：魏晉南北朝的爵制與政治秩序. Taipei: Taida chuban zhongxin, 2013.

Wang Yongping 王永平. *Dong Jin Nanchao jiazu wenhuashi luncong* 東晉南朝家族文化史論叢. Yangzhou: Guangling shushe, 2010.

Wang Zhenglu 汪征魯. *Wei Jin Nanbeichao xuanguan tizhi yanjiu* 魏晉南北朝選官體制研究. Fuzhou: Fujian renmin chubanshe, 1995.

Wang Zhongluo 王仲犖 (1913–86). *Song shu jiaokan ji changbian* 宋書校勘記長編. Beijing: Zhonghua shuju, 2009.

Watson, Burton. *Ssu-ma Ch'ien: Grand Historian of China*. New York: Columbia University Press, 1963.

Weaver, Richard M. *In Defense of Tradition: Collected Shorter Writings of Richard M. Weaver, 1929–1963*. Edited by Ted J. Smith. Indianapolis, IN: Liberty Fund, 2000.

———. "To Write the Truth." *College English* 10, no. 1 (1948): 210–16.

Wells, Matthew V. "From Spirited Youth to Loyal Official: Life Writing and Didacticism in the *Jin shu* Biography of Wang Dao." *Early Medieval China* 21 (2015): 3–20.

White, Hayden. *Metahistory: The Historical Imagination in Nineteenth-Century Europe*. Baltimore, MD: The Johns Hopkins University Press, 1973.

Woolf, Daniel. *A Global History of History*. Cambridge: Cambridge University Press, 2011.

Wright, Arthur F. "Values, Roles, and Personalities." In *Confucian Personalities*, edited by Arthur F. Wright and Denis Twitchett, 3–23. Stanford, CA: Stanford University Press, 1962.

Yan Buke 閻步克. *Pinwei yu zhiwei: Qin Han Wei Jin Nanbeichao guanjie zhidu yanjiu* 品位與職位：秦漢魏晉南北朝官階制度研究. Beijing: Zhonghua shuju, 2002.

Yen Keng-wang 嚴耕望. *Zhongguo difang xingzheng zhidu shi* 中國地方行政制度史. 3 vols. Taipei: Zhongyang yanjiuyuan lishi yuyan yanjiusuo, 1990.

Yoshikawa Tadao 吉川忠夫. *Rikuchō seishinshi kenkyū* 六朝精神史研究. Kyoto: Dohosha, 1984.

Zhang Yuanji 張元濟 (1867–1959). *Zhang Yuanji guji shumu xuba huibian* 張元濟古籍書目序跋彙編. Edited by Zhang Renfeng 張仁鳳. Beijing: Shangwu yinshuguan, 2003.

Zhen Dacheng 真大成. *Zhonggu shishu jiaozheng* 中古史書校證. Beijing: Zhonghua shuju, 2013.

Zhou Yiliang 周一良 (1913–2001). *Wei Jin Nanbeichao shi zhaji* 魏晉南北朝史札記. Beijing: Zhonghua shuju, 1985.

Zhu Dongrun 朱東潤 (1896–1988). *Badai zhuanxu wenxue shulun* 八代傳敘文學述論. Shanghai: Fudan daxue chubanshe, 2006.

Zhu Zongbin 祝總斌. *Cai bu cai zhai shixue conggao* 材不材齋史學叢稿. Beijing: Zhonghua shuju, 2009.

———. "Jin Gongdi zhi si he Liu Yu de guming dachen" 晉恭帝之死和劉裕的顧命大臣. *Beijing daxue xuebao (zhexue shehuikexue ban)* 2 (1986): 55–70. Collected in Zhu Zongbin, *Cai bu cai zhai*.

———. "Liu Yu mendi kao" 劉裕門第考. *Beijing daxue xuebao (zhexue shehuikexue ban)* 1: 50–56. 1982. Collected in Zhu Zongbin, *Cai bu cai zhai*.

Index

absolute (rhetorical quality): defined, 22; and the "definition" of gentry, 128, 153–54, 157; and interiority, 37, 46–47, 61, 74, 79, 103; in negative characterizations, 52, 69–70, 87, 148; as a quality of historical narrative, 31–35, 43–44, 81–82; via synecdoche, 49, 50–51, 53–54, 69

active and passive rhetoric, 64, 67, 102, 108, 112, 115, 202–3; agency and, 98–105, 131, 167, 207–209

allegory, 15–16, 45, 73–77, 111, 235n42

anecdotes: as a core element of historiography, 15–16; function of, 30, 75; instances of, 36–37, 44–47, 50–54, 67–68, 68–69, 86, 109–10, 118–19, 164, 179–80, 191–92, 246n113

annals-biography form: biography as "commentary" to the "classic" annals, 11–13, 26, 30, 72, 79, 108–11, 115, 198, 230n9, 231n18, 240n62; eulogistic nature of biography, 54, 152n87; major elements of, 15–17; as an open form, 17, 23. *See also* historical interpretation

argumentation, 20, 40–44, 133–34, 138, 146, 203. *See also the four rhetorical topics;* enthymeme; stasis

audiences: at court, 110, 161; and fear, 57–58, 197; in historiography, 57–58, 62, 83; of historiography, 4, 16–17

Balazs, Etienne (1905–1963), 2

Ban Gu 班固 (32–92), 12, 202; appraisal of Xiao He, 88, 247n120. *See also Han shu*

bias: competing biases in historical accounts, 186–88; courtesy and the reconciliation of biases, 11, 58, 157, 184, 186, 188, 189–90, 193–94, 208; hidden bias, 115, 206, 207–9; inherent to historical accounts, 9, 169n6, 198, 201–2; inherited by the historian, 11, 14–16, 71–72

Bielenstein, Hans (1920–2015), 2, 16n30, 62n9, 115

biography. *See* annals-biography form

Burke, Kenneth (1897–1993), 25–26, 115, 209

Cai Kuo 蔡廓 (379–425), 76, 119n3, 174n23

Cai Xingzong 蔡興宗 (415–472), as patron of Shen Yue, 119n3, 190

calligraphy, 44–46, 175, 177–78, 198. *See also shu*

Cao Cao 曹操 (155–220), 59–60, 65

Cheng Daohui 程道惠, 94

Chi Sengshi 郗僧施 (d. 412), 76–77, 237n50

Chi Shao 郗紹, 191

cognate historical accounts, 9–10, 36–37, 49n13, 50–52, 56–57, 58–59, 60, 60nn6–7, 64n13, 66–68, 67n19, 70–71, 74, 74n28, 78–79, 78n33, 86n39, 172n16, 183n41, 188, 191–92, 231n12, 231n18, 233n32, 235n39, 238nn52–53, 240n64, 243n91, 246n113

commonplaces (topoi), 20, 39, 41, 80, 110n26, 118, 123n9, 143, 187n50, 190, 247n113. *See also liang shi* (good historian); poverty *under* gentry

Confucius, 126, 147, 161n120, 193n60, 205–6

cross-cultural rhetoric, 201–2

cultural capital, 183, 187

didacticism, 203

Dien, Albert E., 2, 166

documents: as a core "motive" of historiography, 16–17, 26–27, 62n9, 117, 166–75, 200–201; destruction of, 175; incorporation into biographies, 62n9, 114, 121n5, 151n86, 161; knowledge of, 183–84; as a large proportion of the dynastic histories, 16, 168, 175, 197; omens and, 170,

documents (continued)
172; paper and, 166, 198; signing of, 162, 174; and speeches, 16n30, 37–44, 117, 162. See also *shu*

Dubs, Homer H. (1892–1969), 169n6

dynastic history: compilation and finalization of 8n14, 89, 188n53; and dynastic legitimacy, 9n17, 115; forms, principles, and elements of, 11–17; officials in charge of, 8n12, 180, 196; versus chronological history, 11; villains in, 50, 70. See also history and historiography

Eberhard, Wolfram (1909–1989), 2
enargia, 16
endoxa, 22, 52, 71, 88, 115, 186, 190, 192
enthymeme: defined, 22; instances of, 40–42, 81–84, 112–14, 129, 139–41, 144, 146–47, 181, 195–96
epideictic historiography, 28, 200–209. See also eulogy; praise and blame
ethos, 53, 158, 161, 162–64, 181
eulogy, 3, 25, 40, 81, 138, 172, 185; eulogistic orientation of historiography, 3, 28, 30, 54–55, 89, 188, 208
exigence. See rhetorical exigence

Fan Tai 范泰 (355–428), 78
Fan Ye 范曄 (398–445), 73n26, 130n33
focalization, 83, 85, 98, 99, 100, 131, 135, 137
foil. See scapegoats and foils
Founding Ancestor. See Liu Yu
Franke, Herbert (1914–2011), epigraph, 17–18
Fu Liang 傅亮 (374–426), 81, 189, 240n69; downfall of, 119–20

Gai Kuanrao 蓋寬饒 (d. 60 BCE), 231n12
Gan Bao 干寶 (fl. early fourth century), 181, 191
gentry: defined, 5n8, 154; competition amongst, 108–15; conscription of, 131n36; in the early fifth century, 152n89; family as the unit of organization, 91, 151n85; legal versus social distinctions, 153–54;

lower versus elite, 19, 45, 58, 67, 73–79, 86, 110–11, 119; mourning periods of, 152, 162; officialdom and gentry identity, 91, 95–108, 110; and "pure censure" (*qing yi* 清議), 128; relationship with the state, 5–6, 26, 85, 86–89, 115, 122, 124–25, 128, 131–32, 135, 137–38, 142–43, 148, 157; the terms *renshi* 人士 and *shiren* 士人, 124n11; and the topos of poverty, 53n16, 145, 181, 184, 191–92; versus commoners, 129, 133–34, 139–40, 154–57; wayward members of, 133–34, 157. See also slaves and bondservants

good historian. See *liang shi*
Gu Mai 顧邁, 70–71
Guan Yu 關羽 (d. 220), 51–52, 235n41

Han shu 漢書: as a model, 12, 167–68, 182, 202, 247n120; number of histories listed in, 1n1; reliability of, 169n6
He Chengtian 何承天 (370–447), 8, 138n51, 184, 186
He Fasheng 何法盛 (fl. mid-fifth century), 181, 191
He Shangzhi 何尚之 (382–460), 86n39, 112n27, 127n25, 145–48, 158n108
He Wuji 何無忌 (d. 410), 33, 230n10, 234n38
He Yan 何偃 (413–458), 86n39
Hegel, G.W.F. (1770–1831), 28–29
Helian Bobo 赫連勃勃 (381–425), 102
hierarchies, 110–112, 192
historical causation, 23, 44
historical interpretation, 58, 75, 108, 109, 111, 112; of Shen Yue, 11, 86–89, 119n3, 163. See also allegory; annals-biography form; *wei yan*; *hujian fa*; *wei xianzhe hui*
historical narration, 49, 62n9, 107–8
history and historiography: characterizations of the Chinese tradition, 2–3, 168, 200–207; as a family enterprise, 182–84, 186–88; as an ethical value, 175–76, 178, 180; as a form of rhetoric, 201–7; significance and nature of in early medieval China, 1–2, 27, 28–29, 207; terminology

associated with, 193–94; veracity of, 16n30, 62n9, 115. *See also* annals-biography form; cognate historical accounts; dynastic history; politics; *Song shu*; unity of history and historiography
History of the Han. *See Han shu*
History of the Jin. *See Jin shu*
History of the Latter Han. *See Hou Han shu*
History of the Liang. *See Liang shu*
History of the Liu-Song. *See Song shu*
History of the Northern Wei. *See Wei shu*
History of the Southern Dynasties. *See Nan shi*
Hou Han shu 後漢書, 60
hujian fa 互見法 ("theory of mutual illumination"), 14, 58. *See also* cognate historical accounts
Huan Xuan 桓玄 (369–404), 6, 31, 35–36, 40, 94, 101, 102, 113, 118, 170–71, 175, 181n35, 236n47
hyperbole, 148

immediacy (rhetorical quality), 22–23, 31–34, 75, 82, 87; and the narration of time, 108
imperial favorites, 88, 178
imperial schools: of philosophy, 146; of rhetoric, 138
incompletion (rhetorical quality), 27, 190–98. *See also* rhetorical exigence
interiority and exteriority: dangers associated with interiority, 37, 47–55, 72, 175, 176; interiority as a theme, 43, 79, 89, 115, 164, 198–99; the model of, 18–20, 206–7. *See also* irony; prompts; surfaces; threshold
irony: inherent to dynastic historiography, 19–20, 25, 55, 58, 89, 206–7; instances of, 27, 77, 135–38, 170–71, 178, 231n14; instances of dramatic irony, 48–50, 64, 102, 105, 180

Jia Yi 賈誼 (200–168), 131n36
Jiang Ai 江敳 (fl. mid-fourth century?): and the family of, 229n5
Jiang Ao 江奧, 127–29

Jiangzhou 江州, 113–15, 118, 120
Jingkou 京口, 30, 38, 73
Jingzhou 荊州, 113, 118, 120
Jin shu 晉書, 170–71, 192, 233n28; contrasts with the *Song shu*, 49n13, 64n13, 114n30, 172n16

Kong Chunzhi 孔淳之 (372–430), 130n33
Kong Mozhi 孔默之 (b. after 372), 121, 130–32
Kuai En 蒯恩 (d. 418), 109–11, 173

Lewis, Mark Edward, 18–19
Liang Qichao 梁啟超 (1873–1929), 184, 204
liang shi 良史 ("good historian," "good history"), 20, 23, 58, 72, 175–90, 195, 196n65, 201–202
Liang shu 梁書, 186–88
literary writing, 16–17, 162, 172, 208
litotes, 61–62
Liu Daogui 劉道規 (370–412): likely stele inscription for, 229n1, 232n23, 234n38
Liu Daolian 劉道憐 (368–422), 239n57
Liu Jun 劉濬 (429–453), 70
Liu Laozhi 劉牢之 (d. 402), 10
Liu Muzhi 劉穆之 (360–417), 25; chapters 1–2 and appendix passim; association with Cai and Jiang families, 229n5, 246n113; calligraphic specimen of, 239n58; contrasted with Wang Hong, 162–5, 233n24; descendants of, 68–72, 86–87; as foil in Liu Yu's rise, 72–80, 111; as a historian type, 166, 240n65; plotting Liu Yu's rise, 37–46, 48–54; rise of, 30–31, 34–37; Shen Yue's view of, 87–89; social status, 229n3, 246n113, 247n117; the two versions of his death, 56–68, 74–75
Liu Shizhi 劉式之, 69
Liu Xiang 劉祥, 188n53
Liu Xie 劉勰 (d. ca. 522), 162, 202, 205–6. *See also Wenxin diaolong*
Liu Xiuzhi 劉秀之 (397–464), 229n3
Liu Yi 劉毅 (d. 412), 38, 41, 47–48, 50, 113–15, 233n27, 234n38

Liu Yikang 劉義康 (409-451), 103, 120-21, 151, 162

Liu Yilong 劉義隆 (407-453; Emperor Wen, r. 424-453), 8, 95, 176-80, 189; enthronement of, 119-20

Liu Yixuan 劉義宣 (415-454), 105

Liu Yong 劉邕, 68-69

Liu Yu 劉裕 (363-422, the Founding Ancestor, r. 420-22): Duchy of Song, 118, 151; linked to founder of the Han dynasty, 45; quoted, 31-33, 39, 75-76, 77-80, 81-85, 118-19; reign of, 128n29, 162; rise of, 6, 9-10, 38-44, 47-52, 72-80, 115n31, 172-73, 233n25; relationship with Wang Hong, 118; social status, 6, 44-46, 73, 173-74

Liu Yuu 劉瑀 (d. ca. 458), 70-71, 86

Liu Zhan 劉湛 (392-440), 102-3

Liu Zhiji 劉知幾 (661-721), 13, 168n5, 197-98

lodged prefectures, 106

lu 錄 ("record"), 173-75, 182. See also documents

Lu Shuang 魯爽 (d. 454), 105

Lu Xun 盧循 (d. 411), 113, 234n38

Mandate of Heaven, 7, 9n17, 66, 77-79, 101, 116, 118-20, 169-70, 208. See also dynastic history

Mao Xiuzhi 毛脩之 (375-446), 181-82

Meng Chang 孟昶 (d. 410), 38, 41; missing from received historiography, 233n28

Meng Lingxiu 孟靈休, 68

middle voice, 100

mode of emplotment, 28

Nan shi 南史: contrasted with orthodox dynastic histories, 186-88; contrasted with Song shu, 68n21, 77, 85, 122n7, 124n11, 124nn15-16, 126n21, 156n100, 156nn102-103, 158nn109-111, 159n110, 160nn118-119, 161n121, 236n46, 238n54, 239n61, 241n69, 246n111, 246n113

neighborhood groups (fuwu 符伍), 122, 155-57

Nine Bestowals (jiu xi 九錫), 57, 59-60, 64n13, 68, 118

Northern Wei: as threat to the Liu-Song, 4, 119

officialdom, chapter 3 passim; assistants and clerks, 153-60; as a core element of historiography, 17; and local governance, 135, 190; scale of, 105-6; the Secretariat, 127; as a system, 26. See also officialdom, terms of and gentry

officialdom, terms of: bi 辟, qi 起, and qijia 起家, 99-100, 104; in the biography of Liu Muzhi, 91-92; bubai 不拜, bujiu 不就, and buqi 不起, 100-102; chu 除 and bai 拜, 98-99; full list of, 96-97; ellipsis, 95, 98, 108; jian 兼, ling 領, and dai 帶, 107; jia 加, jin hao 進號, and jin wei 進位, 107; jie 階, 106; lei 累, li 歷, xun 尋, e 俄, and fu 復, 108; qian 遷 and zhuan 轉, 106-7; qing 請, yin 引, and ming 命, 105; rang 讓, gui 歸, and xun 遜, 101, 102; reng 仍, 107; rugu 如故 and zhuizeng 追贈, 107; wei 為 and yiwei 以為, 98; xing 行, yuanwai 員外, ban 版, and bu 補, 95, 103-5; zhang 掌 and weiren 委任, 103; zheng 徵, ru 入, and chu 出, 100

passive rhetoric. See active and passive rhetoric

patron-client relationships, 35, 50-54, 61, 66, 70-71, 81, 85, 103-4, 109-11, 229n5, 231n14; and banqueting, 52-54

Pei Songzhi 裴松之 (372-451), 185, 186-88. See also Sanguo zhi

Pei Ziye 裴子野 (469-530), 186-88

Perelman, Chaïm (1912-1984), 23-24

pluperfect (rhetorical quality): defined, 22-23; dreams of Liu Muzhi, 33n4, 230n8; foreshadowing, 75, 80, 109; instances of, 31-34, 43-44, 48, 49-50, 51, 59, 60n6, 80, 81, 111, 172-73, 179, 197, 199; and the term chu 初, 33

politics: as the genus of historiography, 18–20, 54, 151, 181, 201, 207–8
positive and negative rhetoric, 25, 58, 61, 64, 109, 114, 152n87, 163–64, 167, 174, 180, 193, 209. *See also* bias
posthumous reputation, 81–85, 173, 176, 204–6; posthumous titles, 65–66, 71, 86–87
poverty. *See under* gentry
praise and blame (*bao bian* 褒貶), 11, 28, 56, 89, 204–9. *See also* eulogy
primary sources, 2, 11, 28, 117, 165. *See also* documents
prompts: defined, 18–19, 206; instances of, 33, 36, 39–40, 41, 45, 46, 50–55, 61, 69, 75, 79, 80, 82, 85, 89, 141, 164–65, 171, 174, 175n26, 176, 184, 189, 194. *See also* interiority and exteriority, scapegoats and foils
public and private values, 27, 84, 141–43, 157, 158–59, 175–90; and historiography, 202; privately compiled historiography, 184–86, 189–90; relation to "ambition" and "intent" (*zhi* 志), 181–82, 184, 208. *See also* bias; interiority and exteriority
punishments, 125; the term *jing* 竟, 127n27

recluses, 88, 101–105, 130n33, 155
rhetoric: defined, 20
rhetorical exigence: defined, 36; instances of, 10, 38, 51, 110, 112, 125, 161, 174, 189, 190, 193, 194, 208. *See also yi* ("ought"), hierarchies
rhetorical genres: deliberative and forensic, 203; epideictic, 204–7; universal appeal of the epideictic, 209
rhetorical question, 87–88, 141, 158
rhetorical topics: defined, 20–25; as a full set, 36. *See also* commonplaces; topic of analogy and contrast; topic of circumstance; topic of consequence; topic of definition
roles and types: as analogy, 23; blurring of role and type, 63, 111; defined, 62–64;

216; role of the Founding Ancestor, 45; role performance, 63, 117, 167; roles in dynastic transitions, 7; types assigned by historians, 14, 67n19; 208. *See also* scapegoats and foils
Ruan Xiaoxu 阮孝緒 (479–536), 1n1

Sanguo zhi, 65–66; possible influence of the Pei Songzhi edition on the *Song shu*, 52n14, 59, 67, 235n41
Sargent, Clyde B., 169–70
scapegoats and foils, 72–74, 109, 129, 132, 142–43, 162, 192, 198, 205. *See also* slaves and bondservants
Shan Qianzhi 山謙之, 184–85
Shang shu 尚書 ("Hallowed Documents"), epigraph, 168
Shen Yanzhi 沈演之 (397–449), 179
Shen Yue 沈約 (441–513): family of, 101n10, 188n51; and his *History of the Jin*, 190–91, 193; judgments of Liu Muzhi and Wang Hong, 87–89, 162–65; parallels with the life and death of Liu Muzhi, 67n19, 247n113; versus Pei Ziye, 186–88; political views of, 163; presentation of his *History of the Liu-Song* to the throne, 196–98; role in the death of Southern Qi emperor, 172n16. *See also* historical interpretation; *Song shu*
shi 勢 ("propensity"), 45–46
shi 史 ("scribe," "history"), 16, 200–201
Shiji 史記: as a model, 11–12, 17, 167–68, 182, 247n120
shu 書 ("calligraphy," "document," "book," "history"), 16, 167–68, 172; all senses of the word, 177
shu er bu zuo 述而不作 ("relay but do not create"), 14, 190, 193, 197, 198, 209
sign versus symbol, 147–48
Sima Daozi 司馬道子 (364–403), 230n6, 231n17
Sima Dewen 司馬德文 (386–421, r. as Jin Emperor Gong, 419–420), 93–94, 172

Sima Qian 司馬遷 (145/135–86 BCE). See *Shiji*
slaves and bondservants, 129–30, 141–43; owner responsibility for, 141; as a sign of corrupt gentry, 146–48, 158n108; in the Southern Dynasties economy, 134, 143
Song lüe 宋略 (*Brief History of the Liu-Song*), 186n48
Song shu 宋書: contrasted with earlier and later histories, 17; compared with Xu Yuan's history, 9–10; compilation of, 3, 7–11, 121n5, 186–88, 196–97; editions, 142n63, 249–50; predecessors to, 7–9, 179; and related sources, 122n7, 250
Southern Dynasties: nature of, 3–5, 122, 142–43, 155
Southern Qi: contrast with Western Jin, 106; perspective on the Liu-Song, 89, 163, 188n53.
Spring and Autumn Annals, 11, 56, 58
stasis: defined, 43; instances of, 51, 53, 83, 119, 144, 147–48, 153, 185. See also focalization
stele inscriptions, 185–86
Su Baosheng 蘇寶生 (d. 458), 8
Sun En 孫恩 (d. 402), 9–10
surfaces: "agglutination" of, 98, 106, 107, 116; significance of exteriors and surfaces, 17, 19–20, 24–25, 26, 188, 198, 206, 208–9. See also eulogy; interiority and exteriority; irony
suspicion: historiographical function of, 48, 50, 53
synecdoche. See under absolute

Tao Yuanming 陶淵明 (365?–427), 7n10, 157n107
textual criticism: *chang* 常 ("regularly") and *chang* 嘗 ("once"), 46, 61, 237n48; editing, 167; emendations, 45n9, 110n24, 135n45, 139n52–53, 139nn55–56, 140n57–58, 142n63, 154n94, 144n66, 241n72, 242n77, 243n83, 243nn86–88, 243n90, 244nn98–99, 245nn100–101, 245n105; lacunae and eyeskips, 113n28, 126n22, 129n31, 130n5, 136n47, 136n50, 139nn52–53, 139nn55–56, 140n57, 145n67, 146nn69–70, 150n81, 150nn83–84, 155n95, 156n99, 158n110, 159n113, 159n117, 177n30, 242n80; taboo substitutions, 66n18, 126n23, 147n73, 156n102, 243n84; variation due to graphic similarity, 46n10, 124n10, 124n12, 124n15, 124n17, 126n21, 128n28, 132n37, 133n39, 133n42, 134n43, 135n45, 136nn48–50, 139n54, 140n58, 140nn60–61, 142nn63–64, 143n65, 144n66, 147n74, 149n75, 150nn78–80, 150n82, 154n94, 155n96, 156n97, 156n101, 156nn105–6, 158n109, 159nn115–16, 235n43, 240n67, 241n71, 242n76, 242n79, 243n85, 243n89, 245n104, 245n106, 247n119. See also *Nan shi*
theft and plagiarism, 190–93
threshold: defined, 17–18; instances of "thresholding," 24, 26, 44, 51–52, 54, 55, 61, 69, 83–85, 89, 101, 103, 110, 113, 116, 119, 135, 144, 160, 164, 176, 193, 198, 209; and orthodox historiography, 190, 199, 207; and reclusion, 102; the *Song shu* source for this metaphor, 71. See also interiority and exteriority
topic of analogy and contrast: defined, 23–24; instances of, 40, 46, 75, 158, 176; allusions to historical precedent, 52n14, 60–61, 63–67
topic of circumstance: defined, 24–25; instances of, 10, 38, 43, 78, 81–82, 133–34, 152–53, 155; of praise by blame, 205; transformed into the topic of consequence, 33, 42; transforming the topic of definition, 49, 51, 53, 75, 110–11, 126, 161
topic of consequence: defined, 22–23; contrary consequence, 23, 47, 48, 108, 148; combined with definition and circumstance, 38, 52, 53, 71; instances of, 38, 49, 108–9, 131, 154–55; and the term *sui* 遂,

35, 58, 67n19; transforming the topic of definition, 85, 100; undermined, 115
topic of definition: defined, 21–22; instances of, 38, 49, 69, 83, 101, 124n11, 132, 137, 144, 160; versus circumstance, 78, 143, 153–54. *See also* absolute
trope, 20, 66, 77, 111, 135, 137, 183n41, 193–94, 203
Twitchett, Denis (1925–2006), 13–14, 28, 30, 54, 63, 204–205

unity of history and historiography, 1, 15, 17, 20, 28, 30, 39–40, 55, 58, 62n9, 63, 80, 89, 111, 112, 145, 165, 170–71, 196, 201, 203, 209; concept of, 28–29; and the production of documents, 169

Wang Biaozhi 王彪之 (305–377), 183
Wang Dao 王導 (276–339), 117, 233n26; as a possible model for Liu Muzhi, 62–63, 64n13, 236n45
Wang Dun 王敦 (266–324), 231n14
Wang Gong 王恭 (d. 398), 229n5
Wang Hong 王弘 (379–432), 27, 56, 69, 73, 85, 104, 109; life and career of, 117–21, 189–90; political views of, 148–61; Shen Yue's appraisal of, 88–89, 162–64
Wang Hua 王華 (385–427), 102–3, 120, 177, 189
Wang Jian 王儉 (452–489), 163
Wang Jingzhi 王靖之, 86
Wang Mang 王莽 (45 BCE–23 CE, r. 9–23), 169–70
Wang Mi 王謐 (360–407), 38, 233n26
Wang Mingsheng 王鳴盛 (1722–1798), 88n41
Wang Sengda 王僧達 (423–458), 86
Wang Shaozhi 王韶之 (380–435), 7n10, 171–73, 180–84, 189–90; role in the death of Jin Emperor An, 172–73
Wang Tanshou 王曇首 (394–430), 120, 176–77, 181n36
Wang Xi 王錫, 163

Wang Xun 王珣 (349–400), 117
Wang Yin 王隱 (ca. 284–ca. 354), 181, 182–83, 191–92
Wang Zhen'e 王鎮惡 (373–418), 67–68, 85, 246n110
Wang Zhi 王智, 75–76
Wang Zhongluo 王仲犖 (1913–1986), 249–50
Wang Zhunzhi 王准之 (378–433), 132–38, 183; appraised by Shen Yue, 163; versus Wang Hong, 149–53
Watson, Burton (1925–2017), 2, 17, 204
Weaver, Richard M. (1910–1963), 21n36
Wei shu 魏書, 4n7, 67–68
wei xianzhe hui 為賢者諱 ("conceal the failings of worthy men"), 58, 183n41, 205–6
Wei Xuan 韋玄, 101–2
wei yan 微言 ("subtle words"), 13–14, 163
Wenxin diaolong 文心雕龍, 162, 200, 202–6
Wen xuan 文選, 82, 240n69
Wright, Arthur F. (1913–1976), 62
Wu Xi 吳喜 (427–471), 179–80

Xiao He 蕭何 (257–193 BCE): as paradigm for Liu Muzhi, 53, 88
Xiao Sihua 蕭思話 (400–455), 8
Xie Fangming 謝方明 (380–426), 76–77, 78, 86
Xie Hui 謝晦 (390–426), 73–75, 189; downfall of, 119–20
Xie Hun 謝混 (d. 412), 38, 76–77, 94–95, 98, 233n27
Xie Lingyun 謝靈運 (385–433), 101n10, 130n33, 151, 176–78
Xie Shu 謝述 (390–435), 175
Xie Yan 謝琰 (d. 400), 180
Xie Yuan 謝元 (d. after 444), 138–45
Xu Guang 徐廣 (352–425), 7n10, 191n56
Xu Xianzhi 徐羨之 (364–426), 92–95, 101, 104, 108–9, 151, 174n23, 189, 237n50; downfall of 119–20
Xu Yuan 徐爰 (394–475), 8–10, 178–79

Xun Yu 荀彧 (163–212), 59–67, 175, 236n45; as a paradigm for the life of Liu Muzhi 60–61, 167, 234n34, 235n40, 236n44, 240n65, 244n92; differences from Liu Muzhi, 64–67

Yan Yanzhi 顏延之 (384–456), 75, 247n117
Yang Hu 羊祜 (221–278), 175; as a possible model for Liu Muzhi, 244n91
Yang Xuanbao 羊玄保 (371–464), 127n25, 152n87
Yangzhou 揚州, 38, 42–43, 118
yi 義: biographies of the "filial and dutiful," 88; duty, 131; questions of "honor" and "loyalty," 51–52, 54, 65–66, 70–71, 84–85, 171n10; "principle," 144, 145n66; "righteousness," 32, 41, 59, 66, 185, 187–88, 233n25. See also public and private values
yi 議 ("discussion," "debate"), 128, 162; relation to historiography, 185–86

yi 宜 ("ought"), 123, 162, 195–96. See also rhetorical exigence
Yin Jingren 殷景仁 (390–440), 177, 182
Yu Bingzhi 庾炳之 (388–450), 111–12, 173
Yu Yu 虞預, 192
Yu Yue 庾悅 (ca. 374–411), 113–15
Yuan Bao 元豹, 237n50
Yuan Hong 袁宏 (328–376), 66, 191

Zang Tao 臧燾 (353–422): with Zang Xi 臧熹 and Zang Zhi 臧質 (400–454), 228n1
Zhang Fu 張敷 (fl. ca. 430), 173
Zhang Liao 張遼 (169–222), 51–52, 235n41
Zhang Shao 張邵 (d. after 428), 112–13
Zhao Yi 趙翼 (1727–1814), 9, 168n5
Zhu Lingshi 朱齡石 (379–418), 46–47; with Zhu Chaoshi 朱超石, 236n47
Zhuge Zhangmin 諸葛長民 (d. 413), 48–50, 238nn51–53

Harvard-Yenching Institute Monograph Series

(titles now in print)

24. *Population, Disease, and Land in Early Japan, 645–900*, by William Wayne Farris
25. *Shikitei Sanba and the Comic Tradition in Edo Fiction*, by Robert W. Leutner
26. *Washing Silk: The Life and Selected Poetry of Wei Chuang (834?–910)*, by Robin D. S. Yates
28. *Tang Transformation Texts: A Study of the Buddhist Contribution to the Rise of Vernacular Fiction and Drama in China*, by Victor H. Mair
30. *Readings in Chinese Literary Thought*, by Stephen Owen
31. *Remembering Paradise: Nativism and Nostalgia in Eighteenth-Century Japan*, by Peter Nosco
33. *Escape from the Wasteland: Romanticism and Realism in the Fiction of Mishima Yukio and Oe Kenzaburo*, by Susan Jolliffe Napier
34. *Inside a Service Trade: Studies in Contemporary Chinese Prose*, by Rudolf G. Wagner
35. *The Willow in Autumn: Ryutei Tanehiko, 1783–1842*, by Andrew Lawrence Markus
36. *The Confucian Transformation of Korea: A Study of Society and Ideology*, by Martina Deuchler
37. *The Korean Singer of Tales*, by Marshall R. Pihl
38. *Praying for Power: Buddhism and the Formation of Gentry Society in Late-Ming China*, by Timothy Brook
39. *Word, Image, and Deed in the Life of Su Shi*, by Ronald C. Egan
41. *Studies in the Comic Spirit in Modern Japanese Fiction*, by Joel R. Cohn
42. *Wind Against the Mountain: The Crisis of Politics and Culture in Thirteenth-Century China*, by Richard L. Davis
43. *Powerful Relations: Kinship, Status, and the State in Sung China (960–1279)*, by Beverly Bossler
44. *Limited Views: Essays on Ideas and Letters*, by Qian Zhongshu; selected and translated by Ronald Egan
45. *Sugar and Society in China: Peasants, Technology, and the World Market*, by Sucheta Mazumdar
49. *Precious Volumes: An Introduction to Chinese Sectarian Scriptures from the Sixteenth and Seventeenth Centuries*, by Daniel L. Overmyer
50. *Poetry and Painting in Song China: The Subtle Art of Dissent*, by Alfreda Murck
51. *Evil and/or/as the Good: Omnicentrism, Intersubjectivity, and Value Paradox in Tiantai Buddhist Thought*, by Brook Ziporyn
53. *Articulated Ladies: Gender and the Male Community in Early Chinese Texts*, by Paul Rouzer
55. *Allegories of Desire: Esoteric Literary Commentaries of Medieval Japan*, by Susan Blakeley Klein
56. *Printing for Profit: The Commercial Publishers of Jianyang, Fujian (11th–17th Centuries)*, by Lucille Chia

57. *To Become a God: Cosmology, Sacrifice, and Self-Divinization in Early China*, by Michael J. Puett
58. *Writing and Materiality in China: Essays in Honor of Patrick Hanan*, edited by Judith T. Zeitlin and Lydia H. Liu
59. *Rulin waishi and Cultural Transformation in Late Imperial China*, by Shang Wei
60. *Words Well Put: Visions of Poetic Competence in the Chinese Tradition*, by Graham Sanders
61. *Householders: The Reizei Family in Japanese History*, by Steven D. Carter
62. *The Divine Nature of Power: Chinese Ritual Architecture at the Sacred Site of Jinci*, by Tracy Miller
63. *Beacon Fire and Shooting Star: The Literary Culture of the Liang (502–557)*, by Xiaofei Tian
64. *Lost Soul: "Confucianism" in Contemporary Chinese Academic Discourse*, by John Makeham
65. *The Sage Learning of Liu Zhi: Islamic Thought in Confucian Terms*, by Sachiko Murata, William C. Chittick, and Tu Weiming
66. *Through a Forest of Chancellors: Fugitive Histories in Liu Yuan's* Lingyan ge, *an Illustrated Book from Seventeenth-Century Suzhou*, by Anne Burkus-Chasson
67. *Empire of Texts in Motion: Chinese, Korean, and Taiwanese Transculturations of Japanese Literature*, by Karen Laura Thornber
68. *Empire's Twilight: Northeast Asia Under the Mongols*, by David M. Robinson
69. *Ancestors, Virgins, and Friars: Christianity as a Local Religion in Late Imperial China*, by Eugenio Menegon
70. *Manifest in Words, Written on Paper: Producing and Circulating Poetry in Tang Dynasty China*, by Christopher M. B. Nugent
71. *The Poetics of Sovereignty: On Emperor Taizong of the Tang Dynasty*, by Jack W. Chen
72. *Ancestral Memory in Early China*, by K. E. Brashier
73. *'Dividing the Realm in Order to Govern': The Spatial Organization of the Song State*, by Ruth Mostern
74. *The Dynamics of Masters Literature: Early Chinese Thought from Confucius to Han Feizi*, by Wiebke Denecke
75. *Songs of Contentment and Transgression: Discharged Officials and Literati Communities in Sixteenth-Century North China*, by Tian Yuan Tan
76. *Ten Thousand Scrolls: Reading and Writing in the Poetics of Huang Tingjian and the Late Northern Song*, by Yugen Wang
77. *A Northern Alternative: Xue Xuan (1389–1464) and the Hedong School*, by Khee Heong Koh
78. *Visionary Journeys: Travel Writings from Early Medieval and Nineteenth-Century China*, by Xiaofei Tian
79. *Making Personas: Transnational Film Stardom in Modern Japan*, by Hideaki Fujiki
80. *Strange Eventful Histories: Identity, Performance, and Xu Wei's Four Cries of a Gibbon*, by Shiamin Kwa
81. *Critics and Commentators: The Book of Poems as Classic and Literature*, by Bruce Rusk
82. *Home and the World: Editing the Glorious Ming in Woodblock-Printed Books of the Sixteenth and Seventeenth Centuries*, by Yuming He

83. *Courtesans, Concubines, and the Cult of Female Fidelity*, by Beverly Bossler
84. *Chinese History: A New Manual, Third Edition*, by Endymion Wilkinson
85. *A Comprehensive Manchu-English Dictionary*, by Jerry Norman
86. *Drifting among Rivers and Lakes: Southern Song Dynasty Poetry and the Problem of Literary History*, by Michael Fuller
87. *Martial Spectacles of the Ming Court*, by David M. Robinson
88. *Modern Archaics: Continuity and Innovation in the Chinese Lyric Tradition, 1900–1937*, by Shengqing Wu
89. *Cherishing Antiquity: The Cultural Construction of an Ancient Chinese Kingdom*, by Olivia Milburn
90. *The Burden of Female Talent: The Poet Li Qingzhao and Her History in China*, by Ronald Egan
91. *Public Memory in Early China*, by K. E. Brashier
92. *Women and National Trauma in Late Imperial Chinese Literature*, by Wai-yee Li
93. *The Destruction of the Medieval Chinese Aristocracy*, by Nicolas Tackett
94. *Savage Exchange: Han Imperialism, Chinese Literary Style, and the Economic Imagination*, by Tamara T. Chin
95. *Shifting Stories: History, Gossip, and Lore in Narratives from Tang Dynasty China*, by Sarah M. Allen
96. *One Who Knows Me: Friendship and Literary Culture in Mid-Tang China*, by Anna Shields
97. *Materializing Magic Power: Chinese Popular Religion in Villages and Cities*, by Wei-Ping Lin
98. *Traces of Grand Peace: Classics and State Activism in Imperial China*, by Jaeyoon Song
99. *Fiction's Family: Zhan Xi, Zhan Kai, and the Business of Women in Late-Qing China*, by Ellen Widmer
100. *Chinese History: A New Manual, Fourth Edition*, by Endymion Wilkinson
101. *After the Prosperous Age: State and Elites in Early Nineteenth-Century Suzhou*, by Seunghyun Han
102. *Celestial Masters: History and Ritual in Early Daoist Communities*, by Terry F. Kleeman
103. *Transgressive Typologies: Constructions of Gender and Power in Early Tang China*, by Rebecca Doran
104. *Li Mengyang, the North-South Divide, and Literati Learning in Ming China*, by Chang Woei Ong
105. *Bannermen Tales (Zidishu): Manchu Storytelling and Cultural Hybridity in the Qing Dynasty*, by Elena Suet-Ying Chiu
106. *Upriver Journeys: Diaspora and Empire in Southern China, 1570–1850*, by Steven B. Miles
107. *Ancestors, Kings, and the Dao*, by Constance A. Cook
108. *The Halberd at Red Cliff: Jian'an and the Three Kingdoms*, by Xiaofei Tian
109. *Speaking of Profit: Bao Shichen and Reform in Nineteenth-Century China*, by William T. Rowe
110. *Building for Oil: Daqing and the Formation of the Chinese Socialist State*, by Hou Li
111. *Reading Philosophy, Writing Poetry: Intertextual Modes of Making Meaning in Early Medieval China*, by Wendy Swartz

112. *Writing for Print: Publishing and the Making of Textual Authority in Late Imperial China*, by Suyoung Son
113. *Shen Gua's Empiricism*, by Ya Zuo
114. *Just a Song: Chinese Lyrics from the Eleventh and Early Twelfth Centuries*, by Stephen Owen
115. *Shrines to Living Men in the Ming Political Cosmos*, by Sarah Schneewind
116. *In the Wake of the Mongols: The Making of a New Social Order in North China, 1200–1600*, by Jinping Wang
117. *Opera, Society, and Politics in Modern China*, by Hsiao-t'i Li
118. *Imperiled Destinies: The Daoist Quest for Deliverance in Medieval China*, by Franciscus Verellen
119. *Ethnic Chrysalis: China's Orochen People and the Legacy of Qing Borderland Administration*, by Loretta Kim
120. *The Paradox of Being: Truth, Identity, and Images in Daoism*, by Poul Andersen
121. *Feeling the Past in Seventeenth-Century China*, by Xiaoqiao Ling
122. *The Chinese Dreamscape, 300 BCE–800 CE*, by Robert Ford Campany
123. *Structures of the Earth: Metageographies of Early Medieval China*, by D. Jonathan Felt
124. *Anecdote, Network, Gossip, Performance: Essays on the* Shishuo xinyu, by Jack W. Chen
125. *Testing the Literary: Prose and the Aesthetic in Early Modern China*, by Alexander Des Forges
126. *Du Fu Transforms: Tradition and Ethics amid Societal Collapse*, by Lucas Rambo Bender
127. *Chinese History: A New Manual (Enlarged Sixth Edition), Vol. 1*, by Endymion Wilkinson
128. *Chinese History: A New Manual (Enlarged Sixth Edition), Vol. 2*, by Endymion Wilkinson
129. *Wang Anshi and Song Poetic Culture*, by Xiaoshan Yang
130. *Localizing Learning: The Literati Enterprise in Wuzhou, 1100–1600*, by Peter K. Bol
131. *Making the Gods Speak: The Ritual Production of Revelation in Chinese Religious History*, by Vincent Goossaert
132. *Lineages Embedded in Temple Networks: Daoism and Local Society in Ming China*, by Richard G. Wang
133. *Rival Partners: How Taiwanese Entrepreneurs and Guangdong Officials Forged the China Development Model*, by Wu Jieh-min; translated by Stacy Mosher
134. *Saying All That Can Be Said: The Art of Describing Sex in* Jin Ping Mei, by Keith McMahon
135. *Genealogy and Status: Hereditary Office Holding and Kinship in North China under Mongol Rule*, by Tomoyasu Iiyama
136. *The Threshold: The Rhetoric of Historiography in Early Medieval China*, by Zeb Raft